Water Conservation in Landscape Design and Management

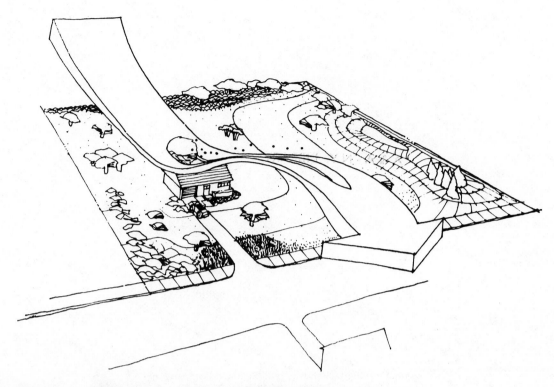

Water Conservation in
Landscape Design & Management

Gary O. Robinette

illustrated by
Kevin W. Sloan

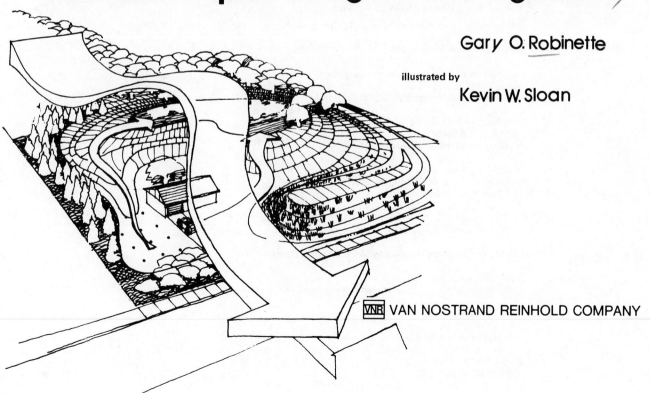

VNR VAN NOSTRAND REINHOLD COMPANY

Copyright © 1984 by Van Nostrand Reinhold Company Inc.
Library of Congress Catalog Card Number 84-13115
ISBN 0-442-22204-1

Printed in the United States of America

Published by Van Nostrand Reinhold Company Inc.
135 West 50th Street
New York, New York 10020

Van Nostrand Reinhold Company Limited
Molly Millars Lane
Wokingham, Berkshire RG11 2PY, England

Van Nostrand Reinhold
480 La Trobe Street
Melbourne, Victoria 3000, Australia

Macmillan of Canada
Division of Gage Publishing Limited
164 Commander Boulevard
Agincourt, Ontario M1S 3C7, Canada

16 15 14 13 12 11 10 9 8 7 6 5 4 3 2 1

Library of Congress Cataloging in Publication Data

Robinette, Gary O.
   Water conservation in landscape design and management.

   Bibliography: p. 250
   Includes index.
   1. Water in landscape architecture.   2. Water conser-
vation.   I. Title.
SB475.8.R63   1984   631.7   84-13115
ISBN 0-442-22204-1

Table of Contents

preface

This is a long overdue reference book. It has taken five years to pull all this together and represents ten years of interest and concern. In seeking to help deal with the problem in many areas of the United States, no such reference book was found, therefore research on this publication was undertaken.

The shortages of water to sustain landscape plants periodically continues to be a recurring problem in many areas of North America. Each summer seems to bring drought conditions to one region or another. Everyone seeks information or assistance when this happens but there is little planning for it ahead of time. In order that all those involved in landscape planning and design and with water use in landscape operations be more aware and better prepared in such situations this book has been written.

This book is in two parts, the first portion is an overview of the problem and what has been done in the past. That section is dated because today, somewhere, someone is doing something which should be included in that section. The second part of the book contains suggestions as to what we all should be doing in the future. The bulk of that section is timeless; since most of these suggestions must be continued, as a matter of course, if we are to act responsibly with the resources we have and will have in the future. A few new techniques and methods may be added in time, but the basic strategies are valid over time, with only some additions and modifications as to how to save water and still have attractive and functional landscapes.

This book is meant for use by everyone who is interested in or involved in landscape operations from the homeowner with a casual interest to the full time professional in the fields of landscape architecture, landscape contracting or grounds maintanance. This book shows:

- what others have done,
- what you can do,
- what you should do.

Dealing with a drought or with water shortages is usually regional; the problem and concern is regional and usually the solutions and dissemination of relevant information are equally regional. Most of those working in one region are usually not aware of what others have done or are doing in other areas. Therefore there is a continual "re-inventing of the wheel". This book is meant to share the readily available information with a much wider audience. There is much out there that we didn't find and an on-going methodology needs to be developed to share information and to find out what is being done on a regular basis in a number of areas. Everyone is well-intentioned, but they operate in a vacuum, there is no overall picture. This book is intended to be one more piece in the puzzle which will help many to save much water and to still have all of the many advantages which an attractive and healthy landscape can provide.

This book was made possible through the cooperation and assistance of a large number of people and recognition and thanks must be expressed to them. Kevin Sloan was responsible for the rough sketches and the final illustrations and did an excellent job in translating complex and confusing scientific data into understandable drawing to help communicate ideas, approaches and concepts. Regina Kurtz was responsible for much of the initial graphic design and layout and established the format. Lois Glick and Jan Bentley were responsible for much of the typesetting. Others such as Larry Caudill of the City of Albuquerque, N.M., Jerry Lawson and Michael Personett

of the City of Austin, Texas, Tom Schultz
of the Irrigation Association and Kathy
Copley, Editor of Grounds Maintenance
magazine were especially helpful in providing information and encouragement
in making this book a reality. Special
thanks needs to be extended to all of those
who shared information and material which
is included in the various sections of this
book. There are some outstanding people
and programs, fortunately they were interested enough in communicating and in
sharing their experience to help make this
a better book.

introduction

LANDSCAPE DESIGN AND MANAGEMENT FOR WATER CONSERVATION

The problem is not lack of water, the problem is that all of the available water is not being used carefully enough on the right plants in the right places. 🙶

In the future we are not going to have as much water for landscape use as we have had in the past. As a greater area of the North American continent is developed and as people continue to move into the more desirable warmer and arid regions, water shortages will probably be a constantly recurring problem. Periodic regional water shortages have caused great difficulty for all segments of society. Landscape development almost always includes some element which requires water in order to thrive or even to exist. Planting of all types requires some water, either at installation or during the growing lifetime of the vegetation. The landscape is a "soft" area. It is usually the first to be eliminated and the last to be funded in a budgetary, energy or water crisis. Therefore in times of water shortage landscape development will suffer unless it is properly designed, installed and maintained.

As competition for available water becomes greater there will be much less to use in landscape situations for the maintenance of plantings. Any time there is a shortage or curtailment of available water, there will be strong competition for that water. With increasing concern for the energy crisis, the energy required to provide water to certain areas or regions will become much more critical. As water becomes more scarce and as competition for it increases, the cost of the energy necessary to provide it will also increase.

In certain perennially dry areas of North America it already costs a great deal to provide water. In tight economic times this cost will be scrutinized more carefully. Traditionally throughout history people have moved to water and away from shortages or drought. This is no longer as feasible as it once was. Water shortages have always occurred periodically in nearly every geographic location and period of time in history. When these shortages occur, those in the landscape industry must cope. The purpose of this book is to provide assistance in doing that.

Vegetation used in landscape development is quite often the first area to suffer in times of water shortage. Much landscape development has taken place in areas which are periodically or perennially dry. Some of the landscape development in these arid areas is basically "wrong" for the area. Landscape development is needed for a variety of reasons. Vegetation and plant materials of all types perform a great variety of services; they quiet, soften, and clean the environment. Therefore strategies need to be developed for doing more landscape development while using less water. The problem is not lack of water, the problem is that all of the available water is not being used carefully enough on the right plants in the right places. The "bad" habits that have developed during periods of abundant and inexpensive water will have to be changed. This book shows how that can be done and how it has been done in other situations and circumstances.

The recognition and acceptance of the water shortage as equal in urgency to the energy crisis is actually very good discipline for the entire landscape industry. It requires more careful use of existing resources and will lead to a more sensitive use of native or indigenous vegetation in each geographic region. This book will discuss the impact of water in human life and activity, the basic water cycle, the predictable recurrences of periodic water shortages, the competition for water between agriculture, industry and urban development, the relationship between landscape development and water use, and finally, the basic strategies or approaches for water conservation in landscape design and management.

There are certain approaches used in dealing with water shortages, and in conserving water in landscape development. There are also a number of ways others have dealt with similar problems in other situations as sporadic water shortages have occurred in different geographic regions of the United States. There are basically three strategies which can be used in dealing with landscape design and management for water conservation. These three approaches or strategies are:
1. To use available water more carefully
2. To design or redesign a landscape so that less water is required
3. To apply water to plants much more carefully and precisely

Detailed strategies based on these three approaches will be discussed in this publication in greater detail. They are:
- Controlling the water falling on the site in order to use it more efficiently and effectively
- Selecting plants which require less water
- Exploring the possibility of leaving plants in a stress condition with minimum water application
- Providing for the erection of wind barriers to reduce the dehydration of the soil around the plants
- Changing the appearance of an area in the landscape so that it will be more naturally manicured and thus will require the use of less water

- Exploring ways to redesign various regional landscapes to require less water

- Altering cultural practices so as to require less water
- Applying mulches or other materials to reduce the transpiration of water from soil
- Applying anti-transpirants to the plant so that existing moisture will remain and be used within the plant
- Exploring the reuse of water on the site
- Evaluating ways to make existing water "wetter" and to increase its effectiveness
- Exploring the options of sprinkler or drip irrigation systems in establishing watering priorities and altering irrigation practices to use irrigation water more efficiently.

Also included is a listing of resources and one of the most complete bibliographies ever developed on this subject. **LANDSCAPE DESIGN AND MANAGEMENT FOR WATER CONSERVATION** is essentially an introductory primer pulling together the experience of many diverse groups or individuals as they have attempted to deal with drought and water shortages in many areas of the United States during the past decade. It is not meant to be a highly technical reference nor is it intentionally biased or prejudiced in any direction. It merely elaborates on some of the strategies which can be used to conserve water and at the same time preserve and enhance planting and plants as used in landscape development.

. . . strategies which can be used are:

1. To use available water more carefully.
2. To design or redesign a landscape so that less water is required.
3. To apply water to plants much more carefully and precisely.

water in human life

❝ . . .with the technology for transporting substantial amounts of water great distances has come the 'Sun Belt' in the United States, an area of warm winters, scanty rainfall or snowfall, abundant sunshine and a limited water supply. ❞

Throughout human history the location, the amount, and the availability of water strongly influenced where people have lived and how they have lived. Once water was used only for drinking. Then, as man's technology improved, water was diverted and used to consciously promote agriculture. Now we have developed many more water-intensive technologies. As society becomes more complex we use more water for more purposes. Also, as technology becomes more complex, it costs more to "treat," clean, or purify water. The higher cost of usable water increases the cost of everything associated with industry, agriculture, and urban development.

Throughout history the lack of water has been a limitation to development. Quite often, because human society did not have the capability to provide water, certain geographic areas were not developed. Generally, as soon as the technology was developed to provide water in a given area, that area was settled. At one time entire societies and cultures moved from place to place to take advantage of available water. In contemporary culture, this kind of mobility is restricted to a much greater extent. A greater investment has been made in infrastructural development which cannot be easily moved or abandoned. Concomitant with this development is a quantum increase in water requirements for various services and activities. While we use more water now for more purposes than in the past, there are also more of us due to an increasing population on a somewhat limited land area. Although people have historically avoided the traditionally dry areas of the world, some of the otherwise most desirable places to live are areas of limited water supply. Thus with the technology for transporting substantial amounts of water great distances has come the popularity of the "Sun Belt" in the United States, an area of warm winters, scanty snowfall, abundant sunshine, and a limited water supply.

Throughout history some technology for moving water has existed. The expansion of the Roman Empire was substantially assisted by the technology possessed by Roman engineers for moving water. There is, however, both a cost and a time factor in transporting large amounts of water great distances. Today we have perfected water moving techniques to an unprecedented degree, at great costs and through the use of a great deal of scarce and expensive energy. Water is still a universal solvent, and it is necessary for drinking, for sanitation, for irrigation, for cleanliness, and for various aspects of industrial development.

In an article entitled, "Our Most Precious Resource: Water," written by Thomas Y. Canby, published in the August 1980 issue of *NATIONAL GEOGRAPHIC* Magazine, the following statement was made.

> Partly because we can take water for granted, partly because it's cheaper than dirt (in most cities 15 cents will get you a ton delivered in your kitchen), we use it lavishly. On an average day you and I each draw about 87 gallons: 24 for flushing, 32 for bathing, laundry, and dishwashing, and 25 for swimming pools and watering the lawn. We use a mere two gallons for drinking and cooking—the only water we actually

require to survive.*

Water is used by agriculture to feed an increasing population. Water is used for industry. Water is used for energy development, especially in the emerging technologies of oil shale and coal gasification processes. Water is necessary for urban growth and development. As life has gotten more complex and technology more sophisticated, the need for water has increased geometrically.

In a cover story from the February 23, 1981 issue of *NEWSWEEK* Magazine entitled, "Are We Running Out of Water?" the hidden cost of water was explained in the following words:

> Just as Americans have discovered the hidden energy costs in a multitude of products—in refrigerating a steak, for example, on its way to the butcher—they are about to discover the hidden water costs. Beginning with the water that irrigated the corn that was fed to the steer, the steak may have accounted for 3,500 gallons. The water that goes into a 1,000-pound steer would float a destroyer. It takes 14,935 gallons of water to grow a bushel of wheat, 60,000 gallons to produce a ton of steel, 120 gallons to put a single egg on the breakfast table. **

Generally, most people think in terms of the amount of water which is used by an individual single family home, rather than the total water consumed both directly and indirectly by residents of certain areas or regions. In a publication produced by the Geological Survey of the U.S. Department of the Interior entitled, "How Much Water in a 12-Ounce Can? A Perspective on Water-Use Information," the following analysis of water use and its variation was made:

* Thomas Y. Canby, "Our Most Precious Resource: Water,"**National Geographic,**Vol. 158, No. 2, August 1980, p. 144-179.
** Jerry Adler, "Are We Running Out of Water?" **Newsweek,** February 23, 1981, p. 26-37.

On a hot afternoon after mowing the lawn, or after returning home from a round of golf, or when just resting from your daily toil, have you ever gone to the refrigerator to satisfy your thirst with a 12-ounce (355-milliliter) can of your favorite beverage? You want to relax and reflect on the activities of the day, but your act of consuming the contents of that 12-ounce can is the culmination of a long chain of processes requiring energy, materials, water, labor, and management. Let us consider your effect as a consumer on the water resources of the Nation and try to answer the question, "How much water is in a 12-ounce can?" Twelve ounces, of course—three-eighths of a quart, or, in the metric system, 0.355 liter (0.000355 cubic meter). But wait a minute; let's rephrase the question to "How much water did it take to manufacture the 12-ounce can?" Doesn't it take water to clean the can before it is filled, water to produce the steel or aluminum used in the can, water to mine the coal that is used in converting iron ore to metallic iron in making steel used in the can, and water for cooling in the thermal electric plants that supply these industries with electric energy?

Let us use that can from which you were about to pour your 12-ounce drink as an example for exploring the ramifications of one of our simple daily water-consumption decisions. The fabrication of metal cans requires a small quantity of water for a variety of in-plant purposes such as cooling and washing. In 1968, nationwide water withdrawals for this industry totaled 7 billion liters(7.4 billion quarts). The average in-plant water use per can is about 0.2 liter of water withdrawn. This small direct use of water is an obvious consequence of your consumption of a beverage in a 12-ounce can. But what of the indirect uses of water necessary to sustain the industries that directly supply the can manufacturers with goods and services?

Using 1967 data, it is estimated that supporting industries directly supplying the metal-can fabrication industry withdraw about 23 liters (24.3 quarts) of water per can produced. Each of these supporting industries, in turn, must purchase goods and services from still other industries. As those purchases "ripple out" through our economy, additional economic sectors become involved. The accumulated water withdrawals for all the indirect suppliers total 40 liters (42.3 quarts) per can, thus increasing water withdrawals by both direct and indirect suppliers to about 63 liters (66.6 quarts) per can.

You might question the need for this type of information; certainly, your individual decision to consume the contents of one can has little impact on water use. In the aggregate, however, the water-use decisions of a large group of individuals, or national policy decisions on water use that affect many individuals, may have a considerable impact. Also, the accumulated indirect effects of an industrial water use are often more significant than the direct water use in that industry, as in the example where an additional 63 liters (66.6 quarts) per can is withdrawn by direct and indirect suppliers to a can manufacturer.*

That same publication goes on to discuss water usage in the home and per capita water use in the following words:

Household uses of water also vary greatly in magnitude. Household uses are internationally expressed in terms of liters (1 liter equals 1.0567 quarts) per day per person, and depend upon such characteristics as climate, accessibility (connected or not connected to a public water-supply system), water quality, water pressure, cost, outdoor needs (lawn, garden, pool), and whether or not the water supply is metered. Although a person needs less than 2 liters (2.1 quarts) of water a day (from liquid and solid foods) to survive, in the United States the actual daily household use (indoor and outdoor) ranges from less than 40 liters (42.3 quarts) per capita in some homes without plumbing to several hundred liters per capita in affluent homes with watered lawns. Lawn watering and toilet flushing are the two largest household uses of water. Table 1 shows a hypothetical example of average daily water use in the future by a family of four (assuming that family has two bathrooms, a garbage-disposal unit, a dishwasher, an automatic laundry, and two automobiles).

Daily per capita water use in the United States is sometimes expressed as a nationwide average for a given year. The average daily per capita *household* use for 1970 was about 280 liters (297 quarts) per person for homes connected to public water-supply systems; however, the total average daily per capita use of freshwater for *all* withdrawal uses—for agricultural irrigation, self-supplied rural homes (domestic and livestock uses), self-supplied industries, and public supplies—was nearly 6,000 liters (6,360 quarts) per capita for the same year (table 2). **

*I.C. James III, et. al., " How Much Water in a 12-ounce Can?, A Perspective on Water-Use Information," pamphlet produced by the Geological Survey of the U.S. Department of the Interior, reprint from the U.S.G.S. Annual Report, Fiscal Year 1976, USGPO 1978-261-226/30, Washington, D.C. 1978.

**Ibid. p.6-7.

—Water withdrawals by direct
and indirect suppliers for the fabrication
of a 12-ounce beverage can. (1 liter equals
approximately 1 quart.)

CAN FABRICATION

AN AVERAGE OF 0.2 LITER OF
WATER IS WITHDRAWN FOR THE
MANUFACTURE OF A SINGLE
CAN

DIRECT INPUTS

WATER WITHDRAWALS IN LITERS
PER CAN(TOTAL IS 22.95 LITERS)

INDIRECT INPUTS

WATER WITHDRAWALS IN LITERS
PER CAN (TOTAL IS 39.99 LITERS)

ROOT BEER

12 OZ.
0.355 LITER

SECTOR

IRON AND STEEL — 19.08 LITERS

THERMOELECTRIC POWER — 3.42 LITERS

OTHER — 0.45 LITER

SECTOR

IRON AND STEEL — 6.13 LITERS

THERMOELECTRIC POWER — 14.75 LITERS

AGRICULTURE — 13.27 LITERS

MINING — 2.18 LITERS

CHEMICALS — 1.44 LITERS

PAPER — 1.32 LITERS

OTHER — 0.90 LITER *

In times when abundant water has been available there was little difficulty in allocating water resources. The water was used as necessary by each of the segments of society or of the economy. However, in times of drought or water shortages, the competition for existing water resources has become severe. Water is needed for agriculture, for industry, for energy development, and for urban development to mention only a few. Water is also needed to grow, to preserve, and to enhance landscape development in most areas of the nation. The allocation of the limited supply of water so as to best serve present and future and future societies becomes a question requiring knowledgeable and carefully thought out decisions.

TABLE 1.—Anticipated daily domestic uses of water by a family of four. (Adapted from Reid, 1965, p. 18.)

Family use of water	Liters per day per family	Liters per day per capita	Gallons per day per family	Gallons per day per capita
Drinking and water used in kitchen	30	7.6	8	2
Dishwasher (3 loads per day)	57	14	15	3.75
Toilet (16 flushes per day)	363	91	96	24
Bathing (4 baths or showers per day)	303	76	80	20
Laundering (6 loads per week)	129	32	34	8.5
Automobile washing (2 carwashes per month)	38	9.5	10	2.5
Lawn watering (180 hours per year)	379	95	100	25
Garbage disposal unit (1 percent of all other uses)	13	3	3	0.75
Total	1,312	328	346	86.5

**

* Ibid., p. 4.

** Ibid., p. 6.

TABLE 2.—Estimated daily per capita use of freshwater in the United States.

	Gallons per person per day	Liters per person per day
Water required for survival	Less than ½	Less than 2
Average personal consumption of water (liquids and water in foods).	About 1	About 4
Domestic uses of all kinds (indoor and outdoor uses), 1970; home connected to public water-supply system.	75	280
	National averages in 1975	
Public water systems, including public-supply water for domestic, industrial, commercial, and public (fire-fighting, parks, etc.) uses and water-system losses (population[1] served in 1975: 175,000,000).	168	636
Self-supplied industrial use (total population[1] in 1975: 217,000,000).	783	2,960
Combined public, rural, industrial, and irrigation uses (excluding hydroelectric power).	1,600	6,000
	(If saline water use is added, per capita use is 1,930 gallons, or 7,310 liters.)	
Water for hydroelectric power	15,200	57,500 *

[1] Includes Puerto Rico and Virgin Islands (U.S.).
Source of data for 1975: Murray and Reeves, 1977.

* Ibid., p. 6.

water cycle

 Water, which was once thought to be free and plentiful, will become increasingly expensive as man is required more and more to interfere in and modify the water cycle.

The entire water supply on the planet Earth is a closed system. Water changes form and location, not always in the form and in the location we desire, but almost no water which has existed on the earth has ever disappeared. It has been said that the water in which John the Baptist baptized Christ still exists and is scattered throughout the earth. In its simplest form the water cycle consists of precipitation and evaporation. Water is evaporated into the atmosphere from oceans, lakes, and other water bodies, from the soil surface and from vegetation. It is transported from place to place in clouds and is then precipitated back to the earth in the form of rain, snow, sleet, or hail. Then it flows across and through the earth either toward rivers, lakes or oceans, or is stored in underground reservoirs or aquifers. Therefore water is endlessly moving and endlessly changing form in a continual cycle powered by the sun and by gravity. Generally, these patterns occur in rather predictable ways and in predictable locations, thus producing chronic situations of too much water in some places and too little water in others. This system generally functions apart from man.

Occasionally, however, it is thought to be advisable to allow for human interference and modification. This may be in the form of cloud seeding to encourage precipitation, of pumping water from underground aquifers, or of irrigation of agricultural or landscape crops in order to provide for their growth in otherwise dry areas. Human interference in the basic water cycle is thought necessary to either speed up the process, to modify it (for instance to clean the water more quickly as it moves through the process), or to desalinate sea water. Generally human interference and modification is both expensive and energy consuming. All of the costs and energy requirements for modification of the water cycle will probably never ever be fully measured. Basically water is almost always available, but the cost may prohibit using it in the traditional way. Water, which was once thought to be free and plentiful, will become increasingly expensive as man is required more and more to interfere in and modify the water cycle.

There is not necessarily a lack of water, there is a competition for available water resources. In an article in the April 4, 1977 issue of *TIME MAGAZINE*, the following statement was made:

> Over 97 percent of the world's water is in oceans and too saline for most uses. Of the 2.7 percent of the water that is fresh, more than three quarters is locked either in glaciers or polar ice. Another large portion is trapped in underground aquifers too far beneath the earth's surface for easy withdrawal. Of all the world's fresh water only .36 percent, in lakes, rivers and streams, is easily accessible and available for human use. The demand for this limited supply of drinking water is increasing and varies greatly among locations. In some African lands, a human may use only .8 gallons of water daily. Metropolitan per capita water-usage figures include:

London 68 gallons, Paris 130 gallons, Moscow 160 gallons, and New York 270 gallons.*

Much of the available water in the drier sections of North America is located in underground aquifers. These aquifers are rapidly being depleted because of excessive pumping for use in agriculture and in industry. Increasingly in the future more water may have to be taken from existing lakes and rivers and even from the oceans to provide for the greater water needs and demands. If water is wasted in caring for landscape development, then the necessary water may not be available for agricultural, domestic or industrial needs. There is only a finite, measurable amount of water which exists in the entire water cycle on earth. It can generally only change from one form to another at a certain predictable rate of speed. Therefore it is essential that the portion of water from the cycle needed for the preservation and growth of landscape development be used most efficiently and effectively.

Water is an emotional issue in many areas and situations. Water is used in a great many ways that are not readily apparent. These many hidden uses are as important as those uses which are readily evident. It is equally vital to allocate water for industrial or commercial uses which are "invisible" as it is for irrigation, car washing or decorative fountains and pools. Irrigation water may be essential to grow the food we eat but it may also be as important to process and transport the food to our tables.

As populations grow, more water will be needed. At the same time, new technology requires more water, so the per capita water use is increasing. Much of this growth is taking place in geographic areas with a limited available supply of water. The availability of adequate water is often a controlling or determining factor in physical development. The amount of water used and the way it is used is increasing exponentially because of these factors.

It is essential to understand the full range of water needs and water usage to put landscape irrigation water needs and usage into perspective. More landscape development generally requires more water usage. Water used in perserving the landscape is water that cannot be used, at the same time, for other purposes.

Water is constantly moving and changing form and location. It goes round and round in a cycle as it changes from liquid to gas to solid depending on the temperature and its location on the globe. Water is polluted and purified over and over again, sometimes naturally and sometimes by human means. Water is purified naturally as it moves through the soil and is purified by man either through chemical means or by helping to speed up the natural processes. In some cases water is pumped from lakes and rivers, used, and then put back into those same lakes and rivers in substantially the same form and purity. In the same way water is pumped from the earth, used, and then returned to the earth for reuse by someone else at a later time or in another place.

The water cycle is in reality a series of spirals moving across and around the globe. There are, at the same time, macro and micro water cycles and each plant in the landscape is a part of the miniature water cycle. Each plant used or found in the landscape is a "water pump", pulling water out of the soil and putting it back into the atmosphere. In times of water shortages this is a substantial problem since the plants "use" water that may be needed for other purposes.

In order to conserve water and to use available water most efficiently and effectively in landscape operations it is necessary to interfere with or modify the small scale aspects of the overall water cycle. In order to do that it is vital to understand the basic cycle at all scales.

* **Time,** April 4, 1977, Vol. 109, No. 14, pp.48-51.

Alan Anderson, Jr., in the **Across the Board** article included a box which explained the water cycle as, "The Water Machine" in the following words:

"The constancy of the earth's water supply is one of nature's great wonders. Our water molecules do not fly apart into hydrogen and oxygen, they don't flee our atmosphere into space, they don't slither down deep-earth crevices. Virtually all the water on earth - about 326 million cubic miles of it - has been present as liquid, ice, or vapor since it spewed out of countless volcanoes 3 billion years ago and more. All of it, whether trapped in dark mile deep in Antarctic ice or drifting high and fast a particle of cloud, is part of the vast, complex machine called the hydrologic cycle.

The machine, by far the world's largest, is powered by the sun. Solar energy provides enough heat to evaporate about 140,000 cubic miles of water a year; the same amount returns to the earth's surface as precipitation.

A water molecule's rate of movement through the cycle depends on weather systems (which are also driven by solar energy). A molecule of water may leap from a foaming ocean wave one moment, and return the next. If it soars clear of the waves, it will float in the atmosphere an average of 12 days before falling back to earth. If it falls on land, it may remain in a stream for a few hours or days, in a glacier for 40 years, in a lake for 100 years, in groundwater for 200 to 10,000 years, a polar ice cap for millions of years. Eventually, however, our molecule will find its way back to the ocean.

For humans, the most important fraction of the hydrologic cycle is that which flows through rivers and streams. About 94 percent of the fresh water we use for all purposes comes from streamflow; the rest comes from groundwater, the vast underground zones of saturated sand and rock. Not until the 17th century did scientists discover that rainfall is the source of all streamflow (and groundwater). Through most of history, humans were baffled that the Nile, for example, could continue flowing through a desert, or that other rivers were constantly replenished long after the most recent rain. Only during the scientific revolution did scientists realize that most natural systems are cyclical, and that water, too, has its cycle - that it evaporates from land and sea, falls again as rain and snow, sinks into the earth to reappear in watercourses, and then drains back into the sea.

An average of 4,200 billion gallons of rain fall on the United States each day. The largest portion of that - some 65 percent - reevaporates or transpires through the leaves of plants. About 30 percent finds its way back to the oceans as streamflow. Much of that quantity is "used"; we humans withdraw about 338 billion gallons a day (bgd) for agriculture, industry, and city water systems. Of that amount, we consume 106 bgd - that is, incorporate it into products or evaporate it for cooling. Another 100 bgd sink into the ground to creep slowly seaward as groundwater, and 15 bgd evaporate from man-made reservoirs. Virtually all of it returns eventually to the oceans - eternally a part of the hydrologic cycle. *

---

* Anderson, Alan, Jr., "New Economic Theorem - There is No Such Thing as Free Water" **Across the Board,** Vol. XVIII, No. 9, October 1981, p. 50.

The water cycle is a never ending spiral moving continuously around the globe. Water is always changing place and form. All plants, including landscape plants are an important and integral component in that overall cycle and they help to speed up and implement the process.

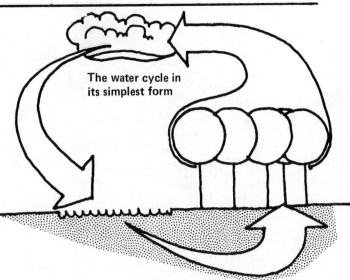

The water cycle in its simplest form

The Water Spiral

In the simplest form, water is pulled out of plants, out of the soil and out of lakes, rivers and oceans as it is converted into a gas or into droplets. It then falls back to earth as rain, snow, sleet or hail. After it reaches the earth it moves through the soil either to plant roots or through aquifers or over land to rivers which carry it to lakes or oceans from which it is once again evaporated or transpired back into the atmosphere.

The plant **is** a very efficient water pump. The many leaves increase the surface exposed to the dry air. The moisture is pulled out of the soil by the roots and moves through the trunks, stems and into the leaves. It then moves out through the openings in the leaves into the air. A mature plant with many leaves can move hundreds of gallons of water per day out of the soil and into the air as a part of the water cycle. That water must be replaced either by rainfall or by irrigation. If it is not the plant suffers and may die. Irrigation takes water from somewhere else and puts it back around the plants and into the cycle in a selected location.

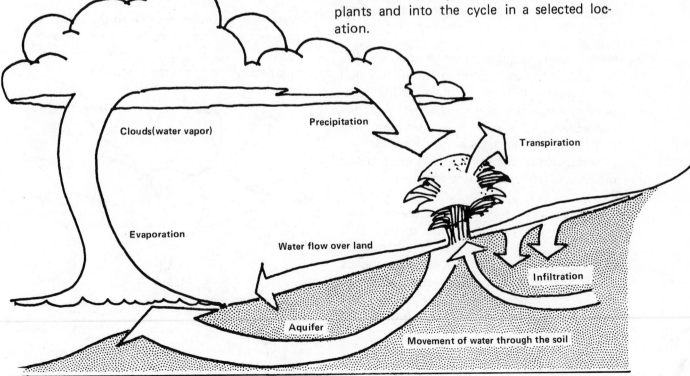

Clouds(water vapor)

Precipitation

Transpiration

Evaporation

Water flow over land

Infiltration

Aquifer

Movement of water through the soil

11

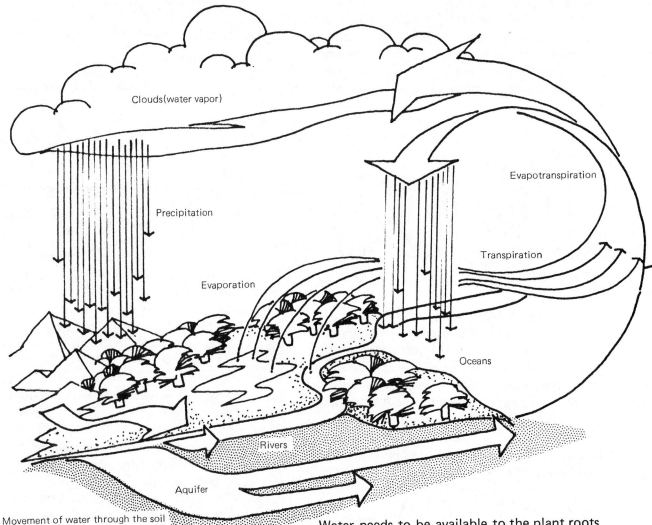

Clouds(water vapor)

Precipitation

Evapotranspiration

Evaporation

Transpiration

Oceans

Rivers

Aquifer

Movement of water through the soil

Plants use a great deal of water and they pull this out of the soil. Some of what they pull out is moved through the plant and is transpired through the plant leaves back into the atmosphere. The plant is a water pump and all plants together use and pump a great deal of water out of the soil and into the air to be moved and used somewhere else.

The entire water cycle is extremely complex. It is quite clearly not possible to discuss it here in all of its detail. But it is important to understand the process, the role landscape plants play in it and the effect it has on irrigation, on water needs and the ways to conserve water or to use it more efficiently.

Water needs to be available to the plant roots to provide nutrients, to be used as a solvent, to move through the plant stems to assist in circulation and to promote growth.

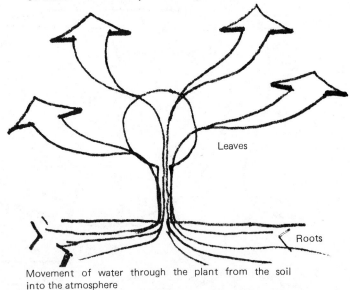

Leaves

Roots

Movement of water through the plant from the soil into the atmosphere

There is no more or less water on the planet than there ever has been. There is only the same water in different forms which has been used over and over again throughout history. Even though there is an abundance of water on the planet, periodic, localized water shortages are "real". They will continue to happen with greater regularity in years to come. They serve to accentuate the competition for available water supplies and they emphasize and heighten water use priorities. Most "water shortages" are a result of inequitable distribution. There is "in fact" only a shortage of available water in one place at one time at one cost for certain purposes, not an actual water shortage on the earth. Shortages will usually drive up the cost of water and as it becomes in short supply expense may make it too expensive or too scarce to use water for landscape growth and preservation. Because of the generally low status of landscape elements in our culture and society, water shortages have a greater impact on its use for landscape irrigation than in nearly any other use of water. Water shortages usually first bring regulation or control of water for landscape preservation and growth.

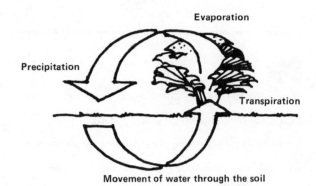

Movement of water through the soil

Even if shortages are less common, the cost of water will increase to cover the expense of construction of water processing facilities and the means to move water from where it exists to where it is needed or wanted. In some cases the extra cost will be to cover to expense of converting salt water to fresh to meet future water needs and requirements. This more expensive water may make it too expensive to use for landscape irrigation in the way it is now used.

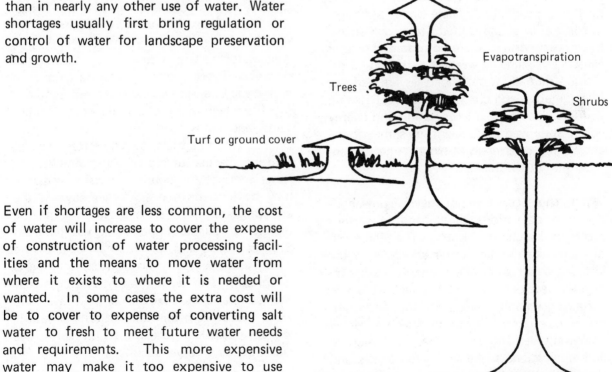

Plants pull water out of the soil to different depths depending on the depth of the roots and the availability of moisture in the soil

water shortages

It is during water shortages that the competition for limited available water resources becomes critical, and it is then possible to see the relative priorities placed by a conserver society.

Almost every summer and fall newspaper and magazine headlines indicate water shortages in some area of the United States or Canada. Each year brings periodic water shortages caused by changing weather patterns and decreased rainfall. Water shortages are periodic in some areas and chronic in others. Dried-up aquifers, increased transportation and energy costs, and overdevelopment in some of the chronically drier areas of North America contribute to the problem.

Water shortages are not new. They have occurred at various times, and in various places throughout history. The increased publicity surrounding water shortages in the last decade or so is due primarily to the increased development that has taken place in certain geographic areas. In the past half-century, contemporary technology has created increasing demands for water, and modern communications make us more quickly and more clearly aware of water shortages wherever they are. In the past such water shortages occurred, but the communications network did not exist for sharing with a wider audience the intricacy of coping with shortages.

When extensive water shortages occur what happens usually depends on how acute the shortage is. Initially, some water priorities are established within the region, and then successive water restrictions, water rationing, and water allocation may be implemented as the situation becomes more serious. In some cases residents have been asked to cut back on water usage by 10, 15, 20, 25, and in some cases, as much as 50 to 60%. In Marin County, in northern California during the severe water crisis which occurred there in the mid-1970's, residents were required, not asked, to cut back on water usage to approximately 37-42 gallons per person per day. One of the first areas to be restricted in any water shortage situation, is the watering of lawns and the use of outdoor water to maintain landscape materials. This, together with restricting the washing of cars, is usually the first sign of a water crisis in any geographic area. As the water crisis becomes more serious or extends in time, various other levels of restraint may be established based on the priorities for "hard" water needs and "soft" water needs. The hard needs for water obviously are for drinking water, cooking and cleanliness, as well as for certain industrial and agricultural purposes. Those "softer" water needs involve appearances and amenities related to automobiles, swimming pools, decorative fountains, and landscaped areas. These are considered non-essentials and therefore do not warrant the use of scarce water supplies. In some areas of the country, outside watering may be limited to every other day. As the crisis becomes more serious, watering may be limited to four hours per week, usually from 8:00 to 10:00 a.m. on alternate days of the week, and eventually no outside watering is permitted. It is during water shortages that the competition for the limited available water resources becomes most critical, and it is then possible to see the relative priorities placed by a conserver society.

Each summer newspaper stories tell of local water shortages. The following is a wire services report during the late summer of 1983.

Towns limit water use in heat's wake

From wire reports

Community officials in at least six states asked residents to conserve water Wednesday as a heat wave, blamed for 10 deaths, wilted corn plants and seared other crops.

Farmers from North Carolina to the Kansas plains, where temperatures reached 107 Tuesday, complained that heat and lack of rain were threatening their livestock and crops.

Almost 100 cattle worth nearly $60,000 died in a feedlot in the south central South Dakota town of Academy when the temperature reached 103.

A federal economist said officials can't predict the impact of the two-week hot spell.

Officials in Edwardsville, Ill., and in Cobb and Fulton counties in Georgia warned residents not to water their parched lawns or wash their cars. Forty towns in Massachusetts, several in New Jersey and Maryland and the town of Kearney, Neb., have restricted water use.

Pepper plants in New Jersey looked as though they had been cooked, said Robert Langlois, the agricultural agent for Gloucester County. He said production could be down 10 to 20 percent.

The heat and dry spell will hurt the corn crop in North Carolina, said an agriculture specialist.

Officials blamed five deaths since Friday on 100-degree weather in the St. Louis area, where 50 emergency shelters have opened.

As a result of these periodic shortages a wide variety of specific programs have been instituted on a local, regional or national basis. Some of these are presented in the following pages to show the extent of the water shortages and the way in which these shortages have impacted on landscape related water use. Among these examples are some very innovative public education and awareness programs in addition to a number of unique and effective means of communication. These are by no means all such efforts but these particular ones are presented here only to show the extent of the water shortages and the diversity of responses which are possible.

More other responses and approaches are mentioned in some of the publications listed in the bibliography.

Grounds Maintenance Magazine instituted a symbol to designate advertised products that contribute to effective landscape management in the face of reduced water supplies. This was used throughout the magazine in individual advertisements for products or materials used in the industry. This helped to focus attention on the problem and identified those who were helping to contribute to the solution in the marketplace.

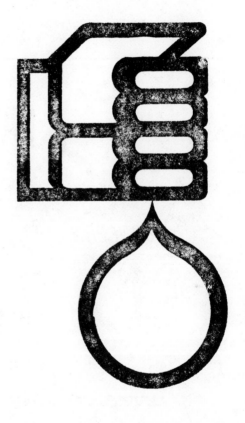

 designates advertised products that contribute to effective landscape management in the face of reduced water supplies.

The Texas Water Resources Institute in their newsletter, **Texas Water Resources,** reproduced a chart which shows the "hydro-illogical cycle" which occurs both when there is a shortage of water as well as when there is plenty. The attitudes of consumers change very quickly and their collective memory is quite short. Water is still subconsciously thought to be "free" and abundant as it was in the past in many areas of the world.

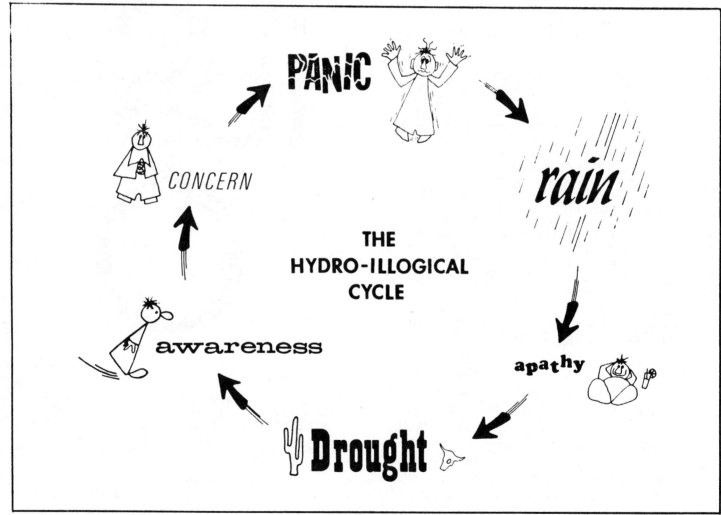

Reprinted from **Water for Texas,** *Vol. 5, No. 10.*

Texas Water Resources, Texas Water Resources Institute, Texas A. & M. University, College Station, Texas, May 1980, Vol. 6, No. 4, p. 3.

During the summer of 1983, the City of Austin, Texas faced potential water shortages. To point up the problem and to help educate the public, a series of activities were coordinated and integrated into an overall program. The **Austin American Statesman,** the major local newspaper, published each day, in the upper left corner of the front page, a chart which showed daily water consumption for the week before. The charts for three different days are shown below. It may be seen that a heavy rain on August 6 decreased substantially the water demands and consumption for the next week. This very visible reminder to the general public each day pointed up the water shortage and the need for conservation.

Austin's water consumption

As the hottest days of summer arrive, the demand on the city's water treatment system is expected to increase. To encourage awareness of water use, the American-Statesman will publish water consumption figures daily. Today's figures show consumption from July 26 through Tuesday, the latest figures available. Mandatory water conservation begins after 3 consecutive days at 150 million gallons.

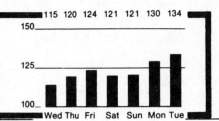

Thursday, August 4, 1983

Austin American - Statesman

Austin's water consumption

As the hottest days of summer arrive, the demand on the city's water treatment system is expected to increase. To encourage awareness of water use, the American-Statesman will publish water consumption figures daily. Today's figures show consumption from July 28 through Wednesday, the latest figures available. Mandatory water conservation begins after 3 consecutive days at 150 million gallons.

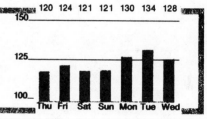

Friday, August 5, 1983 *

Austin American - Statesman

Austin's water consumption

Despite August rains, the demand on the city's water treatment system is expected to increase as summer goes on. To encourage awareness of water use, the American-Statesman will publish water consumption figures daily. Today's figures show consumption from Aug. 7 through Saturday, the latest figures available. Mandatory water conservation will begin if water use is 150 million gallons for 3 consecutive days.

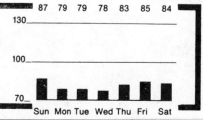

Monday, August 15, 1983 *

Austin American - Statesman

In addition, the Water and Waste Water Department did the following in Austin, Texas during the anticipated water shortage during the summer of 1983:

- published a **Water-Wise Lawn Care** brochure which gave 10 suggestions as to how to maintain a healthy lawn while using less water. This was published in English and Spanish in the same publication; the English translation of this brochure is reproduced on the right of this page.

TEN WAYS TO REDUCE YOUR OUTDOOR WATER USE

Summer water use in Austin is near the treatment and delivery limits of our system. More than twice as much water is used during the summer months than in winter months, with lawn watering the biggest reason for the increase.

The average home lawn is often overwatered. This waste costs you money and does not improve the health of your lawn. Your Water and Wastewater Department suggests the following ten ways to help reduce outdoor water waste and yet maintain a beautiful yard.

1. Check all hose connections, valves and pipes for leaks. Even a small leak can waste hundreds of gallons of water in a single day.

2. Learn your garden's watering needs by studying your yard. How much is topsoil? What is the type of soil? Where are the steep slopes? Which areas have the most shade? etc.

3. Raise the height of your lawn mower. If the lawn is mowed on a regular schedule, only about ⅓ of the grass length needs to be removed. On this schedule, the clippings can remain on the lawn—reducing soil temperatures, helping to retain moisture and providing a natural mulch.

4. Remove weeds before they get large. They not only look bad but they are water thieves—stealing precious water from desirable plants.

5. The best time to water your lawn is early morning. The second best time is evening. However, fungus diseases grow more easily on wet plants and grasses during long evening hours. The most costly time is late morning, midday and afternoon. More water is lost by evaporation during hot parts of the day. Avoid watering when it's windy, as more spray gets on adjoining paving.

6. Be sure the soil is almost dry before watering. Dig down below the surface, rather than just guessing. Moisture sensing devices are easier and more accurate. They tell underground conditions at a glance and come in convenient lengths for shallow and deep-rooted plants.

7. Learn how plants signal for water. Most lawns will lie flat after being stepped on if moisture is low. Many plants lose their shine and start to droop a little before going into wilt. The time to water is when plants need it—rigid schedules waste water.

8. Wait longer times between watering periods. As roots grow deeper, less frequent watering will be required. When watering sloped land, water for a short time only and shut off immediately when runoff begins. Repeat as needed until enough water is applied. If only one spot is dry, water it separately. Remember, water flows through a ⅝-inch garden hose, under normal pressure, at about 10 gallons per minute. This means that an unneeded 30 minutes of watering wastes around 300 gallons of water!

9. Make the most of rainfall. Dig ditches to plants under roof eaves to allow rainwater to reach them. A deep moisture reserve can sometimes carry them through several weeks before more water is needed.

10. Develop a plan to cut waste and stick to it. List the ways you are obviously wasting water. Choose plants that are best suited to your yard. Don't be afraid to make changes—they'll pay off in the long run. Keep a close watch on your water bill to see if your plan is effective.

For more information on water conservation, please call the Water and Wastewater Department's Water Conservation Hotline at 477-7070.

Water-Wise Lawn Care

• published a brochure oulining a 4 stage water conservation program ranging from voluntary conservation to a water alert, to a water warning and to a final stage emergency. The English translation of this brochure is shown below and on the next page.

TO FIND THE WATER CONSERVATION ACTIVITIES FOR EACH STAGE:

1) Use the column for the stage in effect.
2) Read down the column until you find a marked YES block.
3) Read across that row to find the PERMITTED water use.

CONSERVATION REQUIRED

WATER USES*	Stage 1	Stage 2 Water Alert		Stage 3 Water Warning		Stage 4 Water Emergency	
		YES	NO	YES	NO	YES	NO
Wasting Water Prevent water runoff to gutters, ditches or drains	V O L U N T A R Y C O N S E R V A T I O N	●		●		●	
Repair controllable leaks		●		●		●	
ONLY wash sidewalks, driveways, parking areas, tennis courts, patios or any other paved area to remove immediate fire hazards.		●		●		●	
Lawn Watering According to your calendar symbol; every fifth (5th) day; ONLY between the hours of 12:01 a.m. to 12 noon and 6:00 p.m. to 12 midnight by any method		●			●		●
On any day; at any time of day; using ONLY a hand-held hose, faucet filled bucket of five (5) gallons or less, or a drip irrigation system		●			●		●
According to your calendar symbol, every fifth (5th) day; ONLY between the hours of 12:01 a.m. to 12 noon and 6:00 p.m. to 12 midnight using ONLY a hand-held hose, hand-held buckets of five (5) gallons or less, a drip irrigation system or a permanently installed automatic sprinkler system			●	●			●
According to your calendar symbol; every fifth (5th) day; ONLY between the hours of 7:00 p.m. and 12 midnight; using ONLY a hand-held hose, hand-held buckets of five (5) gallons or less or a drip irrigation system			●		●	●	
Car Washing According to your calendar symbol; every fifth (5th) day; ONLY between the hours of 12:01 a.m. to 12 noon and 6:00 p.m. to 12 midnight using ONLY a hand-held bucket or a hand-held hose with a positive shut-off nozzle. To prevent bursting and water waste, remove the nozzle when the hose is not in use.		●		●			●
At a commercial car wash; on any day; at any time of day		●		●			●
On any day of the week; at any time; at any location; IF frequent washings are required for health and safety reasons. For example, garbage trucks and trucks that carry food.		●		●			●
ONLY at commercial car washes; between the hours of 12 noon and 6:00 p.m.; any day of the week			●		●	●	
On any day of the week; ONLY between the hours of 12 noon and 6:00 p.m.; at any location; IF frequent washings are required for health and safety reasons			●		●	●	

*Please see note on page 1.

If you have any questions, please call 477-6511.

This brochure was printed in English and Spanish in the same publication and also was available in a large print copy. It outlined a 4 month period showing what water use was allowed on each day under different water usage constraints.

- in addition, the City sponsored a workshop on how to save water in landscape operations, which was attended by a standing room only group of interested local citizens.

conserveconserveconserveconserve conserveconserveconserveconserve conserveconserveconserveconserve

WHY?

Austin is fortunate to have an adequate SUPPLY of water. But summer peak demands approach and often exceed the capacity of our water treatment and distribution system. If these peak demands continue for many days in a row, several things can happen: 1) water pressure that is needed to fight fires may not be available; 2) areas of the City may be without water for periods of time; 3) major equipment failures are more likely to occur causing even more widespread water shortages.

Improvement projects are continuing, but construction of these projects takes time. This means that while capacity limitations exist, water conservation will be necessary to maintain adequate service throughout the system.

Hopefully, voluntary conservation will be successful enough to prevent required conservation. If required conservation becomes necessary, this brochure explains the Emergency Water Conservation Plan as established by Ordinance 021783-E. Violations of this Ordinance are punishable by a fine not to exceed $200.

PLEASE KEEP THIS BROCHURE AND REFER TO IT THROUGHOUT THE SUMMER.

WHEN?

The Emergency Water Conservation Plan has four stages. These stages are determined by the combined pumpage levels of our water treatment plants, how long this demand lasts, the overnight refill rates for our water reservoirs and any unexpected system failures.

Stage 1, voluntary conservation, begins annually on June 1 and continues through September 30. Stages 2 through 4 require conservation. A specific description of the conditions necessary to begin and end any stage requiring conservation is available for inspection at the Water and Wastewater Administration Building, the main and branch offices of the Utility Customer Service Office, all City of Austin public libraries and the City Clerk's Office. The Water and Wastewater Utility will monitor these conditions and announce the water conservation stage in effect. Throughout the summer months, customers should frequently check the public news media for the stage in effect.

NOTE: *Required water conservation activities for golf courses, swimming pools and ornamental fountains, commercial nurseries and restaurants are also available at the above locations.*

HOW?

The Plan is based upon a calendar symbol system. Although your calendar symbol is especially important for yard watering it also determines many other water conservation activities.

Your symbol is determined by the LAST NUMBER of your house or property address.

If your LAST NUMBER is:	Your Symbol is:
0 or 1	(circle) ●
2 or 3	(triangle) ▲
4 or 5	(diamond) ◆
6 or 7	(square) ■
8 or 9	(star) ★

For example, if an address is 904 East 60th Street, the LAST NUMBER is 4: a diamond.

For your calendar symbol, YOU CAN ONLY WATER ONCE EVERY 5 DAYS. The times and ways you can water are determined by the water conservation stage in effect.

So memorize your symbol; it's important! The calendars that follow show you what days you can water (for multi-unit properties, the lowest address number determines your symbol).

JUNE, JULY, AUGUST, SEPTEMBER calendars showing symbols on each day.

LARGE PRINT COPIES ARE AVAILABLE BY CALLING 477-6511.

The cities of Colorado Springs and Denver in Colorado have developed prototypical water conserving landscapes which serve as guides to local residents and designers. The term, **Xeriscape,** which was defined as the conservation of water through creative landscaping was coined by the staff of the Denver Water Department. With the help and guidance of a large number of groups and individuals the Denver Water Department organized, planned, designed and constructed a Xeriscape demonstration garden outside the Department offices in Denver. The garden was to "offer ideas on water savings in conventional lawn situations; new kinds of grasses that require less water; typical, moderate and low water consuming plants; and ideas for materials that may substitute for some lawn areas.

The staff of the Office of Water Conservation prepared a full color brochure which illustrated the plan of the overall garden and focused on certain areas with perspective sketches to show what was done and why it would help to conserve water. The theme of the Xeriscape garden was "Water Conservation Through Creative Landscaping". *

The same staff also prepared one other booklet which was entitled "Xeriscape - An Overiew of How the Program was Proposed, How it Developed, and Benefits to Date"(October 1982) which provided complete information and background on this very innovative method of public education and awareness. **

The Denver Xeriscape garden has received wide recognition and a number of awards and citations. It was featured on the cover of the American Water Works Association Journal for July of 1983. In a feature story in that issue R. D. Wiley, Manager of General Planning for the Denver Water Department made the following introductory remarks:

> "The most obvious means of conserving water throughout the Denver Water Department's service area is to curb the thirst of homeowner's bluegrass lawns, which consume 80 percent of the residential water used during the summer months. In response to water shortages and a court decree, the water department has undertaken a variety of programs to restrict water use during the growing season and to develop a conservation ethic among customers without imposing unreasonable lifestyle changes." ***

Some of the concepts from the Xeriscape garden were incorporated into landscape design for model homes in the Denver area working with local homebuilders.

XERISCAPE
GARDEN

---

* **Xeriscape,** Office of Water Conservation, Denver Water Department, 1600 West 12th Avenue, Denver, Colorado 80254.

** **Xeriscape Garden - An Overview of How the Program was Proposed, How it Developed, and Benefits to Date.,** Office of Water Conservation, Denver Water Department, 1600 West 12th Avenue, Denver, Colorado 80254.

*** Wiley, R.D., "Denver's Water Conservation Program" American Water Works Association Journal, July 1983, pp. 320-323, JAWWA 5 75(7) 319-382(1983).

"O.K., I give up. What is a Xeriscape?"

Xeriscape (zir'-i-skāp) n. the conservation of water through creative landscaping. [From Greek xeros, dry.] · Xeriscaping, Xeriscaped, Xeriscaper.

This brochure introduces **Xeriscape landscaping**; a word coined to describe the things you can do in your landscape to save water and reduce water bills. Studies show 40% of a total year's average water costs go for lawn and garden watering. Here are tips and materials that will help keep a green oasis around your home, while cutting down the amount of water needed.

Get Organized

Before buying anything, draw a plan of your yard. If you have trouble doing this yourself, contact your local landscape contractor, architect or nurseryman for assistance. Ask yourself how much time and money you want to spend developing and maintaining your landscape. Decide on those areas you want in low, moderate or typical water consuming plantings. Do you have a problem that **Xeriscape** landscaping could solve? How much high-use lawn area do you need? Could a coarser grass with lower water requirements be used in light traffic areas? Could a **Xeriscape** shrub or tree help provide privacy, reduce wind velocity or reduce traffic noise? Consideration of these questions is important for a successful **Xeriscape**.

Design in Mind...Then on Paper

A visit to the Denver Water Department's **Xeriscape** demonstration garden at 1600 West 12th Avenue, just northeast of the Sixth Avenue, Valley Highway interchange will introduce you to some of the plantings and materials available for **Xeriscaping**. Professionals, including local landscape architects, contractors, nurserymen and sod growers, in cooperation with the Associated Landscape Contractors of Colorado and the Rocky Mountain Sod Growers Association, designed and planted this demonstration garden to give you some fresh ideas.

Xeriscape offers ideas on water savings in conventional lawn situations; new kinds of grasses that require less water; typical, moderate and low water-consuming plants; and ideas for materials that may substitute for some lawn areas.

XERISCAPE

XERISCAPE

Xeriscape Considerations

An early part of your plan should consider slope and grade changes. Proper grading will save water and direct drainage away from building foundations. Terracing and retaining walls can be effective in correcting steep slopes, thus allowing for maximum water penetration. Or consider plants that can survive on little water and at the same time control soil erosion.

Factors affecting the location of the plants (i.e. their relationship to buildings, the sun, other plants, etc.) need to be considered. Keep low water-consuming plantings and materials away from those requiring conventional irrigation. Problems with small isolated areas, narrow strips, etc. that are difficult to water efficiently can be eliminated by substituting more effective landscaping. Your nurseryman can help you; he knows the "X-rated" (Xeriscape) plantings that reduce water use.

For grassy areas, you may want to inspect the various types of grasses found in the Denver Water Department's Xeriscape demonstration garden; some require less water than others.

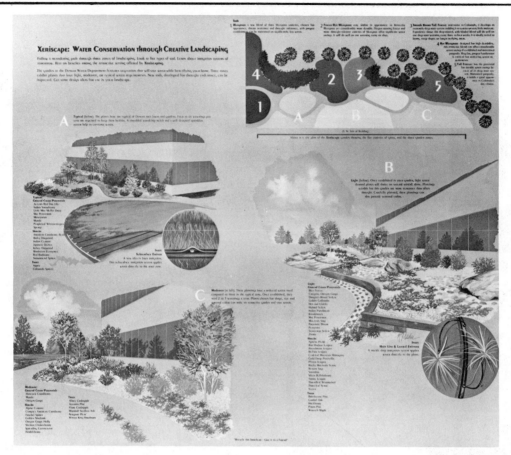

Above: Full color explanatory drawings were included in the Xeriscape brochure which outlined principles, approaches and methods used in the garden.

Below: A sign using the Xeriscape symbol was placed at the entrance to the garden to identify its purpose and plan.

Above: Paved pathways were provided throughout the garden to allow for easy access to each specific area for the greatest number of people with the least destruction or damage to the landscape area.

Below: Shade trees and benches provide a cool place to sit, rest and enjoy the garden which makes it not only educational but shows that a water conserving area can be pleasant and enjoyable as well as responsive and responsible.

Above: This view shows the garden shortly after it has been constructed, installed and planted. In time as the plants mature, it will become a much more finished landscape for the building, but it will continue to be an educational and sensitizing experience for the people of the Denver area.

Below: The types of water conserving trees, shrubs, ground covers and mulches are able to be more clearly seen in a demonstration garden such as this than they ever could in any brochure or publication.

The city of El Paso, Texas is in a very dry area of the nation. The city itself is wedged into a triangle between Mexico and New Mexico. There is little water in west Texas and the city cannot obtain water either from Mexico or from the state of New Mexico. As the city has grown there is almost no water available to maintain landscape plants.

As part of an overall program to encourage water conservation, the El Paso Water Utilities has instituted an awards program to recognize homeowners who have developed low water use landscape development. The program entitled, "Accent-Sun Country" Contest is described in a small brochure as shown below:

"ACCENT-SUN COUNTRY" CONTEST

The "Accent-Sun Country" Landscaping Contest is an annual program directed at spotlighting landscaping materials and techniques that require a minimum of supplemental water. Hopefully, other customers will look at these winners to gain ideas of what can be done to save water, save time and save money and still have an attractively landscaped home.

Over 50% of the water purchased by many residential customers is used for lawn irrigation and about 30% of the total water supplied by the Utility is used for this purpose. This is a "one-time" use of water since there is no significant amount available for a second use like there is when water is used to transport sewage. Let's all get together and help overcome the energy shortage and forestall the water shortage.

Everything points to a higher price for water in the future . . . a short supply, a larger population, increased treatment costs and inflation. Why not plan the type of landscape you can afford? Give yourself a break . . . save energy, water, time and money.

"Accent-Sun Country" Contest endeavors to select the best examples of residential landscaping that requires a minimum of water and yet adds to the beauty of the home. Enter, (even if you've been unsuccessful before) you may be a winner!

"ACCENT-SUN COUNTRY" CONTEST ENTRY BLANK

NAME ———————————————————

ADDRESS ————————————————

ZIP CODE ——————— PHONE ——————

SUB-DIVISION———————————————
MUST BE POSTMARKED BEFORE MIDNIGHT, DECEMBER 31, 1982

MAIL COUPON TO: EL PASO WATER UTILITIES
P.O. BOX 511-EL PASO, TEXAS-79961

RULES FOR
"ACCENT-SUN COUNTRY" CONTEST
(LANDSCAPING FOR LOW WATER USE)

THE WINNERS ARE SELECTED BY QUALIFIED
JUDGES PROVIDED BY THE COUNCIL OF EL PASO
GARDEN CLUBS AND AWARDS ARE PRESENTED IN
APRIL.

1. This contest is open to any occupant of a single family residence located within the city limits of El Paso except employees of the Public Service Board-El Paso Water Utilities, their immediate families, and previous prize winners of the contest.

2. Landscaping to be judged will include only the front yard area.

   (a) Seventy-five (75%) percent of the landscaping must be of low water-consuming plants or materials. (This does not necessarily mean cacti.)

   (b) Grass or other plants requiring more water may complete the landscaping (not more than 25%).

3. Entries may be of any front yard of low water-consuming landscaping completed by December 31, 1982.

4. The plantings must not obstruct the view of traffic or create a hazard to pedestrians.

5. Entries must be postmarked not later than midnight December 31,1982.

6. Entries will be judged between February 1 and March 15, 1983. The decision of the judges will be final.

"ACCENT-SUN COUNTRY" CONTEST
(LANDSCAPING WITH LOW-WATER CONSUMING PLANTS)

SCALE OF POINTS FOR JUDGING

1. DESIGN . . . . 40 POINTS
   a. Composition 20
      Good over all landscape plan
   b. Aesthetic Appeal 10
      Seasonal beauty
   c. Compatability 10
      Relationships of sizes, types
         and colors
      Balance
      Unity

2. SUITABILITY OF MATERIAL . . . . 35 POINTS
   a. Chosen for low-water
         consumption . . . 20
      Must comprise at least
      75% of front yard
   b. Chosen for consideration of
         topography and terrain . . 15
      Relationships of materials
         (plants, ground covers,
         concrete areas, mulches,
         rocks, etc.)

3. MAINTENANCE . . . . 25 POINTS
   a. Chosen for ease of
         maintenance . . . 15
      Minimal care, practicality
   b. Condition 10
      Clean, neat, free of weeds
         and debris.
      Well-groomed, properly
         pruned.
      Evidence of good horti-
         cultural practice—well
         fed, free of disease and
         insect damage.

_____
                                    100 POINTS

The California Water Resources Commission has prepared a checklist for water conservation for use in the review of environment impact statements or reports. This document outlines some of the major considerations which would allow for certain landscape areas to be left in a stress condition or in a natural state. The following is text from a report relating to the use of that checklist.

The following is a guide for EIR reviewers interested in evaluating water conservation in a project. This checklist summarizes those things that affect outdoor water use in urban areas, where 44% of residential water use occurs outside the home. By acting to conserve that water, project by project, through modification of design and choice of plant materials, a cumulative effect will eventually be gained that will result in substantial water savings of a long-term nature.

In reviewing a report with this list, the reviewer is able to note what is lacking or wasteful and to recommend changes in the project, citing the explanations given in each category as the reasons behind the criticism. While strict adherence to these criteria is desirable for water conservation, the reviewer should keep in mind that landscape design needs to respond to a diversity of environmental and social factors which may demand priority considerations in lieu of water conservation needs.

**Checklist for
Water Conservation**

☐ **LAWN**   Turf is not necessary for aesthetic enhancement and can be replaced with low ground cover and other plant materials to achieve the same effect.

☐ **Use**   Is the turf to be used for lawn-dependent activities (sports, active recreation)? If not, it can be replaced with drought-tolerant plant materials.

☐ **Size**   Is the lawn of a size appropriate for its use (i.e. baseball field size, etc.)? The lawn should not spill over unnecessarily into the adjacent landscape.

☐ **Grass Species**   If turf is needed, are drought-tolerant grass species used (e.g. bermuda grass, zoysia, alta fescue)? These grass species still need to be irrigated, but require less frequent waterings than do most grasses.

☐ **LANDSCAPING**

☐ **Use of
Established
Plants**   Are established plants, especially trees, incorporated into the landscape design? These plants are often adapted to low water needed to establish replacement vegetation.

* California Water Resources Commission, **Outdoor Water Conservation for Environmental Impact Reports Review,** Pamphlet, California Water Resources Commission, Sacramento, California, n.d.

☐ **Plant Types**

Are drought tolerant and high water-demanding plants grouped separately? This avoids overwatering the former and allows for efficient application of irrigation water.

☐ **Plant Species**

Are the plant species used fulfilling site needs as well as water conservation goals?
(See the following.)

☐ **Drought-Tolerant**

Are drought-tolerant plant species used when possible? This saves water by requiring little or no irrigation.

☐ **Fire-Retardant**

Are drought-tolerant/fire-retardant species used where environmental conditions present a potential fire hazard to structures and populated areas? Large quantities of water are used when fighting fires. Using fire-retardant vegetation can reduce the frequency and severity of brush fires.

☐ **Erosion Control**

Are drought-tolerant/erosion control species used on steep slopes? These plants protect the soil, facilitate infiltration of rainwater for recharging the groundwater supply, and reduce run-off. Shrubs are more effective than grasses.

☐ **Shade**

Does the landscaping provide shade? Shade reduces the need for irrigation by decreasing the loss of water from both the soil and the plants. How much shade should be provided depends upon the climate and is up to the reviewer to decide.

☐ **CONSTRUCTION**

☐ **Permeable Surfaces**

Are permeable surfaces used for walkways, driveways and parking lots? Use of decomposed granite, wood, or brick discourages run-off and encourages infiltration of water into the soil to recharge groundwater supplies.

☐ **Fire-Resistant Materials**

Are fire-resistant materials used in structures? Concrete is most resistant. Wood is least. Fire-fighting uses large amounts of water. In one fire, on San Rafael Hill, 4 million gallons of water was used—one third of the drought water allotment later issued for the whole district (Marin Municipal Water District).

☐ **On-Site Catchment Basins**

Are on-site catchment basins used? These trap water run-off that can be used for landscape irrigation. Simply catching water from downspouts can catch 15,000 gallons in an area of 20" rainfall from a roof surface of 1,200 square feet. In addition, catching run-off reduces problems of erosion, land-slumping, stream channel scouring, and dangerous storm water levels.

☐ **DEVELOPMENT DESIGN**

☐ **Clustered Development**

Does the development plan use a clustered layout for structures? Clustering saves water by reducing the amount of impervious surface and preserving natural drainage systems—amounting to a 6% reduction over water use by standard grid subdivisions.

☐ **Contiguous Growth**

In general plans and large developments, is growth contiguous? Scattered development creates large amounts of impervious surface and the necessity for long utility extensions.

☐ IRRIGATION.

☐ Low-Output Irrigation Head

Does the irrigation system use low-output irrigation heads (bubbler heads, drip irrigation)? These irrigation heads result in minimum water loss due to evaporation. They should especially be used on serpentine, shallow, or steep soils to encourage plant survival.

☐ Automatic Timing

Is the system timed for early morning irrigation? Irrigation in the early morning results in minimum water loss due to evaporation.

☐ Use of Rainwater

Is rainwater that has been trapped in cisterns, rain-barrels, and ponds used for landscape irrigation? Use of rainwater offers a new and large water supply for landscape irrigation.

☐ Recycled Water

Are there dual plumbing systems that offer the possibility of using rinse water of in-plant cooling water for irrigation? This creates another source of water that offers water of sufficient quality for landscape irrigation.

☐ Use of Reclaimed Wastewater

Is reclaimed wastewater used for irrigation? Chapter 1032, Statutes of 1977, requires the use of reclaimed wastewater for greenbelt irrigation on public lands where it is feasible and there is water of suitable quality available.

☐ MAINTENANCE

A long-term maintenance plan is essential to the water conservation process.

☐ Maintenance of Irrigation System

Is there regular inspection, repair, and adjustment of the components of the irrigation system? Irrigation systems can waste a lot of water if not working properly.

☐ Mulching

Is mulch used on landscaped surface other than turf and pavement? A mulch (wood chips, grass cuttings, etc.) reduces surface evaporation, soil compaction, and weed growth, as well as enriching the soil.

☐ Proper Water Application

Is the irrigation system supplying water when needed? Irrigation systems using timers combined with tensiometers for activation are the most water efficient. Systems using only timers will irrigate regardless of weather or soil moisture conditions.

☐ Thinning of Planting As It Matures

Has the contractor overplanted the new landscape in order to produce a lush effect? If so, there should be plans to properly thin the planting as it matures. Crowded plantings require more irrigation.

☐ Soil Amendment

Has the topsoil been put back or has the mineral soil been amended with organic matter? Soils which have been stripped of topsoil or compacted during construction do not retain water well

☐ Miscellaneous

Have root control boxes been used for trees and large shrubs? This device encourages deep rooting, making the plant more drought tolerant. In addition, it prevents the plant's root system from heaving the sidewalks or driveways.

The Dallas, Texas Water Utilities produced two publications encouraging and guiding water conservation activities as they relate to landscape irrigation. These publications are shown on the following pages and were entitled **19 Ways to Use Less Water Without Really Missing It** and **Water Early in the Morning.** These were small enough to be mailed out with water billings and inexpensive enough to be handed out in great numbers for wide distribution.

Water Early in the Morning

dallas water utilities

Healthy grass is the best cure for weeds, crab grass and other pests.

Here's how to keep your grass healthy:

- Water early in the morning. There is less water loss through evaporation and usually there is little or no wind to blow away some of the water.

- Don't use a sprinkler which "throws" water. Some is lost before it hits the lawn.

- Shallow sprinkling encourages crab grass and weeds, so thoroughly soak your lawn once a week for maximum benefits.

- St. Augustine grass needs an inch and a half of water every 7 to 10 days.

- Bermuda grass needs an inch of water every 7 to 10 days.

- Mow the grass close in early spring and raise the mower blade as the weather gets warmer.

13

Use mulch to retain moisture in the soil and you won't need to water as often. Mulching also controls weeds that compete with plants for water.

14

Use a "soaking hose" to water gardens. You'll use 25-50% less water than with either a regular hose or sprinkler.

15

When you do use a hose or sprinkler, water thoroughly, but only as needed.

16

Use a broom instead of a hose to clean the garage, sidewalks and driveway.

17

Check faucets for drips (both inside and out) and be sure to turn off taps tightly after each use. A slow drip can waste 15 to 20 gallons a day.

18

Repair leaks promptly. Up to 170 gallons a day can leak through a pinhole in a pipe under pressure.

19

The number one water waster in most homes is the commode. To check for a leak, put a few drops of food coloring or vegetable dye tablet in the water closet. If the color shows up in the bowl (without flushing), there is a leak. You should have it repaired promptly.

dallas water utilities

City Hall
Dallas. Texas 75277
651-1441

19

WAYS TO USE LESS WATER WITHOUT REALLY MISSING IT.

It's important that we all use water wisely. A permanent lower level of water consumption will mean savings for all of us because it will prolong the period for which existing Dallas reservoirs can meet system demands and will postpone construction of additional reservoirs.

1

Wash only full loads of laundry. You'll save *time*, too.

2

If you're planning to buy a washing machine, shop for models that use less water (an automatic clothes washer uses 32-45 gallons per load). Don't buy a larger model than you need; look for one with water level controls so you can adjust the amount of water you use. "Suds saver" models save wash water for later loads.

3

Do all handwashing jobs at the same time and make one rinse do the job of two.

4

When buying new clothes, consider those which do not require separate washings.

5

Use a shower instead of tub for bathing. Showers use only 5-15 gallons per minute; a tub bath will take as much as 30-50 gallons. Limit shower time to two minutes, or less.

6

You'll save a lot of water by turning off the tap while you shave, and brush your teeth.

7

When washing fruits and vegetables, fill a bowl instead of using running tap water.

8

You'll get warm water quicker (and use less in the process) if you turn on the hot water first, then mix with cold.

9

You'll use less water in a garbage disposal (they use as much as two gallons a minute) if you peel vegetables, fruits and eggs on a newspaper, and discard in the trash.

10

Don't use more water than called for to cook such foods as frozen vegetables and stews. This will also help preserve nutritional value. Plan more one-dish casserole meals in which vegetables are cooked without adding water. Use drinking water for meals only if people really want it. If you have a pressure cooker, use it often. You'll save time and water. Select the proper size pans for cooking. Utensils that are too large naturally require more water.

11

A good way to save water in hot weather (when consumption is high) is to chill drinking water in the refrigerator. People tend to let the water run if they drink more than one glass.

12

Don't use your dish washer until it's full. It'll use about 16 gallons per load.

As these water shortages or potential water shortages occur or have occurred in various regions, governmental units or water districts have prepared publications to educate or sensitize local citizens as to how to conserve water. These usually deal both with interior and exterior water use and are focused on local conditions and requirements. The Texas Department of Water Resources prepared a small pamphlet entitled, "Water . . . half-a-hundred ways to save it", which included a section on of-of-doors water conservation suggestions and methods. The text of that part of the publication is shown below:

Out-of-doors. . .

♦ Water your lawn early in the morning during the hot months. Much water used on the lawn can simply evaporate between the sprinkler and the grass. (Watering late in the day to avoid evaporation can invite plant disease.

♦ Use a sprinkler that produces drops of water rather than a fine mist, to avoid evaporation.

♦ If you use a soaker hose, turn it so the holes are on the bottom, again to avoid evaporation.

♦ Water slowly for better absorption, and never on windy days.

♦ Forget about watering the streets or walks or driveways. They won't grow a thing.

♦ Condition the soil with compost before planting grass or flower beds so that water will soak in rather than running off.

♦ Fertilize lawns at least twice a year for root stimulation. Grass with good root systems make better use of less water.

♦ Learn to know when your grass needs watering. If it has turned a dull grey-green and when footprints remain visible as you walk across it, it's time to water.

♦ Don't water too frequently. Too much water can overload the soil so that air cannot get to the roots, and can encourage plant diseases.

♦ Don't over-water. Soil can absorb only so much moisture and the rest simply runs off. A timer will help, and either your kitchen timer or an alarm clock will do. An inch-and-a-half of water applied once a week will keep most Texas grasses alive and happy.

♦ Automatic sprinkler systems should be operated only when the demand on your town's water supply is lowest. Set the system to operate between four and six a.m.

♦ Don't scalp your lawn during hot weather. Taller grass holds moisture better. Grass cut fairly often, so that only 1/2 to 3/4 inch is trimmed off will produce a better looking lawn.

♦ If small areas in your yard need more frequent watering (those near walks or driveways or in especially hot, sunny spots), use a watering can or hand water with the hose only in those areas.

♦ Learn what types of grass, shrubbery and plants do best in your area, and in which parts of your yard, and then plant accordingly. If you have a heavily shaded yard, no amount of water will make the roses bloom. In especially dry sections of the state, consider attractive arrangements of plants that like arid or semi-arid climates.

♦ You don't have to be a horticulturist to have an attractive yard, but do learn about the plants you have so that you can water just enough to keep them healthy, and not enough to waste water and injure the plants at the same time.

♦ Consider decorating areas of your yard with rocks, gravel, wood chips, or other materials which are now available and which require no water at all.

♦ Never "sweep" your walks and driveways with the hose. Use a broom or rake.

♦ When washing the car, use a bucket of soapy water and use the hose only for rinsing.

Remember that saving water also saves energy. About 50 percent of the water used in a home is hot water. Providing energy to fuel your hot water heater is a major drain on your utility bill. So save water and you save energy and money at the same time.

Poor Richard also tells us to "Beware of little expenses: a small leak will sink a great ship." And he warns that, "Necessity never made a good bargain." Let's not wait to conserve water in Texas until there is not enough water to conserve.

C-9
1978

WATER...
half-a-hundred
ways to save it

TEXAS DEPARTMENT OF WATER RESOURCES
P.O. Box 13087
Austin, Texas 78711

The Colorado State University Cooperative Extension Service produced a small brochure entitled, "Conserve". It featured the cupped hand symbol around a drop of water and contained sections dealing with bathrooms, kitchens, all around the house, lawn and yard and vegetable and flower garden water conservation opportunities. The latter two sections are reproduced below and are appropriate for most sections of Colorado.

CONSERVE

Lawn and Yard

A lush, green lawn requires about 1½ inches of water a week, applied ½ inch at a time, three times a week. But, in years of water shortages, homeowners will have to accept a lawn which is not as green. Experts estimate that most Colorado lawns can survive on ¾ inch of water a week, or less.

If water is rationed or otherwise restricted, lawns should receive the lowest priority for outside watering. Trees and shrubs die more quickly and are more expensive to replace.

Bluegrass lawns are fairly drought tolerant and can recover after a prolonged dry period.

It is estimated that approximately 40 per cent of the domestic water supply goes for lawn and yard watering. Wise use of water outside can save significant quantities.

Don't over-water your lawn — and don't water until the lawn needs it. When grass turns a dull grey-green, and when footprints remain when you walk across the lawn, it's time to water.

If most of the lawn still looks green and only spots or areas near concrete are grey, root-water or hand-water just the dry spots.

Hand watering should be done with a soaker or a two-pronged aerator which attaches to the garden hose, rather than a sprinkler.

Use root-watering devices on shrubs, trees, strips of grass and areas near concrete. Soakers help prevent runoff on slopes.

When watering near concrete, push a root feeder or aerator into the soil 12 to 16 inches from the concrete. Force the water jets down to a depth of four to six inches. When the grass rises like a bubble, remove spike and repeat operation 12 to 16 inches further along grass edge.

Less frequent but heavier lawn watering encourages a deeper root system to withstand dry weather better.

If a ½-hour setting with a sprinkler is what your lawn needs, keep track of the time. A sprinkler left on overtime in one spot wastes water. Set an alarm clock or timer as a reminder.

With an automatic sprinkling system, make sure it is not soaking the lawn too often and too long.

Much of the soil in Colorado is clay. This heavy soil usually can absorb no more than ½ inch of water per hour. For slopes and heavy clay soils, let the water run for 30 minutes, then come back in an hour and water for another 30 minutes.

Sandy soils need watering more often but for shorter periods of time.

If water starts to run off, turn off the sprinkler until the lawn needs watering a few days later.

Lawns should be watered during hours when the water system experiences the least demand — usually from 4 a.m. to 6 a.m.

Adjust lawn watering to the weather. Following a heavy rain, skip the regular watering schedule until the grass needs it. Know how to turn off an automatic sprinkling system until needed again.

Avoid watering when windy or in heat of day.

Delay regular watering of your grass during the first, cool weeks of spring to encourage deeper rooting.

Sunny, south sides of buildings, or slopes, or areas near sidewalks and driveways usually require watering more often. Shady or north locations need watering less frequently.

Forget about watering streets, walks and driveways. They won't grow a thing.

Keep grass length fairly long — two inches or higher. Cut lawn fairly often so that no more than 1/3 of the grass blade is cut off. Otherwise, grass blades turn yellow from excessive shock.

Taller grass provides more food for deeper rooting if deep-watering is practiced.

Sprinklers throwing large drops of water in a flat pattern are more effective than those with fine, high sprays.

Water flow can be controlled at your water outlet, by the type of sprinkler used, and by the size of the garden hose. More is dispensed faster with a larger diameter hose.

High nitrogen fertilizers stimulate lawn growth and increase water requirements.

Mulch your shrubs and other plantings so the soil holds moisture longer.

CONSERVE

Vegetable and Flower Gardens

When possible, flood irrigate your vegetable and flower gardens rather than using sprinklers. Irrigation allows deeper soaking with less water. Sprinklers result in high evaporation loss of water.

Garden irrigation is best accomplished with shallow ditches next to the plant rows or by use of a soaker hose.

Prevent irrigation water runoff and waste by damming the ends of the ditches with soil. Fill the ditch with water and let it soak in.

Polyethylene (black plastic) mulch between your vegetable garden rows conserves water. (Avoid plastic thicker than four mils as it reduces air exchange.)

Mulches which stay open and porous (leaf mold, wood chips, loosely-applied lawn clippings) conserve water and discourage weeds in your flower and vegetable gardens. Mulches such as finely-textured peat moss or sewage sludge will compact and form a surface crust which prevents water from soaking into the soil.

Certain flower and vegetable varieties can tolerate shade and thus require less frequent watering. (Consult a CSU Extension Service county agent for variety recommendations.)

Leafy vegetables (lettuce) generally require more water than root crops (beets).

Vegetables requiring more water should be grouped together in the garden to make maximum use of water applications.

Vegetables can be combined with flowers and shrubs to prevent watering a separate vegetable garden or to utilize space more effectively.

Vegetables for small families can be grown in tubs, thereby avoiding the need to water a large garden.

CONSERVE

Issued in furtherance of Cooperative Extension work, Acts of May 8 and June 30, 1914, in cooperation with the U.S. Department of Agriculture. Lowell H. Watts, Director of Extension Service, Colorado State University. By law and purpose, the Colorado State University Cooperative Extension Service is dedicated to serve all people on an equal and nondiscriminatory basis.

550M 3/77

In California, the East Bay Municipal District also prepared a public information brochure entitled, "Water Conservation Today - And Tomorrow". In this there was a section on "Gardens and Outdoor Use" which gave suggestions which were appropriate for the San Francisco Bay area and particularly in the drier hills of the East Bay. This particular publication provided a list of publications dealing with native plants of California.

WATER CONSERVATION TODAY—AND TOMORROW

EAST BAY / MUNICIPAL UTILITY DISTRICT
P. O. BOX 24055 · OAKLAND, CA 94623 · (415) 835-3000

A COMPENDIUM OF PRACTICAL ADVICE FOR PERSONAL WATER CONSERVATION

gardens and outdoor use

About half the residential water from EBMUD goes into the garden, and east of the Oakland-Berkeley hills it is an even higher proportion. Plants consume more water than any other category of use.

The basic principle to follow when watering the lawn and garden is not to give it more water than it needs. Some people irrigate their lawns with double the water the lawn actually needs to thrive.

Rather than following a fixed schedule to water the lawn, water it only when it shows the first signs of needing it. You don't need to water the lawn as often in cool weather and on cloudy days. Watch the weather and the lawn before you decide to water it.

Heat and wind will rob your lawn of the water before it can use it. Avoid watering on windy days and you will avoid having most of the water going somewhere besides the garden. Water in the cool of the day, both to avoid excess evaporation and the chance of harming the lawn. Weeds are water thieves also, so keep your garden free of them.

Let the water sink in slowly. Lots of water applied fast will only run off into the gutter where it does no good. If you let the water sink deep, you won't need to water as often and your lawn will develop deeper roots which will let it go longer without water. Mulch on the garden will hold water longer.

You don't need to water the garden until it is flooded. At that point all the water you add will run off, and the garden already has as much as it can use. A kitchen timer is handy to remind you to turn off the sprinklers, and there are sprinkler timers available on the market.

Make sure your sprinklers and hoses are adjusted to water just your lawn and garden. Irrigating sidewalks and gutters will not make them turn green, or grow either.

When you water shrubs and trees, find out how much water they actually require, and let the water flow slowly so that it will penetrate deep into the ground. "Drip" irrigation uses this principle and it might be the best way to water your garden.

Try planting California native plants or other plants from Mediterranean climate zones in your garden. These are plants which don't require much water and thrive on the long dry season we have in the Bay Area. Because they can survive naturally without watering, you won't have to water them much either. You can have a green garden with flowers that doesn't need a lot of water. It isn't necessary to have a backyard desert to conserve water in your garden.

Water Conservation in your garden is common sense. Water only when you need to, and use only as much as you need.

Here are a few titles on California Native Plants and their use in gardens:

"Native Plants in Our Garden," Robert and Betty Hoover;

"Native Plants for California Gardens," Lee Lenz, Rancho Santa Ana Botanic Gardens;

"Native California Plants for Ornamental Use," Mildred Mathias, University of California Extension;

"Sunset Western Garden Book," Lane Magazine and Book Company.

Libraries and nurseries may have these titles or other information. The California Native Plant Society also is a good source for information.

The Southern Arizona Water Resources Association(SAWARA) also prepared a "SAWARA Plant Guide" which dealt with "Using Less Water in Your Garden". In addition to the majority of text in English an announcement concerning more available information was printed on the back in Spanish. This publication outlined, generally and specifically, drought resistant or drought tolerant vegetation appropriate for use in the Tucson desert environment. It also explained the SAWARA endorsement of a water conserving plant and the program for tagging nursery plants to advise potential consumers that a particular plant was water conserving.

Este folleto de agua adjunto es publicado solamente en Inglés. Los ciudadanos que hablan Español están invitados a comunicarse con el Departamento de Tucson Water para recibir asistencia. Nuestros empleados bilingues le ayudarán a traducir este documento. Favor de llamar al 791-3242 o visite el Departamento de Tucson Water, El Annexo del Edificio Municipal, tercer piso, 111 E. Pennington.

"MAKE EVERY DROP COUNT"

NEXT MONTH
BEAT THE PEAK

Chamber of Commerce Building
465 W. St. Mary's Rd. Suite 100
Tucson, Arizona 85705

624-9000

SAWARA

S·A·WA·R·A
PLANT·GUIDE

"USING LESS WATER IN YOUR GARDEN"

If you are planning to buy plants this spring, why not buy low water use plants... Drought Resistant plants can look the same as other plants that use greater amounts of water. These plants will probably fill the need you have in mind for your yard. When you go to the nursery, look for a blue tag. The tag represents an endorsement from the Southern Arizona Water Resources Association (SAWARA). SAWARA has endorsed 35 low water use plants that are affordable, diverse, attractive and fulfill common landscaping needs.

Drought Resistant plants encompass a much greater variety of plants than is commonly thought and in many cases they will require less maintenance as well. Such plants can be as colorful and as functional as you desire... low water requirements do not necessarily mean dull colors and thorns.

Local nurseries have the plants tagged with the SAWARA endorsement and have an information sheet which outlines some basic characteristics of each plant. Such characteristics may include flower color, blooming season, sun requirements, the plant's tolerance to cold, its water requirements and what height and width one can expect the plant to reach.

On the cover are some examples of the plants that are receiving the SAWARA endorsement. The vine, called Queen's Wreath (1) is a nice example of broad leafed greenery that needs considerably less water than other similar plants, and is in full color in early fall. The Desert Marigold (2) is a beautiful flowering spring plant that requires very little additional watering Aloe Saponaria (3) also has an outstanding bloom during most of the year and makes a very effective accent plant. The Mexican Evening Primrose (4) is a groundcover plant and can serve as an attractive alternative over many other typical groundcovers. The Fairy Duster (5) and Jojoba (6) are excellent foliage shrubs to be used as foundation plants or as boundary plants to set off areas of the yard. The tree featured in our cover logo is a Blue Palo Verde (7) and if you desire shade or shelter, this is a beautiful means to obtain it. These specific plants are only meant to be examples taken from a huge range of drought resistant plants.

SAWARA is interested in low water use and drought resistant plants because water conservation is an important area of concern in Tucson. Water will be significantly more expensive in the future and this project will tend to encourage less water use. Other encouragement will come from the Arizona Department of Water Resources which has the authority to require further reductions in water use to balance the supply and demand conditions in our underground water sources by 2025. Lower water use is something we will have to adapt to, but our lifestyles will not change as much as one might imagine. A few small changes by all of us can add up to significant overall savings.

One easy way to reduce your water needs to is to place low water use plants in your yard. Forty percent of the water used residentially is used outside the home, so landscaping and plant watering methods represent a good area for potential water savings and outdoor conservation.

For more information, please call SAWARA at 624-9000.

The Utah Water Research Laboratory published a book on "Water Conservation Information Dissemination During the 1977 Drought Emergency" which was a definitive overview of what was being done at that time. More material from that publication is mentioned elsewhere in this book. *

A conference on Xeriscape was sponsored by the California Landscape Contractors Association(Orange County) and the Municipal Water District of Orange County on April 29, 1983. This covered such subjects as , **Water Shortages and Costs and the Need for Conservation, Xericulture not Zeroculture** and **Design for Xeriscape.** This symposium resulted in proceedings bound in a looseleaf notebook with an extensive bibliography and a listing of arboreta and botanical gardens in California where more information might be obtained. **

The City of Davis, California prepared a list of low water maintenance ornamental plants which were appropriate for that inland California location. ***

The Coachella Valley Resource Conservation District and the Desert Water Agency have cooperated to prepare a listing of "Drought Tolerant Ornamental Plants for the Coachella Valley". They have also prepared a self guided plant tour so that interested persons or groups can see some of the plants growing in the area. ****

The Water Conservation Office of the Water and Waste Water Department of the City of Phoenix developed and published a booklet entitled "More Green Per Gallon" which gave guidelines for water conserving landscape development in Phoenix as well as a listing of arid-country plants. *****

*T*he sun: it's a big part of the Phoenix lifestyle. Suntans. Bicycling nearly any weekend. Coffee and Sunday newspaper on the patio. Golf, jogging, backyard barbecues, gardening. Our abundant sunny days are one reason many Phoenicians choose to live here.

The sun has also created our desert. Blue skies day after day mean little rain, making water precious nourishment for life in the Valley. Water is available, but it is limited.

Natives in the Valley of the Sun know how to use water wisely, cherishing each drop and guarding against waste. Those natives are the desert plants, flourishing here long before people arrived. Newcomers may think the local flora are all cactus, but actually the desert sprouts many kinds of greenery: Palo Verde and Mesquite trees, Creosote and Desert Broom shrubs, grasses, and Poppies and other flowers.

Those natives show it is possible to live vibrantly in the desert while conserving water Using water wisely is essential to living in the desert— to the Phoenix  lifestyle. This booklet is designed to help you make the most of precious water in your landscaping and outdoor living.

Arid doesn't mean brown

Some people think that "conserving water" in their yards means brown yards. That's a misconception, as many others have discovered. You'll see three kinds of yards around Phoenix: the traditional fence-to-fence grass yard with leafy shade trees; the "arid-country" landscaping with low-water-use plants and trees; and the cactus garden. Wise water use is possible, and important, with all three types of landscaping.

* James, L. Douglas and Wade Andrews, **Water Conservation Information Dissemination During the 1977 Drought Emergency,** Water Resources Planning Series, Report P-78-002, Utah Water Research Laboratory, College of Engineering, Utah State University, Logan, Utah 84322, June 1978.

** **Xeriscape,** available from Municipal Water District of Orange County, P.O. Box 15229, 525 N Cabrillo Park Drive, Suite 124, Santa Ana, California 92705.

*** **Draft List of Low Water Maintenance Ornamental Plants,** Available from the City of Davis, City Hall, 226 F Street, Davis, California 95614.

**** **Drought Tolerant Ornamental Plants for the Coachella Valley,** Available from the Desert Water Agency, P.O. Drawer 1707, Palm Springs, California 92263.

* **More Green Per Gallon,**Published by the City of Phoenix Public Information Office for the Water Conservation Office of the Water and Wastewater Department - September 1982, Phoenix, Arizona.

ARID-COUNTRY PLANTS

Many kinds of arid-country plants thrive in the Valley. This list is by no means complete, but gives you a starting point for shopping. More detailed information can be found in gardening books available at nurseries and hardware stores.

Most people know plants by their common names, but the best way to shop for them is by their botanical names. That's the only way to make sure you get what you want, because several different plants may have the same common name. Local availability of arid-country plants sometimes is limited, so many plants on this list may be difficult to find at times.

TREES

Common Name/ Botanical Name	Mature Height	Mature Width	Deciduous/ Evergreen	Flowers	Notes
Whitehorn Acacia (Acacia constricta)	15'	18'	Evergreen	Yellow	Generally shrub, can be trained as a tree.
Sweet Acacia (Acacia faresiana)	20'	15-25'	Evergreen	Yellow	A. smallii is cold tolerant, can be trained as a tree.
Catclaw Acacia (Acacia greggii)	10'	12'	Evergreen	Yellow	Curved thorns, can be trained as a tree.
Shoestring Acacia (Acacia stenophylla)	15-20'	15-20'	Evergreen	Creamy	Weeping, shoestring foliage.
Willow Acacia (Acacia salicina)	25-30'	15-20'	Evergreen	Yellow	Weeping habit.
Blue Palo Verde (Cercidium floridum)	30'	30'	Deciduous	Yellow	Plant away from walks.
Foothill Palo Verde (Cercidium microphyllum)	15'	15'	Deciduous	Yellow	Good patio tree.
Sonoran Palo Verde (Cercidium praecox)	20'	20'	Deciduous	Yellow	Develops umbrella canopy.
Mexican Fan Palm (Washingtonia robusta)	60-100'	10'	Evergreen		Narrow trunked fan palm. 1-2' trunk diameter.
California Fan Palm (Washington filifera)	50-60'	15'	Evergreen		Heavy trunked fan palm. 3-4' trunk diameter.
Date Palm (Phoenix dcatylifera)	60-80'	30'	Evergreen		Uses more water than the fan palms, gray green fronds, edible fruit.
Desert Willow (Chilopsis linearis)	25'	15'	Deciduous	White, Pink, Rose	Weeping form. Lavender.

1. Aleppo Pine

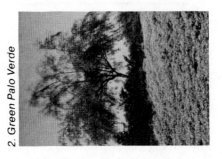

2. Green Palo Verde

9

The Water Conservation Office of the City of Phoenix, Arizona Water and Wastewater Department provided homeowners a series of water conservation ideas which related both to the inside and the outside of the home in the Phoenix climate and desert water conditions.

Our Water is Our Future

Water Conservation ideas for:

RESIDENCES

Outside

1. Water during the cool time of day. Early morning is best. Avoid the peak watering time (4:00 p.m. to 9:00 p.m.).
2. Don't water on windy or rainy days.
3. Don't water every day. To determine if your lawn needs water, step on the grass. If it springs back when you move your foot, your lawn doesn't need water.
4. When you do water, let the water soak down to the roots.
5. Call your local nursery to find out about drought resistant plants, how much water different plants need, and what irrigation and watering systems are best for your needs.
6. Adjust sprinklers so they only water your lawn and plants, and not the sidewalk, street or side of the house.
7. If you have flood irrigation, keep your berms in good shape and get rid of rodents immediately.
8. Use a broom instead of a hose to clean your driveway and sidewalk.
9. Don't leave the hose running while you wash your car. Use a shut-off nozzle on your hose or use a bucket and rag.
10. Check for leaks in pipes, hoses, faucets and couplings.
11. Cover your pool with styrofoam sheets or a pool cover to cut down on evaporation.
12. If you have an evaporative cooler, adjust your runoff so it waters your lawn and plants. (Be sure to check your nursery first to see which plants won't be harmed by cooler water.)
13. Consider installing a recirculating pump on your evaporative cooler.

Inside

1. Check all faucets and pipes for leaks.
2. Check your toilet for leaks. Put a few drops of food coloring in the tank. Wait a few minutes. If the color shows up in the bowl, you have a leak.
3. Call your local hardware store and ask about water-saving devices for toilets, showers, and faucets.
4. Don't use the toilet as a wastebasket or ashtray.
5. Turn off the water while shaving, washing your hands or brushing your teeth.
6. Take shorter showers — turn off the water while you soap yourself up.
7. Wrap your hot water pipes and water heater with insulating material to speed up delivery of hot water to your tap.
8. Always wash full loads of dishes. Or if you wash dishes by hand, don't let the water run.
9. Keep a bottle of cold water in your refrigerator for drinking purposes.
10. Wash only full loads of clothes — or adjust the water level in your washer for smaller loads.
11. Remove food from the freezer before it's needed rather than using running water to thaw it.
12. Use your garbage disposal sparingly.
13. Use leftover drinking water on your plants.

Water Conservation Office, City of Phoenix Water & Wastewater Department
125 East Washington Street • Phoenix, Arizona 85004
Water Saver Hotline 256-3450

Water Conservation Ideas for Residences, Water Conservation Office, City of Phoenix Water and Wastewater Department, 125 East Washington St., Phoenix, Arizona 85004.

The City of Aurora, Colorado prepared a book entitled "Landscaping for Water Conservation in a Semi-arid Environment." * This book covered planning and design, the use of native plants and methods of watering. It was specifically developed for the Denver region and used very clear illustrations to show basic principles of design and management. Water conserving design concepts were shown for remodeling the landscape of an older home and illustrated appropriate plants with a series of full color photographs.

Conceptualized designs were also developed for new cluster homes, for new suburban homes and for older farmsteads. This book contained a series of small cartoon sketches which gave guidance for maintenance and cultivation practices. This report also contained one of the most clear and understandable plant lists which provided information on the need of each species of plant for moisture and irrigation.

These are typical conceptual sketches as contained in the Aurora study which show ways to use water more efficiently in landscape operations. They are accompanied by extensive explanatory text.

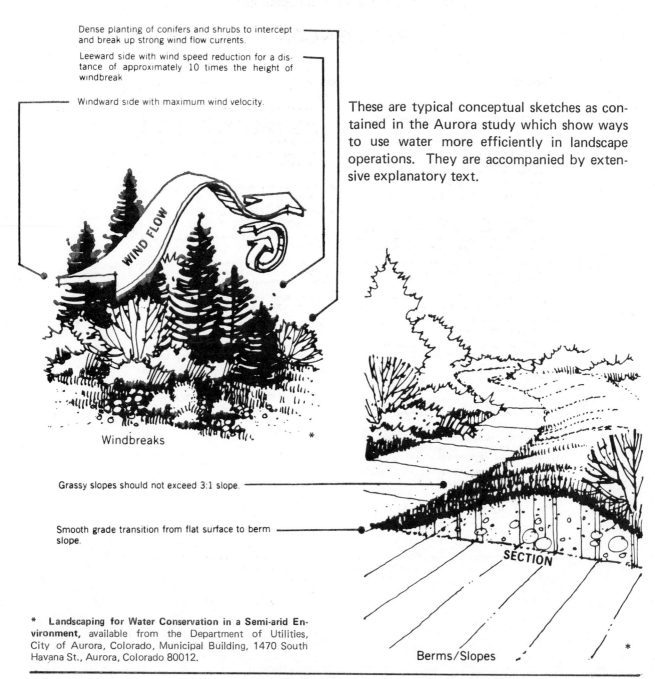

Dense planting of conifers and shrubs to intercept and break up strong wind flow currents.

Leeward side with wind speed reduction for a distance of approximately 10 times the height of windbreak

Windward side with maximum wind velocity.

WIND FLOW

Windbreaks

Grassy slopes should not exceed 3:1 slope.

Smooth grade transition from flat surface to berm slope.

SECTION

Berms/Slopes

* **Landscaping for Water Conservation in a Semi-arid Environment,** available from the Department of Utilities, City of Aurora, Colorado, Municipal Building, 1470 South Havana St., Aurora, Colorado 80012.

These are some of the cartoon sketches which were used in the Aurora study to supplement the text to explain basic concepts in water cserving grounds maintenance practices.

PLANT LIST LEGEND

SOIL MOISTURE

— Exceptionally drought-enduring **once established**. No more than natural rainfall needed.

◐ Dry, well-drained soils; two to three waterings per year.

◗ Moist, well-drained soils; four to six waterings per year.

● Moist, cool soils, never dry.

Note: Soil **moisture** and soil **texture** are interrelated. A heavy clay soil even though somewhat moist, may result in drought injury to a plant because the water is held to the soil particles under high tension (like a magnet) and is not available to the plant. Clay soils tend to hold water longer than sandy soils; thus less frequent watering is advised on clay than on sand. It is also easier to overwater a plant in a clay soil than in sand.

SUN TOLERANCE

✲ Full Shade

✲ Partial Shade

✿ Full Sun

* Limited Plant Availability

TREES

SIZE IN 40 YEARS:
Small -
    Less than 25 feet
Large-
    Greater than 25 feet

This shows the basic plant list information in the Aurora study. It was meant for a lay audience and helped to convert complex technical horticultural information into a form that was quickly and easily understandable. The legend was made very graphic and did relate to the soil moisture or irrigation requirements of each of the plants.

TREES - EVERGREEN

PLANT NAME	SOIL MOISTURE	SUN TOLERANCE	SIZE IN 40 YEARS	DESCRIPTION AND AND COMMENTS
DOUGLASFIR* *Pseudotsuga menziesii*	◗	✲	(large)	Sharply pyramidal in habit; bluegreen soft needle foliage; small bracted cones; tolerates poor soils; shade as well as sun, wind, best grown on dry side
EASTERN REDCEDAR *Juniperus virginiana*	◐	✿	(small)	Densely pyramidal or columnar; scale-like foliage; blue berries female; named varieties available; tolerant of wind and poor soil; slow to establish
FIR, WHITE *Abies concolor*	◐	✲✲✿	(large)	Narrow pyramidal; horizontal branching; blue-green soft needled foliage; not tolerant of heavy clay soils; growth rapid in comparison with other conifers; cones borne upright at top of tree
JUNIPER, ONESEED* *Juniperus monosperma*	—	✲✿	(small)	Upright, dense habit; from large shrub to tree. Tolerates wide variety of soils and adverse conditions; slow to establish
JUNIPER, ROCKY MOUNTAIN *Juniperus scopulorum*	—	✿	(small)	(Same as Eastern Redcedar)

OLDER HOME

Lot Size: 50' x 125' = 6250 sq. ft.

Family Members

- Adults - Young Couple
- Children - none
- Pets - Cat

Existing Conditions

- Home located on terrace with detached garage
- Corner lot
- Small front and back yards
- Narrow sideyards
- Steep slope with hot, south exposure
- Large trees on adjacent street right-of-way and private property
- Narrow parkways
- Good protection from winds

Desires, Needs, Uses

- Private outdoor living space with good interior views
- Vegetable and fruit garden
- Flower garden
- Service area adjacent to alley
- Minimum maintenance and water requirement
- Active and passive outdoor use areas - cooking eating, sitting, games

Landscape Components

The landscape of this older single family residence was renovated to make use of the following components and concepts:

- Remove existing walks to permit creation of lawn and deck areas
- Pavement and decking in high activity areas to reduce amount of irrigated areas and to create more useful areas
- Remove unused lawn areas
- Planting beds to replace lawn to reduce water requirement and maintenance
- Water-conservative plantings in parkways to replace lawn
- Large canopy deciduous trees for summer shade
- Planting masses for privacy screening
- Flower bed as visual focal point

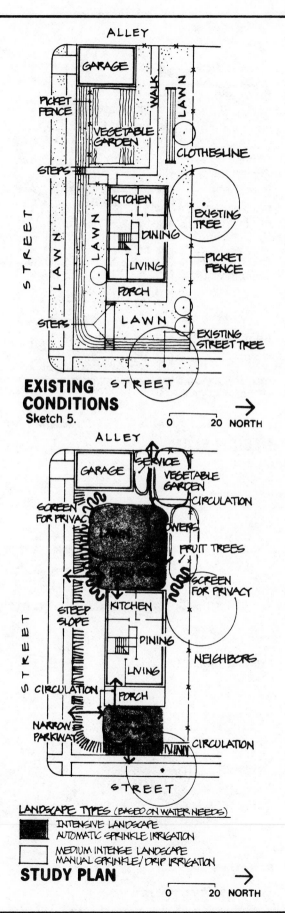

EXISTING CONDITIONS
Sketch 5.

0   20 NORTH

LANDSCAPE TYPES (BASED ON WATER NEEDS)

INTENSIVE LANDSCAPE
AUTOMATIC SPRINKLE IRRIGATION

MEDIUM INTENSE LANDSCAPE
MANUAL SPRINKLE/DRIP IRRIGATION

STUDY PLAN

0   20 NORTH

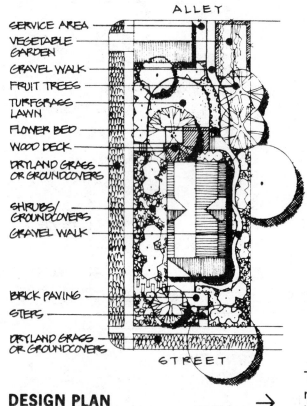

SERVICE AREA
VEGETABLE GARDEN
GRAVEL WALK
FRUIT TREES
TURFGRASS LAWN
FLOWER BED
WOOD DECK
DRYLAND GRASS OR GROUNDCOVERS

SHRUBS/ GROUNDCOVERS
GRAVEL WALK

BRICK PAVING
STEPS
DRYLAND GRASS OR GROUNDCOVERS

ALLEY

STREET

DESIGN PLAN

0   20 NORTH →

Construction Sequence

- Remove existing walks
- New wood deck
- New walks and steps
- Remove old lawn
- Soil preparation (if needed) in planting areas
- Irrigation system
- New lawn
- Parkway planting
- Plantings and mulch

These two pages show the suggestion for the redesign of the landscape around an older home to improve the outdoor usability and liveability and at the same time to save water.

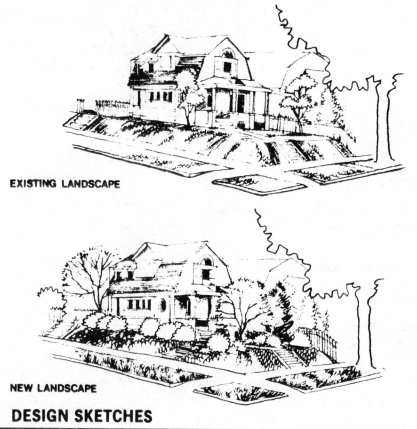

EXISTING LANDSCAPE

NEW LANDSCAPE

DESIGN SKETCHES

The Southern Arizona Water Resources Association has instituted a very visible and effective multi-part education and awareness program. A few facets of this overall effort are most appropriate to mention here. Among them are: *

- a billboard program that emphasizes water conservation and the use of plants native to southern Arizona with the slogan, "Replace a Mulberry with a Mesquite".

- an innovative nursery tagging technique which identifies a "low water use plant".

Nurserymen boost desert plants' use

By TONY DAVIS
Citizen Staff Writer

Tucsonians can buy a wide range of low-water-use plants that cost the same and provide as much comfort, shade and privacy as their thirstier counterparts, a group of plant experts said here yesterday.

At a press conference, the Southern Arizona Water Resources Association trotted out a host of nursery owners, landscape architects and other plant specialists to explain how residents can reduce outdoor water use and why they need to do it. The session was called to launch a three-month campaign to get residents to use less water outdoors.

"The more people who conserve voluntarily, the more we can balance the withdrawal of water with recharge," said SAWARA Executive Director Maribeth Carlile. A state law requires the Tucson area to do that by the year 2025.

She indicated that 60 to 90 gallons a day of the average Tucsonians' 160-to-165-gallon daily water usage is at home. Of that, about 40 percent goes outdoors, she said.

The association and 14 Tucson nurseries are cooperating to label with blue tags 35 species of plants which need little water, so consumers can easily identify them.

Warren Jones, of the UA's landscape architecture program, suggested that residents use acacia or mesquite instead of mulberry for shade and shelter, dense plants such as the mescal bean or rosewood for privacy and jojoba or the Texas ranger as space-defining plants.

Several of the plant experts said these desert plants use at most half as much water as non-desert plants. They stressed that these varieties, which come from as far away as Australia, are not necessarily native plants, but should more properly be called desert plants.

They also said that the desert plants will need watering when first put in the ground and will grow more if they are watered afterward, but can survive without water.

And they warned that residents should not be lulled by this year's unusually heavy rainfall into thinking that they don't need to conserve water in plant use.

"One aspect of the desert is that you get a lot of rain at once and then you get three days of hot weather and wind and the water is all gone," said one speaker. "We will have to conserve like any other year."

They said the use of desert plants peaked after water rates went up sharply in 1976.

**

* **Southern Arizona Water Resources Association,** Suite 100, 465 W. St. Mary's Rd. 85705.

** **Tucson Citizen,** April 14, 1983, Page 5C.

● the development of a listing of drought resistant plants for distribution to homeowners, designers and others with an interest in the subject.

southern
arizona
water
resources
association

SUITE 100
465 W ST MARY'S RD
TUCSON, ARIZ 85705
624 9000

DROUGHT RESISTANT PLANTS

These are low water use plants. If planted properly and well established, they will require less maintenance than plants you may be used to. If you don't give them water, they won't die, but with additional water, they will grow much more quickly. These plants may not look their best in in a container. Please refer to the photographs for a better idea of what they look like in the ground. Check with your nursery personnel for planting care and instructions.

SAWARA

NOTE: THESE PLANTS NEED REGULAR WATERING TO GET ESTABLISHED!

VINES

BEDDING PLANTS

ACCENT

VINES

	Deciduous or Evergreen	Sun	Water	Flower Color	Flowering Season	Height	Spread	Cold Tolerance
Queens Wreath, Mountain Rose, Coral Vine (Antigonon leptopus)	D	F,R	M	P	Sp-S			T
Arizona Grape Ivy (Cissus trifoliata)	D	F	L-M	I				H
Drummond Clematis (Clematis drummondi)	E	F	L-M	W	Sp-S	CLIMBING		H
Yellow Orchid Vine (Mascagnia macroptera)	E/D	P,F	L-M	Y	Sp-S	VINES		T
Mexican Serjania (Serjania mexicana)	E	P,F	L-M	I				T

BEDDING PLANTS FOR COLOR

	Deciduous or Evergreen	Sun	Water	Flower Color	Flowering Season	Height	Spread	Cold Tolerance
False Sand Verbena (Verbena tenuisecta)	E	F,P	M	Pur	Sp-S	5"-6"	3'-4'	H
Red Autumn Sage (Salvia greggi)	D	P,F	L	R	Sp-S	3'-4'	3'-4'	H
Desert Marigold (Baileya multiradiata)	D/E	F	L	Y	Sp	12"-18"	12"-18"	H
Penstemons								
Parry's Penstemon (Penstemon parryii)	E	F	M	P	Sp	3'	2'	H
Eaton's Penstemon (Penstemon eatonii)	E	F	M	R	Sp	3'	2'	H
White Brittle Bush (Encelia farinosa)	E	F	L	Y	Sp	2'-3'	3'-4'	T
Gazanias								
Trailing Gazania (Gazania ringens leucolaena)	E	F-P	L	Y,W,O	All	3'		T
Clumping Gazania (Gazania ringens)	E	F-P	M	Y,W,O	Year	12"		H
Mexican Evening Primrose (Oenothera berlandieri)	E	S,P,F	M	W-R	Sp	1'-2'	Spreads	H

PLANTS FOR ACCENT OR EMPHASIS

	Deciduous or Evergreen	Sun	Water	Flower Color	Flowering Season	Height	Spread	Cold Tolerance
Aloes								
Aloe saponaria	E	F,P	M	R	3/yr	12"	Spreads	T
Aloe barbadensis	E	F,P	M	Y	1/yr	12"	Spreads	H
Ocotillo (Fouguieria splendens)	D	F,P	L	R	Sp	10'-20'	10'-15'	
Yuccas								
Soap Tree Yucca (Yucca elata)	E	P,F,R	L-M	W	Sp	8'-12'	V	H
Blue Yucca (Yucca rigata)	E	F	L-M	W	Sp	8'	V	H
Banana Yucca (Yucca baccata)	E	F	L	W	Sp	4'-5'	6'	H
Schott's Yucca (Yucca schotti)	E	F	L	W	S	6'-20'	4'-10'	H
Joshua Tree (Yucca brevifolia)	E	F,P,R	L	W	Sp	15'-20'	15'-20'	H
Agaves								
Century Plant (Agave americana)	E	F,R,P	L	Y	Bloom	4'-6'	6'-8'	H
Octopus Agave (Agave vilmoriniana)	E	F,P	L	W-Y	once	3'-4'	4'-6'	T
Huachuca Agave (Agave huachucensis)	E	F,R,P	L	Y	only	24"-30"	3'	H
Desert Spoon or Sotol (Dasylirion wheeleri)	E	F,R	L	W	S	2'-3'	3'-4'	H
Bear Grass (Nolina microcarpa)	E/D	P,F,R	L-M	I	Sp	3'-4'	4'-6'	H
Palms								
Mediterranean Fan Palm (Chamaerops humilis)	E	F,P,R	L-M	I	S	15'	8'-15'	H
Mexican Blue Palm (Brahea armata)	E	P,F,R	L	W	S	30'	8'-10'	H

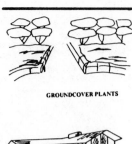

GROUNDCOVER PLANTS

Plant	Deciduous or Evergreen	Sun	Water	Flower Color	Flowering Season	Height	Spread	Cold Tolerance
Rosemary (Rosmarinus officinalis)	E	F,P,R	L-M	B	W,Sp	12"-15"	3'	H
False Sand Verbena (Verbena tenuisecta)	E	F,P	M	Pur	Sp,S	5"-6"	3'-4'	H
Fairy Duster (Calliandra eriophylla)	E	F	L-M	R,W	W-Sp	2'-3'	3'-4'	H
Prostate Indigo Bush (Dalea greggi)	E/D	F,P,R	L-M	R	W-Sp	2'-3'	3'-4'	H
Mexican Evening Primrose (Oenothera berlandieri)	E	P,F	M	P	S		1'-2'	H

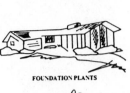

FOUNDATION PLANTS

Plant	Deciduous or Evergreen	Sun	Water	Flower Color	Flowering Season	Height	Spread	Cold Tolerance
Feathery Cassia (Cassia artemisioides)	E	F,P	L	Y	W-Sp	4'-6'	4'-6'	T
Desert Cassia (Cassia eremophila)	E	F,P	L	Y	W-Sp	5'	5'	H
Jojoba (Simmondsia chinensis)	E	F	L-M	Y	Sp	4'-8'	4'-8'	H
Fairy Duster (Calliandra eriophylla)	E	F	L-M	R,W	W-Sp	2'-3'	3'-4'	H
Texas Ranger (Leucophyllum frutescens)	E	F,R	L-M	Pur	S	5'-12'	4'-6'	H

SPACE DEFINING PLANTS

Plant	Deciduous or Evergreen	Sun	Water	Flower Color	Flowering Season	Height	Spread	Cold Tolerance
Arizona Rosewood (Vauquelinia californica)	E	F,R	L-M	W	S	10'-30'	5'-15'	H
Clammy Hop Bush (Dodonaea viscosa)	E	P,F	M		F	12'-15'	12'-15'	T
Jojoba (Simmondsia chinensis)	E	F	L-M	Y	Sp	4'-8'	4'-8'	H
Texas Ranger (Leucophyllum frutescens)	E	F,R	L-M	Pur	S	5'-12'	4'-6'	H
Texas Mountain Laurel (Sophora secundiflora)	E	P,F,R	L-M	Pur	Sp	20'-30'	5'-10'	H
Desert Hackberry (Celtis pallida)	E/D	F	M	I	Sp	5'-10'	5'-10'	H
Desert Broom (Baccharis sarothroides)	E/D	P,F	L	W	F	6'-8'	7'-10'	H

SHADE & SHELTER

Plant	Deciduous or Evergreen	Sun	Water	Flower Color	Flowering Season	Height	Spread	Cold Tolerance
Chilean Mesquite (Prosopis chilensis)	D	F,R	L-M	W-Y	Sp	25'-30'	30'-40'	H
Mexican Palo Verde (Parkinsonia aculeata)	D	F,R	L-M	Y	Sp-S	20'-35'	20'-35'	H
Desert Willow (Chilopsis linearis)	D	F	M	W,Y,P	Sp-S	15'-30'	10'-20'	H
Blue Palo Verde (Cercidium floridum)	D	F	L-M	Y	Sp	15'-30'	15'-30'	H
Southwestern Sweet Acacia (Acacia minuta)	E	F	L-M	Y	Sp	18'-25'	10'-18'	H

KEY

Deciduous or Evergreen

D = Deciduous
E = Evergreen

Water

L = Low; infrequent
M = Medium; likes some additional water

Flowering Season

F = Fall
W = Winter
Sp = Spring
S = Summer

Flower Color

B = Blue
Pur = Purple
R = Red
W = White, cream
P = Pink
Y = Yellow
O = Orange
I = Insignificant

Sun

P = Partial Sun
S = Shade OK
F = Full Sun
R = Reflected, such as near paved areas

Cold Tolerance

H = Hardy; not bothered by cold periods in the Tucson Area.
T = Tender; will die back with frosts, but recovers quickly

* the preparation and dissemination of a series of news releases which resulted in newspaper articles explaining the water savings possible through the use of appropriate landscape design and plant selection for the desert Southwest.

* Ibid.

* **Tucson Daily Star**, April 23, 1983, Page E1.

Water-conserving plants urged for Tucson area homes

By Gene Varn
Southern Arizona Bureau

TUCSON — A water-conservation group on Wednesday started a campaign urging southern Arizona residents to use desert plants that consume little water in place of water-guzzling imported plants.

Officials of the Southern Arizona Water Resources Association, a private group of business and government officials and residents, said the campaign is another step in the conservation effort aimed at reducing the demand on the Tucson area's dwindling ground-water supply.

The campaign will feature billboards with the motto, "Make every drop count — replace mulberry with mesquite," in English and Spanish.

Marybeth Carlile, the association's executive director, said the campaign is an attempt to make southern Arizona residents aware that "every time you turn on the tap, you have to consider you are living in a desert community."

As part of the campaign, 14 Tucson plant nurseries will promote 35 desert plants that need little or no watering to be used in place of popular imported varieties, such as fruitless-mulberry and citrus trees, which require generous amounts of water each year.

The nurseries will attach the water association's blue logo to the containers of each of the recommended plants to aid prospective purchasers, said Sarah Brown, coordinator of the association's conservation effort.

The recommended plants provide shade, shelter and space definition equivalent to, or better than, the popular water-consuming imported varieties, according to Warren Jones, a professor of landscape architecture at the University of Arizona.

Among the recommended trees are the blue and Mexican paloverdes, Chilean mesquite, desert willow and Southwestern sweet acacia.

Space-defining plants recommended by the association include the Arizona rosewood, jojoba, Texas ranger and desert broom.

Other recommended plants include the fairy duster, false-sand verbena, desert and feathery cassia, yuccas, agaves, ocotillo, aloes, Mexican blue palm, desert spoon, Arizona grape ivy and yellow orchid vine.

Nursery operators at the press conference announcing the association's campaign said the recommended plants use from 10 inches of water per year, equivalent to the area's average rainfall, to 20 inches.

*

Conservation is an important part of landscaping in Arizona desert

By WALT NETT
of The Territorial

The Southern Arizona Water Resources Association last week kicked off the second phase of its water conservation-education program, which leans heavily on changing landscaping from high-water-demand greenery to desert vegetation.

Marybeth Carlile, executive director of the local water lobbying group, told reporters that "conservation is an integral part of the water management program in Tucson. All users will be required eventually to conserve."

Conservation actually becomes mandatory in January with the passage of the first state water management plan.

The campaign includes billboards in English and Spanish encouraging the public to "Replace Mulberry with Mesquite," while interior and exterior bus signs encourage people to use drip irrigation and to "Think desert landscape."

At the direct consumer level, SAWARA has appointed a conservation committee to advise the organization on low-water-use vegetation selections, devised a tag identifying those plants, and enlisted nurseries in town to place the tags on SAWARA-approved vegetation.

In all, 35 varieties of plants — hedges, ground cover, trees, vines, bedding plants and accent plants — have been tabbed by SAWARA as low-water-use.

Warren Jones, faculty member at the University of Arizona's landscape architecture program, said one facet of SAWARA's program will be to "push the idea of a mini-oasis. A small area of green is still valid."

He said that shade and other desired effects can be accomplished with low water-use plants replacing many of the water-intensive plants now seen around Tucson.

Nurseryman Bill Harlow suggested that his business' participation has been extended "because the bottom line is profit. The tag makes the plants easy to identify, and the tag gives you a second source that tells you it's a good plant. We'll sell more plants."

One side effect might be a diminished pollen count, as two of the more thirsty transplants to Tucson — Bermuda grass and mulberry trees — also fill the air with pollen.

Jones said the pollen problem probably wouldn't entirely go away, but he pointed out that most of the plants on the SAWARA-approved list are bee-pollinated.

Several reporters asked about the potential for skeptical public response to the continuing call for water conservation, since Tucson again opened the year with about twice as much rainfall as normal for the first four months.

Harlow said the inclement weather has caused him to withhold judgement on the public's attitude about water conservation since "nobody's been out in their gardens yet."

Joe Patterson, of Desert Survivors, took a more psychological view of it.

"We work out of a basic mental retardation model," he said. "Mentally retarded people don't mean to do bad things when they do them. Like children, we will forget the long-term punishment and glut up on all the candy in the kitchen when Mom's gone. The stomachache comes later."

Other members of the committee are George Brookbank of the University of Arizona Cooperative Extension Service, Carol Dorsey of the Pima Association of Governments, Mickey Fontes of Desert Trees, Joan Johnson from Johnson & Crowley, Gene Joseph of the Arizona Sonora Desert Museum, Jim Miller of Anderson, Passarelli and MacVittie, and Lester Snow of the State Department of Water Resources.

The SAWARA campaign is designed to supplement the Beat the Peak and Slow the Flow programs operated by local governments.

**

---

* **Daily Territorial**, April 28, 1983, Page 22.   ** **The Arizona Republic**, April 14, 1983, Page B4.

52

One other response to water shortages which related to landscape development was a booklet published by the Metropolitan Water District of Southern California. This 24 page booklet was entitled "How to Have a Green Garden in a Dry State" and dealt with the use of tensiometers, moisture sensors and soil samplers; it covered irrigation systems, methods of retaining rain water, a summer starvation program, weed removal, mulching and soil conditioning. It also contained a very general list of drought resistant plants and some garden design guidelines with individual plant suggestions.

The cover of that publication, which was printed in color, is reproduced in black and white below. Some of the illustrations from the brochure are shown in the right hand column and an example of a two page spread is shown on the next page.*

---

* **How to Have a Green Garden in A Dry State,** Metropolitan Water District of Southern California, P.O. Box 54153, Los Angeles, California 90054.

Water Doesn't Grow On Trees.

Eucalyptus Red-Cap Gum

The winter of 1977-78 brought desperately needed rain to California in record amounts. It filled rivers and lakes and reservoirs. It deposited tons of welcome snow in the mountains. And once the danger of floods and landslides had passed, it lulled us into a false sense of security. The drought was over. We turned on the faucets and fountains and sprinklers. We watered our lawns, gardens and, sometimes, sidewalks. And we forgot rather quickly just how dry California can be.

California's weather patterns are anything but predictable. Perhaps heavy winter rains will come again. Perhaps not. But the experts tell us that even normal rainfall may be incapable of filling our needs in years to come. Our demand for water continues to rise. But the state's history of lower than average rainfall and drought virtually guarantees a limited supply for future generations.

What can we do?

Conserve. During wet years as well as dry. And a good place to start is in the garden. Nearly half the water used in a typical home is used outdoors, soaking lawns, trees, shrubs, flowers, backyard vegetable gardens. And perverse as it may seem, our gardens don't really appreciate all that water. Eight out of ten plant problems are caused directly or indirectly by too much water. So breaking the overwatering habit will save both plants and water. But not quite enough.

The obvious solution is to use plants that require less water — much less. That doesn't mean turning your backyard into a miniature Death Valley. Many drought-resistant plants are green, lush and almost shameless in their production of blooms. They come in every shape, color and size — from clinging ground cover to towering shade trees. And most of them can go as long without water as a camel. Which means less work in the garden once it's become a water saver.

Creating a water-saving garden takes a little knowledge and some careful planning. It doesn't require plowing under everything presently living in your yard. It can be a gradual process — replacing tired old plants with young drought-resistant ones. Whether you do it gradually or start from scratch, you'll need to know the best plants to use, where and when they should be planted, and the most economical ways to water both thirsty and unthirsty gardens. You'll find all that information in the following pages. Because that's what this little book is all about — keeping California green, but only a little bit wet.

The Cooperative Extension Service of Colorado State University utilized a symbol for conserving water and prepared a series of "Service in Action" brochures for wide distribution. They also prepared a series of illustrations which were used in a slide presentation and in a series of overhead transparencies which utilized the character "Johnny Waterwise" who presented '12 Ways to Save Water in the Garden''.

CONSERVE

JOHNNY WATERWISE PRESENTS...

12 WAYS TO CONSERVE WATER IN THE GARDEN

SPRINKLERS with COARSE, LOW SPRAY ARE BEST

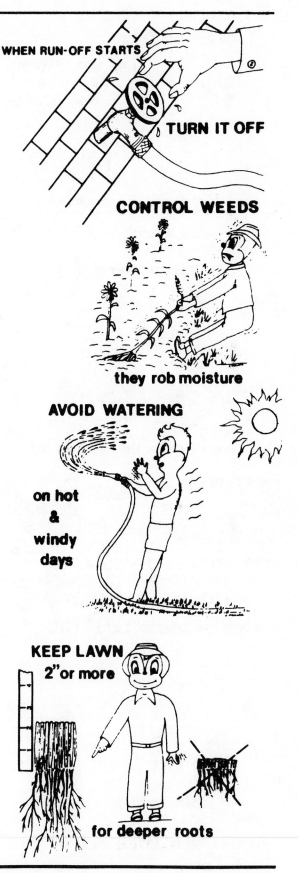

WHEN RUN-OFF STARTS

TURN IT OFF

CONTROL WEEDS

they rob moisture

AVOID WATERING

on hot & windy days

KEEP LAWN
2" or more

for deeper roots

* Available from Cooperative Extension Service, Colorado State University, 909 York Street, Denver, Colorado 80206.

DEEP WATER

trees & shrubs

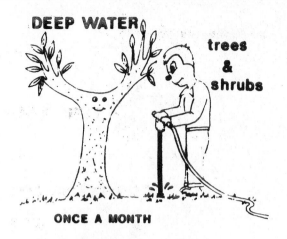

ONCE A MONTH

MULCHES CONSERVE WATER

Organic Matter

COMPACTED SOILS

waste water through run-off

improves the

WATER EFFICIENCY of your soil.

WATER ONLY

HEY! I NEED A DRINK!

when the plants "TELL" YOU

DON'T GET LAZY ABOUT WATER

BE AWAKE!

a BIG garden

takes more WATER than .....

....a small one

CAN YOU GET BY WITH LESS?

The City of Albuquerque, N.M. passed a waste water ordinance in 1978 and since that time has been very diligent in enforcing it. The following two pages show the text of that ordinance. On the page immediately after the ordinance, a sample letter which is sent to anyone found to be wasting water in Albuquerque is shown. An entire, staffed, program of public education and awareness as well as enforcement has resulted in significant water savings in times of shortage or drought. *

ARTICLE XVI
WATER WASTE

8-16-1   SHORT TITLE.

This ordinance shall be known and may be cited as the "Albuquerque Water Waste Ordinance". (56-1978)

8-16-2   DECLARING A NUISANCE CONDITION TO EXIST.

The flow of excess landscape water, fugitive water, and water wastage from any water supply, transport, or delivery system, installation or facility onto adjacent property or public right-of-way of the City of Albuquerque is hereby declared a nuisance. (56-1978)

8-16-3   DEFINITIONS.

For purposes of this ordinance, the following definitions apply:

A. "Waste" shall mean the non-beneficial use of water supplied by the municipal water supply system.

B. "Fugitive Water" shall mean the pumping, flow, release, escape, or leakage of any water from any pipe, valve, faucet, connection, diversion, well, from any water supply, transport, storage disposal or delivery system of facility onto adjacent property or the public right-of-way.

C. "Non-beneficial Uses" include but are not restricted to the following:
1. Landscape water applied in such a manner, rate and/or quantity that it regularly overflows the landscaped area being watered and runs onto adjacent property or publi right-of-way.

2. Landscape water which leaves a sprinkler, sprinkler system or other application device in such a manner or direction as to spray onto adjacent property or public right-of-way.

3. Washing down or hard surfaces such as parking lots, aprons, pads, driveways or other surfaced areas when water is applied in sufficient quantity to flow from that surface onto adjacent property or the public right-of-way.

D. "Public Right-Of-Way" shall mean paved or unpaved streets, alleys, drainage, or other public easements and lined or unlined drainage channels, which comprise the municipal storm drainage system.

E. " Responsible Party" shall mean the owner, manager, supervisor, or person in charge of the property, vacility or operation during the period of time the violation(s) are observed.

F. " Mayor" shall mean the Mayor or Albuquerque, or his designated representative. (56-1978)

8-16-4   WASTE WATER PROHIBITED.

After the effective date of this ordinance, no person, firm, corporation, or municipal facility or operation shall waste, cause or permit to be wasted any water furnished by the municipal water supply system of the City of Albuquerque. (56-1978)

---

* Environmental Health and Energy Department, Consumer Protection, City of Albuquerque, P.O. Box 1293, Albuquerque, N.M. 87103.

8-16-5 FUGITIVE WATER FLOW PROHIBITED

After the effective date of this ordinance, no person, firm, corporation, municipal, or other government facility or operation shall cause or permit the flow of excess or fugitive water onto adjacent property or public right-of-way. (56-1978)

8-16-6 EXEMPTIONS.

A. "Fugitive Water" shall not include:
1. Storm run-off allowed under provisions of City Council Resolution 55-1976 or 59-1976.

2. Flow resulting from temporary water supply system failures or malfunctions.

3. Flow resulting from other emergencies.

B. "Waste" shall not include:

1. Flow resulting from fire fighting or routine inspection of fire hydrants or from training activities.

2. Water applied as a dust control measure as may be required under Section 8.0 - Air Pollution Control Regulations.

3. Water applied to abate spills of flamable or otherwise hazardous materials.

4. Water applied to prevent or abate health, safety, or accident hazards when alternate methods are not available.

5. Water which reaches or flows onto adjacent property or public right-of-way when caused by vandalism, wind, or other uncontrollable circumstances or condition.

6. Flow resulting from a routine inspection or maintenance of the municipal water supply system.

7. Occasional flow resulting from commercial or individual residential applications such as washing of vehicles, boats, driveways, sidewalks or municipal flushing of streets.

8. Water used by the Traffic Engineering Division, City of Albuquerque, in the course of installation or maintenance of traffic flow control devices.

9. Water used by contractors or utilities in saw-cutting or pavement, compaction, or otheruse required under terms of their contract. (56-1978)

8-16-7 ADMINISTRATION OF THE ORDINANCE.

The Mayor shall be responsible for the enforcement of this ordinance. He shall prescribe policies, rules, or regulations to carry out the intent and purposes of the ordinance.

A. SUSPENSION OF SERVICE. On determination by City Staff that a health or safety hazard exists, and failure by the responsible party to abate the nuisance, municipal water service may be suspended at the discretion of the Mayor.

B. VARIANCES. A variance may be issued by the Mayor, provided that all options for abatement through modified water management have been exhausted. The variance may be issued for a period not to exceed one year and shall stipulate both corrective measures and a schedule for completion. (56-1978)

8-16-8 PENALTY.

Any responsible party who violates any of the provisions of this ordinance shall be deemed guilty of a misdemeanor and upon conviction thereof shall be punished by a fine not exceeding three hundred dollars($300.00). Each occasion this ordinance is violated shall be considered a separate offense. (56-1978)

City of Albuquerque

P.O. BOX 1293   ALBUQUERQUE, NEW MEXICO 87103

Date--------------/------/198----

----------------------------------   RE: Water Waste

Dear--;

Water has been observed flowing from the above address at--a.m.
p.m.

on---,   coming from---
        Day(s), Date(s)

The cause appears to be---

Repeated flow onto adjacent property and/or the public Right of Way is a violation of the Municipal Water Waste Ordinance(Ord. (8-16)), copy attached.

Your cooperation in correcting this problem is requested. Please contact me at 766-7433 within
five(5) working days of receipt of this notice. Hopefully we can reach agreement on intended
corrective measures and a mutually acceptable time frame for compliance. Alternately, failure to
respond will close the option of informal resolution of the problem and necessitate formal enforcement action.

cc:File   Sincerely,

Enclosure   --
                                                     Larry T. Caudill

Notice Date--Response Date----------------------------------

Intended corrective measures/time frame:--

The following are sections of the model ordinance prohibiting non-essential uses of water prepared by the State of California for possible adoption by local communities. It demonstrates the impact this has on residential water use to maintain landscape development.

MODEL ORDINANCE PROHIBITING NONESSENTIAL USES OF WATER

ORDINANCE _____

An Ordinance of the _____ (agency) Declaring a Water Shortage Emergency, Establishing Rules and Regulations Prohibiting Nonessential Uses of Water, and Providing Penalties for Violations Thereof.

The (governing body) of _____ (agency), does enact as follows:

Section 1. *Purpose and Intent.* The _____ (governing body) of _____ (agency) hereby declares that a water shortage emergency condition prevails within the _____(agency) due to drought conditions prevailing throughout the State of California and that the ordinary demands and requirements of water consumers cannot be satisfied without depleting the water supply of the _____ (agency) to the extent that there would be insufficient water for human consumption, sanitation, and fire protection.

In order to conserve the water supply for the greatest public benefit with particular regard to domestic use, sanitation, and fire protection, and to allocate, distribute and deliver water for other purposes in a manner which will not discriminate between consumers using water for the same purpose or purposes, this _____(governing body) adopts the following regulations and restrictions on the delivery and consumption of water to take effect immediately and remain in effect until October 15 of this year or until rescinded, whichever occurs first.

The specific uses regulated, or prohibited in this Ordinance are nonessential, if allowed would constitute wastage of water.

Section 4. *Prohibition on Sprinkling and Watering.* No person or customer shall sprinkle, water, or irrigate any shrubbery, trees, lawns, grass, ground covers, plants, vines, gardens, vegetables, flowers, or any other vegetation, except as follows:

(a) Such irrigation, sprinkling, and watering shall be permitted by _____ (even-numbered residences or certain location) on even-numbered days of the calendar.

(b) Such irrigation, sprinkling, and watering shall be permitted by _____ (odd-numbered residences or certain locations) on odd-numbered days of the calendar.

(c) Such person or customer is a commercial nursery, golf course, park, cemetery, school, community garden, or similar school, recreational or memorial-type facility.

Section 5. *Large Water Users.* The requirements of this Ordinance to the contrary notwithstanding, no person whose historic monthly average water use for the period _____ through _____ exceeds _____ (i.e., one million) gallons per month, herein called "large water users," shall irrigate, sprinkle, or water any shrubbery, trees, lawns, grass, ground covers, plants, vines, gardens, vegetables, flowers, or any other vegetation except on days assigned in each week during which this Ordinance is in effect, said days to be assigned by the _____ (chief Officer) after consultation with the individual large water users.

* **Model Ordinances,** Water Conservation Information Bulletin, Department of Natural Resources, Box 388, Sacramento, California 95802.

The Office of Appropriate Technology and the Department of Water Resources of the State of California developed, in Sacramento, a model Urban Water Conservation Garden. In a guide to that garden they gave the rationale for this project as an educational and awareness tool in the following words:

> Drought years such as those Californians experienced in 1976 and 1977 reinforce the need to conserve water while maintaining a green and healthy landscape. Although some winters produce ample rains, we know that long-range planning and careful use of water is essential in this mediterranean climate which experiences long dry spells, fluctuations in water supply from year to year as well as "droughts" every summer.
> The Office of Appropriate Technology and the Department of Water Resources have developed this demonstration garden as a working model for people throughout the state who want to know how to create and maintain a beautiful yet water conserving landscape. We hope to encourage care for all our city's limited natural resources - the soil, water, air, wildlife, plants, and energy. This garden serves as a model for urban park design which provides food, recreation, and a pleasant mix of settings as well as open space for a downtown neighborhood. *

A plan of that garden is shown on the following page.

Guide to the Model Urban Water Conservation Garden

sponsored by: OFFICE OF APPROPRIATE TECHNOLOGY and DEPARTMENT OF WATER RESOURCES

* **Guide to Model Urban Water Conservation Garden,** State of California, Office of Appropriate Technology, 1530 10th Street, Sacramento, California 95814; Department of Water Resources, P.O. Box 388, Sacramento, California 95802.

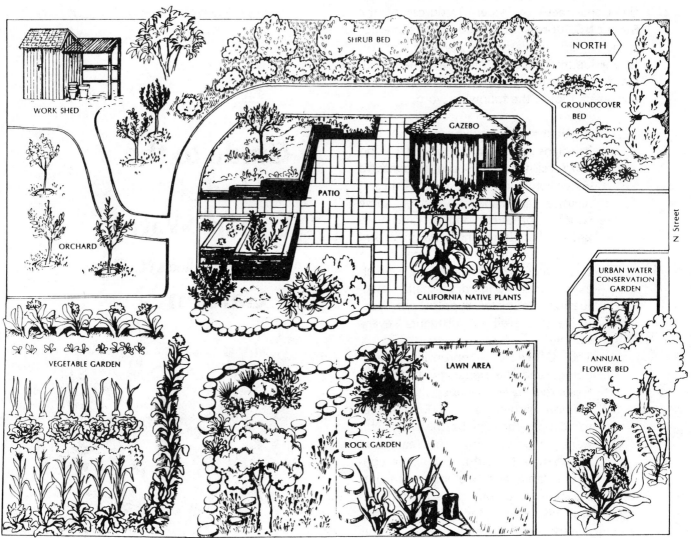

WORK SHED

SHRUB BED

NORTH

GROUNDCOVER
BED

GAZEBO

ORCHARD

PATIO

CALIFORNIA NATIVE PLANTS

N Street

URBAN WATER
CONSERVATION
GARDEN

VEGETABLE GARDEN

LAWN AREA

ANNUAL
FLOWER BED

ROCK GARDEN

17th street

Marin County California developed in the late 1970's a water conserving garden near their government center complex. They provided an explanatory plan which guided visitors and illustrated concepts of water conserving landscape and planning appropriate for coastal Northern California. *

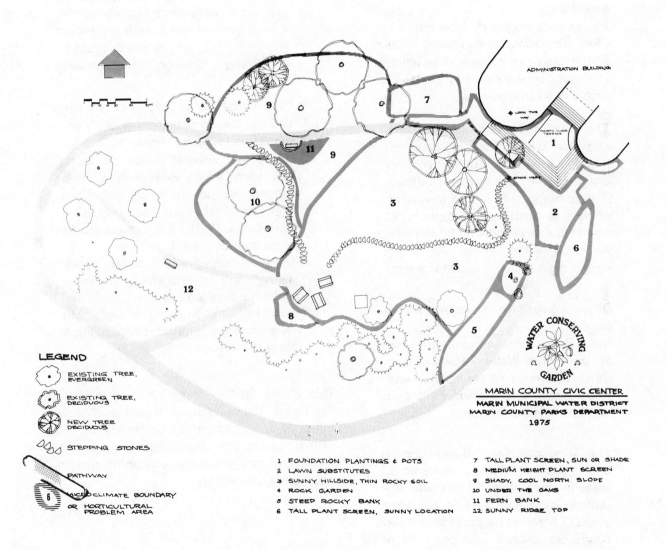

LEGEND

- EXISTING TREE, EVERGREEN
- EXISTING TREE, DECIDUOUS
- NEW TREE DECIDUOUS
- STEPPING STONES
- PATHWAY
- MICROCLIMATE BOUNDARY OR HORTICULTURAL PROBLEM AREA

ADMINISTRATION BUILDING

WATER CONSERVING GARDEN

MARIN COUNTY CIVIC CENTER
MARIN MUNICIPAL WATER DISTRICT
MARIN COUNTY PARKS DEPARTMENT
1975

1 FOUNDATION PLANTINGS & POTS
2 LAWN SUBSTITUTES
3 SUNNY HILLSIDE, THIN ROCKY SOIL
4 ROCK GARDEN
5 STEEP ROCKY BANK
6 TALL PLANT SCREEN, SUNNY LOCATION

7 TALL PLANT SCREEN, SUN OR SHADE
8 MEDIUM HEIGHT PLANT SCREEN
9 SHADY, COOL NORTH SLOPE
10 UNDER THE OAKS
11 FERN BANK
12 SUNNY RIDGE TOP

* **Water Conserving Garden,** Marin County Civic Center, Marin Municipal Water District, 220 Nellen Avenue, Corte Madera, California 94925, p.5-6.

Henry Eason in the cover story in the August 1983 issue of **Nation's Business** on the "Approaching Water Supply Crisis" points up the periodic water shortages and outlines conservation as one aspect of proper water management in the following words:

Over the past 30 years, the United States has doubled its consumption of water to a staggering 450 billion gallons a day - 2,000 gallons for every American.
The experts expect those numbers to keep increasing, precipitating a resource crisis that could have as serious an impact on the economy as did the energy crisis a decade ago.

'The crisis of the 1990's on the domestic side will be lack of water for domestic use,' says Interior Secretary James G. Watt. He warns 'All efforts to promote growth and employment, to increase agricultural prosperity, to protect the environment and to revive our cities will mean nothing, unless we can meet society's need for water.'

Other voices are sounding similar themes.
Rep. Robert Roe(D-N.J.), chairman of the House Water Resources Subcommittee, says of water shortages: 'People say it is a crisis waiting to happen. It is a crisis now.'

The American Farm Bureau Federation predicts that 'a number of areas in the United States could face critical water shortages in the years ahead.' A report by the federal Water Resources Council lists problems of inadequete surface water supply in all 21 of the nation's water resources regions. And, the report says, 38 out of 106 subregions are now experiencing moderate to extensive groundwater overdrafting - withdrawals at a faster rate than replenishment."

"Conservation is another aspect of proper water management needed to avert shortages. The General Accounting Office states:
'Traditionally, our nation solved water supply problems either by building new projects, thus creating additional holding and delivery capacity, or developing technologies whereby water that was formerly unusable can be used. However, these approaches are very costly and time-consuming An alternative solution is to reduce the demand on present supplies, principally through conservation.'

"The user-fee principle is closely tied to the conservation goal. Consumers who learn, from their bills, the actual market value of water will soon adopt conservation techniques, just as motorists did when the price of gasoline quadrupled during the 1970s, the experts in the water-supply predict.
Increased recycling of water by industry and development of more agricultural processes that reduce the need for large amounts of water will be among the important conservation steps. *

This article, in this magazine is particularly significant since **Nation's Business** is published by the Chamber of Commerce of the United States and represents business interests and an economic viewpoint toward water and water supply.

* Eason, Henry, "The Approaching Water-Supply Crisis", **Nation's Business**, August 1983, Vol. 71, No. 8, p.22-23.

There are a vast number of other projects and programs which cannot be mentioned here because of space limitations. People accommodate to water shortages in a variety of ways. Water shortages are a fact of life now and in the future. There will be many more water shortages in the future for a variety of reasons and in many different locations. Plans should be made now for that eventuality and it should be understood that landscape development will be one of the first areas or facets rationed, cut, curtailed or limited in such shortages. No matter how much water there is, it still should be used carefully, conscientiously and responsibly. If there were unlimited water in any geographic area, care should still be taken, since, in other areas there are or will be shortages. There is no longer unlimited water in all geographic areas which can be wasted or used profligately. Water conservation should be a matter of con-science and of responsible stewardship. Careful water use may become necessary for economic or financial reasons or it may become mandatory because of rationing or other legal controls. In any case, the landscape industry and the consumers and users of landscape products will never again have the limitless water to nuture, sustain and enhance landscaped areas. Water shortages are here, and they are "reality", they do provide good discipline and help to enforce responsible design guidelines and principles that should have been used all along in most areas of the country. The landscape industry needs to understand and accept water shortages and to learn to cope in an active way. Part of that learning is from what others have done and are doing. This chapter has shown that in a small way and the information presented should serve as a guide to the future which will include increased water shortages.

Rain Dance Doesn't Work Here Anymore

The title is meant to convey the shifting realities of the urban Southwest. The first inhabitants of this area lived in close harmony and profound awareness of basic resources, particularly water. Today urbanization has provided this resource in an abundance beyond the dreams of the Old Ones. It also led to a loss of awareness, for water appears to most people as simply another commodity available in overflow supply at the turn of a tap. Those who still live in fundamental harmony with the Earth Mother and the Sky Father however, know that the rain dance works. It is alive and well, living on the forgotten mesas and in the hidden valleys of New Mexico. He simply prefers not to work in cities.

*

---

* Lupsha, Peter A., Don P. Schlegel and Robert U. Anderson, **Rain Dance Doesn't Work Here Anymore,** Water Use and Citizen Attitutdes Towards Water Use in Albuquerque, New Mexico, Division of Government Research, Institute for Applied Services, The University of New Mexico, Albuquerque, New Mexico, December 1975., p. 51.

the competition for water

> No matter how much people love trees, shrubs, flowers and lawns, if they must give up drinking, cooking or bathing water to have them, they will give up the plants.

It seems that everyone wants all of the clean, pure water they can get for as little cost as possible. When we see all of the water in rivers, lakes and oceans, it is easy to think of it as abundant and free. It does cost money to purify, store and transport water. That cost is not paid proportionally by those who use the water.

The competition for water is one of the major problems facing many societies, governments and regions in the world today. Competition for water may do more to limit the use of growing landscape elements than any other factor. No matter how much people love trees, shrubs, flowers and lawns, if they must give up drinking, cooking or bathing water to have them, they will give up the plants. To use water for irrigation is acceptable if there is plenty of inexpensive water available. If water is scarce, expensive or needed for other uses then the competition becomes apparent, obvious and "real".

There is an intense competition for water and it is(and will to a greater extent) affecting landscape irrigation practices. This competition is illustrated in a number of recent quotations and illustrations. In the article, "New Economic Theorem - There is No Such Thing as Free Water", the following chart shows graphically the competition for water from industry, recreation, navigation, hydroelectric, fish and wildlife, thermal electric as well as domestic water users.

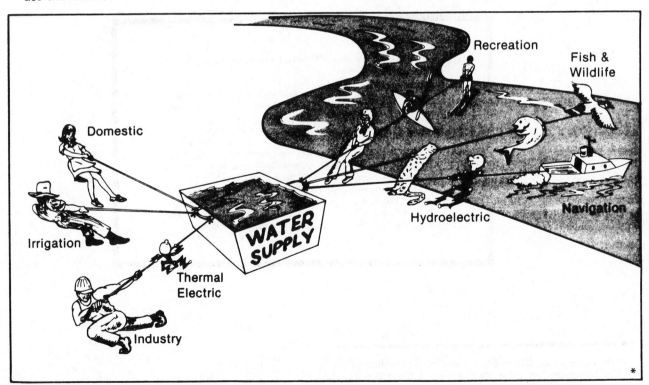

*Anderson, Alan, Jr. **New Economic Theorem - There is No Such Thing as Free Water,** Across the Board, October 1981, Vol. XVIII, No. 9.,P. 53.

That same article amplifies on the premise of the title in the following words:

Traditionally we have regarded fresh water as part of nature's bounty, falling free like sunlight to nourish life on earth. Fresh water falls in quantities greater than we can imagine ever using; global reserves(streams, lakes, groundwater, vapor and ice) add up to enough to fill the Mediterranean 10 times over.

But, being human, we have polluted our supplies of water where they are abundant and drained them where they are scarce. Water is indeed free and renewable, when it falls from the sky, but it is also finite. We cannot increase the amount now on and around the earth. When we use - or demand - more than nature supplies, we change its traditional status as a gift. No longer free, it is being treated like a commodity to be bought and sold. *

That same author outlines the total quantity of water on the earth and indicates the distribution of this water in the following words:

. . . The total quantity of water on earth seems virtually infinite - some 326 million cubic miles. Only about 2.5 percent of this is fresh water, however, and of that amount more than three quarters is bound up in polar ice. Of the total water budget, then, only about 0.6 percent is liquid fresh water.

Still even this tiny percentage is a huge volume of water. Even if all nations used as much as the United States for irrigation - our single largest consumer of water - the daily world rainfall could support a population of 20 billion to 25 billion. In the United States alone, some 40,000 billion gallons of water per day(bgd) pass overhead as water vapor. About 10 percent, or 4,200

bgd, falls as rain, snow, sleet or hail - enough to build a nationwide lagoon 30 inches deep each year. Total average streamflow is estimated at 2,248 bgd - more than 10 times our estimated consumption through the year 2000. Likewise, the total groundwater supply is enormous - equal to about twice the flow of the Mississippi into the Gulf of Mexico for the last 200 years.

But the flaw in this picture of plenty is the implication that water is distributed according to human needs. In fact, distribution is radically uneven, both in time and space.
**

The Southern Arizona Water Resources Association in the newsletter "Waterworks" uses the following illustration to show the allocation of the world's water supply.

THE WORLD'S WATER

97% = Salt Water

0.3% Fresh Water Available to Man

0.77% = Polar Ice
0.22% = Ground and Soil Water
0.003% = Rivers and Streams

***

---

* Ibid. , p.40-42.
** Ibid., p.42.
*** SAWARA waterwords, Vol. 2, No. 7, July 1983, Southern Arizona Water Resources Association, 465 St. Mary's Road, Suite 100, Tucson, Arizona 85705., p. 6.

The same organization indicated the competition for water in a residential situation with an indication of the demands inside and outside the home for each 100 gallons in the following diagram:

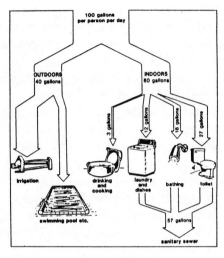

Average Residential Consumption

*

In the State of California, the statewide water demand by type for 1972 was shown in the following diagram. This puts the competition for water into perspective.

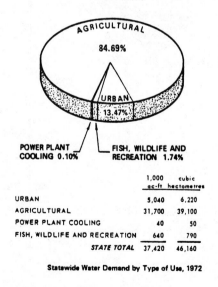

	1,000 ac-ft	cubic hectometres
URBAN	5,040	6,220
AGRICULTURAL	31,700	39,100
POWER PLANT COOLING	40	50
FISH, WILDLIFE AND RECREATION	640	790
STATE TOTAL	37,420	46,160

Statewide Water Demand by Type of Use, 1972   **

The urban water use in that same state was shown in the following way:

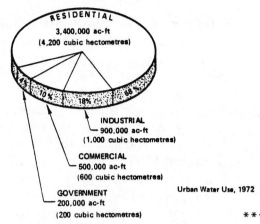

Urban Water Use, 1972

***

In the same publication residential water allocation was illustrated. All of this shows the competition and the "pull" on existing resources in the most populous state in the nation.

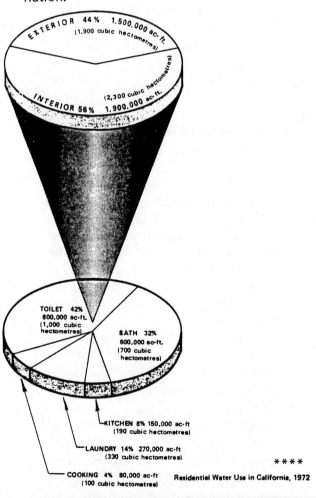

Residential Water Use in California, 1972

****

* Ibid. p.3.

** Water Conservation in California, Department of Water Resources, The Research Agency, State of California, Bulletin No. 198, May 1976. p. 11.

*** Ibid.,p. 14.

**** Ibid., p. 17.

Henry Eason in the **Nation's Business** article on "The Approaching Water-Supply Crisis" also points up the competition by geographic region and by sector of the economy.

"Much of the availability problem stems from the misalignment of water supplies and people. More than 75 percent of the population and most manufacturing activity are concentrated on less than 2 percent of the land, and bringing water to those sections grows increasingly expensive.

Industry and agriculture are by far the two largest water-consuming sectors of the economy, accounting for more than 90 percent of the daily total. Within those sectors, power generation and irrigation are the major end uses. Public water supplies represent most of the balance of the consumption.

Among regions, water-use patterns vary widely, as shown by the U.S. Geological Survey's recent report which covers 1980.

Although 90 percent of all irrigation water is drawn in the western United States, 90 percent of all water for industrial purposes is used in the East.

Per capita use ranged from 19,000 gallons a day in Idaho, a thinly populated state with large tracts of irrigated land, to 180 gallons per day in Rhode Island, the smallest and one of the most densely populated of the states.

Three of the fastest-growing states - California, Florida, Texas - are the largest water users, in that order. Those states, combined with Idaho withdrew 25 percent of the water used in the United States in 1980.

*

Competition for water drives up the price, it limits the uses of available water and it creates friction among potential water users. But in the forseeable future, competition will increase. It will cause some to make do with less or go without. Landscape irrigation will suffer most in such competition. It is among the first water uses to be cut back in periodic water shortages. Landscape irrigation will suffer even more and the water for it will be more expensive as the competition increases, especially in the growing areas of the Sunbelt. In such situations all of the possible alternatives and strategies for conservation need to be explored, examined and utilized to the fullest extent possible. In the competition for water there may not be any so it is best to develop a conservation ethic and attitude as early and as completely as possible.

Eason, Henry, "The Approaching Water-Supply Crisis" **Nation's Business,** August 1983, Vol. 71, No. 8, p. 22

landscape development & water use

Landscape development is one of the first areas cut back during time of shortage for at least two reasons:

1. It is a visible use of water, and

2. Landscape development is regarded as a luxury.

Landscape development is desired and needed in almost all geographic areas. The claim that it is considered desirable is supported by the proliferation of parks, golf courses, landscape development around commercial and public buildings, the planting of street trees, and the extensive landscape development around individual single family residences, apartment buildings, and houses. There is a psychological need within most people to have some degree of contact with natural growing elements. Plant materials and landscape development serve many needs. Plant materials provide atmospheric purification, noise control, glare and reflection reduction, shade, wind control, privacy, and screening of objectionable views and objects. They are also used to create outdoor spaces, and to provide attractive color and form in the outdoor environment. The functional uses of plant materials are covered extensively in a number of documents, and particularly in the book, *PLANTS, PEOPLE AND ENVIRONMENTAL QUALITY.** The extent of a landscape development as well as its form will usually be determined by climate

* Gary O. Robinette, **Plants, People and Environmental Quality,** U.S. Government Printing Office, Stock No. 2405-0479, Washington, D.C., 1972.

and available water. As urbanization and crowding increase, the need for landscape development becomes greater because of the need for screening, noise control and for natural "oases" to relieve the pressures created in a crowded and complex world. Landscape development almost always includes living plant materials. These plants require a certain amount of water to grow and thrive. As water becomes scarce during water shortages landscape plant material suffers to varying degrees. In addition to the basic need of plants for water, water assists the growth processes by dissolving fertilizer and by transporting nutrients within the plants. The increased growth and development in the perpetually water-short "Sun Belts" of the southern and western parts of the United States has created in those areas a demand for landscape development which cannot be sustained by existing water supplies. Often the type of landscaping done is basically inappropriate. Indigenous native plant materials can usually more easily accept the climatic water restrictions for their particular region. Exotic plants introduced from outside an area quite often do not have that same ability to withstand the limitations and restrictions of either climate or water. During times of drought or water shortage these particular plants suffer and require much more water to continue their existence. Concepts of landscape development acquired from other climatic areas of the country may be difficult and costly to impose on an area of limited water.

Professor Russell A. Beatty with the Department of Landscape Architecture at the University of California, Berkeley, in an article entitled "Browning of the Greensward," outlines this problem of the introduction of foreign and exotic species into a basic arid environment:

> Fortunately the garish ostentatious style of the Victorian era is gone. Refinements in garden and park design have been made during the 20th century. Nevertheless, the landscape

plantings we see today have their origins in the earlier styles imported from the East. The dominant theme is the picturesque style of the English landscape tradition. With 20th century affluence, the technological advances in the irrigation industry and development of the turfgrass and nursery industries, the greensward has persisted as the accepted planting motif. Mixtures of drought tolerant plants and thirsty species from less arid climates are combined with the aesthetic effect as the primary concern. We have inherited, without question or re-evaluation, a demand for highly irrigated landscapes. The simplicity and sensible fitness of the Mexican garden style has been largely discarded or forgotten. Newcomers are still lured to this benign climate by claims as exaggerated as those of the 19th century writers. Television and movies influence every American and paint a picture of California as a sunny Eden (the smog notwithstanding).

From Maryland, Missouri, or Connecticut families leave their homes and the expanses of lawn to live in Novato or San Bernardino. Either they, or the developers, make the transition easy by duplicating the lush landscape of their hometowns.

The net result is that we have become a state of people who have forgotten, or have never really discovered, where in the world we live. We have not really come to terms with living in the Mediterranean climate of California. Furthermore, we have become so detached from nature through dependency on modern technology that we have developed a lifestyle largely independent of the climate and landscape.*

*Russell A. Beatty, '' Browning of the Greensward,'' **Pacific Horticulture**, Fall 1977, P. 5-7.

Some sort of landscape development is obviously needed in all geographic areas of the country and one of the strategies which will be discussed later deals with the use of native or indigenous plant materials appropriate to each geographic region. As landscaped areas are developed, the amount of water which is used to maintain plant materials in the landscape is extensive. The Introduction to the book, *PLANTS FOR CALIFORNIA LANDSCAPES*, covers to a certain extent the required water needs for maintaining the landscape planting in that state.

Nearly 50 percent of California's urban residential water use goes towards the irrigation of landscaped plantings—amounting to almost 1,850,000 cubic dekametres (1,500,000 acre-feet) per year. Another estimated 370,000 cubic dekametres (300,000 acre-feet) is used for irrigating governmental and commercial lands. Based on predrought water use figures, new single-family units constructed by the year 2000 will create a demand for an additional 370,000 cubic dekametres (300,000 acre-feet) per year and new multifamily units will need another 308,000 cubic dekametres (250,000 acre-feet) per year. During the drought, various landscaping firms and governmental agencies reported a 25 percent to 90 percent reduction in water use for landscaped plantings due to efficient irrigation and changes in their maintenance practices. If the use of drought-tolerant plants and alternative water supplies, such as rainwater cisterns and gray-water systems, is added to this, outdoor water savings may be as high as 90-100 percent. Based on this high potential for water savings, it is reasonable to estimate that water use in existing landscapes can be reduced by 50 percent by the year 2000. A cutback of 50 percent of the water use in new single-family residences and 20 percent in new multifamily residences should also be possible by 2000. This reduction would result in water savings of 1,350,000 cubic dekametres (1,100,000 acre-feet) each year. (A cubic dekametre of water is approximately what a household of five people use in a year.) Reducing the water needs required for landscaping can, therefore, create substantial savings in our urban water supplies. The increased use of drought-tolerant plants is an important step towards long-term water conservation on the part of the homeowner or landscape designer.*

Another source has estimated that "in semi-arid or arid climates, much and often most water use occurs outside the home (approximately 70% in Salt Lake City) and the amount of water required outside depends largely on the adopted landscaping."**

Another study by Dr. Donald J. Cotter and Donald B. Croft of the New Mexico Water Resources Institute indicates that:

> It was found that residential dwellers use an average rate of 215 gallons of water daily and an additional 160 gallons for landscapes. Arid regions of the west exceed the humid regions of the east in landscape water use by 133%, rainfall being the most important factor in determining the amount of water used to irrigate landscapes. Other factors affecting landscape water use were water price, metering, residence density, other climatal considerations such as temperature, and consumer economic status.***

One other source explains that:

> About 44 percent of California's residential water is used outside the home, principally for lawn and garden irrigation. For several reasons, however, the reduction of exterior water use has not received the same research and attention as has reduced interior use:
>
> 1. In much of the United States, a reduction in interior use has been prompted primarily to reduce waste flows to treatment plants rather than to conserve water.
>
> 2. In many parts of the country, exterior water use is seasonal, and far less exterior water is used than in California, where lawns and gardens may be irrigated the year around.
>
> 3. The variety of exterior fixtures is limited, as compared to the various types of interior fixtures and appliances, which limits the opportunity for research and innovations.
>
> Some 90 percent of exterior water use is for irrigating lawns, shrubs, and home vegetable gardens; the remaining 10 percent is used for car washing, swimming pools, and cleaning driveways, sidewalks, and streets. Following application, water is stored in plants, transpired, and evaporated. Some runs off into storm drains, or percolates to ground water. Part of the percolated water may infiltrate sanitary sewer lines and be carried to wastewater treatment plants.

* **Plants for California Landscapes - A Catalog of Drought Tolerant Plants,** Department of Water Resources Bulletin No. 209, State of California Resources Agency, September 1979, P. 1-3.

** Richard Baldwin, " Conserving Water in the Landscape," California Turfgrass Culture, **Vo. 27, No. 2, Spring 1977, P. 2-3.**

*** Donald J. Cotter and Don B. Croft, "Water Application Practices and Landscape Attributes Associated with Residential Water Consumption, " New Mexico Water Resources Research Institute, **Technical Completion Reports,** Project No. C-4060, NMEX, Los Cruces, New Mexico, November 1974.

Because of this large residential water use for irrigation, significant amounts of water can be saved by eliminating overwatering and reducing evapotranspiration.*

That same study estimates that as much as 20 percent of all applied exterior water may represent overwatering.

Some of the water applied to plants and shrubs evaporates and some is used for growth (transpiration). Water in excess of these quantities either runs off or percolates. Although water deficiency will hinder plant growth and productivity, plants that need only moderate or small amounts of water are usually overwatered. *As a result, as much as 20 percent of all applied exterior water may represent overwatering.*

In 1972, the estimated statewide *excessive* exterior water use resulting from overwatering totaled 272,000 acre-feet (336 cubic hectometres); this excessive use could increase to 418,000 acre-feet (516 cubic hectometres) in 2000 . . . estimated residential overwatering in the Central Coastal, San Francisco Bay, and South Coastal hydrologic study areas totaled 191,000 acre-feet (234 cubic hectometres) in 1972 and could amount to 286,000 acre-feet (352 hectometres) in 2000.

Automatic sprinklers, except those with soil moisture override (sprinklers activated at predetermined soil moisture conditions), are feasible for ordinary home use. The soil moisture override system is best for the irrigation of larger areas, such as parks. All automatic sprinkler systems need periodic adjustment, due to seasonal climatic variations, sprinkler head adjustment, and changes in infiltration rates. The readings from soil moisture testing devices must be carefully interpreted. Soil texture, depth of test, and type of plant are important considerations. Well-controlled, timed sprinkler systems would not entirely eliminate overwatering, but could reduce it by 50 percent.

Eliminating overwatering would not necessarily result in an equal net water savings. In many areas, this excess water is not irrecoverably "lost," because most of it percolates to usable ground water, where it is pumped and reused (although it may have a higher salt concentration). On some coastal areas, it may also help repel sea-water intrusion.**

From all of the above it may be seen that an enormous amount of water is used to maintain areas of the landscape, particularly in the arid regions at certain seasons of the year. Landscape development does not use as much water as is used by agriculture and industry, but for at least two reasons the water used in landscape development is one of the first areas to be cut back during times of shortage. Reasons for this are:

1. It is a *visible* use of water. Water used or even wasted inside a factory or a home or an office is not easily seen by the general public. However, water being used to sprinkle a golf course or a lawn in front of a home or office is visible to all passing by the area.

2. Landscape development is still regarded as a luxury in contemporary society. It is considered a non-essential luxury; something that can be neglected or done without in times of shortage or crisis.

* **Water Conservation in California,** Department of Water Resources, The Resources Agency, State of California, May 1976, Bulletin 198, p. 22.

** Ibid., p. 23.

Both of these reasons are probably not going to be changed in the near future, so that the use of water to preserve landscape areas will always come under sharp attack during shortages. Responsible landscape design calls for the optimum use of all resources, including water, and the waste of little or nothing. Therefore it is worthwhile to explore all of the available strategies for conserving water in the design and maintenance of areas in the landscape. Those in all aspects of the landscape and green industry will find it imperative to recognize and deal with periodic water shortages in a responsible way or the entire field, including design, sales, construction, and maintenance, is going to suffer.

Strategies

**FOR WATER CONSERVATION
IN LANDSCAPE DEVELOPMENT**

Introduction

There are four basic strategies for water conservation relating to landscape development:

1. Preserve the water falling on the site,
2. To modify or reduce the need for water,
3. To use existing water more efficiently,
4. To find new sources of water.

Obviously a wide range of strategies need to be developed not only by designers, but by installation contractors, by grounds maintenance personnel and by homeowners in dealing with conserving water while enhancing and preserving the quality of landscape development. No one approach is going to save all of the water necessary in all circumstances or situations during all types of water crises. Therefore those dealing with landscape development during periods of water shortage need to have a full range of potential strategies to use where necessary and where advisable. There are four basic concepts dealing with all of the strategies for water conservation relating to landscape development. These are:

1. To preserve the water which falls on the site and to use it to preserve and enhance the landscape development on the site.
2. To modify the landscape development so as to reduce the need for water.
3. To use existing water available on the site more carefully and efficiently.
4. To find new sources of water for possible use in preserving the landscape development on any specific site.

The remainder of this book is an explanation of each of these suggested approaches. New strategies will have to be developed in time to come, especially in some geographic areas. However, this is an overview of experience from a wide variety of sources. It is a pulling together of what is now known and readily available at this particular time. It gives an overview of what can be done and what has been proposed at different times and in different places as the water crisis has been felt in different geographic regions. As stated by a number of authors in the literature on this particular subject, we know enough, we just need to do it before, during, and after the periodic water shortages occur. All members of the landscape team need to be aware, knowledgeable, and responsible. No one group can do it all alone in all circumstances and situations. Landscape designers, landscape installation contractors, landscape maintenance personnel, clients and owners all need to be involved in an on-going overall program. No one individual group can save all the necessary water in isolation. The designer must be aware of responsible landscape practices. The landscape contractor, in the installation of the plants, must be aware of what can and should be done to save the maximum amount of water. The maintenance personnel, whether staff or contractor, need to be aware of what can be done, who can do what, and when it can be done, whether before, during, or after installation. Some things mentioned in this book will not be able to be done in each specific situation or circumstance because of time or money, but others can and should be done by the responsible party. If planting suffers because of a lack of water the fault is with the designer or grounds manager, not with the plant. It is possible, with more careful planning, design, and maintenance to preserve landscape development with more efficient use of less available water.

James R. Watson, Vice President and agronomist at the Toro Manufacturing Company, listed in an article in the May 1977 issue of *GROUNDS MAINTENANCE MAGAZINE* a series of suggestions for coping with the water shortage. These outline in a rather perfunctory way some of the strategies which will be covered in greater detail later in this book. These suggestions for coping with the water shortage are as follows:

Establish watering priorities. Give the highest priority to the most intensively managed areas; for example, on a golf course, the greens, the most valuable part of the course and where the most critical play takes place.

On a golf course, give lesser importance, in descending order, to tees, fairways, clubhouse grounds, rough. If there are specimen plantings or trees or plants that have special significance, e.g. those imported at high cost or a gift, give them the same special attention as the greens.

Alter irrigation practices. (This is much easier to do if the course has an automatic irrigation system.) Use only enough water to sustain life, not to stimulate growth. Irrigate when there is the best combination of little wind, low temperature and high humidity. In any 24-hour period, that combination most often exists just before dawn.

Alter mowing and cultivation practices. Initially, test the soil to ensure adequate fertility, especially for phosphorus, which encourages root system growth—deeper roots, thus expanding the area from which the turfgrass can draw nutrients and moisture. Use calcium if there is a deficiency, to bring pH to a range of 6.5-7.2 Maintain a constant and uniform supply of nitrogen at a low to medium level to avoid unnecessary leaf growth. Consider slow-release materials; otherwise apply soluble materials at low rates frequently, rather than at higher rates infrequently. The latter will stimulate excessive leaf growth.

Raise the height of cut for all areas. Although this enlarges the surface area through which moisture is transpired, and under normal moisture conditions may result in stepped-up activity for disease-producing organisms, the benefits gained—mainly root extension—are most important. Raising the height of cut on a golf course green as little as 1/32 of an inch can have a significant effect on the ability of the green to tolerate stress from lack of moisture.

Mow frequently. The combination of reduced irrigation and fertilization, higher height of cut and less frequent mowing can induce "hardening" of the turfgrasses.

Expand use of mulch. Apply heavy layers of mulch—any organic debris that's available—around the base of trees, shrubs and flower beds, to hold in moisture.

Erect wind barriers, especially where there are large expanses of open spaces. Less than 3 percent of the water absorbed by a turfgrass plant is utilized by the plant. Most of it—the other 97 percent, is lost into the atmosphere by transpiration. And the rate of transpiration will rise with an increase in wind speed, radiation or temperature and by reduction in humidity. (Some of the same practices used to trap snow in the northern regions can be applied to reduce wind velocity.)

Aggressively seek additional sources of water. Among the several possibilities are wells and ponds, collections of marginal water and—the most abundant and most wasted supply—treated sewage effluent. There are many golf courses throughout the country successfully using recycled wastewater for irrigation.

Experiment with anti-transpirants. Although techniques for inhibiting transpiration have had mixed results, some reduction in moisture loss through transpiration might be accompanied with the use of chemicals, emulsions or films.*

The publication *WATER CONSERVATION INFORMATION DISSEMINATION DURING THE 1977 DROUGHT EMERGENCY*, prepared by the Utah Water Research Laboratory, collected data on hundreds of types of public information materials which were disseminated throughout the West dealing with public awareness and research efforts. Three different categories of their particular study dealt with water conservation practices outside the home. They categorized all of this information which was disseminated into three specific categories. These were (1) materials on water conservation in home landscaping, (2) materials suggesting water conservation practices in lawn care, and (3) ideas for conserving water in home gardening. The following lists an overview of the major points in 17 selected publications reviewed as a part of this study.

Water Conservation Factors to Consider in Home Landscaping **

1. Landscape to achieve desired functions (space separation, shade, ground cover, etc.), and select plants to achieve each function to minimize water application requirements.
2. Use native plants (or plants grown in arid climates in other countries) whose water requirements do not exceed local water availability as much as possible in landscaping.
3. Use drought-resistant or non-water using ground cover rather than lawns.
4. Vary water applications with stage of plant growth, season, soil structure, land slope, and plant's position in garden.
5. Reduce water applications in heavy clay soils because such soils are scarce in the oxygen needed for good root growth and

excessive watering further reduces vital air and can actually kill plants.
6. Use mulches or plastic films to hold moisture in soil.
7. Carefully use mulches so as not to create a soil nitrogen deficiency.
8. During water shortages, give watering priority to the more drought sensitive trees and shrubs, do not fertilize, and make special effort to control insects and diseases since these inflict greater harm to moisture stressed plants.
9. Provide extra water for small trees and shrubs whose water may be robbed by larger ones nearby.
10. Watch for insects and other pests known to be particularly active during drought periods and implement control measures when they appear.
11. Drought injured trees are best helped by deep-root aeration and watering and temporarily permitting shoots to sprout at the base.
12. Deep water can also help more shallow rooted trees through a snowless cold season provided that the ground has not frozen.
13. Pruning citrus trees saves water, but pruning most other trees does not.
14. Apply antidesicant or antitranspirants to trees and shrubs during periods of moderate temperature; these are not very effective during warm summer periods.

The same study summarized the essential points made in 15 selected publications which listed ideas for conserving water in lawn care:

Listing of Ideas for Conserving Water in Lawn Care ***

1. Water slowly enough to prevent runoff onto adjacent areas, long enough to penetrate the root zone, but not so long as to waste water penetrating beyond the reach of the roots.
2. Water lawns at night or early in the day. Evapotranspiration losses are less, and early watering also spreads water use more evenly over the day and thereby

*Watson, James R.,"Coping with Water Shortage", **Grounds Maintenance,** May 1977, Vo. 12, No. 5, p. 25.

** James and Andrews, op. cit. p. 13.

*** Ibid., p. 15.

reduces the cost to the water utility of system capacity expansions. Morning watering is also less likely to bring turf disease.

3. Water lawns when a moisture test indicates need rather than on a schedule based solely on the number of days since the last watering. Moisture indicators are available commercially.

4. Water sunny areas more often because of higher evapotranspiration rates, lawns, shaded by large trees more deeply to supply moisture for the tree roots, and areas shaded by buildings less often.

5. Overlap areas covered by sprinkler-settings by about one-third.

6. Spread water uniformly over homogeneous lawn areas.

7. Use special care in reducing water application rates to minimize runoff from steep slopes or compacted soils.

8. Hand water dry spots to delay general lawn watering.

9. Use lighter applications for newer lawns whose roots have not yet penetrated very deeply into the soil.

10. Determine the moisture requirements of the root zone and apply the same amount of water each time, but increase the duration between waterings as the weather grows cooler or if rain occurs.

11. Place cans on the lawn where they will catch water in order to measure the amount applied.

12. Do not use fine-mist sprinklers since they cause excessive evaporation.

13. Accept a less-than-lush green color all the time on a lawn.

14. Root-water dry spots when more water becomes available through an aerator attached to a garden hose.

15. Do not begin watering the lawn in early spring. Delaying the first watering encourages deeper root penetration. Roots penetrate most rapidly early in the spring as that is the most active growing season.

16. Give lawns the lowest priority of any landscaping in watering because they are slower to die and less expensive to replace than other vegetation.

17. Delay initial lawn planting around new homes until after the drought emergency.

18. Cut grass higher (approximately 2 inches) because soil shaded by the blades of grass is not dried so much by the sun.

19. Cut lawn fairly often (about 0.5 inch of grass per cutting), and with a sharp lawn-mower to keep grass from turning yellow and losing excessive water through the wounds.

20. Cut dead or dormant lawns around buildings to reduce fire hazard.

21. Leave some leaves and other debris on the lawn to reduce evapotranspiration as long as the cover is not so dense as to prevent water and air penetration.

22. Rake lawn early in the season to remove buildup of surface thatch that restricts free water penetration.

23. Use a mechanical aerator to promote deeper water penetration if other methods for reducing surface runoff fail.

24. Make an extra effort to control insects that attack the lawn, but water the lawn more frequently if it should be damaged.

25. Fertilize with phosphorus and potassium as these elements are particularly recommended for drought hardiness.

Finally these same researchers prepared a listing of ideas for conserving water in home gardening. This list, primarily oriented toward individual homeowners, summarized the information provided in 22 different publications and reports.

Listing of Ideas for Conserving Water in Home Gardening*

1. Select garden site with a deep, well drained soil with plenty of organic matter that will hold water in the plant root zone.

2. Select garden site sheltered by a windbreak to reduce evapotranspiration.

3. Plant rows more closely together.

4. Use other vegetation as windbreaks to reduce evapotranspiration losses.

5. Plant early vegetables and flowers that mature before late summer evapotranspiration rate peaks.

*Ibid., p. 14-15.

6. Plant vegetable crops such as tomatoes and carrots that maximize food value per unit of space.
7. Combine annual flowers and vegetables in the same garden.
8. Cover bare soil areas with mulch to help hold soil moisture.
9. Use trickle systems or other slow irrigation methods to water trees or shrubs. Slow irrigation over a long period is better than flooding, and both are better than frequent brief periods of hand sprinkling.
10. Provide trees and shrubs more water at each irrigation but irrigate less often.
11. Irrigate in furrows along garden rows to use less water than flooding.
12. Allow slight wilting of garden plants as an indicator of need for water as the condition is not injurious.
13. Use warmer irrigation water for earlier germination and faster plant growth.
14. Remove weeds. Each pound of dry weed matter grown consumes several hundred pounds of water in evapotranspiration.
15. Dig basins around trees and shrubs to hold water near the roots.
16. Replant with cool season vegetables that can survive some frost if original garden is killed by drought and water becomes more readily available later.
17. Sprinkle ashes on snow so that it will melt and soak into the soil rather than stay on the surface and evaporate.

Richard Baldwin, farm advisor for Ventura County, California, in an article entitled "Conserving Water in the Landscape" outlines a series of suggestions which are particularly applicable to the problems in that state.

> The available water in California is becoming scarce as our population and varied needs for water increase. The current drought underscores the need to conserve water both now and in the future. Some thoughts on conserving water in irrigation of landscape plants were put together for use in Ventura County and are presented here.

Irrigate only when the plants need water. Irrigation schedules are usually compromises involving times when play areas are not in use, capacity of the irrigation system, convenience, and plant needs. Frequency of irrigation should be flexible because plant needs vary with temperature, wind, rooting depth, leaf surface, and amount of water in the soil still available to the plants.

Most turf would be improved by applying water when the grass shows a subtle change in color or footprints remain impressed for a period of time, indicating the grass is getting dry. Water should then be applied at a slow enough rate that the soil absorbs it as fast as it goes on, without runoff. Apply sufficient water to wet the soil to the depth of the major portion of roots. This is normally 6-8 inches deep for the common cool season grasses.

Irrigation only when the plants show the need for water and then leaving the water on long enough to supply deep roots will stretch the interval between watering and improve the vigor of grass. Since water is lost by evaporation and drift during sprinkling and by evaporation from the wet soil surface, less frequent but deep watering conserves water for plant use.

Check water distribution for uniformity of application. If individual sprinkler coverage is not reasonably even or sprinkler patterns do not overlap sufficiently, the water will be distributed unevenly. "Donuts" of vigorous grass indicate distribution problems. Elongated patterns of turf growth usually indicate the effect of wind in disrupting sprinkler patterns.

Lawn sprinkler systems vary widely but many put out about an inch of water per hour. Some soils will accept water that fast but often the soil infiltration rate is closer to 0.1 inch per hour. A series of cans set out at intervals from a sprinkler head to catch the water will show both how much water is being discharged per hour and the uniformity of application. Typically, some cans will contain ten times as much water as others, indicating poor distribution of water.

Edges are a special problem to irrigate. Either sprinklers wet the sidewalks, driveways, or unused land area or turf at the edge suffers for lack of water. Edge effects can be minimized if attention is given to planning a sprinkler installation and the system is regulated and maintained.

Runoff is a waste of water. Use of low-output sprinklers or other methods of low application of water help considerably. **Lawn aeration and thatch control usually improves soil infiltration rate.** On dry soil, use of wetting agents sometimes temporarily improves infiltration of water into the soil. Use of mulch around trees and shrubs slows water loss.

Some grasses are more drought resistant than others. Tall fescue and bermuda grasses are very hardy turfgrasses. Even dichondra, given deep watering and a light soil will develop a good root system for a foot deep and have fairly good drought tolerance. Shaded plants use less water than those in full sun.

Late winter to early spring fertilization with nitrogen will increase root growth under moderate California climatic conditions which, in turn, will increase drought tolerance. An extensive root system enables a plant to fully utilize available soil water. **Effective weed control conserves water for other plants.** Weeds flourish because they are well adapted to compete with desirable plants for water and nutrients. Even very young weeds set back the growth of desirable plants.

Consider a landscape plan with fewer plants. Designing a landscape plan for low maintenance can be a challenging and rewarding project. Small areas invite the temptation to put in too many plants with loss of open space and high maintenance and water use. Often a simple plan is much more pleasing than one with a crowded appearance. Plants with different irrigation needs should not be mixed.

So what can be done to improve irrigation efficiency? Here are some specific suggestions:

1. For new lawns, be sure to select and install an irrigation system with a low rate of application and uniform coverage.
2. Use an automatic irrigation timer or, for small areas, appropriate timer that can be attached to a hose bib.
3. If water starts to run off, shut the water off, wait an hour or so for the water to soak in then start the water again. On one golf course, runoff occurred after 6 minutes. The irrigation timer was set to activate the sprinklers periodically for 6 minutes until irrigation was completed. Growth of the grass improved immediately, runoff was minimized and less water was used.
4. Water only when needed. For the mechanically minded, water sensing instruments such as tensiometers are available. They can

be connected to a timer to automatically apply water during designated hours, as needed.

5. When irrigating let the system run long enough to replenish the soil water to the depth of the root system. Depth of water penetration can be checked during or after irrigation with a soil tube, irrigator's rod or a long screwdriver.

6. Shrubs and trees should be watered separately. Use of a drip or trickle system is excellent for these plant materials and conserves water, often with improved growth. Depth of water penetration in the soil can be determined with a long metal rod.

7. Use drought tolerant plants.

8. Do not fertilize during the summer. The increased growth from fertilization requires more water and reduces or restricts the root system of cool season grasses.

9. Check irrigation line connections for leaks. Check sprinkler heads to be sure they clear the grass, are upright and functioning as intended.

10. Raise the cutting height of mowers during the summer, especially with cool season turfgrasses. The increased height of grass helps root survival.

11. Control weeds.

Use of these suggestions will improve water application efficiency. Unfortunately, they might not reduce total water use by the plant. Irrigating according to plant needs may result in improved growth of plants rather than use of less water. Improved application of water within a given level of maintenance, however, will result in conservation of water. Certainly water lost in runoff, excessive evaporation, leaks, etc. is wasted.

Maximum water use by plants adapted to drought may not necessarily be lower than that of plants adapted to frequent irrigation. Rather, by various mechanisms, they are better able to survive periods of low water availability. While some savings in applied water may be realized from use of selected plants, the major savings must come from more efficient use of irrigation water.

It is difficult to simply plug plants with drought resistance into a landscape. Such plants need to be watered less frequently or not at all during the summer. Native plants have been disappointing in many landscapes simply because they generally will not tolerate as much water as they are given during the summer. An area set aside for such plants is good because then the whole area can be treated alike.

Junipers are a special case in that water around the base of the plant during warm weather is likely to induce rot. Junipers are able to utilize water from deep in the soil and it has been found best to water junipers infrequently in the summer. Many native plants, such as ceanothus, similarly should be watered infrequently during the summer, for the same reason.

Not all turf managers want a perfectly manicured green sward. Such a turf requires more time and effort than most sites find justifiable. Increased growth means more frequent mowing as well as other attention. Realistically, then, plantings should be planned with a level of appearance, effort, and cost of maintenance in mind. Competent professional design input at the outset of a site installation will more than pay for itself. *

* Baldwin, Richard, "Conserving Water in the Landscape" **California Turfgrass Culture,** Vol. 27, No. 2, Spring 1977, pp. 2-3.

These lists and suggestions form an overview of water conserving strategies. In the remaining chapters of this book we will present the following strategies in greater detail:

- control water falling on the site to use it more effectively
- selection of drought resistant or drought tolerant vegetation
- leave plants in a stress condition
- erect wind barriers
- change the appearance of an area
- expand the use of mulch
- use of anti-transpirants
- reuse water
- make water "wetter"
- modify the soil or growing medium
- alter cultivation practices
- renovate or redesign
- establish watering priorities
- alter irrigation practices

These are obviously not the only things which can be done. They are, however, approaches which have been and can be applied by professional grounds managers, by homeowners and by landscape designers before, during and after periodic drought conditions occur in any geographic area. More research and public information will be undertaken as periodic water shortages occur in different areas.

strategy

CONTROL WATER FALLING ON THE SITE TO USE IT MOST EFFECTIVELY AND EFFICIENTLY

Planted areas should be used as a water collector. The surface planting. . . should prevent rapid runoff and allow for percolation of the falling water into the soil.

This is the surest, least expensive and most environmentally correct strategy to conserve water and to use available water most efficiently. **"**

Obviously the best source of water on each specific site is that water which falls originally on the site. Water which falls on the site and then is allowed to drain off the site without fully wetting the plant material is lost and must be replaced at a later time. Therefore it may be advisable to set aside part of any landscape area, no matter how small, on any site, to serve as a water collector. This is especially true if the site is in water short or drought prone areas. This may be done in any number of ways. Planted areas should be used as a water collector. The surface planting whether turf or ground cover, should prevent rapid runoff and allow for the percolation of the falling water into the soil. In other cases, the paving design for a site or grounds area may be done in such a way as to direct falling water towards the plant. This may mean re-grading of the paving. It also may mean grading of the turf to create saucers. The site should be designed so as to drain falling water toward planting areas and not off the site or onto paved areas. Walks should be graded so as to drain water off the walks or driveways into the planted areas. By the same token standing water should not be allowed or encouraged on the site, except in certain designated areas.

Therefore all areas on the site should be graded so as to allow some drainage onto designated areas on this site, but not off the site. Any site should be designed originally (ARCHITECTURALLY) to direct falling water where it will be needed at a later time. At the same time care should be taken to prevent standing water since any water standing on the site during the heat of the day will probably be evaporated or transpired into the atmosphere and thus be wasted. In some cases permanent retention basins may be integrated into the development. These retention basins should be lined with asphalt or plastic so as to prevent percolation of the water into the soil. In water short areas allowance should be made on the site in the original design for such a cistern pool or pond. Planting should be used to slow run-off time so that it will penetrate the soil to the maximum extent possible. This planting should be done on steep slopes to prevent soil erosion or excessive run-off. Absolutely the best source of water to irrigate plants on any site is that water, no matter how meager, which originally falls naturally on a specific site. Obviously in very dry areas this must be supplemented by other sources, but should not be supplemented unless it has first been most efficiently used.

The aim of this strategy is to use all of the water that falls on the site to the maximum before letting any of it go off the site. This can be done in the following ways:

- slow down falling water so that it can be absorbed into the soil,

- focus the flow of falling water,

- move falling water to where you want it or need it on the site,

- put falling water into the soil where it falls or where you need it on the site,

- store fallen water on the site. rather than letting or encouraging it to run off the site.

In order to "capture" and use all of the water which falls on the site most efficiently it may be necessary to design the site differently originally or to redesign certain parts of it at a later date. An entire chapter is devoted to that subject, but certain aspects such as paving and curbing may more appropriately be covered here in this chapter.

Paving, on most sites, is impervious to falling water. Therefore when rainfall and runoff falls on asphalt or concrete it flows across the paving and into a storm sewer outlet where it is carried to a nearby lake, river or reservoir. Much of it is thus lost to the site.

If the paving was designed to admit water into the soil rather than encouraging it to run off, more water would stay on the site and not have to be replaced. There are a number of types of paving which will admit water into the soil. Gravel, crushed stone and bark paving are pervious but do not always provide a solid paved surface. The simplest pervious hard surface is a brick paving on a sand base which allows water to penetrate between the bricks, through the sand and into the soil.

There are a number of newly developed grass pavers which allow for increased traffic on turf and at the same time provide for increased percolation of water into the soil. When these blocks are used over a large area they help to increase the water which remains available on the site.

New pervious paving materials help to reduce erosion and sedimentation and at the same time enable runoff to move into and through the paving. This makes it possible to have the best of both worlds; paving and percolation.

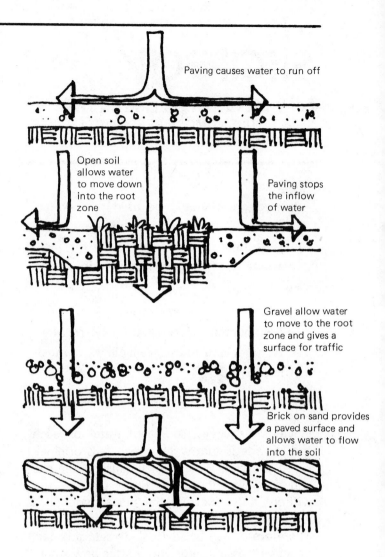

Paving causes water to run off

Open soil allows water to move down into the root zone

Paving stops the inflow of water

Gravel allow water to move to the root zone and gives a surface for traffic

Brick on sand provides a paved surface and allows water to flow into the soil

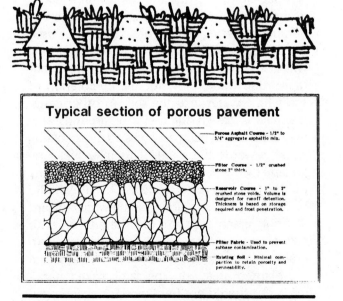

Grass block paving allows trafic movement and also the inflow of water into the soil

Typical section of porous pavement

Porous Asphalt Course - 1/2" to 3/4" aggregate asphaltic mix.

Filter Course - 1/2" crushed stone 2" thick.

Reservoir Course - 1" to 3" crushed stone voids. Volume is designed for runoff detention. Thickness is based on storage required and frost penetration.

Filter Fabric - Used to prevent subbase contamination.

Existing Soil - Minimal compaction to retain porosity and permeability.

* **E & S Bulletin,** Virginia Erosion & Sedimentation Control Program, No. 20, Summer 1983, Richmond, Virginia p.1.

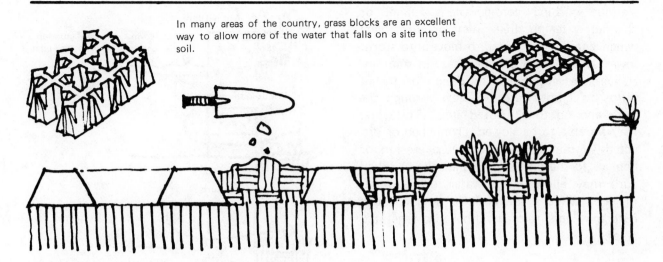

In many areas of the country, grass blocks are an excellent way to allow more of the water that falls on a site into the soil.

Standardized precast blocks are placed on the soil, then the spaces in the open blocks are filled with soil and planted with grass. The areas thus treated are able to absorb limited traffic, such as for overflow parking and yet not create a hard, impervious surface through which water cannot percolate.

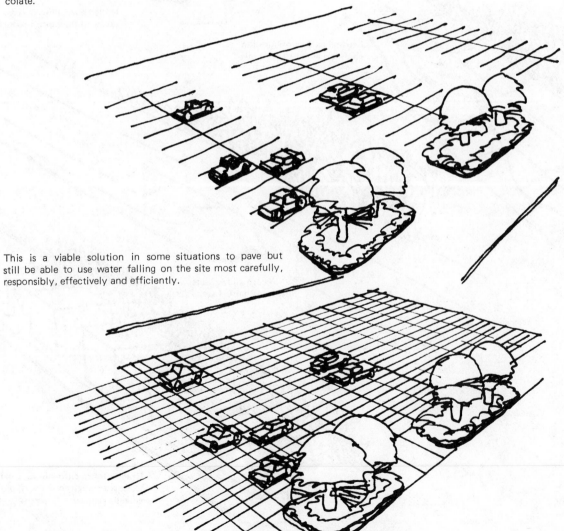

This is a viable solution in some situations to pave but still be able to use water falling on the site most carefully, responsibly, effectively and efficiently.

Various curbing configurations funnel or channel water to drain inlets or curb inlets which enables the water to move into storm sewer systems and off the site. In some instances, it is possible to design or install curbs to allow water to flow through the curb and on to a planted area. The water may be able to be slowed, channelled or directed so that it does not cause erosion or damage to the plants or to the soil. A rolled curb may allow excess water into a planting area while a sawtooth or dragon tooth curb may vent rainfall runoff into vegetated areas.

Water moves into the drain Inlet or curb inlet and into the storm drainage system and is moved away from the site, only to be replaced later with irrigation water.

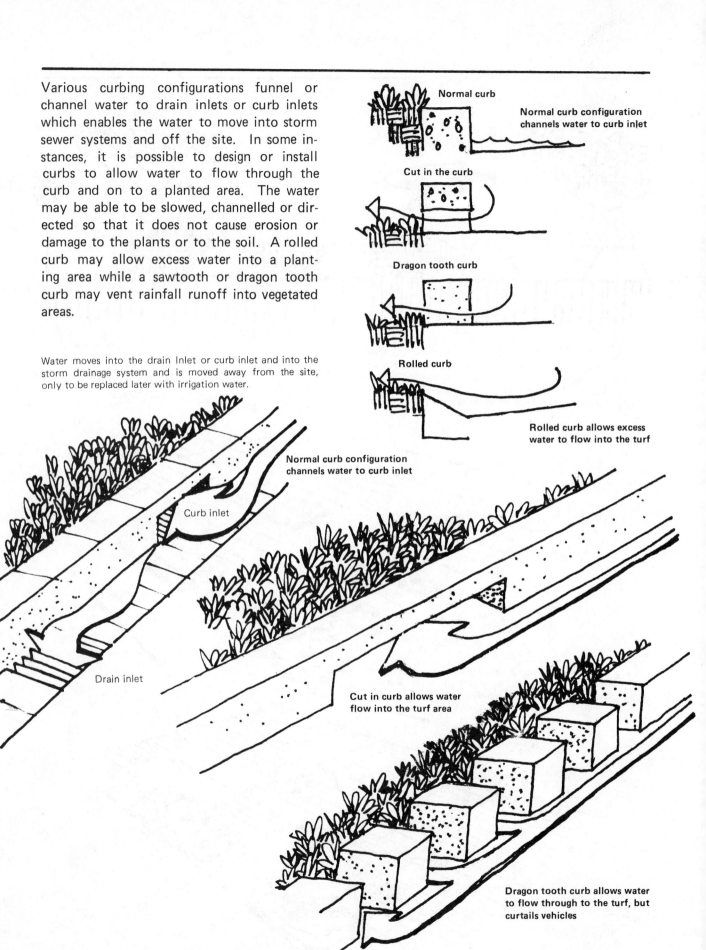

Normal curb

Normal curb configuration channels water to curb inlet

Cut in the curb

Dragon tooth curb

Rolled curb

Rolled curb allows excess water to flow into the turf

Normal curb configuration channels water to curb inlet

Curb inlet

Drain inlet

Cut in curb allows water flow into the turf area

Dragon tooth curb allows water to flow through to the turf, but curtails vehicles

At Texas Tech University in Lubbock, Texas the University Landscape Architect's office developed a program for water collection and reuse. This was described by James Vaughn, who was then University Landscape Architect in an article in LANDSCAPE ARCHITECTURE FORUM in the following words:

The Landscape Architect office at Texas Tech University has developed an unusual solution to a very common problem - water conservation. It has contrived the environmental chamber system, a compatible adaptation of natural West Texas land form and vegetation features. Long-range planning for resource management on the High Plains strongly indicates the need for implementation of a comprehensive water conservation program.

This program will include the obvious, agricultural water use, but must also be developed for direct application to the urban areas. The urban landscape sector of this water conservation program is very important due to both present consumption and graphic illustration of resource awareness by the general public. After planning and construction of several minor water conservation projects as an integral part of other university developments, the landscape architects office, at the request of the Space Committee, completed a Percolation Zone Study. Four general zones of design application emerged as a product of the research. These are as follows:

ZONE I indicates application of a site grading concept which circulates water(rainfall and irrigation) through turf channels with minimal ponding prior to dumping in a Class II, III, or IV percolation zone.

ZONE II is particularly feasible in small landscape islands or peninsulas of parking and other massive paving areas. Functions by grade suppression and architectural penetration of concrete curbing.

ZONE III requires implementation during planning phases of new university facilities or as renovation effort during structural remodeling or general landscape improvement. Some areas of Zone III application may function best with an inanimate ground cover.

ZONE IV(environmental chamber) that is similar to Zone III in design through repeated use of architectural curbing. The addition of a subsurface cavity designed to emulate the natural drainage system of West Texas provides additional percolation. This zone also requires integrated planning and special construction for optimum function.

The environmental chamber is a sub-grade cavity designed to:
- Conserve natural resources(primarily water)
- Recreate natural high plains drainage structure
- Reduce all phases of irrigation costs(installation, maintenance and water loss from evaporation and run-off)
- Create an environmental balance conducive to plant growth by acclimated plant species
- Provide natural filtering of the watershed by preventing the concentration of toxic materials through catchment and breakdown.

The chamber has been developed with the capable assistance of numerous professionals in the fields of plant materials, soils and water studies.

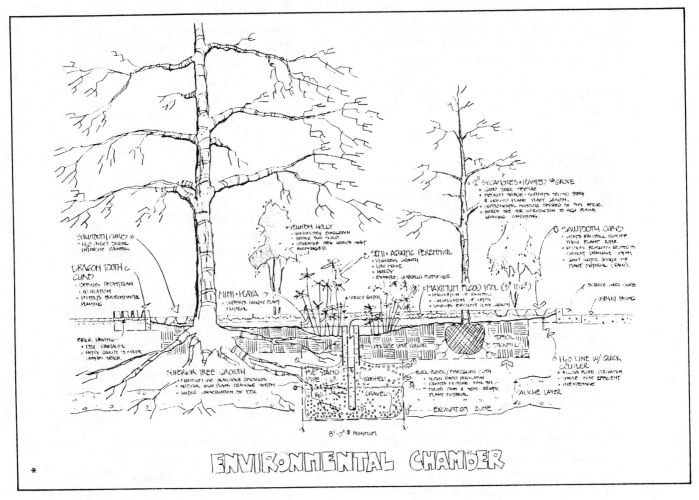

ENVIRONMENTAL CHAMBER

The State of Michigan utilized the landscape architectural firm of Beckett, Jackson and Raeder to prepare a study of sedimentation and soil erosion control which gave guidelines as to methods of grading which moves water and utilizes in on a site in an environmentally responsible way. Even though this study was done primarily to show how to prevent erosion, some of the principles in that study could be used to insure greater utilization of falling water on a specific site. **

Vegetation absorbs the energy of falling rain.

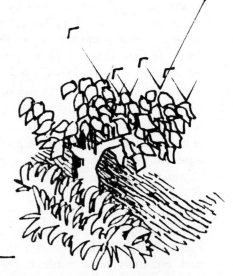

Vegetation slows the velocity of runoff and acts as a filter to catch sediment.

* Vaughn, James, "Problem/Solution", **Landscape Architectural Forum,** Summer 1981, Vol. 2, No.3, pp.40-41.

** **Michigan Soil Erosion and Sedimentation Control Guidebook,** prepared by Beckett, Jackson, Raeder, Inc. Ann Arbor, Michigan; prepared for Michigan Department of Natural Resources, Bureau of Water Management, Lansing, Michigan, 1974, p. 8.

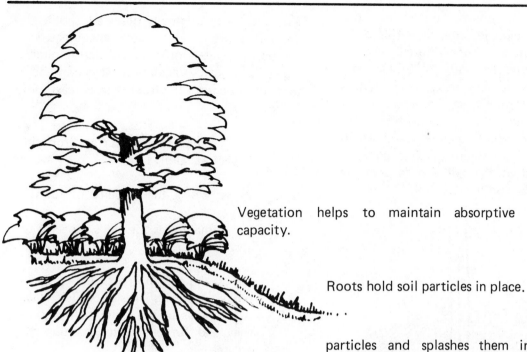

Vegetation helps to maintain absorptive capacity.

Roots hold soil particles in place.

This report spelled out, in some detail, the types of erosion and methods of control of the falling water. The types of erosion which caused runoff and damaged the topsoil were identified as: (1) Raindrop erosion, which was defined as erosion resulting from the direct impact of falling drops of rain on soil particles. This impact dislodges soil particles and splashes them into the air. The dislodged soil particles can then be easily transported by the flow of surface runoff; (2) Sheet erosion, which was defined as the removal of a layer of exposed surface soil by the action of raindrop splash and runoff. The water moves in broad sheets over the land and is not confined in small depressions; (3) Rill and gully erosion, as runoff flows it concentrates in rivulets, cutting several inches deep into the soil

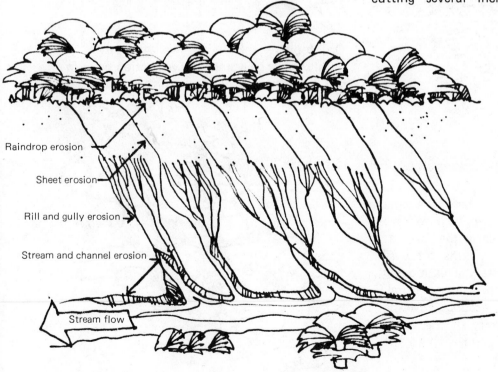

Raindrop erosion

Sheet erosion

Rill and gully erosion

Stream and channel erosion

Stream flow

surface. These grooves are called rills, gullies may develop in unrepaired rills or in other areas where a concentrated flow of water moves over the soil; (4) Stream and channel erosion, as water increases in volume and velocity the runoff may cause erosion of the stream or channel banks or bottom. This erosion and the rapidly moving water which causes it needs to be controlled to alleviate the destruction of the soil and to save the water for later use on the site itself.

Any site, when originally designed, should be developed in such a way as to encourage percolation of water into the soil and minimizing rapid runoff. Vegetation plays an important role in controlling runoff in at least four ways:

1. It shields the soil surface from the impact of falling rain.

2. It slows the velocity of runoff.

3. It maintains the soil's capacity to absorb water.

4. It holds soil particles in place, thus preventing erosion which leads to channels in the soil which encourages and funnels water running off an area.

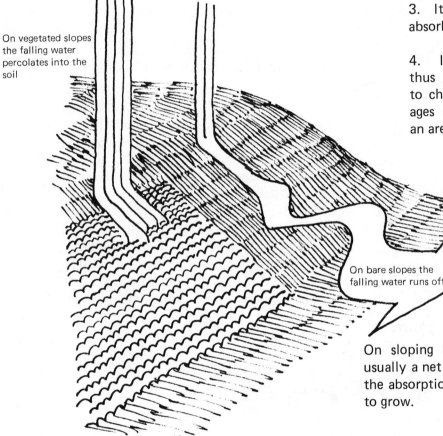

On vegetated slopes the falling water percolates into the soil

On bare slopes the falling water runs off

On vegetated slopes the falling water percolates into the soil

On sloping banks with vegetation there is usually a net gain since the vegetation helps in the absorption of more water than it requires to grow.

Existing stream

Sediment trap

Vegetation on any site uses water at the same time, however, vegetation can help to save water. Falling water either in the form of irrigation or rainfall quickly runs off bare soil and is lost to the site. This moving water erodes and destroys the soil. A naturally occurring or planted ground covering on a bank slows the velocity of the water causing more of it to be absorbed into the soil.

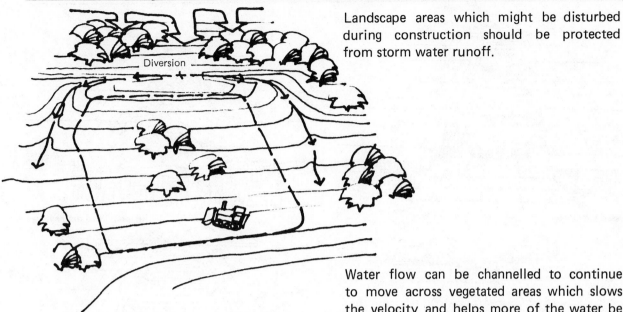

Landscape areas which might be disturbed during construction should be protected from storm water runoff.

Diversions and stable outlets should be provided for water on a site before any construction begins on a site.

Water flow can be channelled to continue to move across vegetated areas which slows the velocity and helps more of the water be absorbed into the soil to be available for use later on the site.

This insures water flow over vegetated and undisturbed areas and a maximum inflow into the topsoil and the underlying aquifer.

Diversion ditches or channels may be provided at the top of slopes to slow water velocity and to keep it off the steep slopes.

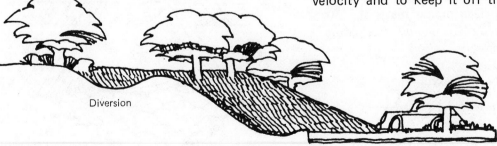

Diversion devices may also be used to keep water off paved areas where it may quickly be moved off the site and into the storm sewer system.

In other instances water can be retained by slowing runoff as it flows through the site.

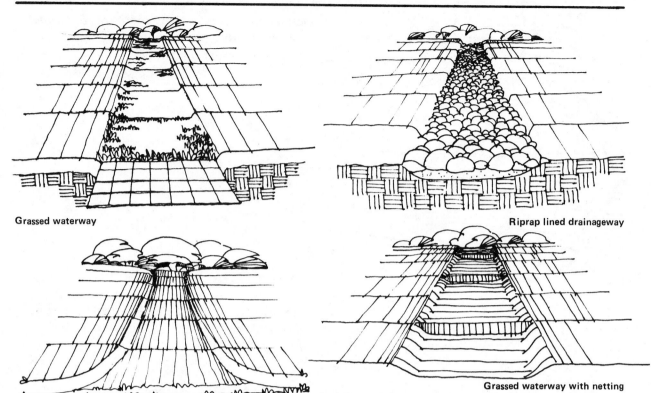

Grassed waterway

Riprap lined drainageway

Chute slope drain

Grassed waterway with netting

Where the runoff cannot be satisfactorily disposed of by conveying it laterally, it can be drained over the face of a slope, but kept in the landscape area if the site is large enough. Slope drains can be run down the surface of the slope as a sectional downdrain, paved chute, or pipe placed beneath the surface of the slope. On-surface sectional downdrains are usually pipes made of corrugated metal, bituminous fiber, or other materials which are usually temporary. Paved chutes are generally covered with a surface of concrete or bituminous material, and these chutes are usually permanent as they are made of a subsurface piping material. At the slope drain outlet, energy dissipators are frequently necessary.

Runoff can be diverted from slopes that are exposed during development by using diversions to intercept runoff and divert it from the slope face. A diversion can consist of a dike, a ditch, or a combination of both.

Surface runoff may be collected by drainageways and directed into stabilized holding areas on the site or to where it might be of use to turf or other plants as it slowly percolates down into the root zone.

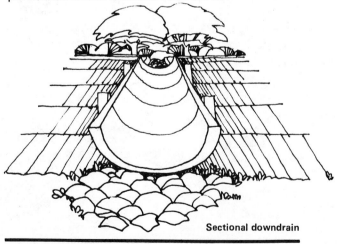

Sectional downdrain

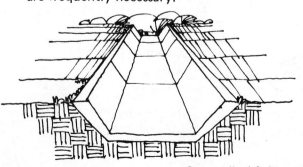

Concrete lined drainageway

* **Michigan Soil Erosion and Sedimentation Control Guidebook,** prepared by Becket, Jackson, Raeder, Inc., Ann Arbor, Michigan; prepared for the Michigan Department of Natural Resources, Bureau of Water Management, Lansing, Michigan, 1973.

This can be done in a variety of ways, including:

grading or shaping the earth on the site initially to prevent rapid runoff, to encourage percolation and to funnel or channel the water where you want it,

regrading on existing sites to correct errors or deficiencies in the original design,

establish storage basins or environmental chambers around trees or throughout the site,

open the soil to encourage percolation of water down into the soil to be stor-for later use. This can be done by introducing more softscape and by exploring alternatives in paving techniques.

Traditionally, in landscape design the concept has been to drain water off a site as easily and quickly as possible so as to provide a dry, usable site as soon as possible after a rain. This approach has been changing since that water which is drained off the site must be replaced with irrigation water which is often scarce and which takes energy to produce. Therefore a more appropriate contemporary approach would be to grade to hold, not to grade to dispose.

This is being done successfully in many areas. In Albuquerque, N.M. where on-site storage or use of water is encouraged and, at times, required, basins are provided in planting areas to accommodate on-site water storage.

In many regions, saucers are designed or constructed around individual plants or around entire planting areas to collect and accommodate the storage of rainfall or irrigation water and to prevent runoff of the water from the site.

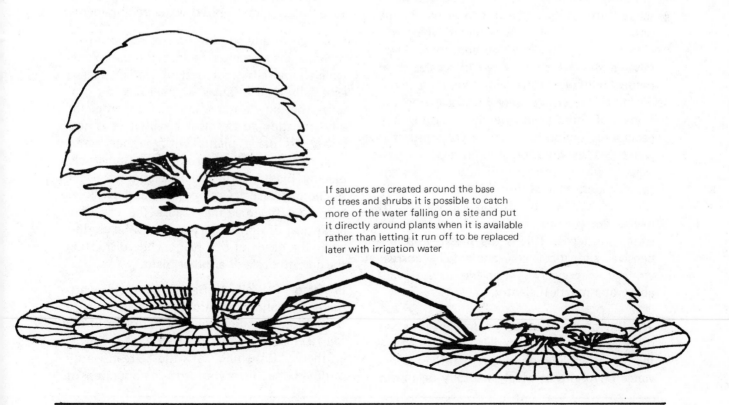

If saucers are created around the base of trees and shrubs it is possible to catch more of the water falling on a site and put it directly around plants when it is available rather than letting it run off to be replaced later with irrigation water

strategy

USE OF DROUGHT RESISTANT OR DROUGHT TOLERANT VEGETATION

Basically the purpose is to replace water-requiring plants in the landscape with those which require less water and irrigation.

If only totally drought resistant or drought tolerant plants were used in a particular area or situation no additional water or irrigation would be required no matter how dry the season. Unfortunately very few landscape settings have been conceived in the past to include only those plants which survive with very little or no additional water beyond that which they would receive from natural rainfall. At the same time there is not a general knowledge among landscape professionals of those landscape plants used in any geographic region which have very restricted water needs. Where possible in areas of persistent water shortage, landscape designs should be developed in the future, using only those plants which, through a variety of means are able to resist or tolerate extreme water shortages. This is the surest, least expensive and most environmentally correct strategy to conserve water and to use available water most efficiently.

The use or specification of drought resistant or tolerant plant materials would require the use or application of very little additional water beyond that which naturally falls onto the site. Over the years there has been a tendency in many geographic areas of the United States to be insensitive or unaware of the inherent esthetic qualities of the different landscape regions. Where no beauty or esthetic appeal is seen, an "artificial" landscape may be created which has been defined as beautiful or attractive in another situation or setting. Therefore, there is a tendency to impose on any area the landscape forms and plant materials of another area which are perceived to be beautiful in the other location. This causes problems by introducing into an area vegetation which is either not hardy or is not able to survive in the area without a great deal of additional water.

The water crisis in California and in many other parts of the western regions in the 1970's prompted renewed interest in the use of indigenous or native vegetation which was much more water tolerant. In order to save water and thus to conserve energy in landscaped areas, it is necessary to evaluate carefully the plant materials used originally in the landscape design. In extreme cases it may even be necessary to remove plants which have heavy water requirements in an area and replace them, where possible with plants which have more limited water requirements.

Redesign of any site in order to reduce maintenance may include replacing those plants which require a great deal of water. This is especially true in areas where irrigation provides the only water available. In order for any irrigation to be most effective it is necessary to place plants with similar water requirements in close proximity. Conversely placing plants with widely dissimilar water requirements(such as cactus and willow) too close together may cause the use of a great deal of unnecessary water to be used to meet the needs of one plant while disrupting the growth cycle of another plant.

Professor Russell A. Beatty of the Department of Landscape Architecture, University of California at Berkeley, in an article in the fall 1977 issue of *PACIFIC HORTICULTURE*, entitled "Browning of the Greensward" outlined the history of the introduction of exotic plants in the State of California. The use of water to maintain these plants was seriously curtailed during the water crisis of the 1970's. Professor Beatty outlined possible approaches in that situation which might be applicable to park managers in other similar situations. He did this in the following words:

Three alternatives seem apparent. First, we can regard the drought as an ephemeral event and make do. The rains will come sooner or later and we have adapted well to this crisis. After all, this phenomenon hasn't been a regularly recurring event. We can adjust temporarily to a brown landscape.

A second philosophy would support arguments to depend more heavily on technological solutions. Supporters of the expansion of the California Water Project have good evidence to justify building more dams and reservoirs and perhaps extend taps to the Northwest or beyond.

A third alternative seems more plausible in the long run. This is to develop a new landscape ethic and aesthetic consciousness. By considering the drought as a welcome opportunity and challenge, we can be more effective in dealing with it directly, as individuals, and with longer lasting, more satisfying results. By learning anew or re-learning what it means to live in a Mediterranean climate where water is a precious limited resource, we can all develop a new consciousness in planting the landscape.

Does this mean that the "Greensward" will turn brown--that our gardens will look like desert scenes? Or will we return to the austere gardens of the padre and the vaquero? None of these are necessary. We still need our fantasies of Eden fulfilled. California is special! It is different and let's celebrate that. The touchstone is ecological fitness. This does not mean aesthetic satisfaction need be sacrificed.

There are a number of positive alternatives to consider. First, extensive plantings of trees, shrubs and groundcovers should follow what Professor Bob Perry of California Polytechnic, Pomona, calls the "ecological alternative." Mesophytic (high water using) plants should not be mixed with xerophytic species (drought tolerant).

Using sensible plant selection and the creative arrangement of plants, landscape plantings at all scales from home gardens to parks and freeways can be designed to be both aesthetically pleasing and ecologically sound, not to mention economically appealing.

Secondly, the "thirsty plants" should be limited to small areas where such plants can be justified on either a functional or aesthetic basis. A lawn is the only plant tolerant of foot traffic. Its use should be restricted primarily for that function—play fields, home lawns for children to play on, park and campus lawns for recreation. Even with such economics of limited planting, turfgrass selection can be based upon water conservation principles. Some grasses such as "tall fescue" require less total irrigation than shallower-rooted species. Unfortunately it must be seeded because it is a bunchgrass. The demand for "instant landscapes" using sod must be tempered with long-range conservation policies. Another modification in turf practices could be to break away from the fine, precise clipped lawn in large parks in favor of a meadow-like turf.

Another way to limit the "thirsty plants" is to rediscover the charms of the California patio. In residential neighborhoods and to a certain extent in business areas so many plantings are purely cosmetic settings—exterior window dressing or "landscape." Building ordinances force a setback of twenty feet for suburban houses. That strip frequently becomes a piece of unused landscape and is usually planted in lawn or flowers with little or no function. A front patio enclosed by a fence or wall would be a more useable family space as well as a pleasant entry forecourt. Here the small beds of flowers, azaleas and other "thirsties" could be grown satisfactorily. Such interior oriented gardens would be low water users compared with planting the entire front yard. The exterior could be planted with a combination of suitable Mediterranean species selected for both appearance and drought tolerance. Lawns could be eliminated or relegated to a small patch in the rear garden. Combinations of broadleaf evergreen shrubs such as rockrose (*Cistus*), rosemary, lavender, ceanothus, arbutus, photimia, dwarf baccharis could be accentuated with California poppies (from seed) or the similar looking gazania for a brilliant floral display. The possibilities are endless and the visual effects every bit as delightful as the shrub and lawn "Eastern" effect.

A third and perhaps less tangible approach to water conserving planting design is to consider the visual fitness of planting relative to the character of the California landscape setting. This concept is more important in areas where the natural or rural landscape predominates as compared with an urban landscape. Again, the sole use of California native plants is not suggested. For lack of a better term, "visual ecology" comes closest to attaching a label. This means what is planted fits the setting both ecologically (low water demand, not invasive, and so on) as well as visually. *

The East Bay Municipal Water District in a brochure entitled, "Water Conservation Today and Tomorrow" estimated that about one-half of their residential water from their district goes into the garden. Plants consume more water than any other category of use. **

The Marin County California Municipal Water District prepared a booklet entitled "Water Conserving Gardening" for use by home owners within Marin County. In that publication they differentiated between drought avoiding plants in the following way:

Drought Resistant plants conserve water which might be lost by evaporation by:
- having waxy and/or hard leaves
- having small and/or upright leaves to minimize direct solar radiation
- having hairy leaves to keep moist air near plant
- having fat, succulent leaves and stems with water-retaining tissues and less surface area to lose water from
- losing leaves

Drought Avoiding plants may keep from suffering stress by:
- growing from seed to flower and setting new seed in one season
- growing from bulb (or rhizome or corm) to flower and over-winter as bulb
- growing at great distance from others of the same species
- having penetrating, super-efficient water gathering roots. **

That same body worked with the Marin County Park Department to prepare a water conserving garden near the Marin County Civic Center for the guidance of homeowners and other residents of the County to assist them in guidelines for water conserving park

---

* Beatty, Russell A., "Browining of the Greensward", **Pacific Horticulture,** Fall 1977, pp. 5-7.

* **Water Conservation Today - And Tomorrow,** East Bay Municipal Utility District, P.O. Box 24055, Oakland, California 94623.

** Cuneo, Katherine, Botanist, Madrone Associates, Box 2970, San Rafael, California 94902, **Water Conserving Gardening,** Marin Municipal Water District, 220 Nellen Avenue, Corte Madera, California 94925, 1978, p. 5.

and landscape development. The Office of Appropriate Technology and the Department of Water Resources for the State of California developed a model urban water conservation garden as a demonstration as to how to create a beautiful yet water conserving landscape. This project was located in downtown Sacramento, California.

SUNSET MAGAZINE had a series of articles on water conservation in landscape development. They also developed lists of appropriate plants to specify so as to use less water in landscape development.

The Department of Water Resources for the State of California prepared a document (Bulletin 209) entitled, "Plants for California Landscape—A Catalog of Drought Tolerant Plants," which explains the premise to this approach or stategy in the following way:

A drought tolerant plant is a plant that can survive with little or no water other than available rainfall. The degree of drought tolerance varies from site to site, from species to species, and from plant form to plant form.

Plants contain within them a continuous column of water which extends from their root hairs to the pores in their leaf surfaces. This water supports the plant's structure and transports materials through the plant. Upward movement of the water column occurs when water evaporates from the pores in the leaf surfaces. When evaporation exceeds the amount of water being absorbed by the roots, the plant suffers water stress. Prolonged water stress eventually leads to the death of tissues or to the entire plant.

Drought tolerant plants are able to cope with scarcity of water by a variety of physiological adaptations.

Some plants, including many trees in this plant list, survive dry conditions with the aid of deep, large root systems which tap water stored deep in the soil. Such plants will require nearly equivalent amounts of water as non-drought tolerant plants, but need little or no artificial irrigation. Infrequent, deep watering, with shallow water basins around the plant fulfills these plants' water needs. In time, with the development of a deep root system, these plants may need no supplemental water. Problems arise, however, when the soil depth is too shallow. In such a case, the use of drought tolerant plants which have other adaptations is advisable.

Other adaptations for water stress involve the leaves. Some plants have developed leaves with thick, heavy cuticles which reduce water loss. Others have hairy surfaces, which slow air flow over the leaf, thereby increasing the leaf humidity and reducing the evaporation rate. Still other plants have developed means to reduce the amount of radiation from the sun heating their leaves, thus cutting the rate of evaporation. This is done either by white hairs that reflect sunlight or by leaves that fold when exposed to sunlight. A few plants—exerophytes, the lowest water users—drop their leaves and enter a dormant state under dry conditions. Later, with the return of moisture, they send out new leaves. Through the use of one of these adaptations or a combination of them, the plants in this list are able to cope with dry growing conditions.

A number of environmental conditions affect the amount of water available to a plant. The soil type, the soil depth, the local microclimate, the degree of exposure to sun and wind, and competition with other plants for water all affect the plant's available water supply and ultimately determine its drought tolerance in a particular location. Distinctions as to the degree of drought tolerance of the plants in this list have not been made here because of this relationship between site conditions and water needs. This plant list is designed to be used as one tool in the plant selection process. It is advisable to consult local landscape specialists for particular information on the tolerance and availability of plants for the environment that you wish to landscape. Information sources are included at the end of this paper.

It is important to remember that most plants, even drought tolerant ones, need water initially in order to become established. In addition, some drought tolerant plants need occasional watering—infrequent, but deep soakings to encourage a deep root system. Drought tolerant plants should be grouped separately from water demanding plants in order to provide each planting with irrigation to fit its needs. Many drought tolerant plants suffer when overwatered.

Contrary to the popular image of a water conserving landscape consisting solely of cactus plants or resembling a dusty scene of rocks and pebbles, drought tolerant plants are usually highly attractive, with lush foliage and showy flowers. This list contains plants to fit every landscaping need— offering a variety of form, size, foliage color, flower color, and fruit color.

In addition, a number of the plants can serve functional needs, such as erosion control and fire retardance (which result in additional water savings). Drought tolerant plants, once established, have the added virtue of requiring relatively little care—a useful attribute for people with second homes or little time for gardening.*

This publication then goes on to list some of the demonstration gardens which exist throughout the State and goes on to list trees, shrubs, ground covers, annuals and perennials, vines, ornamental grasses and plants for special purposes for use to lessen the need for additional water for the survival of the plants.

Obviously the first step in conserving water and thus energy in park areas is to select those plants which will require less water through their effective lifetime.

In an article entitled, "Water Use by Plants" by S. L. Gulmon and H.A. Mooney of the Department of Biological Sciences at Stanford University in Palo Alto, California, the following statement was made:

> When fully saturated, one cubic yard of loam soil contains about 55 gallons of water available to plants. On a warm July day (85° F, 40% relative humidity) a single corn plant growing in this yard of wet soil would use about 1.4 gallons of water per day. If the plot were covered by annual herbs with characteristically high transpiration rates, such as desert evening primroses, water use would jump to about 4.3 gallons per day. However, if we filled our plot with corn, daily water use would increase still further to seven gallons. By contrast, a six foot tall toyon shrub would get by on a meagre half gallon per day.**

Work is currently underway at the University of Arizona to develop, identify and support more drought resistant ornamental

* Plants for California Landscapes - A Catalog of Drought Tolerant Plants," **Department of Water Resources Bulletin,** No. 209, State of California Resources Agency, September 1979, pp. 1-3.

** Gulmon, S.L. and H.A. Mooney, "Water Use by Plants," **Pacific Horticulture,** (reprint), Fall 1977, p. 11.

plants for use in landscape design. As drought conditions exist or persist in different sections of the country, nurserymen, landscape designers and grounds managers need to work with university research personnel to identify drought tolerant species for any geographic region. Generally it is advisable to check with local extension service staff in any state to have them identify the most drought tolerant plants for a specific region or area. The Texas Water Resources Newsletter, Vol. 6, No. 4 in May 1980, dealt with the drought tolerant native or indigenous vegetation in an article entitled, "Planting Texas Style."

As pioneers moved to Texas from damper, cooler, climates, they learned to adapt their housing, their clothing, and their diets.

Many a pioneer woman, however, brought with her a lilac bush or some other living momento of a far-away home. She placed the bush in her barren Texas yard, then lovingly gave it as much moisture as it would have received from rain in her native state.

Today, Texans with "roots" in other regions of the country have yet to change imported attitudes on landscaping. We must, for instance, have dark green bushes around our houses rather than the gray-green beauties of the desert. Our lawns must be of grasses as soft and thick as those of Kentucky or England—not tough native grass which can survive the dry Texas summers. Areas around schools, public buildings, and commercial offices must also be lush and green to give the impression that rainfall is more than adequate. Even in the driest areas of the state, cities must maintain parks with acres of green lawn and areas of dense foliage.

We will, of course, continue to landscape around houses and buildings. Besides providing aesthetic benefits, living plants help us to physically survive the extreme temperatures in the state. Plants around buildings reduce the amount of energy needed for heating and cooling and also protect buildings from wind and sun.

But why must we make the same mistake as the pioneer woman with the lilac bush? She could have saved herself precious water and effort by transplanting a flowering shrub from nearby. A native plant would have required little care and probably would have thrived with no extra water.

Many horticulturists in drought-prone states suggest that using native plants is the best way to reduce outside water consumption. Scientists here in Texas, still in the collection and propagation phases of studying native plants, know very little about the water requirements for specific plants. It stands to reason, however, that native plants from areas with low annual rainfall require very little water.

Benny Simpson, research scientist at the Texas A&M University Research and Extension Center in Dallas, is one of a handful of experts on propagating native Texas trees and bushes. He has collected and studied plants from all over the state for the past 30 years.

Simpson now has close to 200 species of native trees and shrubs at the Dallas Center. All have come from seeds or cuttings from the native habitat of each plant, and many have become part of the Center's landscaping. The entire Dallas Center grounds, as a matter of fact, are landscaped with plants native to Texas.

Most months of the year, some part of Simpson's collection is especially showy with bright colored blooms, leaves or berries. Two of the most promising flowering bushes for future Texas yards are the Texas madrone and the cenizo. The madrone has bell-shaped white flowers, red fruit, and smooth red bark. The cenizo is a shrub with gray or dark green leaves and blossoms of purple, red, or white.

Simpson is interested mainly in native bushes and trees which are attractive enough to be adopted as ornamental landscape plants. A plant is attractive, according to Simpson, because of its leaves, flowers, fruits, bark or shape. He explains that as native plants are introduced into public and private yards, they will first be noticed because of their appearance. Later, however, they will become popular because of how little care they require, how well they thrive, and how well they survive droughts.

Native plants should be purchased from nurseries, not taken from nature, warns Simpson. Anyone tempted to dig up a native plant and transplant it into a yard (1) may not be successful in saving the plant, (2) may be breaking the law, and (3) may be endangering a particular species. A few native bushes and trees are now available through commercial nurseries and are common in landscaped areas. These include oak, sage, yaupon, magnolia, and mesquite.

It makes sense to landscape with plants which require little extra water or care—especially if they can survive a Texas-style drought.*

Dr. John P. Baumgardt, writing in an article of the November 1978 issue of GROUNDS MAINTENANCE Magazine, entitled "Native Grasses for Low Maintenance" also touched on the drought tolerances of some native vegetation.

Ideally, turfgrasses are evergreen or nearly so, mat-forming rather than growing in clumps, and of spreading growth or tolerant of close clipping. Over the years, a very small number of grasses have been selected from the vast world-wide population of grasses to be used for ornamental or utility turf. With the exception of some hot summer, mild winter grasses, most of the turfgrasses used in the United States and Canada are introduced species.

There are problems with growing plants away from their natural habitats, where they are subjected to different rainfall patterns, humidity levels, soil conditions and more. Under these alien conditions their culture becomes more difficult. When we look at the place turf takes in our annual maintenance budgets, we become only too aware of this.

Soaring costs are forcing us to re-evaluate turf-growing programs. Expanses of grass are critical to landscape design, especially in the more moist areas of the North Temperate Zone. People are conditioned to expect generous areas of mowed grass in parks, cemeteries, golf courses, industrial parks and around public and commercial buildings. One only has to compare the arid, moonscape appearance of pavement surrounding a typical shopping center to come to

* "Planting Texas Style," **Texas Water Resources**, Texas Water Resources Institute, Texas A. & M. University, College Station, Texas 77843, Vol. 6, No. 4, May 1980, pp. 1-2.

a quick appreciation for grass as a living, attractive ground cover. But the problem remains; mowed lawns are absorbing far too much of the maintenance budget. Where do we go from here?

Prairie Grasses

Why prairie grasses? It seems logical. Being native species, they are especially adapted to American growing conditions and should require less maintenance from a standpoint of insect and disease control or irrigation. Quite handsome stands are developing where native grass species have been brought into cultivation in areas of Kansas, Missouri, Nebraska and other plains and prairie states. These stands of native prairie species have little in common with the popular concept of a well-maintained lawn, yet there are good reasons for growing such grasses.

Maintenance of Established Stands

Maintenance is low once the grasses are established. Native grasses grow naturally on soils that are moderately low in mineral salts of nitrogen, phosphorus and potassium. Often, the prairie soils are rich in clay, so they are relatively slow to drain. Because American prairie areas are often watered generously in winter but poorly in summer, native prairie grasses grow quite satisfactorily without supplementary irrigation.*

Dr. James Beard in a later article refers to another study which ranks Kentucky bluegrass cultivars by their water use rate during exposure to desiccating conditions.

RANKING OF KENTUCKY BLUEGRASS CULTIVARS BY THEIR WATER USE RATE DURING EXPOSURE TO DESICCATING CONDITIONS*

Kentucky bluegrass cultivar	Water use rating
Merion Birka Sydsport Majestic Nugget Bonnie Blue	Very high
Bristol NuDwarf South Dakota Certified Enprima Geary Fylking Park	High
Vantage Victa Delta A-34 Enmundi Aquila Parade Pennstar Enita	Intermediate
Glade Cougar Entopper Touchdown Cheri Banff Plush Baron Galaxy	Low
Adelphi Newport S-21 A-20 Enoble	Very low

*Low water use by a cultivar does not necessarily imply drought tolerance, but turf quality can be maintained with less water.

Technical credit: University of Nebraska-Lincoln

* Baumgardt, John P., "Native Grasses for Low Maintenance," **Grounds Maintenance,** November 1978, Vol. 13, No. 11, pp. 54-56.

The changing of the landscape esthetic to one which contains primarily indigenous plants may entail the adoption and acceptance of different esthetic tastes for a specific geographic area. This may require an education program for users and for home owners to show them the beauty of native, indigenous or drought tolerant plantings. There is now no industry to promote native or drought tolerant plants at the present time. The most drought tolerant plants require less fertilizer and irrigation equipment, so they represent some economic sacrifice to suppliers in the field. However, in time to come, they may become a major alternative since all of the possible options have to be considered. In the article by Dr. James Beard in the March 1981 issue of *GROUNDS MAINTENANCE* Magazine which dealt with preparing turf for drought, Dr. Beard lists the drought resistance of 22 turfgrasses as follows:

EXCELLENT	Buffalograss
	Bermudagrass
	Zoysiagrass
	Bahiagrass
GOOD	Crested wheatgrass
	Hard fescue
	Sheep fescue
	Tall fescue
	Red fescue
MEDIUM	Kentucky bluegrass
	Redtop
	Timothy
	Canada bluegrass
FAIR	Perennial ryegrass
	Meadow fescue
	St. Augustinegrass
POOR	Centipedegrass
	Carpetgrass
	Italian ryegrass
	Creeping bentgrass
	Rough bluegrass
	Velvet bentgrass *

Dr. Victor A. Gibeault in an article entitled "Preparing Turf to Survive Drought" deals with drought tolerance of turf grasses.

---

* Beard, James, "Preparing for a Drought - Water Conserving Turf Maintenance Practices," **Grounds Maintenance,** March 1981, Vol. 16, No. 3, p.22.

Drought Tolerance

One of the first questions that must be answered in an impending dry year is the drought tolerance of the various commonly used grass species. To produce a quality sward, all turfgrasses require applied water or rainfall in amounts equal to or greater than the water they use and lose through evapotranspiration in a given time. When drought conditions exist and total water application is less than evapotranspiration or is eliminated, grasses do differ in their responses to these conditions. Turfgrasses commonly used are ranked according to their drought tolerance in Table 1. In general, warm-season or subtropical grasses are more drought tolerant than cool-season or temperate grasses. Grasses with deep root systems have better drought tolerance than shallow-rooted grasses. Bermuda and zoysia, for example, frequently have root systems that penetrate 6 to 8 feet deep, providing them with a tremendous soil water reservoir for plant growth and survival. In contrast, well-maintained Kentucky bluegrass has a 6 to 12-inch root system.

In a study at the University of California, Davis, Dr. John Madison removed all irrigation from selected turf plots for 120 days. Thereafter, he resumed normal watering and observed the recovery of various turf species. Under his conditions, he found that bermuda, zoysia, and tall fescue recovered well in 15 days. "Highland" bent recovered in five months, while Kentucky bluegrass and red fescue showed poor recovery. Note that the deepest rooted species recovered fastest. There are limits to the drought tolerance of each species beyond which the grass sward will not survive, as was evident from the Kentucky bluegrass and red fescue plots.

Madison concluded that there is a "high genetic potential for drought tolerance among turfgrass species but it has not been exploited." Fortunately, current research at Colorado State University by Dr. J. Butler is examining the drought tolerance of turfgrass species and varieties as well as the influence of management practices on drought tolerance.

To conclude this discussion, grasses do differ in their drought tolerance, their ability to survive extreme drought conditions is in large part due to their root system depth, and there is a drought limit beyond which sward survival is affected.*

Table 1 - (Gibeault)

—THE COMPARATIVE DROUGHT TOLERANCE OF COMMONLY USED TURFGRASSES

Good Drought Tolerance

Improved bermuda
Zoysia
Common bermuda
Tall fescue
Red fescue
Kentucky bluegrass
Meadow fescue
St. Augustine
Colonial bent

Poor Drought Tolerance   **Creeping bent**

One of the most effective strategies for using water most efficiently in maintaining landscape development is not to have to use any water at all. The way to do this is to use plants in the original design which require no extra water at all during drought conditions. This can be done in the original design, in a redesign or through a piecemeal replacement of plants which cannot survive a drought with those which can.

Obviously, drought tolerant, drought resistant and low water use plants will be differ-

ent in each climatic or geographic region of the country. What would be appropriate in New Jersey would not be the same as what could reasonably be specified in Texas, or in Arizona, Colorado or California. There are too many other variables such as cold adaptation, ecological communities and topographic acceptance of different plants.

Unfortunately there is no one definitive listing of water conserving plants for all regions. Local groups or state extension services are in the process of preparing or developing these as the demand develops as a result of periodic water shortages which occur in different regions. Some of these lists have been mentioned in the earlier chapter dealing with "Water Shortages". For those homeowners or grounds managers using this strategy in dealing with water shortages very localized resources should be checked to find lists of such plants. Local native plant societies, botanic gardens, universities and nurserymen's associations are appropriate groups which might be able to provide such information for a finite area. Great care should be taken not to use, arbitrarily, a list from another area since a plant which is drought tolerant or resistant in one area may not be hardy or adapted in other ways in another area.

"Xeric adapted" has been suggested as more appropriate terminology for plants which are able to survive and flourish with limited water.

In all cases and in all regions the specification, selection and installation of xeric adapted or low water use plants should always be one of the first strategies suggested.

The use or selection of a plant or a series of plants which can survive periodic droughts in a specific area will, in the long run, preclude the use of other strategies. Over a period of time a landscape design made up of such plants will be more attractive since it will have a certain unity and all of the plants will survive and not have to be replaced when they die for lack of water.

---

*Gibeault,Victor, "Preparing Turf to Survive Drought," **California Turfgrass Culture,** Vol. 27, No. 2, Spring 1977, p. 9.

The native plant movement throughout North America has grown dramatically in recent years in response to a number of factors including the desire to use plants which will live and flourish in an area no matter what the weather or natural rainfall. Wherever and whenever possible the use of drought tolerant plants should be one of the very first strategies considered when planning a new landscape or renovating or redesigning an older one where water shortages are a concern. It is a responsive and responsible approach which deals with the water limitation problem once and for all in most cases.

Drought Tolerant

Plants tolerate drought conditions by dying and regrowing each year, by storing energy in a bulb or root, by growing at a great enough distance from each other so that they do not compete with each other and by developing deep roots which can seek more available water.

Losing leaves

Losing leaves lessens the need for water

Annuals

Annuals grow and die in a single year to regrow from seed the next year.

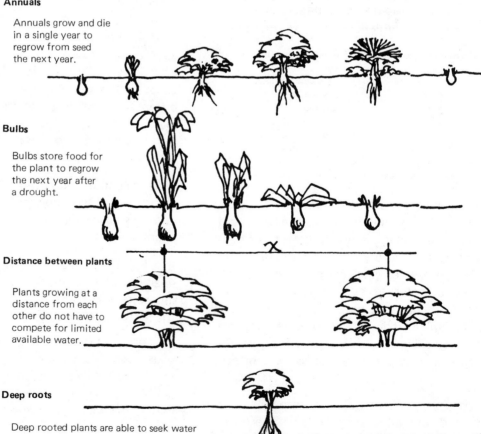

Bulbs

Bulbs store food for the plant to regrow the next year after a drought.

Distance between plants

Plants growing at a distance from each other do not have to compete for limited available water.

Deep roots

Deep rooted plants are able to seek water at depths where it is not available to shallow rooted plants.

Drought Resistant

Plants resist drought conditions by keeping moisture in the leaves, by holding moisture on the leaves, by storing moisture in the leaf cells or by losing their leaves and limiting the need for water.

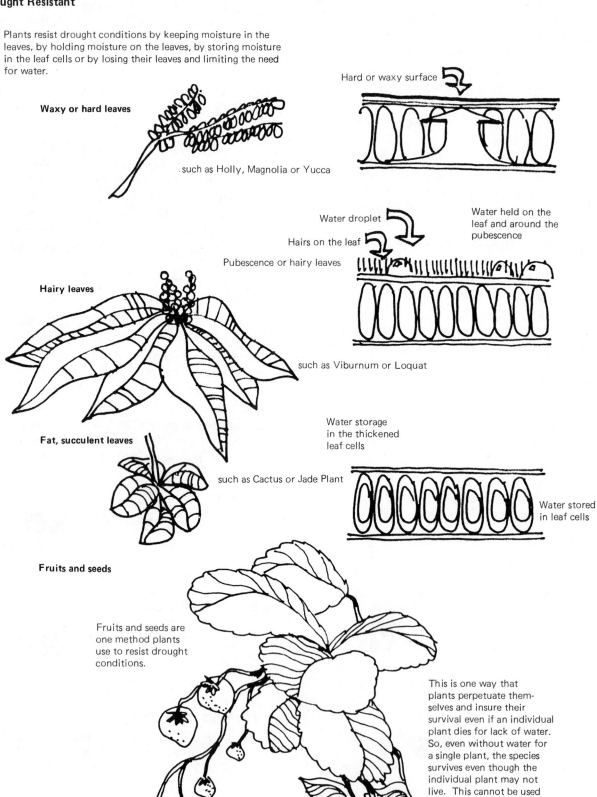

Waxy or hard leaves

.such as Holly, Magnolia or Yucca

Hard or waxy surface

Water droplet

Hairs on the leaf

Pubescence or hairy leaves

Water held on the leaf and around the pubescence

Hairy leaves

such as Viburnum or Loquat

Water storage in the thickened leaf cells

Fat, succulent leaves

such as Cactus or Jade Plant

Water stored in leaf cells

Fruits and seeds

Fruits and seeds are one method plants use to resist drought conditions.

This is one way that plants perpetuate themselves and insure their survival even if an individual plant dies for lack of water. So, even without water for a single plant, the species survives even though the individual plant may not live. This cannot be used in large scale landscape situations or with large plants.

The University of California has defined the characteristics of drought tolerant plants in the following way:

- Plants that survive a drought use a combination of mechanisms to limit water consumption, including:

  - Thick, waxy cuticle that reduces water loss.

  - Hairy covering of leaf surfaces that reduces water loss directly or by reducing air flow over leaf surfaces.

  - Stomata that are few in number, sunken into the leaf surface or covered by hairs, or that close rapidly and completely when water stress occurs.

  - Formation of colloidal gels that bind the water(cacti and succulents).

- Folding or cupping of leaves(rhododendron) or leaf orientation(some eucalyptus) to present a minimum surface to the sun.

- Gray or silvery leaf color that reduces absorption of radiant enrgy

- Gray or silvery leaf color that reduces absorption of radiant energy reducing the heat load and water loss.

- Remaining dormant as seeds or storage organs(rhizomes, corms, or bulbs) until soil moisture will support growth. *

The Cooperative Extension Service of the College of Agriculture at the University of Arizona has developed a series of information pamphlets on the plants of Arizona. On each of these information sheets, they have indicated the growth rate, the water requirements, the desired exposure and the cold hardiness of each of the plants. The following indicates how that is graphically communicated.

Cold Hardiness Zones
(expected min. winter temps.)   °F

FLAGSTAFF	1	(−20°)
PRESCOTT	2	(− 5°)
GLOBE	3	(+10°)
TUCSON	4	(+20°)
PHOENIX	5	(+24°)

Water requirement

dry   ample   moist

Exposure

sun   part shade   shade

Mexican Palo Verde

Growth rate

slow   moderate   fast

Blue Palo Verde

Growth rate

slow   moderate   fast

Foothills Palo Verde

Growth rate

slow   moderate   fast

**

* Copley, Kathy, "Landscape Design for Water Conservation", **Grounds Maintenance,** July 1981, Volume 16, No. 7, p. 24.

** Brookbank, George, **Native Palo Verde Trees,** Cooperative Extension Service, College of Agriculture, University of Arizona, Tucson, Arizona 85721,(Q 47). p. 2.

strategy

LEAVE PLANTS IN A STRESS CONDITION

In essence, this strategy involves just barely watering the landscape plants enough to keep them alive, but not enough for them to grow and flourish apart from the available natural water sources.

In some ways this is the simplest and easiest strategy. In other ways it is most difficult and complex. In essence, this strategy involves just barely watering the landscape plants enough to keep them alive, but not enough for them to grow and flourish apart from the available natural water sources.

This is a strategy which should be employed only in extreme drought situations and should not continue to be used all during the life of a plant or landscape unless the planting is totally native, indigenous or fully adapted to the region. This is a strategy of design as much as it is of maintenance. Using this strategy, the plants should be given just exactly enough water, at the appropriate time, to keep them barely alive and no more than is absolutely necessary at the maximum. In this strategy, if the plants die they die, and should be replaced with plants which are able to survive without additional water, or maybe they should not be replaced in the same place or even replaced at all.

From a design standpoint, if plants are left in a stress condition, they may die and if certain plants die they leave gaps in a planting design. Some of these may be critical in the structure or overall framework of a landscape project. In such cases, critical shade trees, individual plants in a screening hedge or a major specimen plant may die. All of

this significantly changes any basic landscape design beyond the intent and control of the original designer. Therefore the maintenance personnel or anyone else adopting this strategy of leaving plants in a stress condition becomes, in fact, the ultimate designer, since they determine which plants live and which plants die and thus the ultimate form of the landscape.

The landscape should be designed initially to be left in a stress condition during its lifetime and then maintenance personnel should be sensitive as to the minimum level of water required at the appropriate times to just barely preserve the planting even during extreme drought conditions. Even though leaving the plants in a stress condition can be done accidently by just not watering it is a more effective strategy if it is done consciously and understood fully by all designers, contractors and maintenance personnel who will be involved in a project during its lifetime.

Using a more naturalistic and less formal design theme and employing native, indigenous plants or plants adapted to a geographic or climatic region will make it much easier to use the strategy of leaving the plants in a stress condition if water is not available.

This is obviously another very strong arguement for the use of native plants. Any plant species which was existing in an area for hundreds of years without additional water beyond that which is available from natural sources will probably be able to survive periodic water shortages in the future.

In an article in Journal of the American Society for Horticultural Science research on minimum irrigation requirements of landscape plants was reported in the following words:

> In many crop plants there is a direct, although not linear, correlation between consumptive water use

and yield. That is, maximum yields per unit land area are attained generally with high irrigation frequency to prevent water stress... For landscape plants yield is not a factor, only appearance and ultimately, survival. We wish to maintain the minimum leaf area consistent with acceptable appearance and shading and screening functions. Thus, irrigation requirements for established landscape plants should be quite different from and, overall, considerably less than for comparable areas of crop species. Nevertheless, in many areas of California deep and shallow irrigation, particularly for species indigenous to humid regions, are made monthly, or even more frequently in warm weather from May through September.

The authors report that:

"Our data suggest that a bimonthly or less frequent irrigation schedule, totally 9.4 to 18.8 cm during the 'dry' season, was suitable for maintaining established plantings of several landscape species grown on deep, well-drained soils. Compared to monthly irrigation schedules considerable savings in water were realized, and vegetative overgrowth, a costly maintenance problem, was reduced substantially. .*

Leaving plants in a stress condition is an extreme strategy to be employed to save water and to use available water more effectively, but it is one which should be considered very seriously and carefully especially in times of drought. Planning for this option should, however, be made in the early design stages and it should not be applied insensitively.

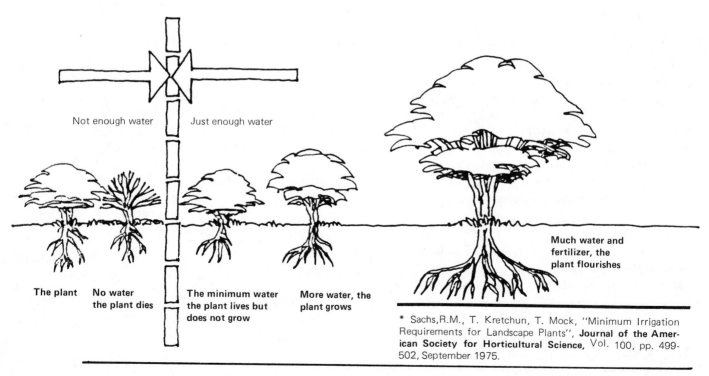

Not enough water   Just enough water

The plant   No water the plant dies   The minimum water the plant lives but does not grow   More water, the plant grows   Much water and fertilizer, the plant flourishes

* Sachs,R.M., T. Kretchun, T. Mock, "Minimum Irrigation Requirements for Landscape Plants", **Journal of the American Society for Horticultural Science**, Vol. 100, pp. 499-502, September 1975.

A Plant Growing Normally

The Same Plant in a Stress Condition

Prune carefully to reduce top growth and mass

Do not prune heavily or drastically

Do not fertilize

Mulch if possible

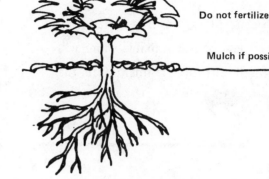

Not all plants experience stress at the same level of water deprivation

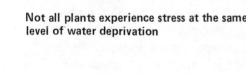

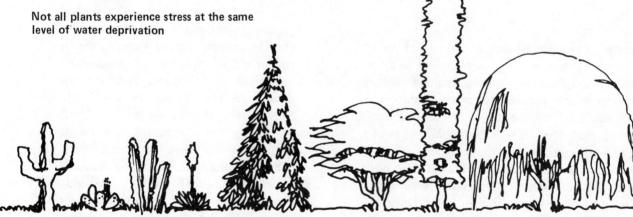

Leaving plants in stress condition is a short term solution during periods of extreme drought or severe water shortages. This strategy may be combined with other options including increasing the use of mulch, the alteration of cultural practices, especially careful pruning and the curtailment of the use of fertilizer as well as the modification of the soil and the use of anti-transpirants.

The object is to maintain enough life so that the plant can come back when water supplies are more abundant. Even though this is not necessarily a normal condition for some plants, many do develop a series of mechanisms to deal with such situations. Each plant type may be a different level of tolerance. It is difficult to know just exactly what the allowable stress point is for each plant or type of plant. Observation or testing at times is advisable on each site. Consultation is also advisable with local extension, horticultural, botanic or agricultural personnel. Often a mistake may be made and the plant may pass beyond the stress point and die. This is not as catastrophic as it may seem, since, if the drought is extended in time or regularly recurring maybe the plant shouldn't have been in that climatic situation or location. It might better be replaced with one which is more tolerant of water short or drought conditions.

strategy
ERECTING WIND BARRIERS

> " . . . the concept . . . is that by reducing wind speed less of the available water will be transpired out of the plant into the atmosphere. "

Quite often most people feel that plant materials use all of the water applied to them. More often, however, only a small percentage of the water applied to plant materials is actually used by the plant. It has been estimated that 3% of the water applied to plants is actually used by the plant, whereas 97% of the water is transpired through the plant back into the atmosphere. Obviously, solar radiation on a plant causes transpiration. However, less well-known is the fact that wind causes a drying out of the soil and increases the rate of evapotranspiration from the plant. If the plant is continuously exposed to high winds it will dry out not only the plant, but the top level of soil around the plant. The concept of erecting wind barriers to assist in water conservation in landscape development is that by reducing wind speed less of the available water will be transpired out of the plant into

the atmosphere. If, at the same time, the wind is slowed down and shade is provided for a specific plant the amount of transpiration is reduced even further. Wind screens also slow down deposits of snow in the colder sections of the country. This snow deposited on the leeward side of the wind barrier will also melt in place, providing additional soil moisture.

In a paper entitled, "Trees Outside the Forest" by Johan Van Der Line in the book, *FOREST INFLUENCES*, published by the Food and Agriculture Organization of the United Nations, the following is stated in relationship to evaporation and wind speed:

Evaporation

The rate of evaporation depends on the velocity of the wind, the temperature and the relative humidity of the air. Bodroff, who writes with special authority on conditions in the Russian steppes, attaches great importance to the effect of windscreens on evaporation, which he regards as a sure indicator of the dryness of a climate. There is general agreement that, in the whole, evaporation is much smaller in the lee than in the open. 'The influence of stands on evaporation' Bodroff states, 'extends over a distance which, in wind velocities of 2.5 to 3 meters per second in the open exceeds 60 times the height of the windscreen, and which amounts to 100 times the height of the windscreen in wind velocities of 5 to 10 meters per second.' Smolik found a decrease in evaporation over a distance equal to 33 to 46 height. According to Iizuka, Tamate, Takakuwa and Sato, who made their

Fast moving dry winds moving across the bare surface of moist soil pulls water out of the soil.

By reducing wind speed, less of the available water will be transpired back into the atmosphere.

As moisture from the top layer of the soil is pulled out, water is brought up from the root zone of the smaller landscape plants.

investigations in Japan, reductions extend over a distance of 20 to 25 height from the screen. They also found that at a distance equal to 1 height from the screen, evaporation amounted to 40 percent of the value in the open. At a distance of 5 height it was 60 percent, and at a distance of 10 height it was 80 percent.

Bates reached a conclusion which should be quoted here. 'The distance from the windbreak to the area of greatest protection,' he wrote, 'depends upon the position of the mass of foliage which affords the protection. With a dense grove, it is immediately in the lee of the trees; with a narrow belt of trees that lack lower branches, it may be as far from the trees as five times their height and it moves outward as the velocity of the wind increases.'' His conclusion accords with the theory of the windfields behind screens of different density. It also indicates that, to a great extent, the influence of windscreens on evaporation corresponds to their influence on wind. *

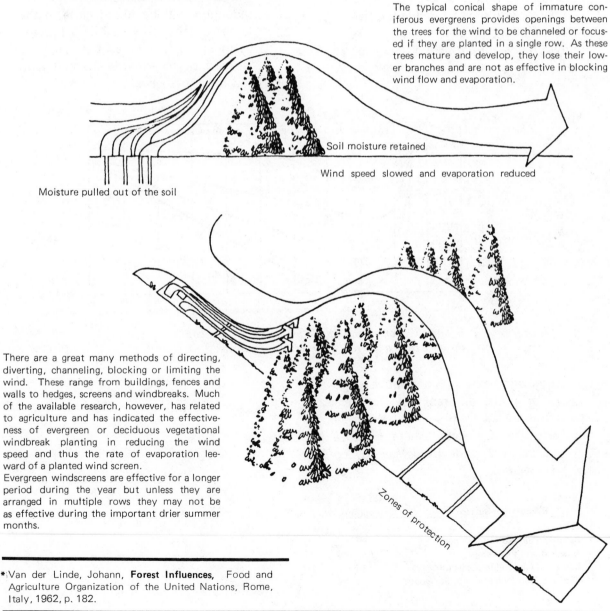

The typical conical shape of immature coniferous evergreens provides openings between the trees for the wind to be channeled or focused if they are planted in a single row. As these trees mature and develop, they lose their lower branches and are not as effective in blocking wind flow and evaporation.

Soil moisture retained

Wind speed slowed and evaporation reduced

Moisture pulled out of the soil

There are a great many methods of directing, diverting, channeling, blocking or limiting the wind. These range from buildings, fences and walls to hedges, screens and windbreaks. Much of the available research, however, has related to agriculture and has indicated the effectiveness of evergreen or deciduous vegetational windbreak planting in reducing the wind speed and thus the rate of evaporation leeward of a planted wind screen.

Evergreen windscreens are effective for a longer period during the year but unless they are arranged in multiple rows they may not be as effective during the important drier summer months.

Zones of protection

* Van der Linde, Johann, **Forest Influences,** Food and Agriculture Organization of the United Nations, Rome, Italy, 1962, p. 182.

Joseph Kittredge, in his classic book, *FOREST INFLUENCES*, also gives basic information concerning the relative effectiveness of the forest and vegetation on evaporation of the soil. He covers extensively the research that had been done before 1948 to show the relative effectiveness of wind breaks in reducing evaporation of water from the plant and the soil. He does this by referring to a number of other studies which had been done relating to the effect of forest and vegetation on evaporation of the soil:

Effects of Forest and Vegetation on Evaporation from Soil

It has been shown that, on forested as compared with unvegetated areas, the solar radiation, the maximum temperatures, the vapor-pressure differences, and the wind velocities are reduced.

The reductions are greater as the density of the vegetation increases. Evaporation decreases with a decrease in each of these factors. Therefore, it may be expected that there will be a decrease in evaporation as the density of the cover increases.

In the simple case of windbreaks, Bates has shown that the reduction in evaporation is proportional to the density of the windbreak, and also that the reduction in evaporation and the distance at which such reduction is found increases with the wind velocity. Thus the area of greatest reduction will be found close in the lee of a dense grove, while it may be as much as five times the height to leeward of a narrow shelterbelt with few lower branches.

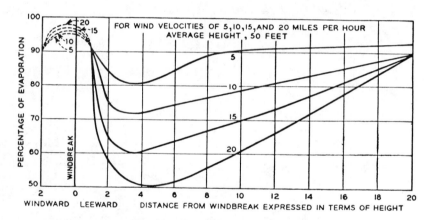

Relative evaporation in relation to wind velocity and distance from a one-row cottonwood windbreak.

Interesting examples of relative evaporation under different kinds of cover are reported from some of the older work in Germany where measurements were made from May to September.

Evaporation Surface	Relative Evaporation, %
Free water	100
Saturated bare soil in the open	93
Free water in the woods	39-39
Saturated bare soil in the woods	35
Saturated soil under litter in the woods	13

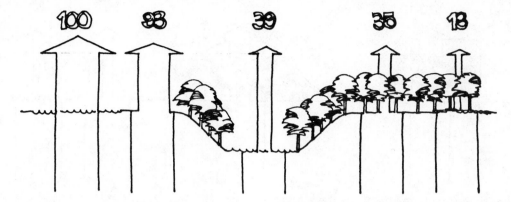

Records from lysimeters 21 in. deep at North Fork, California, for 1934-1936, with average precipitation of 48 in., gave average annual evaporation from bare soil of 17.1 in. compared with 12.3 in. from the same soil covered with 2 in. of ponderosa pine litter.

The relative evaporation at Lincoln, Nebraska, from a silt-loam soil for 4 selected days in August, 1938, was as follows:

Kind of Litter	Relative Evaporation, %
None	100
Beech	55
Spruce	40
Pine	33

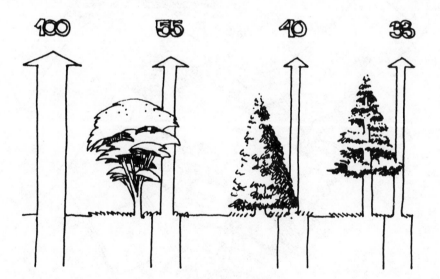

When a litter layer of equal depth of 5 cm was used for the three species, the beech and spruce showed relative evaporation of 11 per cent and the pine 15 per cent, as compared with 100 without litter.

Differences between species are illustrated by German records for 4 years of monthly mean evaporation from sandy soil at capillary saturation under an open cover.

Condition at Surface	Relative Evaporation, %
From bare soil (0.19 in. equals 100)	100
Bare soil shaded	64
Bare soil shaded and sheltered from wind	47
Straw mulch, 1½ in.	27
Soil mulch, 1½ in.	9

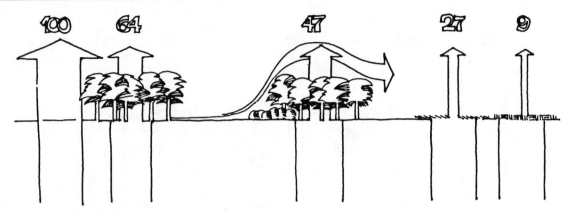

As in Germany the depth of the straw mulch had little effect after it was increased above 3 in., corresponding to 8 tons per acre. Coarse sand or gravel has been shown to be as effective as soil, straw, or litter in reducing evaporation.*

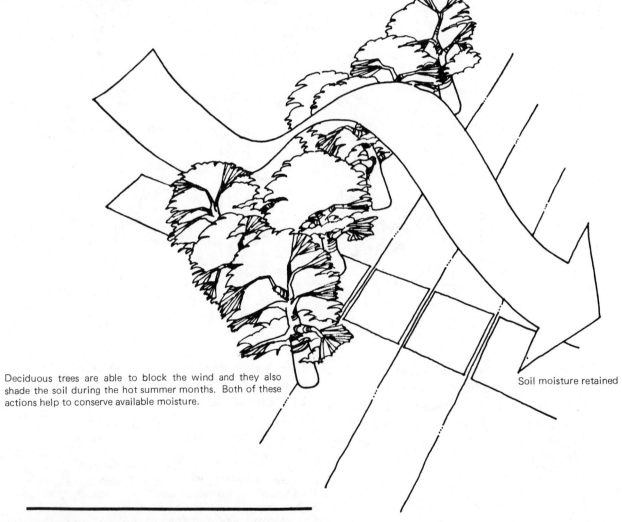

Deciduous trees are able to block the wind and they also shade the soil during the hot summer months. Both of these actions help to conserve available moisture.

Soil moisture retained

* Kittredge, Joseph, **Forest Influences,** McGraw-Hill Book Co., 1948, p. 151-153.

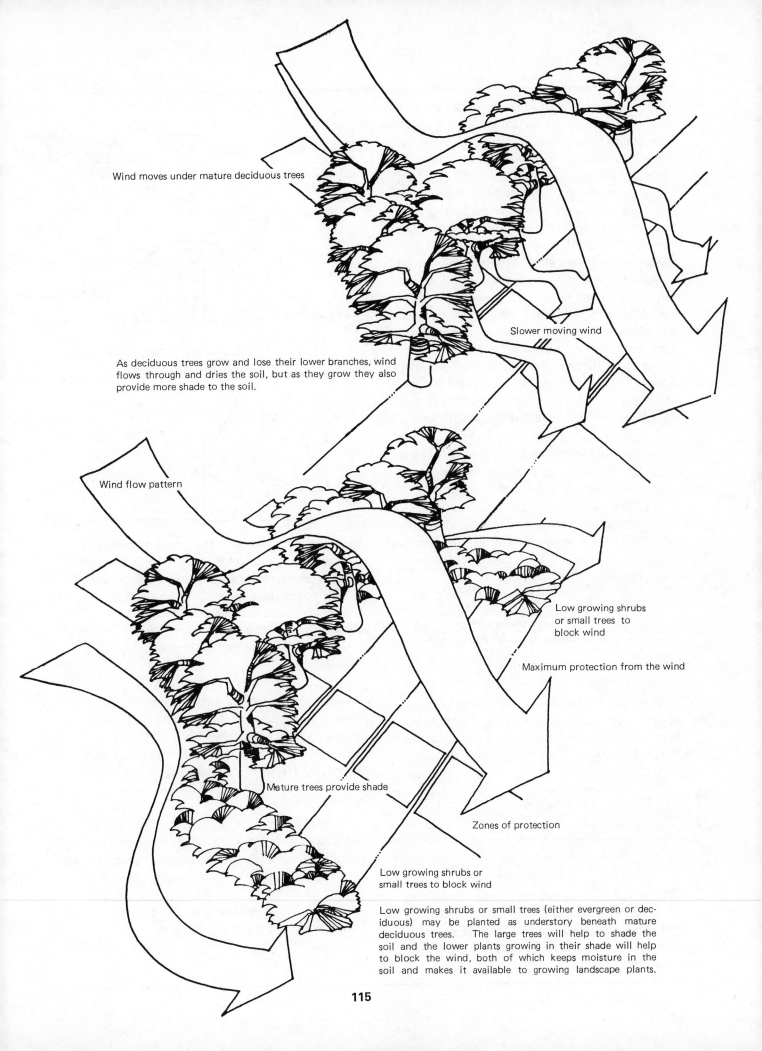

Wind moves under mature deciduous trees

Slower moving wind

As deciduous trees grow and lose their lower branches, wind flows through and dries the soil, but as they grow they also provide more shade to the soil.

Wind flow pattern

Low growing shrubs or small trees to block wind

Maximum protection from the wind

Mature trees provide shade

Zones of protection

Low growing shrubs or small trees to block wind

Low growing shrubs or small trees (either evergreen or deciduous) may be planted as understory beneath mature deciduous trees. The large trees will help to shade the soil and the lower plants growing in their shade will help to block the wind, both of which keeps moisture in the soil and makes it available to growing landscape plants.

115

This research shows that windbreaks are much more effective in protecting soil moisture where winds have a fairly high velocity. This also shows that windbreaks used in isolation are relatively effective in protecting the soil moisture. But where windbreaks are used in conjunction with shading devices and mulches; they may, in combination, reduce the relative evaporation from 100% down to from 9-13%. A windbreak, to be effective does not necessarily need to be large, dense or wide. All types of natural and man-made materials which can be used to block or divert excessive winds, may help to preserve moisture in the soil. This is one more strategy that needs to be seriously considered in any landscape design to preserve the maximum amount of moisture and to use water most effectively and efficiently.

Growing wind screens such as trees or shrubs help to preserve moisture but they also use much in order to grow and develop. They also require a great deal of water even in dry periods and may have to be irrigated to survive to provide wind screens in the future.

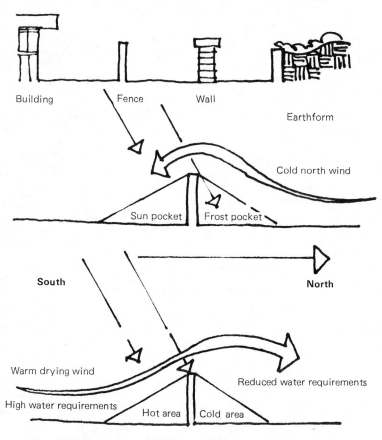

The net water balance with vegetation may be zero since they use as much as they save.

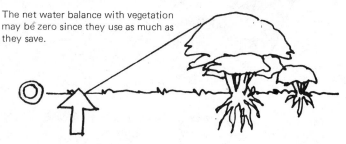

The net water balance using plants as wind screens may thus be balanced. Sometimes they use more than they save, at other times they save more than they need to grow.

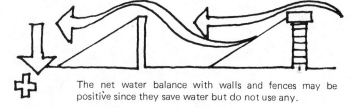

The net water balance with walls and fences may be positive since they save water but do not use any.

Non-growing wind screens, such as fences or walls help conserve soil moisture and do not use or need any water themselves. This gives a positive water balance between what they use and what they save.

Blocking or screening the wind to prevent moisture loss is one more strategy that should be considered in every situation. It will not always save all of the water that is needed but it may save some, and coupled with other methods or strategies, a great amount of water may be conserved on any site.

Where wind barriers exist on a site they should be used and high water use plants should be placed in their lee. If windbreaks do not exist and if they are needed to save water, they should be included in the initial design or in the redesign of the landscape.

This one use of vertical elements cannot be considered in isolation. Certainly orientation, prevailing wind direction, height, porosity, and relationship to horizontal elements should be carefully considered and assessed as a part of an overall site design with efficient water management in mind.

strategy

REDESIGN
OR RENOVATE TO REDUCE
WATER REQUIREMENTS

Specific plants which require too much water, whether it be a tree, a shrub, ground cover or even a turf variety, may have to be replaced in times of extreme water shortage.

In some instances landscape areas have been designed in another era of generally much more rainfall and more readily available water. Therefore, even though redesign or renovation of the landscape area to conserve water may be a drastic and expensive approach, it may be justified and worthwhile over an extended period of time. The redesign and renovation may be extensive and expensive or it may be reasonably inexpensive and easily accomplished. Basically the purpose is to replace water-requiring plants in the landscape with those which require less water and irrigation. Generally the redesign of any garden or landscaped area can be divided into redesign dealing with plants, growing medium or mulch, or redesign to change irrigation devices or irrigation methods.

Specific plants which require too much water, whether it be a tree, a shrub, ground cover or even a turf variety, may have to be replaced in times of extreme water shortage. The replacement needs to be done with types or varieties of plant material that require less water. In other instances plants may need to just be removed because they compete for water with other plants or because there are too many plants in an area for the water available. This is especially the case, for instance, when a shrub is growing within the drip line of a shallow rooted tree. It may also be the case with turf or a ground cover growing under a shallow rooted tree. The tree roots are so invasive that they take water from the other plants and if the smaller plants are not removed they may die because of lack of water.

In other instances planting within a landscape area may be rearrranged or reorganized. This is normally done either to simplify the planting or to group plants with like water requirements. Those plants requiring a great deal of water should be placed near other plants which also require a great deal of water. In this way the irrigation process would be greatly simplified. By the same token, those plants which require little or no water should be placed near other plants which require little or no water. In this way it will not be necessary to provide any water for those plants in this area for longer periods of time. It is also advisable, in drought situations, to simplify planting to enable it to be more easily irrigated or cultivated. It is also possible, and many times advisable, to provide for a more natural quality or appearance in the landscape. Generally, a very green, lush, highly manicured landscape requires a great deal of water. One which has a less pruned, trimmed, sheared and manicured appearance may take much less water and certainly require less energy to maintain over its effective lifetime.

Planting may be modified to provide for windbreaks which would shield smaller plants in the lee of the windbreak from the drying effect of harsh summer winds. It may be also possible, in some instances, to provide shade to plantings within a landscape situation so that it would be possible for the plants to survive with much less water than if they were placed in the direct sun.

One other aspect of redesign or renovating an area so it will require less water has to do with the replacement of the growing media. In either extremely compact or extremely light soils the effort may be worthwhile to replace individual plants or planted areas and replant them into better soil or better growing media so that they will require less water in time to come. Obviously the planting should be done late in the fall or early in the spring so that normal rainfall will be available to help establish the plants. In some instances it may also be very worthwhile to modify the standard planting details so as to provide more treated growing media around the base of the plant than would normally be the case. In this way the plant has a longer period of time to send out roots into the new growing media. In extremely small holes the plant roots would very quickly reach the surrounding soil which may or may not be conducive to rapid root growth. In water short areas this extra investment to provide more and better initial growing material for the plant may be entirely justified.

In other instances landscaped areas may be redesigned or renovated to provide more mulch around the base of existing or newly installed planting. In such instances you may have more staff, more time or even more mulch than you have water. This would help considerably in conserving water over the effective lifetime of the plant.

It also may be advisable to make the effort to redesign a garden or landscaped area to install mechanized sprinkler systems and tensiometers. In this way, the proper amounts of water will be applied regularly and the water levels can be checked in a more careful way. This extra effort in redesign of a garden may result in a considerable savings of scarce and expensive water in time to come. For instance, it has been suggested that if it is found that after relatively short periods of time (say within 6 minutes), water begins to run off from a specific area, that automatic irrigation system can be established to allow for 6 minutes of water and then be shut off. After this water is absorbed into the soil, an automatic irrigation system would once again be turned on. In this way water would be saved, the plants would be saved, and the water would be used much more efficiently.

Dr. Victor A. Gibeault has suggested a number of possible areas of redesign in *PREPARING TURF TO SURVIVE A DROUGHT:*

Possible Redesign

Drought can be defined as a prolonged period of abnormal moisture deficiency. This definition implies that normal moisture conditions will return to an area in time. Such a situation means that temporary, minor design changes can assist a manager ride out the current water shortage.

Conversely, many areas in the western states face what can be foreseen as "permanent drought conditions." That is, because of jurisdictional or political action, they do not have sufficient water to supply existing or increased demand. Turf managers in such water districts may consider major design changes so as to continue operation. Of course, a landscape architect will be helpful in this regard.

Listed below are some changes that may be considered:

- Line water storage lakes to reduce water loss.
- If your facility is considering the installation of a new, more effective and efficient irrigation system, then this may be the time to act.
- Redesign the irrigation system to increase control over water application. As examples, sun vs. shade areas should be on different stations; reduce fairway width and cap sprinkler heads in roughs on golf courses; remove from irrigation, or reduce irrigation, on other areas not essential to play.
- Level mounds and redesign other hard to irrigate topographic features.

- Investigate the possible availability of effluent water, if state or local law permits its use.
- Remove poor performing plants from the landscape.
- If establishing plant material, group plants with similar water requirement so all can be irrigated for optimum performance.
- Use mulches 1-2 inches thick to reduce evaporation water loss in plant beds.
- Selectively eliminate plants, if necessary, by carefully identifying which plants are most important to the total landscape.
- When conditions necessitate, select turfgrass species and varieties that perform well in your area and are known to have good drought tolerance.

In summary, each turfgrass manager has special, specific problems and opportunities on his facility. To deal with a drought condition effectively, the manager must know the local water availability condition, he should be aware of turfgrass management practices that will be of assistance, and he should be ready to implement major or minor design changes so the facility and play can continue.*

This redesign or renovation of an area certainly is one option or strategy that should be considered in every circumstance or situation. It may be expensive, it may be drastic and it may be time consuming, but in time, certain types of design use less water than do others. As water continues to be a concern and as a new and more sensitive generation of designers develops a new ethic and a new attitude, more initial designs will be more water conscious and water efficient. This is another professional generation way in many parts of the country and existing designs may have to be modified so they will be able to survive without so much water. Guidelines

need to be developed to show how initial designs should be planned and implemented so as to be more water conscious and water conserving. In the interim, the following are a few illustrated suggestions.

Site design elements can be divided into "hardscape" such as paving, walls, fences, and graded surfaces and "softscape" which is usually plant material such as trees, shrubs, ground cover and turf. Site elements can also be divided into vertical and horizontal elements. Horizontal can be under foot or overhead while vertical elements can be short or tall.

Horizontal hardscape elements are usually paving, decking or canopies. Water can be saved by converting areas of turf or ground cover to a porous paving material or to a mulch. Turf or ground cover allows water into the soil but also uses precious water, while mulch or porous paving allows water into the soil, uses none and prevents it from evaporating back into the atmosphere.

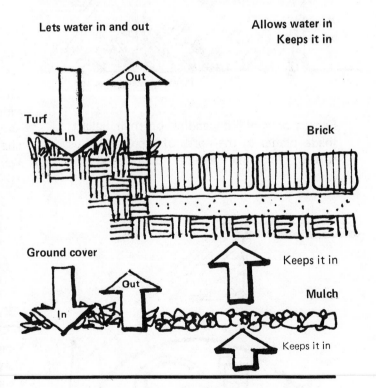

* Gibeault, Victor A., "Preparing Turf to Survive Drought", **California Turfgrass Culture**, Vol. 27, No.2, Spring 1977, p. 11.

Decking may also be used to shade the soil or to provide a level space without disturbing the underlying grading and water drainage patterns.

Free standing walls and fences deflect or channel the wind and this windbreak effect decreases the amount of water which is pulled through the plant from the soil.

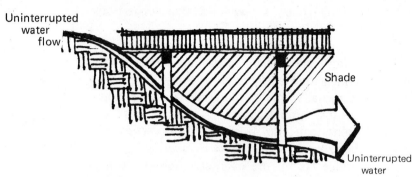

Uninterrupted water flow

Shade

Uninterrupted water flow

Shaded areas use and transpire less water than areas exposed to the sun. A shade tree may use more water than it saves, where a trellis, either with a vine growing on it or without, will provide shade and not use as much water as a growing plant.

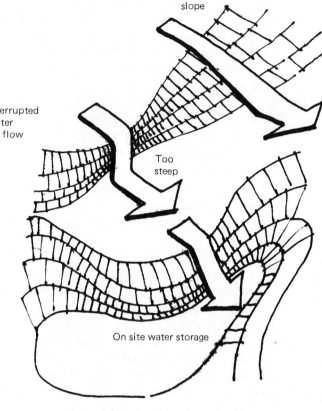

Gentle slope

Too steep

On site water storage

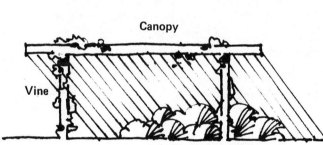

Canopy

Vine

Plants growing in shade

Fences or walls, depending on their height, shade plants to the north of them and thus curtail, to some extent, their need for water.

Generally, grading should be done to provide gentle, not drastic or harsh slopes and should be done either to keep water on the site or to direct it to where it is needed or wanted.

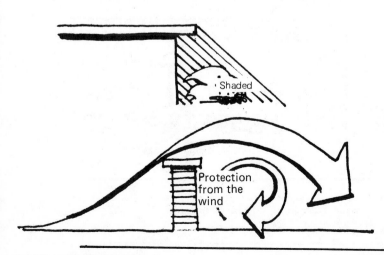

Shaded

Protection from the wind

Planted areas should not be so narrow that they cannot efficiently be watered with existing mechanical equipment, because they will either not be watered or water will be wasted as it runs off on to the adjacent paving.

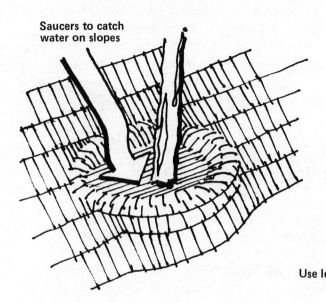

Saucers to catch water on slopes

Turf or other ground covering which use a great deal of water should be removed and replaced with turf or ground covers which take less water or with mulch, paving or decking.

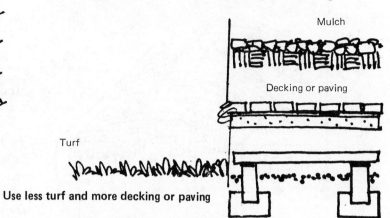

Mulch

Decking or paving

Turf

Use less turf and more decking or paving

One design alternative which might be considered in such situations is to create permanent "saucers" around trees on berms or slopes. This would allow extra water for the needs of the trees to be placed in the saucers either through rainfall or in the irrigation process and for the turf to be watered periodically to the appropriate depth.

Softscape elements use water, pump it out of the soil and transpire it back into the atmosphere.

Plants with like water requirements should be grouped together so they can most effectively and efficiently be irrigated at one time. That is, plants which take a great deal of water should be arranged together and those which take little should also be put in one place or area. This makes it easier to maintain the plants and makes it possible to irrigate all of them at the same time and rate.

Some planting areas should be converted from a very formal design containing a great deal of introduced plant material to a more naturalistic design using native, indigenous xeric adapted, drought tolerant or drought resistent plant material. This may change the entire character of a site but that may be entirely appropriate in most cases.

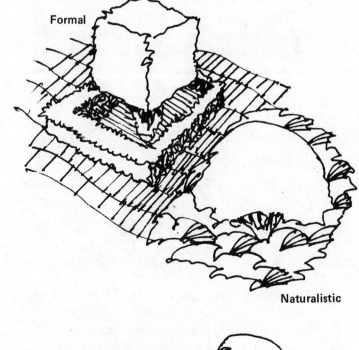

Formal

Naturalistic

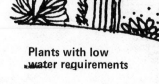

Plants with low water requirements

Plants with high water requirements

Earth should not be bermed up between curbs or between walks and curbs if turf is to be grown on them since irrigation water will run off and be wasted.

Don't berm narrow turf areas

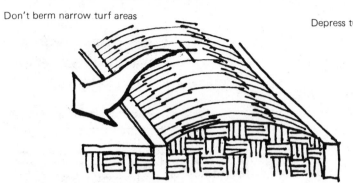

Water quickly runs off narrow bermed turf areas

Rather, if possible, they should either be channelled or scooped out to form a shallow basin which may retain the excess which may be available to percolate into the soil at a later time.

Depress turf area to hold water

If these areas must be level to be easily mowed or maintained they should be depressed below the surrounding curbs so that water can be retained and not have to be replaced because it ran off.

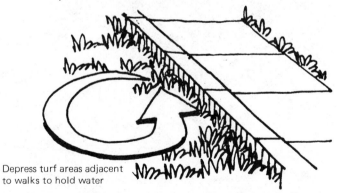

Depress turf areas adjacent to walks to hold water

Since turf and trees root to different levels trees should not be planted on berms or slopes. If you put on enough water to irrigate the turf, the tree either does not get any water or develops a very shallow rooting system. If you water deeply enough to saturate the tree roots, then excess water runs off the turf and is wasted.

If possible, turf should be depressed adjacent to walks. This prevents the water from running off the growing area and on to the paving to be wasted to the site.

Depress turf areas adjacent to walks to hold water

Turf has shallow roots and trees have deeper roots. If water is applied so as to irrigate the turf, the excess water runs off and never reaches the tree roots. If enough water is applied so as to reach the tree roots all of the excess water runs off the turf area.

Don't put trees on turfed berms

In instances of extreme water shortage, plantings should be thinned, that is, in mass plantings, certain plants can be taken out without destroying the overall effect.

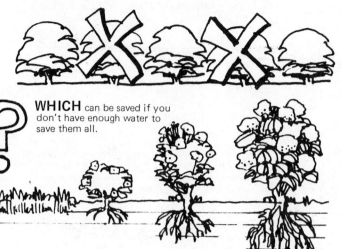

WHICH can be saved if you don't have enough water to save them all.

In almost all cases, when water shortages occur, plants which require too much water for a region should be removed and eliminated and be replaced with those which require less water. These may not always be "native" plants, but they should be those plants which are able to grow and prosper and which have landscape potential in a region. They should be tolerant or growing with the amount of water which is available or which can be applied in a region or they should be drought tolerant or drought resistent.

A site may also be redesigned in order to make it easier to irrigate. Most systems for irrigating plants are mechanical and have limitations as to how they can apply water or where they can reach. If any designer tries to fit an irrigation system to a landscape design, water may be wasted. On the other hand, if the landscape designer uses the irrigation system limitations as one more form determinant or as a guide, it is possible to have a landscape design which has sufficient water in all parts and doesn't waste water, over water or neglect to water any part of the landscape.

Most irrigation equipment can now be modified to fit nearly any landscape design.

Many times irrigation is easier and more efficient if the landscape design initially recognizes and accepts the limitations of conventional equipment and configurations.

It is possible, through careful initial design or redesign, to use water which falls on the site or which is placed on the site in irrigation, over and over again. This can be done through terracing, through grouping plants along natural drainage channels or by having plants whose roots grow to different depths arranged together. In the latter case, water is used by plants which have shallow roots, then the excess water flows down through the soil to be used by the plants with deeper roots.

If water is applied here it is designed to reuse the water over and over again as it falls downhill.

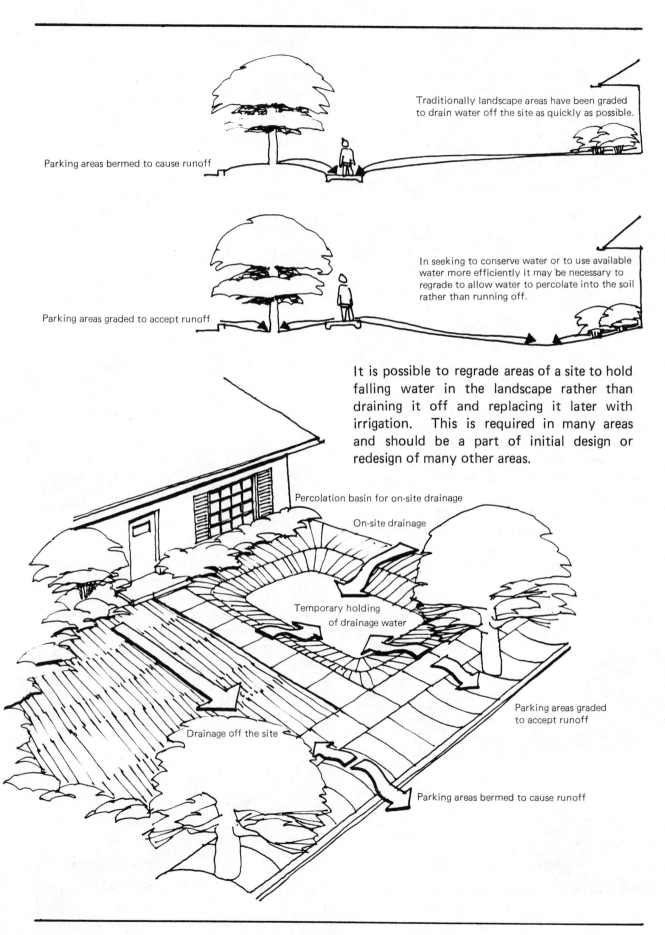

Traditionally landscape areas have been graded to drain water off the site as quickly as possible.

Parking areas bermed to cause runoff

In seeking to conserve water or to use available water more efficiently it may be necessary to regrade to allow water to percolate into the soil rather than running off.

Parking areas graded to accept runoff

It is possible to regrade areas of a site to hold falling water in the landscape rather than draining it off and replacing it later with irrigation. This is required in many areas and should be a part of initial design or redesign of many other areas.

Percolation basin for on-site drainage

On-site drainage

Temporary holding of drainage water

Drainage off the site

Parking areas graded to accept runoff

Parking areas bermed to cause runoff

Great care should be taken, however, not to plant small shrubs, turf or other ground cover, which require a great deal of moisture, under the branches of large trees with dense canopies or with shallow roots. In such cases, the trees shed rain and their roots compete with those of the smaller plants for limited available water.

Remove shrubs from under spreading trees

One of the most effective redesign strategies is to develop zones, some of which are small, highly used and fully irrigated and others of which require minimal maintenance and irrigation. In such instances, small turf areas may be used for sunbathing, for recreation or for viewing while larger areas of a site require little or no water. Using this approach, it is possible to tailor irrigation and maintenance to usage and have a series of small landscapes with different needs and requirements on the same site.

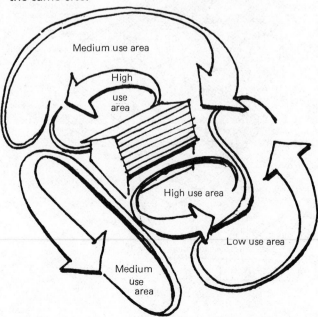

Medium use area

High use area

High use area

Low use area

Medium use area

Entire sites maybe should be redesigned, portions of a site should be redesigned or sequentially a site should be redesigned, section by section so as to use less water. This eventuality and investment should always be a viable strategy.

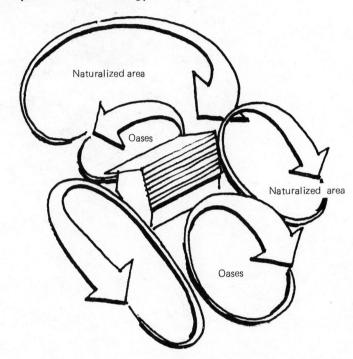

Naturalized area

Oases

Naturalized area

Oases

If sufficient water is not available to maintain an existing landscape in the condition in which it was designed and installed, then the redesign or renovation of the site is a viable option and an appropriate strategy. How to do this is the subject of an entire book and cannot be adequately covered in a single chapter. Redesign can save water and can save enough water, over time, to justify the cost of considering the inevitable continuing water shortages.

What should not be done in the redesign of any landscape area to use less water is:

- to take out of all the plants,

- to replace growing plants with plastic reproductions or plastic "plants",

- to replace all of the turf or ground cover with gravel.

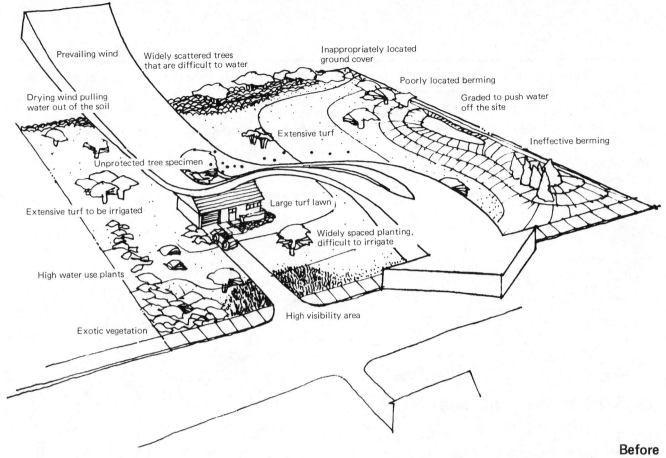

Prevailing wind

Widely scattered trees
that are difficult to water

Inappropriately located
ground cover

Drying wind pulling
water out of the soil

Poorly located berming

Graded to push water
off the site

Extensive turf

Ineffective berming

Unprotected tree specimen

Extensive turf to be irrigated

Large turf lawn

Widely spaced planting,
difficult to irrigate

High water use plants

High visibility area

Exotic vegetation

Before
Single family residence
Redesign of the landscape to conserve water
After

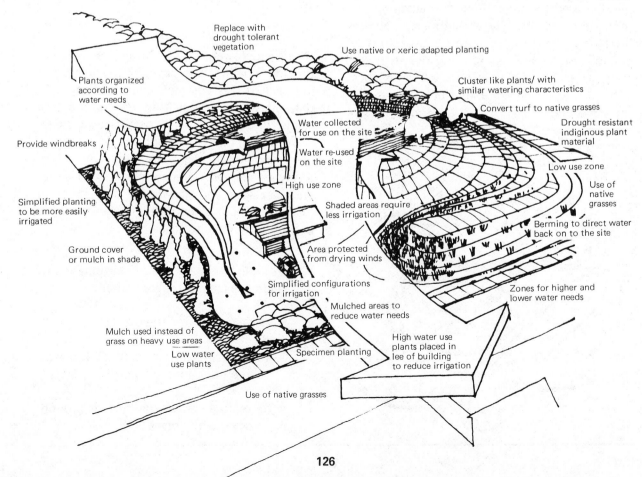

Replace with
drought tolerant
vegetation

Use native or xeric adapted planting

Cluster like plants/ with
similar watering characteristics

Plants organized
according to
water needs

Convert turf to native grasses

Water collected
for use on the site

Drought resistant
indiginous plant
material

Provide windbreaks

Water re-used
on the site

Low use zone

High use zone

Use of
native
grasses

Simplified planting
to be more easily
irrigated

Shaded areas require
less irrigation

Berming to direct water
back on to the site

Ground cover
or mulch in shade

Area protected
from drying winds

Simplified configurations
for irrigation

Zones for higher and
lower water needs

Mulched areas to
reduce water needs

Mulch used instead of
grass on heavy use areas

High water use
plants placed in
lee of building
to reduce irrigation

Low water
use plants

Specimen planting

Use of native grasses

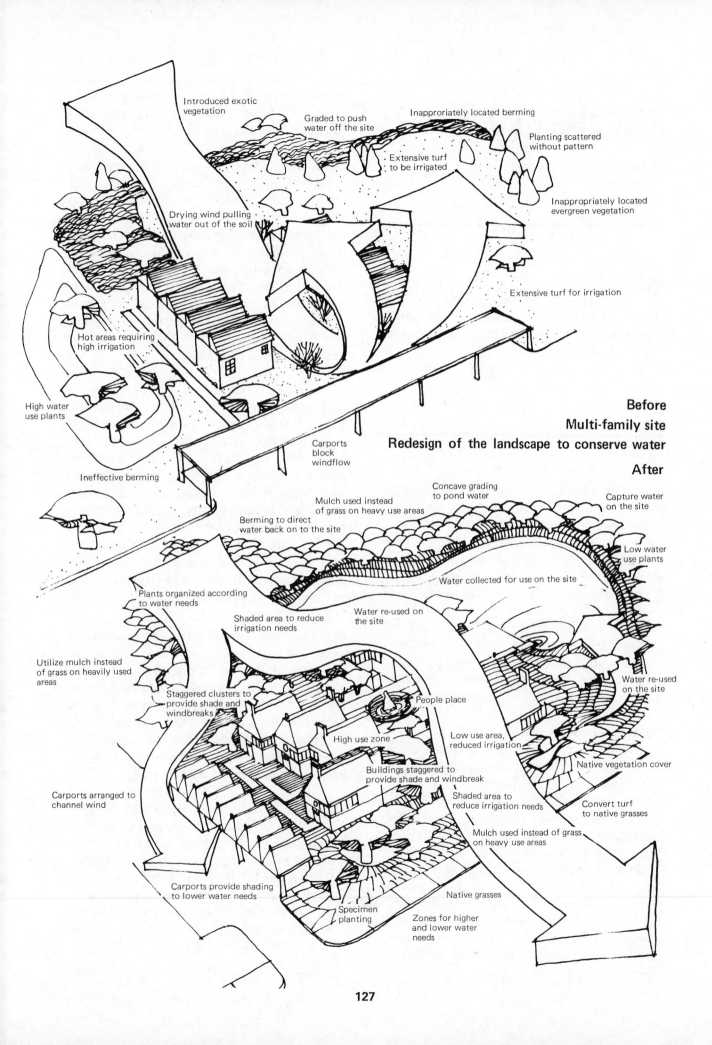

Introduced exotic vegetation

Graded to push water off the site

Inapproriately located berming

Planting scattered without pattern

Extensive turf to be irrigated

Inappropriately located evergreen vegetation

Drying wind pulling water out of the soil

Extensive turf for irrigation

Hot areas requiring high irrigation

High water use plants

Before

Multi-family site

Redesign of the landscape to conserve water

After

Ineffective berming

Carports block windflow

Mulch used instead of grass on heavy use areas

Concave grading to pond water

Capture water on the site

Berming to direct water back on to the site

Low water use plants

Water collected for use on the site

Plants organized according to water needs

Shaded area to reduce irrigation needs

Water re-used on the site

Utilize mulch instead of grass on heavily used areas

Staggered clusters to provide shade and windbreaks

People place

High use zone

Water re-used on the site

Low use area, reduced irrigation

Native vegetation cover

Buildings staggered to provide shade and windbreak

Shaded area to reduce irrigation needs

Convert turf to native grasses

Carports arranged to channel wind

Mulch used instead of grass on heavy use areas

Carports provide shading to lower water needs

Specimen planting

Native grasses

Zones for higher and lower water needs

strategy

ALTER CULTIVATION PRACTICES

. . .it is possible to save a great deal of water and to use available water much more efficiently through more careful study of cultivation practices.

It may be advisable and necessary in times of extreme drought to substantially alter the cultivation practices normally used in landsscape, site and grounds areas. This may help to conserve water and to use water more efficiently. In some cases this may be, in effect, trading hand labor for water. By spending more time in cultivating and maintaining plant material, it may be possible to use less water. However, it is very possible to save a great deal of water and to use available water much more efficiently through more careful study of cultivation practices.

Obviously in some cases it may be necessary in extreme water shortages to leave some plants or areas in a stress condition. However, water can be saved by altering the fertilizing, pruning, mowing and cultivating practices. The healthy, growing plant with a great deal of available water will benefit from the use of timely and balanced fertilization. However, in times of drought, grounds managers should generally fertilize much less. Fertilization stimulates growth and usually is activated by the addition of water. If water is not available it is possible through excessive fertilizing to burn and kill plants which are

in a stress condition. If fertilization is to be done in a drought condition a relatively low nitrogen fertilizer should be used. Nitrogen is primarily responsible for the growth of leaves and the visible portion of any plant. Fertilizer with high nitrogen content obviously will stimulate the growth of leaves or blades of grass which would then require the addition of more water. If any fertilizer is to be used it should be one with a relatively high phosphorous content to stimulate additional root growth below the ground surface. Also, where possible, it has been suggested that you use a slow or timed release fertilizer which will be available to the plant over an extended period of time.

When water is not available it may be advisable or necessary to prune plants more severely than otherwise would be the case if water were plentiful and available. In this way, by pruning, the stress on the plant is reduced and the plant is able to continue growing and living without the necessity for greater amounts of water. Care should be taken, however, that the plants are not too severely pruned which would cause either the death of the plant or a deformity of the natural plant form growth habit. Weeding is suggested to remove competition from ornamental landscape planting areas. Obviously, a weed, like a plant is a small water pump, pumping water out of the soil and transpiring it into the atmosphere. Weeds compete with ornamental landscape plants for available water in the soil. Therefore the fewer weeds which are in a specific area the more water that is available to desirable landscape plants. This is especially true in ground cover beds, in turf areas and in shrub borders.

The June 1977 issue of *GROUNDS MAINTENANCE* Magazine, in an article entitled, "Turfgrass Water Stress and Drought," under a section dealing with No Irrigation Water Available, they suggested a series of altered cultivation practices which would assist in conserving limited water supplies in turf management.

There are portions of the country where priorities in water usage will be established and there may be no water available for turfgrass irrigation during the upcoming summer. What does one do in this situation? The primary steps should involve preparing the turfgrass so that it has maximum hardiness against the anticipated drought stress, ensuring maximum effective infiltration of what rainfall does occur, and enhancing root growth so that water can be obtained from greater soil depths. The possible alternatives can be summarized as follows:

1. *Cultivation.* Hopefully some rainfall will occur during the spring period. Coring or slicing, particularly on compacted fine textured soils, will assist in achieving the maximum possible soil penetration of what rainfall is received. This procedure is particularly helpful on sloping areas where the percentage water loss by runoff is greatest.

2. *Use minimal nitrogen levels.* This may restrict shoot growth somewhat and result in a partial loss of color, but will maximize the extent and depth of root penetration.

3. *Provide adequate amounts of potassium.* The depth and extent of rooting as well as drought hardiness are maximized by relatively high potassium nutritional levels. There is also evidence that iron applications, particularly under high nitrogen levels, will enhance the tolerance to water stress.

4. *Raise the cutting height.* Under these conditions the main concern is not the highest quality turf possible but rather survival. Thus, a higher cutting height will permit increased rooting which is so vital in maximizing water absorption from greater soil depths. In addition, the higher cutting height will result in increased shoot growth above ground, thus enhancing wear tolerance. This could be very important during the subsequent summer under intense traffic when there is no recuperative rate due to dormant turf.

5. *Avoid the use of herbicides.* Many pre-emergence herbicides have a certain degree of toxicity to turfgrass roots. It would be advisable to avoid herbicide applications during the spring period if one of the major objectives is to achieve maximum root growth and the weed problem is not too objectionable.

6. *Adjust soil pH, if needed.* Adjust the pH, as near as is practical, to the desirable range of six to seven for maximum rooting.

7. *Control serious root feeding pests.* Be sure that root feeding pests, particularly grubs and wireworms, are controlled. But don't apply a pesticide unless a critical infestation has been accurately diagnosed.

8. *Finally,* it is hoped that adequate thatch control has been achieved during previous summers. It is probably too late to change if a thatch problem exists at this time.*

Other suggestons which may be made to alter vegetation cultivation practices to conserve water would include the aeration of turf areas to allow available water to penetrate through the thatch to the roots. This should be done generally only in spring and fall when water is apt to be available and not in summer when it is more apt to be dry. If done during the summer time the aeration process would allow the soil roots to dry out to a greater extent. It is also advisable, in managing turf during periods of water shortage, to remove thatch from the lawns to allow for better water penetration to the roots.

---

* Beard, James, "Turfgrass Water Stress and Drought", **Grounds Maintenance,** June 1977, Vol. 12, No. 6, pp. 73-74.

It has been suggested that it is unwise to plant new vegetation during the dry season since these newly installed plants would require regular irrigation water. It is much more advisable to plant in the fall when the water demands are lower and when the possibility of rainfall occurs in some areas of the country. It is also suggested that it is wise to use pesticides to decrease the pests which would provide a drain on plants. It has also been suggested that it is advisable to use weed control chemicals to lessen weed competition within turf plantings.

The publication SAVING WATER IN LAND-SCAPE IRRIGATION, published by the Division of Agricultural Sciences of the University of California in Berkeley (Leaflet 2976) suggests one other cultural practice which might be considered extreme in some situations in the following words:

> Remove some of the plants in crowded beds or low-priority plants that are growing close to others you want to save. This reduces competition for soil moisture. Turf may be the first to go but is easiest to re-establish later.*

This may be especially true where a shrub planting exists underneath a large shade tree with shallow, invasive roots. A decision may have to be made as to whether to keep the larger tree or the shrubs. The tree probably deprives nearby shrubs of available water but would be expensive to replace and slow to grow to mature size.

It has been suggested that grounds managers should mow less often and allow turf areas to achieve a more natural appearance to conserve water. If this is not done, one other solution may also be considered. This would be to mow turf areas much more frequently and mow at a much lower level to the ground. In this way, the lawn area would require much less water and would, in effect, be in a near stress condition. This may take more manpower, equipment and energy, but it would maintain the lawn or turf area during the limited periods of drought.

Another approach to altered cultivation practices would be to encourage the naturalization and a less manicured appearance of any outdoor area. If an area is not mowed, trimmed or fertilized, some plants may be lost, but other plants may become predominant, in an area. The entire landscape area might, over a period of time, require less water. In a public landscape area, however, this would take very careful education of the public or the users so that it does not appear that the area is no longer being maintained at all.

Robert E. Danielson and Charles M. Feldhake, in their Completion Report No. 106 entitled, "Urban Lawn Irrigation and Management Practices for Water Saving with Minimum Effect on Lawn Quality," made some statements concerning cultivation practices of turf during drought conditions:

> Grass maintained at a 5 cm mowing height used about 15% more water than grass at 2 cm when irrigation was provided for maximum use. However, the taller grass remained at high quality longer than the short grass when irrigation was limited.

> Grass receiving adequate nitrogen fertilizer used 10% more water than nitrogen deficient grass. This was likely a result of the difference in rate of leaf elongation after mowing. Adequately fertilized grass had a minimal reduction in visual quality when irrigation was decreased to 70% of maximum evapotranspiration but quality decreased rapidly with further decrease in irrigation. Grass with a nitrogen deficiency showed a linear decrease in quality beginning at irrigation equal to 90% of maximum evapotranspiration.

---

* Harris, Richard (Editor), **Saving Water in Landscape Irrigation,** Leaflet 2976, Division of Agricultural Sciences, University of California, Davis, California, April, 1977, p. 7.

Bermudagrass used about 20% less water than bluegrass during the summer months. This may be due to differences in stomatal control or warm season compared to cool season grasses; but, is probably mainly due to differences in advective energy received due to canopy geometry. Warm season grasses like bermudagrass are only green during the frost free period of each summer while bluegrass greens up much earlier in the spring and continues to grow a couple of months after the first frost in the fall. During 1979 the bermudagrass had a quality rating of 1.5 by October 7 when the bluegrass was still rated at the maximum of 10.

Grass grown in clay soil used slightly less water than grass grown in the sand-peat mix. This was probably due to slower growth after mowing so that the time average height of the clay grown grass was lower. In general, clay is unsatisfactory for growing turfgrass because root growth is restricted and frequent irrigation is necessary to maintain high quality. Thus drought tolerance is reduced. The infiltration rate of clay is low, especially if compacted, and urban irrigators may lose a large percent of their water to runoff. A non-compacted sandy loam soil is best for developing and maintaining a healthy, vigorous lawn.

Decreasing irrigation below maximum usable levels increases surface temperature. For every 10% decrease in evapotranspiration the surface temperature increased as much as 3°F.

In the solar radiation studies lysimeters were placed under shade cloth to compare radiation levels of 100, 73, 54, 33% of maximum possible solar radiation. All treatments were irrigated to provide for maximum ET within each environment. The following results were obtained.

Water use increased linearly with increase in incident radiation.

Advective energy from air movement was constant for all treatments and provided an ET component of about 2 mm/day for both summers. This was approximately 30% of maximum ET.

There is no indication that grass would adapt to the shade environments in any way that would affect water use in relation to energy available for evaporation.

Trees and shrubs are in a position to use more water than when grass only covers the same area. A water conserving landscape should have a minimum of woody plants and those should be species adapted to dry areas. Woody plants need some irrigation to survive drought even though some grasses may not.

In drawing conclusions from the results of this study it is helpful to put into perspective why we irrigate in urban areas. The region along the Front Range of Colorado contains cities where most of the state's population lives. Ecologically this area developed as a short grass prairie. There are few naturally occuring bushes and trees except along streams because precipitation is insufficient to ensure their survival.

A town built on the natural short grass prairie with vegetative areas given no supplemental irrigation would soon be lacking even grasses as a result of foot traffic incurred by outdoor activities. Therefore grasses have been planted that grow more vigorously than native and are irrigated to maintain a good ground cover. With the increased irrigation, trees and shrubs are able to survive and add to the appearance of residential areas. Lush vegetation provides a low dust environment and pleasing appearance. The evaporation of water from leaf surfaces contributes considerable cooling and makes the urban environment more pleasant during the summer. *

Dr. Victor A. Gibeault in his article on "Preparing Turf to Survive a Drought," suggests reviewing management practices.

Review Management Practices

Mowing, fertilization, irrigation, vertical mowing and coring are the five primary management practices regularly used in turf management. During dry periods, these practices should be evaluated and adjusted in terms of maximizing turfgrass drought tolerance.

With respect to mowing height and frequency, the first consideration must be the requirements imposed by the use of the facility. Using a golf course for example, a putting green must be maintained in the 3/16 to 5/16-inch height range, a tee slightly higher, and a fairway from ½ to 1¼ inches depending on player preference and the grass species used. If it becomes necessary to prepare a turfgrass for drought tolerance, increase its cutting height to the highest allowable height within the use-mandated range. This will result in a deeper root system with an increased soil water extraction capability. Also, the higher cutting height will shade crowns and soil during periods of high temperature. It should be understood that research indicates the higher cut turf will use more

water by evapotranspiration. However, I believe that the deeper root system will result in a stronger plant with a greater water foraging potential and, therefore, greater drought tolerance.

Research has shown that water use increases as mowing frequency increases; therefore, it is best for drought tolerance to mow as infrequently as possible, again within the confines of facility use.

As for a drought tolerance nutritional program, a soil test will indicate needed addition or adjustments of phosphorous, potassium, pH, and salt load for optimum turfgrass growth. Such correction should be made immediately, before temperatures increase. Nitrogen fertilization should be eliminated whenever possible from the management program during late spring and through the summer, especially on cool-season turfgrasses. If it is determined that nitrogen must be applied because of play or use, then light, infrequent applications should be considered, because moderate or heavy nitrogen application during the spring and summer will reduce the depth and amount of rooting and will result in a higher water use because of stimulated topgrowth. Certainly, lush topgrowth is to be avoided if drought tolerance or water conservation is a consideration.

Thatch control and coring are important management practices in a dry year because both processes tend to increase irrigation efficiency. Thatch and compaction can reduce water entry into a soil profile, thereby resulting in wasted water from runoff or evaporation. Similarly, thatch and compaction restrict nutrient and air entry into the soil which reduces the rooting needed for maximum drought tolerance.

* Danielson, Robert E. and Charles M. Feldhake, **Urban Lawn Irrigation and Management Practices for Water Saving with Minimum Effect on Lawn Quality,** Colorado Water Resources Research Institute, Colorado State University, Fort Collins, Colorado, Completion Report 106, May 1981, pp. 43-45.

Irrigation is by far the most important management practice when preparing for drought; every effort should be made to increase watering efficiency. The following checklist can be helpful in this regard. While pursuing the points mentioned in this checklist, remember that the objective of irrigation is to replace water used by evapotranspiration of the turf as infrequently as possible.

Determine rooting depth. Since the objective of irrigation is to replace water in the soil profile to the depth of turfgrass roots, knowledge of root system depth is essential.

Determine soil water holding capacity. Soils differ in their ability to hold water for plant absorption. The following table indicates the amount of available water per unit depth.

AVAILABLE AND UNAVAILABLE WATER PER FOOT OF SOIL

| | INCHES PER FOOT | |
SOIL TEXTURE	AVAILABLE	UNAVAILABLE
Sand	0.4-1.0	0.2-0.8
Sandy Loam	0.9-1.3	0.9-1.4
Loam	1.3-2.0	1.4-2.0
Silt Loam	2.0-2.1	2.0-2.4
Clay Loam	1.8-2.1	2.4-2.7
Clay	1.8-1.9	2.7-2.9

Evapotranspiration (ET) rate. The rate of water used is largely governed by the climate. Of extreme importance are factors such as: radiant energy (ET increases as radiant energy increases), temperature (ET increases as temperature increases), humidity (as humidity increases, ET decreases) and wind (as wind increases, ET increases). Other factors such as rainfall, soil fertility, growing season, cutting height and frequency also influence water use.

The ET rate for turf in much of the western United States can be estimated on a daily basis at a location by multiplying evaporation loss from a Class A U.S. Weather Bureau Evaporation Pan by a factor of 0.8. This will give an approximate use amount for turf areas of low humidity.

Calculate irrigation amount and frequency. As an example, a cool-season grass with a 6-inch effective root system growing on a soil with 1½ inches of available water per foot of soil would have the following soil water reservoir:

$$H_2O \text{ available/ft (inches x} \\ \text{root depth (feet) =} \\ \text{soil water reservoir}$$

$$eg., 1.5 \text{ inches x } 0.5 \text{ feet =} \\ 0.75 \text{ inch available}$$

If the daily water use is 0.15 inch (March-May in Southern California), then

$$\frac{soil\ water\ reservoir}{water\ use} = \frac{irrigation}{frequency}$$

$$e.g., \frac{0.75\ inch\ available}{0.15\ inch/day} = \frac{5\ day\ water}{supply}$$

Of course, the amount of water to be resupplied would be equal to, or slightly greater than, the amount used in that unit time.

Tensiometers and other devices. In addition to the preceding mathematical method to determine irrigation needs, soil moisture measuring devices such as tensiometers or soil probes can be used. Tenisometers also are useful to identify dry or wet spots in a golf course landscape where special irrigation design and programming may be necessary.

Other points to consider to increase watering efficiency.

- Late night or early morning irrigation is most effective. At these times water loss by evaporation is minimal and distribution is usually good because of good water pressure and limited wind.
- Avoid runoff by matching water application rates to soil infiltration percolation rates. Cycle water application if necessary to ensure infiltration.
- Practice good weed control methods. If they are not controlled, the weeds, not the desired turf species, will use the water.
- Calibrate all parts of the irrigation system so water application amounts and distribution are known. A can test is useful in doing this.
- Shaded areas will use much less water than turf in open sun. Therefore, shaded areas will require less irrigation. Tensiometers can be used to determine water needs of shaded areas.*

In summary then, landscape maintenance is a cycle based on the annual or lifetime growth and decline of vegetation. At the same time maintenance is an interruption or arresting of this cycle. In order to grow most effectively plants need light, nutrients, a growing medium (soil) and water. Without human interference in the plant growth cycle, various types of plants grow, flower, fruit, die or rejuvenate themselves and replicate the cycle over and over again. Generally this natural cycle appears to be disorderly, unkempt and haphazard. Therefore, humans intervene in the cycle and "maintain" an area in a state of suspended animation.

All landscape maintenance is a "freezing in time" of the natural processes of growth and decay. We put extra fertilizer on a plant to make it grow faster then we cut or mow it back when it grows too fast or too large. When we do that it takes extra water to dissolve or break down the fertilizer to make it available to plant roots in the soil. Highly fertilized plants use more water. Therefore to reduce fertilization levels may help to reduce the need for water. The three principal ingredients in fertilizer are:

Nitrogen(N) - which promotes the growth of leaves and foliage,

Phosphorous(P) - which promotes the growth of roots,

Potash(K) - which promotes the flowering and fruiting of plants.

To put fertilizer high in nitrogen on plants will cause the foliage to grow if sufficient water is available. This will require additional maintenance and the use of even more water to sustain the added foliage. To apply a high phosphorous fertilizer may be more appropriate before an anticipated water shortage since new roots may be encouraged to reach out and down into the soil to seek additional water. Such high phosphorous fertilizer should be applied long before a drought and be adequetely "watered in" so as to dissolve the fertilizer and move it down into the soil close to the roots.

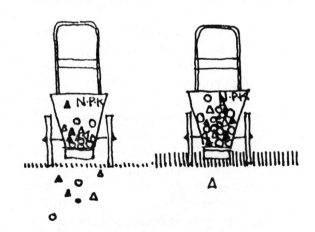

* Gibeault, Victor,"Preparing Turf to Survive a Drought", **California Turfgrass Culture**, Vol. 27, No. 2, Spring 1977, pp. 9-11.

Much fertilizer is wasted, as is a great deal of water, because the water and fertilizer is applied at the wrong time in the growing cycle of plants. Not all plants grow at the same time or have dormant periods at the same time. Certain varieties of turf, trees, shrubs or ground cover begin growing at one time, maintain that growth for a time, then become dormant. Water applied while the plants are dormant or nearly dormant is almost always totally wasted or underutilized.

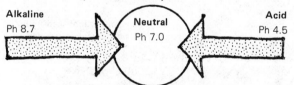

Fertilizer and water can be wasted if the soil chemistry is not correct. Therefore the soil *Ph* may need to be adjusted to use water most effectively during water shortages. In order to be used most fully and effectively fertilizer and water should be added to soil which has the appropriate chemistry and acidity or alkalinity.

| Alkaline Ph 8.7 | Neutral Ph 7.0 | Acid Ph 4.5 |

When turf is fertilized and watered, the grass grows and must be mowed. If less water and fertilizer is applied, the grass will not grow as much or as rapidly. Therefore mowing frequency needs to be reduced and the turf should be cut to a higher level so as not to dissipate the strength of the turf plant while water is witheld. Therefore the cultivation of turf during drought needs to be altered to mow higher and less often.

Therefore, to use less water, you need to fertilize less, use the right fertilizer and to use it at the right time in the growing cycle.

At the same time turf should be aerated and the thatch should be removed more often to allow for maximum penetration of the available water into the soil and to the plant roots.

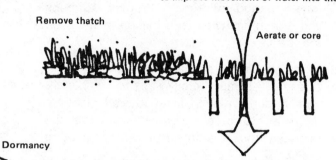

In order to relieve the strain on plants produced during water shortages, the trees and shrubs should be thinned and pruned more heavily than normal. The plants should not be scalped or pollarded, but the top mass of the trees or shrubs should be reduced to lessen the stress on the roots and the rest of the plant.

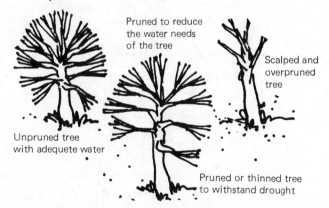

The application of water is much more important before and during the growing period of plants than it is when the plants are dormant.

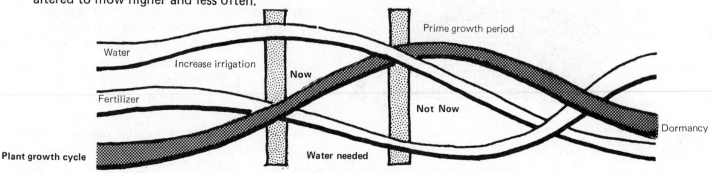

If there is less water available in the soil, roots can only take in a limited amount to support twigs, limbs, and leaves on the top which manufacture chlorophyll and distribute nutrients within the plant. If the leaves, branches and twigs are reduced the roots have less to feed and support the plant and therefore the plant may be able to survive a drought condition for a longer period of time. Pruning, thinning and trimming helps to bring the plant back into balance.

In some cases, as mentioned elsewhere in this book, it may be advisable to completely remove some plants, in an overall planting, in order to save water and preserve the rest and thus the integrity of the planting design.

Mulch is an important means of reducing water loss and it may have to be applied more extensively and deeply when water is short.

Weeds pull a great deal of water out of the soil and compete with desired landscape plants. Therefore weeding may need to be done more carefully and more often when water is short or scarce. Every gallon of water used by a weed is one which is not available to a landscape plant or one that must be replaced in the soil.

Weeds which are pulled do not take moisture from the landscape plants

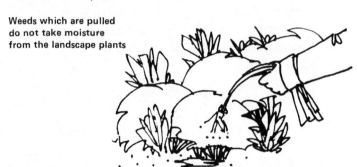

Irrigation systems can malfunction and when they do they may waste a good deal of water or they fail to water certain areas. During times when water is short, special care needs to be paid to making certain that all parts of an irrigation system are functioning properly.

Malfunctioning sprinkler head may waste water

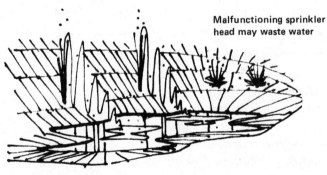

Altering cultivation practices may help to save a great deal of water if it is done sensitively and carefully. Special maintenance guidelines may need to be developed. Additional training for maintenance personnel may have to be initiated during water emergencies. No single list of guidelines can suggest all of the the potential changes or alterations in cultivation practices which could ultimately save water. It is a viable strategy, however, and will help to save a good deal of water and a large number of plants when sufficient water is not available.

Mowing higher may save water during droughts

strategy

SOIL MODIFICATION

An ideal soil for conserving water or using water most efficiently would be one with a high percentage of organic matter and which is a deep friable loam.

Obviously, one of the best ways to use moisture or water most effectively would be to have all landscape planting done originally in an optimum soil. An ideal soil for conserving water or using water most efficiently would be one with a high percentage of organic matter and which was a deep friable loam. However, it is very expensive and difficult to create this type of soil in all landscape situations if it does not exist. Many times plants have been originally placed in a very small hole in the ground which contains fairly adequately prepared soil As the plant grows, however, the roots move into the surrounding soil material which may be sandy or may be hard and compacted. In such situations excessive water is used to keep the plant alive and to help it to grow. A soil which is too sandy will not hold water but will allow it to pass through the root zone where it is most usable to growing landscape plants. A soil which is too compacted will not allow the water to penetrate to the root level of the plants. Water which is applied to a heavily compacted soil may run off the soil surface and be wasted or lost as far as specific plants are concerned. Obviously, some soils are much more effective growing media than are others.

In a section entitled, "What is Good Soil" in the book *ALL ABOUT FERTILIZERS, SOILS & WATER*, the following statement has been made.

It's easy to talk at great length about soil in general without ever defining the specific qualities of a "good" soil. In fact, the properties of problem soils are probably better known than the properties of good soils, because unfortunately, more people have poor soils than good ones.

But if you look at soil improvement as an ongoing, long-term program, it's a good idea to know what the ultimate goal is, so that each step is a step in the right direction. Obviously, there are different optimums of soils for different groups of plants, but it's surprising how many plants are content to grow in a range of soils with the same basic qualities: a "good" soil.

Qualities of a good soil are closely related to the functions of soil in general: (1) Soil serves as anchorage for the plant: the roots must be able to penetrate far enough into the soil to anchor the plant securely. (2) The structure of the soil must be such that the roots can readily develop, assuring the plant its full quota of water and minerals. The structure of the soil is related to water percolation and retention characteristics—whether water can move into the soil and whether the soil holds too much, too little or just the right amount—so structure is doubly important. (3) The fertility of the soil: the nutrients necessary for plant growth that are not naturally available in the soil must be added in their proper amounts. *

---

* **All About Fertilizers, Soils and Water,** Ortho Books, San Francisco, California, 1979, p. 18.

In short, some main points to consider are depth of the soil, its structure and its fertility.*

That same publication, in discussing "Getting and Keeping Good Soil," made the following statement.

Any discussion of the characteristics of good soil ultimately gets into the subject of organic matter, because *the addition of organic matter is probably the single most important method of improving soils*. Soil particles are held together in aggregates mainly by a by-product of soil microorganisms that use organic matter as their food.

Adding organic matter to your soil as an amendment or conditioner that you incorporate into the soil—or as a mulch that you spread over the top of the soil—is what the gardener can do to help keep the structure of a good soil good.**

That same publication outlines the basic type of soil particles ranging from clay to silt to fine sand to medium sand to coarse sand. That same publication states the following concerning "How Does Your Soil Rate in 'Good Drainage'?"

The ideal soil is one that holds moisture and at the same time allows a constant flow of air through the soil —bringing oxygen to the roots and removing carbon dioxide from the soil. The ideal soil is a combination of the good points of sand and of clay. Sand provides fast drainge and good aeration, but fails in the water-holding department. Clay is tops in water-holding ability, but dangerously low in supplying air to the soil.

Packed soil may have individual, non-aggregated particles packed into a solid mass with no space for air or water. Crumbly soil may respond to cultivation and the addition of organic matter to help aggregate the particles into porous crumbs or granules. When water fills all the spaces in the soil, air is forced out and plants may drown. In well drained soil there is a film of water and air in each space within soil.***

In order to modify the soil most effectively to help plants withstand drought conditions it is advisable where possible to create an ideal water-retaining soil to the depth necessary around each plant. The addition of more organic material is usually an answer to improving the soil moisture retention and release. Organic material will help in both heavy clay and in light, porous, sandy conditions. In order to modify the soil to assist in plant growth during drought conditions, it is advisable to use soil with a better mixture of sand, clay, loam and humus material when plants are initially installed. Also the planting hole or opening should be large enough and be backfilled with a good growing media. In this way the plant will be able to establish roots in this material in the shortest period of time with the least amount of water. In some cases where plants in a drought or stress condition are in extremely poor soil, it may be advisable during water shortages to replant individual plants in better soil to improve the water holding potential in the soil around the plant. In order to modify the soil to make it more effective in using limited amounts of water it is wise to add humus and to work in organic materials in the areas around the plants. This may be done either area by area within a large landscape, or it may be possible to rennovate sections of a large area from year to year. Generally, if the soil is modified, it is able to provide better water storage and better water movement and thus more efficiently use the available water.

---

* "What is Good Soil", **All About Fertilizers, Soils and Water,** Ortho Books, Chevron Chemical Company, 575 Market Street, San Francisco, California 94105, 1979, p. 18-19.
** Ibid., p. 19.

*** Ibid., p. 15.

Good, well drained and water retentive soil is one of the best ways to preserve landscape plants during times of water shortages.

To improve existing soil or to replace problem soil is a very effective long term strategy for conserving water through landscape design and management. The most appropriate soil for the geographic region and the plants utilized in an area should always be used initially since that is often the most cost effective over time no matter what the initial cost. In cases where the soil is not the best, corrective action may be justified to save existing water. Both the designers and the grounds managers need to know the soil in a given area and they need to know how to correct it to use water most effectively and efficiently, either through the addition of sand or organic matter or through the modification of soil chemistry. Compacted soil wastes water, causing it to run off and not be used by plants. Soil that is too loose causes water to be wasted because it is not retained for use of the plants.

Soil that is too tight

Soil that is too loose

Soil that is too wet

A correct mixture of soil, moisture and air

Soil particle size and the amount of space between particles determines both the water holding capacity and percolation rate of soils.

Topsoil depth needed for good roots

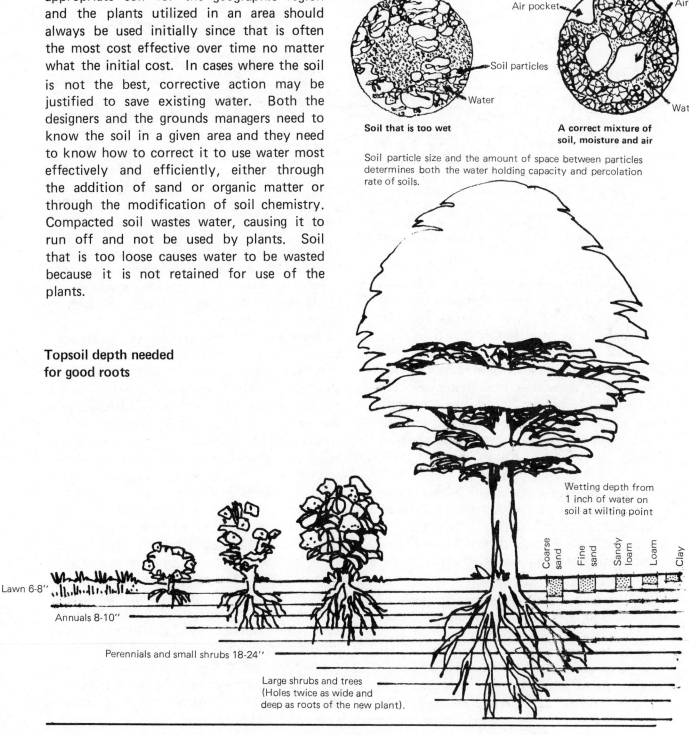

Wetting depth from 1 inch of water on soil at wilting point

Lawn 6-8"

Annuals 8-10"

Perennials and small shrubs 18-24"

Large shrubs and trees (Holes twice as wide and deep as roots of the new plant).

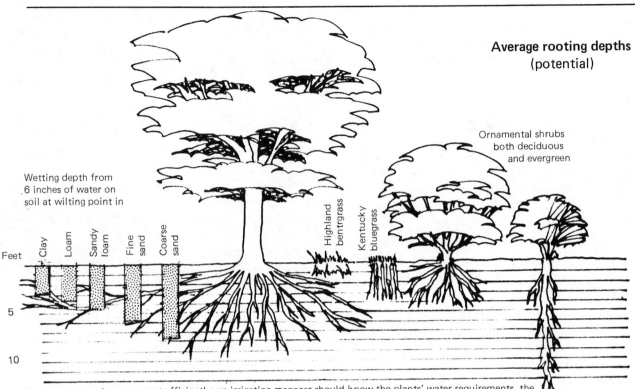

Average rooting depths
(potential)

Ornamental shrubs
both deciduous
and evergreen

Wetting depth from
6 inches of water on
soil at wilting point in

Clay
Loam
Sandy loam
Fine sand
Coarse sand

Highland bentgrass
Kentucky bluegrass

Feet

5

10

To use water and energy most efficiently, an irrigation manager should know the plants' water requirements, the water absorption capabilities of various soils, the optimum timing for irrigation and the background information necessary to make the best selection of irrigation techniques.

Generally the roots of turfgrasses will grow approximately 6-8″ deep. Annuals may have roots from 8-10″ into the soil, whereas perennials and small shrubs may have roots growing down to 18-24″ below the ground level. Large shrubs may have roots 4-5′ deep and major trees may have extremely deep roots of 5, 10 or even 20 feet deep. Obviously the soil at each of those depths should be of an appropriate quality and character to allow water penetration down to the root level. It is obviously not possible to modify soils to any extent at the depth where major tree roots grow, but it certainly is possible to modify soil at the depths at which the roots of turf, annuals, perennials, and small and medium sized shrubs would grow.

It is not possible to alter, amend or change all of the soil in a landscape to make it more ideal for water use and retention. In areas where water shortages have occurred or are likely to occur, greater care than usual should be taken to insure that the best and most water retentive soil mixture be used in in-itial landscape planting. Special care should be taken in containers or plant boxes where plants would suffer most in a drought or would require extra water or attention with-adequate rainfall.

In some cases it may be advisable to dig up plants and replace them in better soil so that they will be prepared to withstand water shortages. This is expensive and time-con-suming, but it may be a good insurance in the long run. This especially true with small shrubs, ground covers, annuals, bulbs and even turf in some cases. Larger shrubs, small trees, vines, perennials and specimen plants represent a more expensive problem to place in a better soil. It can be done but may not warrant the cost or the time. In any case, not all of the soil in a landscape needs to be modified or re-placed. Only that soil in the root zone of the specific plants is most critical for water retention or movement. Obviously the soil layer immediately beneath the root zone can also effect water movement, if it forms a hard pan or if it is too porous, but the prime soil which can and should be control-led is immediately around the plant roots.

The best possible soil to hold the water most effectively for the optimum period of time and with the correct porosity should be used initially in installing any landscape plant. If such soil is not used initially, it may be necessary to dig up a planting or an individual plant and replace the soil around it with more appropriate and effective soil to withstand water shortages and drought conditions. This may be expensive and time consuming, and will only be possible with relatively small plants or plantings, but it is a fully possible and feasible strategy to protect landscape plants during times when water is short or not available at all.

When water is placed on the soil either naturally or mechanically, the water moves down through the soil by wetting one soil particle after another as it moves down through the growing medium. The holding capacity of any soil will determine how much water is retained by each particle and how rapidly the water moves down into the soil.

Until the particles above are thoroughly wetter the water will not move down to wet lower particles. Obviously different types of soil will have different holding capacity and the water will move down through the soil at different rates and to different levels depending upon how much water is applied.

Practical Interpretation Chart for Soil Moisture

Amount of readily available moisture remaining for plants	Sand	Sandy loam	Clay loam	Clay
	(gritty when moist, almost like beach sand)	(gritty when moist; dirties fingers; contains some silt and clay)	(sticky and plastic when moist)	(very sticky when moist; behaves like modeling clay)
Feel or appearance of soils				
Close to 0%. Little or no moisture available.	Dry, loose, single-grained, flows through fingers.	Dry, loose, flows through fingers.	Dry clods that break down into powdery condition.	Hard, baked, cracked surface. Hard clods difficult to break, sometimes has loose crumbs on surface.
50% or less. Approaching time to irrigate.	Still appears to be dry; will not form a ball with pressure.	Still appears to be dry; will not form a ball.	Somewhat crumbly, but will hold together with pressure.	Somewhat pliable, will ball under pressure.
50% to 75%. Enough available moisture.	Same as sand under 50%.	Tends to ball under pressure but seldom will hold together.	Forms a ball, somewhat plastic; will sometimes stick slightly with pressure.	Forms a ball; will ribbon out between thumb and forefinger.
75% to field capacity. Plenty of available moisture.	Tends to stick together slightly, sometimes forms a very weak ball under pressure.	Forms weak ball, breaks easily, will not become slick.	Forms a ball and is very pliable; becomes slick readily if high in clay.	Easily ribbons out between fingers; feels slick.
At field capacity. Soil won't hold any more water (after draining).	Upon squeezing, no free water appears but moisture is left on hand.	Same as sand.	Same as sand.	Same as sand.
Above field capacity. Unless water drains out, soil will be waterlogged.	Free water appears when soil is bounced in hand.	Free water will be released with kneading.	Can squeeze out free water.	Puddles and free water forms on surface.

Soil that is too loose and light may be made more able to hold water by mixing it with heavier clay or loam in addition to organic materials. On the other hand, soil that is too tight and compacted may be modified to make it more open by mixing it with sand or lighter material in addition to some organic material. All soil is made up of a mixture of mineral and organic materials. The organic materials break down but are able to be replenished by plant material parts which are incorporated into the soil either naturally or mechanically. The mineral material is the base and determines to a great extent, the texture and the permeability of the soil. To modify this basic soil mixture, organic material needs to be integrated, replaced and periodically incorporated into the mineral base to increase the water holding capacity of the soil and to allow available water to move through the soil to the roots of landscape plants.

The size of the individual soil particles determines the water holding capacity of soil. Clay soil may be made up of individual particles of less than 1/12,500 inch in size, silt particles may range up to 1/500 inch, fine sand to 1/250 inch, medium sand to 1/50 inch and the largest sand particles may be as much as 1/12 inch.

In order to modify existing soil around specific plants or in a small scale landscape setting to help plants withstand drought it may be necessary to add amendments to the soil.

Organic soil amendments, such as peat moss, leaf mulch, well rotted manure, straw, lawn clippings, sawdust or wood chips help to "fluff up" tight soil and open up spaces in fine textured clay or silt soils. They may also bind sandy or large particled soil. Mineral soil amendments such as gravel, vermiculite, perlite, coarse or sharp sand help to introduce larger particles into tight, small particled soil, thus increasing their permeability to water. Mineral amendments do not increase the water holding capacity of the soil in the same way as organic amendments, but they often do not disintegrate and become integrated into the soil as quickly or as readily.

In compacted soil the individual particles are pressed tightly together so that little or no space is allowed for air or water to move or be stored. In saturated soil the water does not drain and plants may not receive enough oxygen and drown or become waterlogged. In crumbly soil the disintegrating organic material helps combine with the mineral particles adding textural variation and nutrients to the soil. In moist soil a thin film of water is formed around each soil particle thus insuring adequate water to the individual plant roots as they grow and move through the soil particles.

Soil should be amended or modified as necessary to allow for the retention and movement of water and air to the roots of the landscape plants during times of water shortages or drought. This may be through loosening tight soil or binding loose soil and providing the optimum mixture of organic, mineral, air and water film.

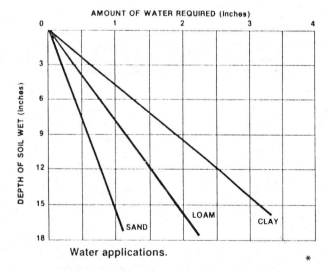

Water applications.

*

* **Saving Water in Landscape Irrigation,** Division of Agricultural Sciences, University of California, Davis, California, Leaflet 2976, April 1977, p. 4.

142

An article entitled "Preparing for a Drought: Water-conserving Turf Maintenance Practices," in the March 1981 issue of *GROUNDS MAINTENANCE* Magazine contained a section on amendments to enhance water retention.

Amendments are commonly used to improve compaction, but they are equally important as materials to enhance aeration, and nutrient and water retention. Such amendments should be evaluated on their ability to improve soil texture and structure, their long-term stability, availability, quantity required and cost.

Peat humus, reed-sedge peat and hypnum peat are common organic materials for soil modification. The organic content should be above 90 percent and the material should be relatively fine to allow uniform mixing.

Other organic amendments are manures, processed or unprocessed sewage sludge, sawdust, hulls, bark, leaves, green manures, and various byproducts of animal and vegetable processing. Their disadvantage is that large quantities of undecomposed material are necessary to provide a sufficient amount of residual matter, and most should be composted in advance of large amounts being incorporated into soil. *

One of the longest term and most effective ways in which a landscape area may be modified to make it more drought resistant is to modify the basic soil in which the plants of all types are growing. Obviously it is not possible to modify or change significantly the soil in which large established major trees are growing. However, turf, ground covers, and even relatively small shrubs may be "drought proofed," at least to some extent, by improving the quality of soil in which they are growing.

In an article by Dr. James Beard in the June 1981 issue of *GROUNDS MAINTENANCE* Magazine, a number of factors affecting evapotranspiration were outlined. These included soil, plant shoot and atmospheric factors.

FACTORS AFFECTING TRANSPIRATION

Transpiration →

SOIL	PLANT SHOOTS	ATMOSPHERE
Soil water content	Internal water content	Light intensity
Soil water retention capacity	Stomatal density	Temperature
Salinity	Vascular system translocation rate	Relative humidity
Root —depth —extension rate —number		Wind

That same article emphasized the depth of water penetration in various types of soil.

How Deep the Water Penetrates
In dry soil, 1 inch of water will penetrate as follows:

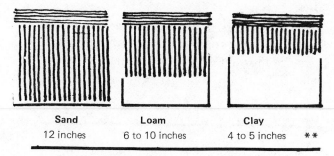

Sand	Loam	Clay
12 inches	6 to 10 inches	4 to 5 inches **

TYPE OF PEAT	WATER ABSORBING CAPACITY,%	DESIRABILITY FOR SOIL MODIFICATION
Peat humus	150 — 500	Excellent
Reed-sedge peat, high pH	400 — 1,200	Good
Reed-sedge peat, low pH	500 — 1,200	Good
Hypnum peat	1,200 — 1,800	Good

* Beard, James, "Preparing for a Drought: Water-conserving Turf Maintenance Practices", **Grounds Maintenance**, March 1981, Vol. 16, No. 3, p. 24.

** Beard, James, "Water Use Rates and Turf Breeding Programs, **Grounds Maintenance**, June 1981, Vol. 16, No. 6, p. 84.

In an article in the September 1980 issue of *WEEDS, TREES AND TURF* Magazine dealing with the turf grass environment, water relating to the plants is divided horizontally into the water which is available in the atmosphere or above the plant and that water which is available to the plant in the soil. Above the plant is atmospheric water. Precipitation falls on the soil around the plant, it then infiltrates into the soil and becomes soil moisture. As it moves down through the soil it percolates and becomes ground water. That same article indicates that:

> The texture and structure of a soil has a great effect on drainage, movement of chemicals in the soil, upward movement of water (capillary action), rooting ability, and presence of needed gases in the soil. Loam soil is actually a combination of sand, silt and clay.*

That article then goes on to discuss the layers or horizons of the soil:

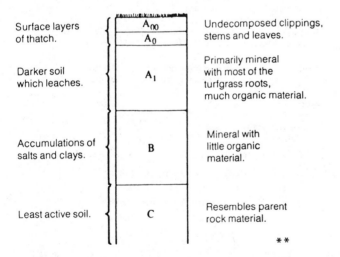

Then it discusses and illustrates how the depth of the topsoil affects retention of water following irrigation or natural rainfall.

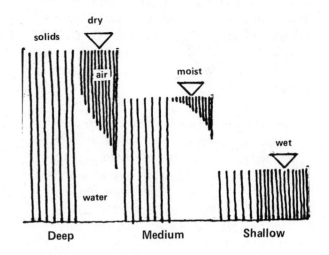

The same article also states that:

> The composition of the soil affects water accumulation and drainage. Sand soils do a poor job of holding water. However, they have the advantage of aiding drainage when added to other soils. Clay soils hold water but this water may not be available to the plant roots. Silt soils retain water well but also tend to compact easily. The pore space between soil particles determines the ability of the soil to hold and pass water. The organic matter content of the soil also aids in water retention. The ability of the soil to let water in is called infiltration. If soils are compacted, pore space is limited and water will not flow into the soil easily. Water can be treated with wetting agents to reduce its surface tension and allow for easier entry.

> The ability of the soil to allow water to pass through is called percolation. If soil layers are significantly different in texture, water movement downward can be hindered. If surface water is applied faster than the soil can take it in or let it flow through, puddling or runoff will occur. ***

---

* ''The Turfgrass Environment'', **Weeds, Trees and Turf**, Cleveland, Ohio 44102, p. 18 and 20.

** Ibid., p. 18.

*** Ibid., p. 18.

This article indicated that in dry soil 1″ of water will penetrate 12″ of sand, 6-10″ of loam, and 4-5″ of clay. In the same way soil water holding capacity varies:

SOIL WATER-HOLDING CAPACITY
The capacity of 100 square feet
of soil 1 foot deep is:

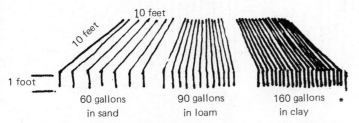

That same article made the following statement:

Water loss from turf areas in regions of mild summer averages approximately 1″ per week. Two or more inches per week will be lost in hotter regions. The frequency with which this water must be replaced depends on the soil capacity to retain water and the depth to which it will penetrate, all other factors being equal.**

It is also important to know the relationship between the types of soils and the average rate of absorption. The water needed to penetrate 1 foot of soil and the average time between waterings under average summer conditions is shown on the chart below.

Generally soil modification which assists in causing the roots to grow deeper will cause any type of landscape plan to be more drought resistant. The larger trees and shrubs quite often are able to find ground water moisture at extreme depths in even the most severe droughts. The grounds manager or homeowner should try to make certain that roots are not confined in shallow subsoil, but have proper soil deep enough for optimum root development for the individual species or type of plant. At the same time watering practices should encourage deep root growth. Frequently light sprinklings or shallow watering will encourage shallow root growth, while on the other hand less often or occasional deep watering practices will encourage deeper root growth.

The various facets of the following chart are illustrated graphically on the next page.

Type Soil	Average Rate of Absorption	Water Needed to Penetrate 1 foot	Under Average Summer Conditions Water
Light Sandy	1½″-2″ per hr.	¾″ water	every 5 days
Average Loam	½″-¾″ per hr.	1½″ water	every 10 days
Heavy Clay	¼″-½″ per hr.	2½″ water	every 17 - 18 days

*Ibid., p. 19.
**Ibid.,p 20.

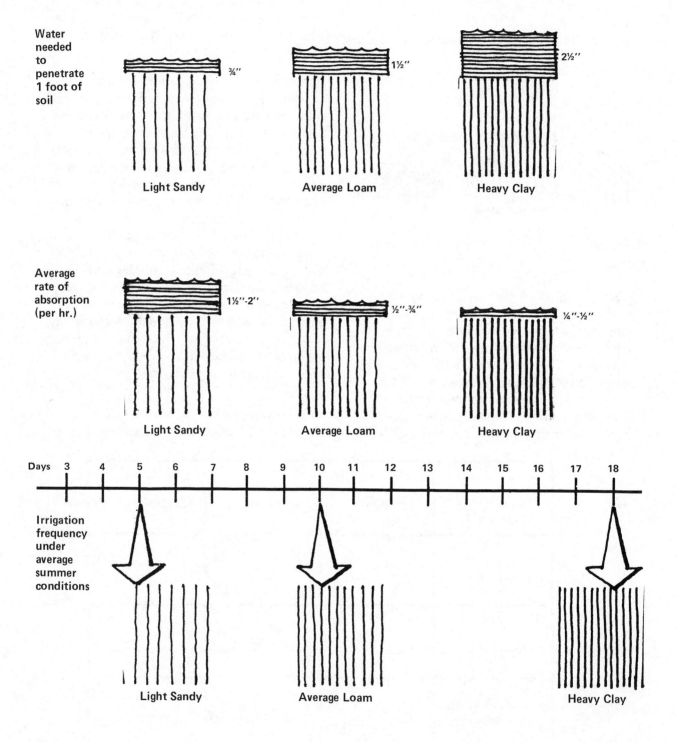

Water needed to penetrate 1 foot of soil

¾″

1½″

2½″

Light Sandy

Average Loam

Heavy Clay

Average rate of absorption (per hr.)

1½″-2″

½″-¾″

¼″-½″

Light Sandy

Average Loam

Heavy Clay

Days 3   4   5   6   7   8   9   10   11   12   13   14   15   16   17   18

Irrigation frequency under average summer conditions

Light Sandy

Average Loam

Heavy Clay

strategy

EXPAND THE USE OF MULCH

... mulches (are) effective in helping to conserve existing water supplies ... and to use more efficiently that (which) falls around the plants or is placed there...

The concept of using mulches to help conserve water is very simple yet it has a great number of permutations and possibilities. The concept is that if a blanket of organic, inorganic or man-made material is placed to varying depths over the soil and around the roots of the plant or planting, the heat in the soil will be reduced, weeds will be controlled and the soil around the plant will be much less compacted. Mulches *do* help to retain the water which is in the soil and keep it from evaporating or transpiring back into the atmosphere. Therefore, mulches have proven, in many instances, to be very effective in helping to conserve existing water supplies already in the ground and to use more efficiently that water which either falls naturally around the plants or is placed there through various irrigation devices.

Mulches may reduce the heat of the soil by insulating the plant roots, they may control erosion of the soil around the base of plants, they hold moisture in the soil by controlling evaporation and transpiration, they assist in improving the quality of the soil by providing amendments of organic materials in the upper layers of the soil. Mulches may also help to conserve water by controlling weed growth which competes with landscape plants and finally mulches reduce the compaction of soil and thus improve the permeability, allowing water to move into the soil.

Mulches may be basically of three types—these are organic mulches, inorganic mulches or man-made mulches. Organic mulches are generally those materials which have been derived from growing plants or vegetative materials. Examples of organic mulches would be wood chips, bark mulch, straw, peat moss, lawn clippings, and pine needles. Inorganic mulches generally are those natural materials derived from a non-plant base. This would include rocks, gravel, aggregate, decomposed granite, pebbles, brick chips or other sorts of mineral based mulching material including sand. Man-made mulching material would include plastic, paper or composition asphalt paper products. The plastic may be clear or black; the paper products may be brown paper mulch or it might be an aluminum coated plastic or foil.

The Office of Appropriate Technology in the Department of Water Resources in the State of California, has produced a small pamphlet entitled, "Compost and Mulch." In that publication they outline some of the basic principles of the use of mulch and also give a short synopsis of the relative availability, advantages and disadvantages of various types of mulch.

Mulch

Mulch is usually applied to the top surface of the soil and can be of organic matter in a decomposed or non-decomposed state, it can be an inert material such as plastic, or it can be a living plant covering the soil.

The best mulches are those that are inexpensive and readily available, preferably from your own garden or neighborhood.

When choosing a type of mulch, consider its aesthetic as well as functional qualities. A coarse, large-particled mulch will be overwhelming in a flower garden, though quite useful in the orchard.

There are only a few materials to avoid as mulch: diseased plants, vigorous weeds such as bermuda grass, or material with toxic substances.

Nitrogen, an essential element for plant growth, is also used by soil bacteria in decomposing organic matter. Small-particled or quickly decomposing mulch may create a nitrogen deficit. Watch for signs of yellowing mature leaves. A top dressing of fertilizer can solve this problem.

Listed below are suggested materials to be used as mulch, along with their qualities.

Straw—from barns or an animal supply store; inexpensive; good for large areas; coarse texture.
Woodchips—from tree prunings or a nursery supply; inexpensive from municipal prunings; attractive near shrubs; redwood is stable but expensive.
Seaweed—in coastal regions; excellent fertilizer; unattractive in ornamental beds.
Peat moss—from nursery supply; expensive; attractive; fine texture and color.
Pine needles—good for acid-loving plants.
Lawn clippings—readily available; lightly layer to prevent matting.
Compost—homemade or from nursery supply; attractive; inexpensive; good soil conditioner.

Rice hulls—from rice mills; inexpensive; unstable—add nitrogen.
Farm refuse—locally available—try nut orchards; use caution, look for disease or pesticides.
Rock and gravel—from quarries or aggregate supply; attractive; stable; permanent, not decomposable.
Black plastic—expensive; unsightly when exposed; effective weed control; soil heat buildup; disposal problem.
Decomposed granite—from aggregate supply; stable; attractive.
Dry leaves—available in gardens, parks; attractive; can tend to mat.
Manure—from barns, nurseries; contains nitrogen, soil conditioner; can burn plants if too "green."
Sawdust—from lumberyards, saw mills; attractive; fine texture; good soil conditioner.
Green manure plants, i.e., alfalfa, clover, birdsfoot trefoil, fava beans—nitrogen-fixing ground covers for orchards, crop rotation, or soil reclamation.*

In a discussion of strategies or techniques for water conservation in landscape design and development there are primary and secondary uses of mulch. In the present discussion the primary purpose of mulches is to prevent evaporation and to reduce soil temperature. By doing that it is possible to hold a greater amount of moisture around the base of the individual plant. The secondary purpose in this particular discussion has to do with soil improvement, control of weeds, reduction of maintenance and alleviating wind erosion from the top layer of the soil.

Generally organic ground cover or mulching materials help significantly in the granulation of the soil. Over a period of time the mulching material placed on top of the ground surface is worked into the lower levels of soil as a

* **Compost and Mulch**, edited by Mary Lou Van Deventer, Designed by Donna Rivers, printed by the Office of Appropriate Technology and the Department of Water Resources, for a Growing Concern and Community Interaction Program, 1401 21st Street, Suite 400, Sacramento, California 95814, p. 2.

soil amendment. This significantly improves the porosity and water holding capability of the soil.

Mulch, placed on top of the soil and later incorporated into the soil as an amendment helps prevent soil crusting. This is a problem in some of the drier areas of the country. When heavy clay soil dries out it forms a sort of crust over the soil which prevents easy passage of air and water into the soil around the base of the plant. Mulching is able to reduce that crusting as the top level of soil dries out around the plant.

The book, *GARDEN SHORTCUTS*, gives a chart which deals with the pluses and minuses of mulch as it relates to soil temperature. It does not, however, deal to a great degree, with the relative ability of mulches to preserve moisture within the soil.

During periods of drought, dust is formed and is blown around during windy periods. By using or placing mulching material around the base of the plant this blowing dust is prevented. This helps to hold the topsoil around the base of the plant. Mulching and its improvement of the soil helps minimize both water and wind erosion. As the individual water droplets reach the ground their fall is buffered by the mulching material and the water is able to percolate down into the soil in a more easy and less destructive manner, thus preventing soil erosion.

One of the suggestions which has been made in regard to the alteration of cultivation practices to conserve water is, to the extent possible, control the growth of weeds in any planting area. The weeds pull moisture out of the soil and rob the landscape plants which need that moisture. One of the other functions of mulches is that they help to keep down or prevent the growth of unwanted weeds in planting areas. This is especially true in ground cover beds and in shrub beds. The sprouting of many of the small weed seeds is limited because it is not possible for the sun to reach the weed seedlings through the mulching material.

A combination of mulching materials may be more effective than any single type. Plastic mulch to control weeds and decorative mulch for appearance may be better than either in isolation.

Because of all of the above factors it may be seen that the use of mulch significantly reduces maintenance requirements. A permanent or long lasting

The pluses & minuses of mulches

Mulch	Change in soil temperature	Performance
CLEAR PLASTIC	+10	Short rays of sun penetrate clear plastic and warm soil; plastic traps evaporating water. Increases early growth in cool season, also stimulates weed growth beneath plastic.
BLACK PLASTIC	+6	Short rays heat black plastic which in turn warm soil. Solves weed problem. Increases crop yields of many crops. Protects fruit of vine crops from rot. See text.
BROWN PAPER MULCH	as much as –8	Light brown paper mulch with thin plastic coating reflects most of the short rays from the sun. It's biodegradable. Soil temperatures are as much as 8° cooler than first inches of exposed soil. No weeds.
ALUMINUM COATED PLASTIC & FOIL	as much as –10	Reflective surface bounces back short rays from the sun. Soil temperatures are as much as 10° cooler than top inches of exposed soil. Research findings show that reflective surfaces repell aphids.
ORGANIC MULCHES	as much as –10	Thick mulch of organic matter stops sun's rays before they hit the soil. Soil surface layer as much as 10 degrees cooler than exposed soil. Stops most annual weeds if applied thick enough. Needs yearly additions. *

* **Garden Shortcuts**, Editorial Staff of Ortho Books, Chevron Chemical Company, San Francisco, California, 1977, p. 22.

mulching material may be used around shrub beds where it would not have to be replaced every year. On the other hand organic mulching material which would help to improve the soil, might be worked into the top layer of the soil each year in an area which would contain annuals, bulbs or seasonal flowers. A word of caution, however, is in order in using mulches, especially organic mulches. These may deplete nutrients from the soil. Quite often, if fresh sawdust is placed on the soil before any decomposition has taken place, nitrogen may have to be added. Otherwise, as sawdust decomposes, it draws nitrogen out of the soil.

Some mulching materials such as dry peat moss, may become impermeable to water. When the top layer of the peat moss is dried out and used as a mulch it is very difficult for water to penetrate through it to the lower levels of the soil. In such cases it may be necessary to sprinkle very lightly this top layer of the peat moss to enable moisture to penetrate more easily through it.

At the present time no significant definitive, usable research data on the relative water retention capability of various type of mulches exists. Information is available as to heat retention capabilities of different mulching materials. However, in time to come it is anticipated that more and more research will be undertaken to show the relative capability and merits of different mulching materials on retaining moisture in the soil around plants. Mulching is one of the most effective and beneficial strategies for conserving water and for using water more efficiently in landscape, grounds or site situations.

Generally, the thickness of a mulch that needs to be placed around a plant relates to the type of mulch used. Obviously a plastic or paper mulch will be extremely thin though it may be covered by other materials or even by more soil to improve its unsightliness. An organic mulching material however, which is of a very light texture, may be placed more thinly on the soil than would be a coarse mulching material with larger particles. Generally 2-4'' of mulching material is recommended, however, in some instances a mulching material of 4-6'' may be appropriate. The mulch should be spread evenly over an area and the mulching thickness should be maintained throughout the year. Some materials such as straw or grass clippings may pack down onto the soil. In these instances the materials which were originally used whether they were wood chips, corn cobs or bark mulches, should be replenished as necessary throughout the year to maintain the original mulching thickness.

Some form of mulching is absolutely mandatory in any garden or landscape design to conserve the maximum amount of water no matter what else is done or whatever strategy is attempted. The soil around the base of the plant not covered by turf or some other form of ground cover, needs to be protected by some form of mulching material.

A mulch which is ideal for conserving water or which is most helpful in using water most efficiently is not necessarily a mulch which:
> looks the best
> is least expensive
> is most readily available
> adds to the quality of the soil
> reduces heat alone
> or performs any single function in isolation.

The ideal mulch for conserving water would be one which opens vents to accept water in and closes vents to prevent water from going out.

open - water in

closed - no water out

There is obviously nothing like that available at this time, therefore the aim is to find something as close to that as possible with existing mulching materials.

The criteria for evaluating mulch for water conservation is different from that used for choosing mulch for any other purpose.

The concept of using mulch for water conservation

Mulch may be used in landscape settings for a variety of purposes. It is one of the most effective methods for controlling water usage and limiting the need for irrigation. The concept of expanding the use of mulch as a strategy for conserving water is to allow the maximum amount of water into the soil and to keep that water in the plant root zone as long as possible.

A strategy of expanding the use of mulch means to:

- use thicker layers of mulch,
- use mulch in more areas,
- use more different kinds of mulch.

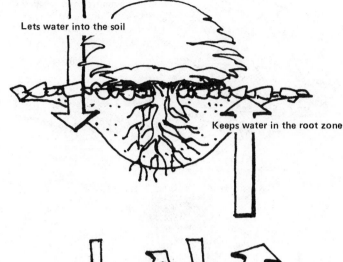

Lets water into the soil

Keeps water in the root zone

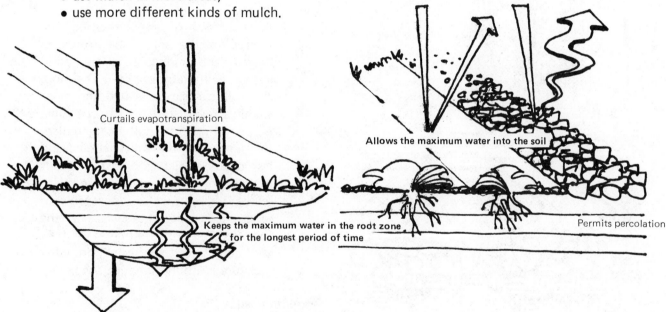

Curtails evapotranspiration

Keeps the maximum water in the root zone for the longest period of time

Allows the maximum water into the soil

Permits percolation

The ideal mulch for water conservation:

- limits reflectivity,
- curtails heat,
- prevents weeds,
- holds soil,
- builds soil,
- keeps water in the root zone,
- controls erosion,
- reduces maintenance
- improves appearance
- uses no water as would a ground cover planting

thicker

more area

more options
either/or

The ideal mulch for water conservation

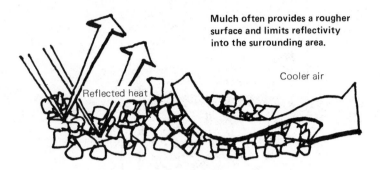

Mulch often provides a rougher surface and limits reflectivity into the surrounding area.

Reflected heat

Cooler air

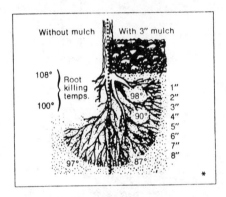

Without mulch   With 3" mulch

108° } Root killing temps.

100°

98°   1"
       2"
90°   3"
       4"
       5"
       6"
       7"
97°   87°   8"

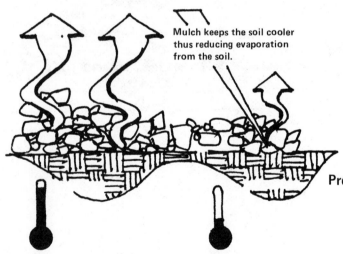

Mulch keeps the soil cooler thus reducing evaporation from the soil.

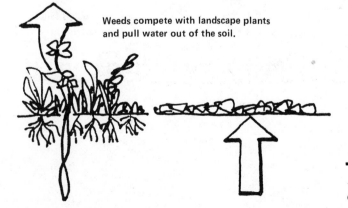

Weeds compete with landscape plants and pull water out of the soil.

Limits reflectivity

During the hot summer months the uncovered surface of sand or clay soil develops a very light reflective surface. This bounces the heat and light of the sun back onto plants, buildings, paved surfaces and into the atmosphere. Mulch serves to give a darker and more fragmented surface, thus cutting down on the reflectivity and cooling the area around the plant stems and leaves. This, many times, cuts down on the amount of water pulled out of the soil.

Curtails heat

As the rays of the sun strike the surface of the soil, the ground is heated and moisture is transpired back into the atmosphere. The more the soil surface is heated the more water is pulled out of the root zone. By covering the soil with mulch, the surface of the soil is cooled and less of the moisture is lost and thus it does not have to be replaced with scarce irrigation water. Most mulches serve to insulate the surface of the soil, keeping from extremes of heat and cold and thus sealing in what moisture is around the root zone.

Prevents weeds

All plants growing in the soil pull water out of the soil and use some of it while they transpire or pump more of it back into the atmosphere. This is true whether the plants are desirable trees, shrubs, ground covers or whether they are undesirable and unwanted weeds. Mulch placed on the surface of the ground helps to keep down the weeds, thus allowing more of the soil moisture to be available to desirable and wanted plants.

* **Weather-Wise Gardening,** Ortho Books, San Francisco, California, 1974, p. 16.

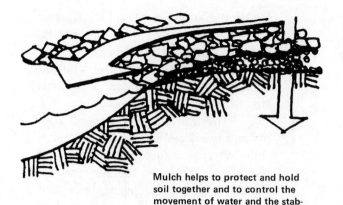

Mulch helps to protect and hold soil together and to control the movement of water and the stability of the soil as a water reservoir.

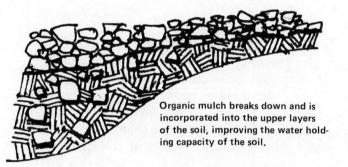

Organic mulch breaks down and is incorporated into the upper layers of the soil, improving the water holding capacity of the soil.

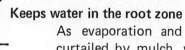

Root zone - varies depending on the type of plant and depth of the roots of the plants growing in an area.

Holds soil

Mulch insulates the soil against freezing and thawing and prevents cracks or other disruption of the soil surface. It helps to keep moisture in the soil to encourage root growth into the soil, thus stabilizing it. It also enables more of the water applied to the soil to move in an orderly way down into the root zone. Mulch often provides a protective layer which limits the mixing of the soil horizons which would disrupt the natural textural relationships. Mulch may reduce compaction of the soil and thus enable it to absorb and hold water more effectively.

Builds soil

Organic mulch applied to the surface of the soil eventually breaks down and is incorporated into the upper layers of the soil, often improving its water holding capacity. This is one of the advantages and the disadvantages of using organic mulches. It is an advantage because it improves the quality of the soil, and it is a disadvantage because the mulch must continually be replaced and replenished on the surface of the soil.

Keeps water in the root zone

As evaporation and transpiration is curtailed by mulch, water is retained in the upper layers of the soil. This is normally the zone in which the roots of ground covers, perennials, annuals, and small shrubs draw their moisture. Evaporation may be reduced by 30 percent on mulched soil compared to bare soil. A straw mulch has been estimated to reduce evaporation by up to 70 percent.

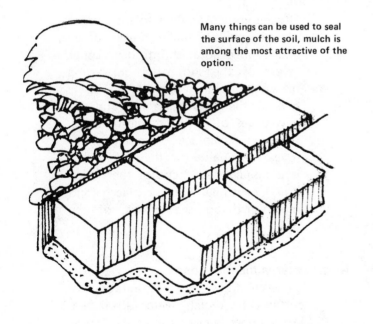

A mulching material on the soil protects soil from splash and flow erosion and encourages water flow into the soil.

Many things can be used to seal the surface of the soil, mulch is among the most attractive of the option.

Maintenance activities use water indirectly, less maintenance often means the use of less water.

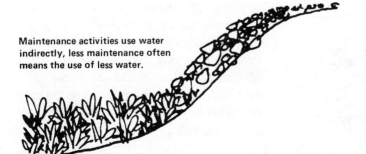

Controls erosion

If the upper layers of soil wash away in heavy rainstorms they will not be there to nurture the plants. Mulch on the bare soil helps to soften the impact of falling water and allows for the orderly flow of water into the soil. This curtails erosion and run-off and preserves the quality and character of the surface soil surrounding the plant. If water rapidly runs off the soil it has to be replaced later with irrigation water. If soil is washed away from around plants it must be replaced to preserve the growing medium. The use of mulch prevents this, thus using available water and soil more efficiently.

Improves appearance

This is a minor factor in conserving water, but mulch is more attractive than any other method of sealing the surface of the soil to prevent water loss. Mulch is less harsh than paving such as asphalt, concrete, or brick and because it is usually of organic or mineral derivation it blends with the growing landscape elements. Using mulch it is possible to seal the soil surface attractively.

Reduces maintenance

Mulch lessens the need for additional water. At the same time it usually takes less maintenance than does a similar area of planting of any type. Usually periodic weeding and occasional replacement is all of the on-going care that is required. Water is used directly in grounds care, but it is also used indirectly in cleaning equipment, to cool engines, and by maintenance workers.

Mulch holds water in the soil for use by nearby plants, so the soil is a water bank, with mulch controlling deposits and preventing withdrawals.

Mr. Harleigh Kemmerer in an article on "Managing Mulches" in GROUNDS MAINTENANCE magazine points up the effectiveness of mulches in stretching available water resources in the following way:

The amount of water that can be lost by evaporation from the soil surface is given in this breakdown of what happens to rainfall. In an area with 40 inches of annual rainfall, the breakdown would be:
- 20 inches(50 percent) lost by percolation and runoff.
- 10 inches(25 percent) lost by evaporation.
- 10 inches(25 percent) available for plants.

Applying a mulch to the soil surface is one way to save some of the water that would otherwise be lost. Not all water can be saved, but with mulching some is retained and available during periods of stress when bare soils are dry. *

Uses no water as would a ground cover planting

Ground cover, turf or other plant material soil covering are growing and thus take water out of the soil and use it while mulch does not take water but seals the soil surface. Therefore, mulch helps to realize a net gain by holding the available water in the soil and not using it but making it available to nearby plants.

Mulch should be considered and used more often as a part of an overall strategy for conserving available water resources. These various mulching materials should be used on slopes, on uncovered soil, around the base of trees and shrubs and in place of vegetative ground covers which use water. A landscape entirely covered with mulch is unattractive. However, when used with landscape construction material and water conserving vegetation, it attractive and effective.

Mulch used under groves of trees will preserve moisture and will not take water out of the soil as would turf or ground covers

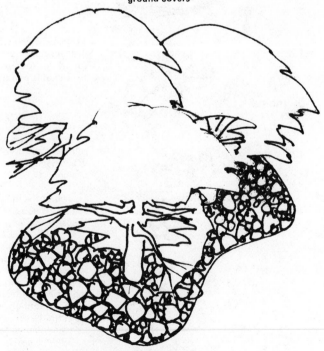

Mulch can be used under groves of trees to preserve moisture in the soil, to prevent erosion and to reduce maintenance in an area where either grass or ground cover will not grow.

* Kemmerer, Harleigh, "Managing Mulches", **Grounds Maintenance,** April 1979, Vol. 13, No.4, p. 62.

A Comparison of the Water Conservation Potential of Various Mulching Materials

It is possible to evaluate the effectiveness of mulches in conserving water by indicating their effectiveness in allowing water into the soil, in holding water in the soil and how much water the mulching material holds itself rather than allowing it to pass through to the root zone of the plants.

There are a wide variety of mulching materials which can be used to conserve water and manage available water more carefully and efficiently. As mentioned previously these may be divided into man-made, natural - inorganic and natural - organic. The following chart gives an overview of these mulches and focuses on their ability to control water flow into and out of the soil.

Mulching material	Water conservation advantages	Water conservation disadvantages	Most effective depth
Man-made			
Polyethelene film	Holds water in very effectively, can be used under other mulches thin, light, easily transportable, works well on initial installations, holes can be punches in it to allow water into the soil, is best used under ground cover and in small shrub beds.	Unsightly and must be covered or masked by other materials. Heat is increased, does not allow water in very easily, is labor intensive to install.	3 -10 mm.
Fiberglass	Lets water into the soil, holds it in, more attractive than film and can be used on slopes.	Expensive, labor intensive to install and allows some weed through, must be pegged down, mats when wet and best used in small areas.	½'' - 1''
Kraft paper	Keeps water in, reflects sun if two sides are of different materials.	Doesn't let water in, must have holes punched in it to let water in, labor intensive to install, most effective on flat surfaces, disintegrates in a year or two and must be replaced, can be unsightly.	5 - 10 mm.
Newspaper	Keeps some water in, lets little in, controls erosion, can be incorporated into the soil as it weathers.	Short-term mulch, disintegrates, unsightly, dries out and blows, trashy, not commercial but may be used on small areas for a temporary mulch.	1'' or less
Inorganic			
Gravel	Lets water in very well, holds none itself, keeps water in the soil, does not decompose, comes in a variety of sizes and is long lasting.	Can be pushed down into the soil, does not help the water holding capacity of the soil, unsightly if used in too large an area.	1''-3''
Crushed stone	Lets all of the moisture into the soil, holds none of it itself and keeps the water in the root zone,	May change the soil chemistry when it breaks down, can be very reflective if it is too white,	1''-3''
Sand	Tight, so not all water gets in, holds a lot of water itself, lets some water in but keeps in what is in the soil, dries on the surface forming a dust mulch, eventually incorporates into the soil, improving its water-holding capacity.	Dries out quickly and blows away, erodes and runs off, highly refelctive and somewhat unsightly.	1''-2''
Decomposed granite	Holds a certain amount of water itself, allows water in, and holds water in the soil, long lasting.	Regionally available, a variety of colors are possible, does disintegrate in a number of years.	2''-3''

Mulching material		Water conservation advantages	Water conservation disadvantages	Most effective depth
	Pumice	Holds some water in the pores but alllows a great deal of water into the soil, cools the soil, the most porous and the lightest of the inorganic mulches.	Regionally available, in a variety of colors, does break down in a few years, does not integrate into the soil to improve the water holding capacity of the soil.	2'' - 3''
Organic	Wood chips	Lets water in effectively, keeps some in the mulch layer, allows little out, cools and seals the soil and improves the water holding capacity of the soil and keeps down weeds, many sizes available but largest and smallest should be avoided.	Breaks down and disintegrates in a year or two depending on derivation and type, small sizes require nitrogen if they break down too quickly.	3'' - 4''
	Sawdust	Lets water in slowly, holds a great deal itself, not all of it reaches the soil, does help the water holding capacity of the soil as it disintegrates, forms a barrier which compacts in time.	Breaks down rapidly, blows in the wind when it is dry, and crusts, regionally available, nitrogen must be added either to the soil or to the sawdust to avoid nitrogen depletion, certain varieties are slower to disintegrate than others.	1'' - 3''
	Shredded bark	Binds the soil, lets water in, holds it in the soil well, builds the moisture holding capacity of soil and is looser than wood chips and much more open than sawdust.	Expensive, may compact in time and can be unsightly and ineffective if applied in too thin a layer.	3'' - 4''
	Chunk bark	Coarse texture, large size lets more water in but does not hold water in as well as finer textured materials, can be long lasting and does not hold much water in the mulch layer but allows it to pass through.	Fairly expensive, not always available except on a regional basis, breaks down slowly so is not able to improve soil texture.	4'' - 6''
	Pine needles	Loose, light, but binding, lets in a lot of water, holds little and keeps some in, allows some to be transpired, binds the soil and does break down.	Regionally available, acid, settles and forms a mat, lasts a short time	2'' - 3''
	Leaves/leaf mold	Lets some water in, keeps it in holds the soil, readily available in some areas, shredded is more compact and easier to use, improves the water holding capacity of the soil.	Can be a fire hazard, regional availability, mats and causes run off, dries and blows, unshredded are difficult to handle.	2'' - 4''
	Lawn clippings	Readily available, lets some water in, holds little itself and inhibits transpiration and best used in small areas	Best used dry, mats, heats, offensive odor, needs to be spread in thin layers, may contain weed seeds.	1'' at a time
	Straw	Easily lets water in, cools the soil, holds some water in the soil though not as much as other mulches, good for temporary cover over grass seeding.	Not always attractive, will blow and scatter, will mat, flamable, may contain weed seeds.	4'' - 6''

Mulching material	Water conservation advantages	Water conservation disadvantages	Most effective depth
Hay 	Holds little or no water itself, lets much water in but lets some water out in transpiration, good color especially if marsh hay is used.	Regionally available, expensive and straw performs the same functions less expensively.	3'' - 5''

Waste

Strawy manure 	Actually a waste product, low level fertilizer, improves the water holding capacity of the soil, a dual use mulch which will be incorporated into the soil and have to be renewed each year.	Needs to be aged or treated, regionally available and can have an unpleasant odor.	2'' - 4''
Compost 	Readily available on most sites and can be made from waste generated on the site, an excellent method of incorporating organic matter into the soil, improving its future water holding capacity, is average at letting water in, holds some itself but is excellent at holding it in the soil.	Needs to be stored and aged on or near the site, is unsightly, bulky, can have an unpleasant odor, takes time to collect and compost, but costs little other than labor and storage, may contain weed seeds.	2'' - 4''
Corncobs Spent hops Peanut hulls Pecan shells Mushroom compost Rice hulls	A series of regionally available mulching materials, which are attractive and effective in letting water into the soil, holding little itself, can be a low level fertilizer, some are excellent soil conditioners.	Will depend on what is available locally, cost will depend on transportation costs and costs for purchase(if any), may change the soil chemistry and may be slow to break down, may need to be ground or processed before use.	2''- 3''

Peat moss

Sphagnum 	One of the best mulching materials, holds water in the soil very effectively, holds a great deal of water itself, is a superlative soil conditioner and can be worked into the topsoil each year and be replaced to improve the water holding capacity of the soil.	Expensive, sheds water when dry, may blow in windy sites may not let water in when it is wet, cannot easily be used on slopes as it erodes, is best used in small confined areas.	1'' -3''
Bog	Is much less expensive where it is regionally or locally available, hold water itself but is effective at holding water in the soil, lets water in slowly, and hold a great deal, may not drift as much as sphagnum when dry.	Not always weed free, can be bought in bulk, is some coarser than sphagnum and is not as uniform or predictable as to texture or quality.	

strategy

USE OF
ANTI-TRANSPIRANTS TO REDUCE
EVAPOTRANSPIRATION FROM
PLANTS

. . . anti-transpirants will lock in whatever moisture is already in the plant. **99**

Each plant is, in essence, a large or small water pump, bringing water out of the soil, moving the water through the plant and transpiring the water out of the leaves, needles, or blades through microscopic openings. Each plant leaf contains stomata through which the plant takes in and gives off air and water. In drought conditions quite often the air is very dry, therefore, plants pump water out of the soil and transpire moisture into the drier air. If this can be controlled to any extent, it is possible to maintain the plant in a living condition with the use of much less water. Therefore, over the years many grounds managers have explored the possibility of using anti-transpirant spray all over the leaves and branches of the plant.

Anti-transpirants have quite often been used in colder climates to protect plants from freezing or from drying out during the winter time. Quite often if the air temperature is warm in the winter time while the soil is sometimes still frozen, moisture may be pulled out of the soil through a plant. Then when an extremely cold snap occurs, the air temperature is lowered and the dehydrated

plant is killed. Therefore in order to protect somewhat delicate and sensitive plants in extremely cold climates the plant is sprayed with an anti-transpirant. These materials are usually water-soluble petroleum or paraffin based products that form a film over the leaves and branches of the plant, thus inhibiting transpiration from the plant and evapotranspiration of water through the plant. These anti-transpirant materials usually do no damage to the plant, if carefully used, but do protect them.

The use of anti-transpirants is not a substitute for watering plants. Basically the anti-transpirants will lock in whatever moisture is already in the plant. Therefore it will not be as effective on plants which have already wilted. These materials are also not as effective on young or rapidly growing plants, but are best used on mature plants during the summer when the plant has fully leafed out. It has been estimated that anti-transpirants will reduce evaporation from plants as much as 80%. Various studies have given estimates for various species and varieties from 40-80% effectiveness in reducing evaporation. The transpiration rates will be retarded at least 25-30% for 3 weeks under the most difficult conditions. Generally anti-transpirants have been used on agricultural crops and in some cases have been sprayed on entire forests to reduce transpiration from watersheds.

As drought conditions develop in many sections of the country, grounds managers and personnel have explored the possibility of using anti-transpirants on plants to prevent them from transpiring great amounts of water and thus being damaged by drought conditions or to lessen the need for requiring additional irrigation. The use of anti-transpirants for drought protection thus far has had mixed results. More research undoubtedly will be conducted on this strategy or method as drought conditions spread to other regions. This, however, is an option or an alternative to consider in some circumstances. It may supplement other options or approaches.

Generally it can be recommended for use on specific critical or important plants during times of extreme drought to supplement other methods or techniques. For best results anti-transpirants should be sprayed on plants at the onset of a drought condition, then the plants should continue to be watered to a limited degree and protected through either windbreaks or shading. In this way the plant can be maintained with minimum watering until the drought conditions subside.

An anti-transpirant acts as a seal around the plant to seal in moisture

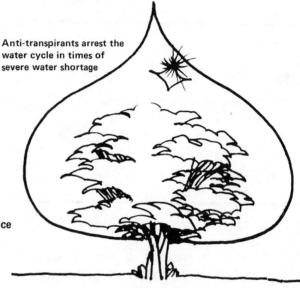

Anti-transpirants arrest the water cycle in times of severe water shortage

The concept of anti-transpirants - a seal on the leaf surface

An anti-transpirant does not provide more water it just seals in the water which exists in the plant

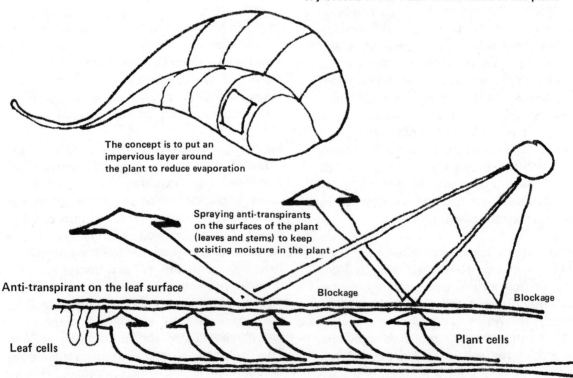

The concept is to put an impervious layer around the plant to reduce evaporation

Spraying anti-transpirants on the surfaces of the plant (leaves and stems) to keep exisiting moisture in the plant

Anti-transpirant on the leaf surface

Blockage

Blockage

Leaf cells

Plant cells

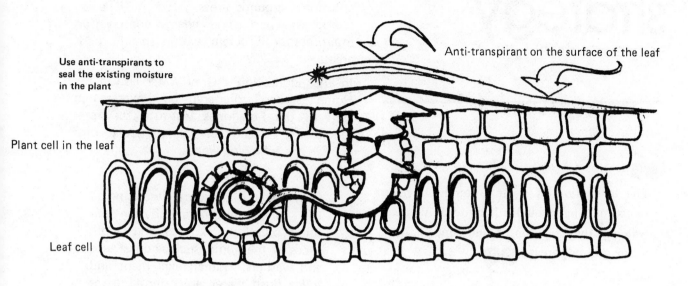

Use anti-transpirants to seal the existing moisture in the plant

Anti-transpirant on the surface of the leaf

Plant cell in the leaf

Leaf cell

Cross section of a leaf showing how water is sealed in a leaf by applying anti-transpirant to the leaf surface

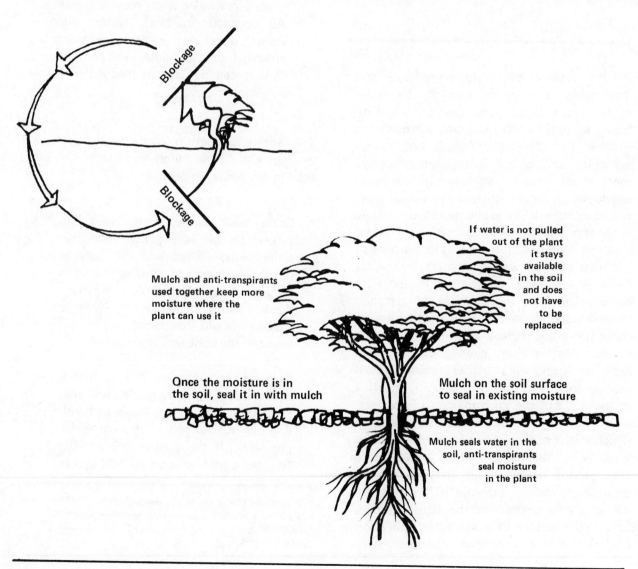

Blockage

Blockage

Mulch and anti-transpirants used together keep more moisture where the plant can use it

If water is not pulled out of the plant it stays available in the soil and does not have to be replaced

Once the moisture is in the soil, seal it in with mulch

Mulch on the soil surface to seal in existing moisture

Mulch seals water in the soil, anti-transpirants seal moisture in the plant

strategy

RE-USE OF WATER

> The utilization of waste water is . . . a re-use of what would otherwise be waste water in the irrigation of landscape plants in the grounds areas.

All the water in the world is used over and over again as it moves through the water cycle. Many times water used for irrigation has been purified to the point of making it suitable for drinking. This is not always necessary and is not sound water management in all cases. A strategy which is being employed in certain areas is the use of what would otherwise be waste water to irrigate landscape plants. The utilization of water that has been used for some other purpose to water plants before it re-enters the water cycle is a "re-use" of water. In some instances this may be the use of partially treated water or even of untreated water for other purposes before returning it to the cycle. This is short cycling of the water cycle or "using water before its time." Even though this water may not be fully purified to make it suitable for drinking, it is perfectly satisfactory to meet the needs of vegetation which might otherwise not have access to any water at all. One concept which was used to a great extent in the western states during the drought period of the mid-1970's was the use of "grey water" in the home garden. This is the essence of waste water utilization applied at a residential scale. Obviously grey water would not be able to be used in institutional grounds areas, but it may be explored as a part of an energy conservation interpretation program within specific park areas.

In the publication, "Grey Water Use in the Home Garden" prepared by the research staff of the Farallones Institute, they presented the concept of this particular program in the following words:

> Grey water is the term describing all the waste water generated by the non-toilet plumbing fixtures and appliances of the home, such as sinks, tubs and washers. Human excrement and toilet flush water are referred to as "black water" and are not to be included in a waste water recycling plan. As opposed to black water, grey water does not require extensive chemical or biological treatment before it can be used in the garden as irrigation.*

The same publication contains one section dealing with "How much grey water can be used in the home garden?"

> Scale your waste water recycling efforts to suit your garden water requirements; collect and use only as much grey water in your garden as is required for reasonable irrigation. Waste water in excess of what is needed should be discharged in the sewer in the conventional manner.

> A good, conservative rule is that a square foot of loamy garden soil, rich in organic matter, is capable of handling one-quarter gallon of waste water per week. If the garden area suitable for grey water irrigation is 400 square

---

* **Grey Water Use in the Home Garden,** prepared by the research staff of the Farallones Institute under the direction of Tom Javits, Graphic by Andrea Thrams, Berkeley, California, 1977, p. 2.

feet, then up to 100 gallons of water may be used in the garden each week. This rate may be greater in the summer months when surface evaporation and plant transpiration is considerable, and should be less during the winter when there is rainfall.

A program of waste water recycling should be coupled with garden water conservation measures. Using mulches of compost, planting in depressions, and landscaping with plants native to your area will reduce your garden's need for water. Frequently check soil moisture to determine precisely when the garden is in need of irrigation.*

They also cover in that same publication information on "How should grey water be applied to the soil?"

Several principles govern the best usage of the water for garden irrigation. They are:

A. Apply waste water directly to the soil surface; do not overhead sprinkle or allow the recycled water to splash off the soil and contact the above-ground portion of plants. Grey water is not suitable for drip irrigation as the solid matter it conveys would clog the emitters in the pipe.

B. Distribute the grey water to flat garden areas; avoid steep slopes where run-off may be a problem.

C. Disperse the waste water over a broad area: avoid concentrating it on one particular site.

D. When available, use fresh water for garden irrigation on rotating basis with grey water to aid in leaching the soil of contaminants.

E. Apply thick compost mulches to areas receiving grey water to facilitate natural decomposition of waste residues.

F. Grey water is alkaline. Do not use it on acid-loving plants such as rhododendrons, azaleas and citrus fruits. Lawns and deciduous fruit trees may receive grey water in rotation with fresh water.

G. If you must use waste water for irrigating food plants restrict its application to the soil around plants of which only the above-ground part is eaten; such as corn, tomatoes or broccoli. *Do not* apply it to the soil around leafy vegetables or root crops. The best idea is to use grey water for your ornamental foliage and use what fresh water is available for your vegetable garden.

H. And, finally, use the waste water on well established plants. Seedlings as well as houseplants will not tolerate the impurities in household waste water.**

This same publication also deals with the question, "Must any precautions be taken to protect against damage to the soil resulting from long-term use of grey water?" This question is answered in the following words:

Yes. Over extended periods of grey water application, sodium levels may build up in the soil resulting in poor soil drainage and potential damage to plants. High levels of sodium may be detected by conducting a pH test of the soil using pH paper (commonly available from pharmacies or nurseries). A pH of 7.5 or above indicates that your soil has become overloaded with sodium. You can correct this problem by spreading gypsum (calcium sulfate) over the soil at a rate of 2 pounds per 100 square feet per month. Continue treatment until the pH of the soil drops to 7.0. As a precaution against further sodium buildup, gypsum may be applied to the soil receiving grey water at a rate of 1 pound per

* Ibid.,p-2.

** Ibid., p. 3.

month for every 20 gallons per day discharge. (This means that if you are discharging waste water to the garden at a rate of 50 gallons per day then a monthly application of 2½ pounds of gypsum is required to neutralize the detrimental effect of the sodium.) Normal dilution of waste water by rainfall or fresh water irrigation also will help leach the soil of sodium and excess salts.*

The publication "Are You Using Grey Water During the Drought?" contains a diagram which shows a system using underground tubing for grey water application in the home landscape. The following is the actual drawing from that pamphlet:

A system using underground tubing for grey water application must use well filtered water in order to prevent clogging.

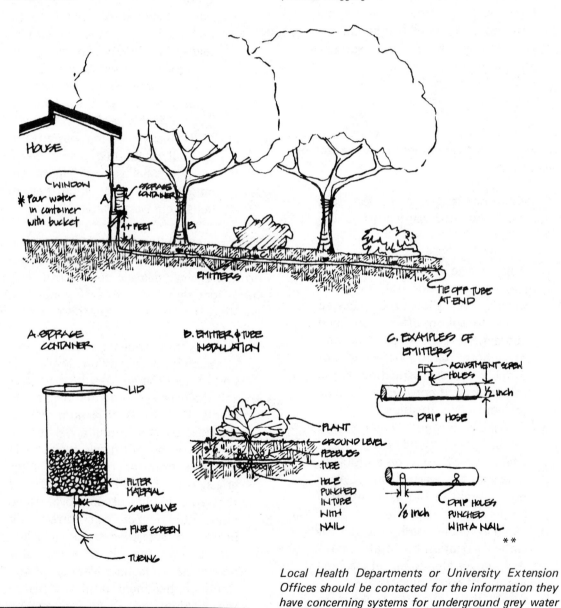

Local Health Departments or University Extension Offices should be contacted for the information they have concerning systems for underground grey water application.

* Ibid., p. 3.

** **Are You Using Gray Water During the Drought?,** Health Considerations Using Household Waste Water, Department of Water Resources, Sacramento, California, 1978, p. 4.

The July 1983 issue of SAWARA **waterwords**, contained an article by Dr. A. Richard Kassander on "Residential Water Recycling and Runoff Uses" which spelled out residential reuse options and the potential water savings which can be realized using this strategy:

"Mr and Mrs. Average Taxpayer (the A. T.'s) are confused. They want to do their share toward reducing our groundwater overdraft, but the initiative seems to be in the hands of politicians, power groups, courts and above all, the federal congress. There seems little for the "A.T.'s" and their friends to do but look forward to paying the bill, their ultimate perogative. In the face of massive water use in other sectors, over which they have little control, is there nothing they can do except put rubber washers in their shower heads and plastic bags in their toilet tanks? That doesn't seem like much. However, carried a step further, it might make a big difference.

Residential water reuse is something we've heard a bit about. It has been suggested that the 'grey water' waste from clothes-washers could be used for outside landscaping irrigation. A variant of this is the much discussed use of treated effluent for golf courses. Could additional options be available at home?

First of all, one needs to be reminded of the supply and demand budget of the Tucson Basin area. By the year 2025, by Arizona statute, this must be in balance. However, our present projections have us in a deficit position of 100,000 acre-feet, assuming we receive our full CAP allocation. Moreover, that also assumes that all of the projected 135,000 acre-feet of municipal sewage effluent is reused, including the 30,600 acre-feet which has been allocated to the Papago Tribe. 100,000 acre-feet is the residential water use of over 1 million people! The City's consultant

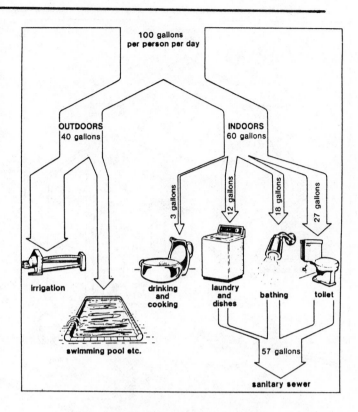

Figure 1. Average Residential Consumption

report, entitled 'Tucson Metropolitan Wastewater Reuse Assessment', 1983, addressed essentially nothing but golf course irrigation, and found use for only 43,000 acre-feet by the year 2030, assuming the Papago Indians use their entire wastewater allocation of 30,600 acre-feet of the municipal effluent. Thus the 100,000 acre-foot deficit projection might be optimistic by 50,000 acre-feet per year, a serious matter.

Now take a look at Figure No. 1, a possible per capita usage scenario at the "A.T.'s" household. Obviously the variation will be tremendeous, but the 'bathing and personal' use does make up a good fraction of the toilet flushing requirement and the "laundry" requirement is nearly one-third of the outdoor consumption(but not including swimming pools). It could be possible in housing and certain existing homes, especially mobile homes, to use

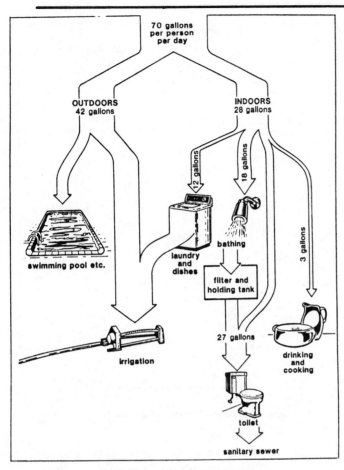

70 gallons
per person
per day

OUTDOORS
42 gallons

INDOORS
28 gallons

2 gallons

18 gallons

3 gallons

swimming pool etc.

laundry
and
dishes

bathing

filter and
holding tank

irrigation

27 gallons

drinking
and
cooking

toilet

sanitary sewer

Figure 2. A Partial Reuse Scheme

soapy bathing water to flush toilets, probably with some sanitary benefits, and use laundry water for outdoor irrigation, see Figure No. 2.

With no changes in use patterns, the result is a 30% reduction in water consumption and nearly a 50% reduction in sewage effluent! If we could accomplish this only in the new housing required for the 884,300 people projected from 1990 to 2025, we would save 28, 372 acre-feet of water per year with a large reduction in capital outlay for transportation and treatment otherwise needed for the resulting savings of 28,372 acre-feet of sewage effluent. Cumulatively the "A.T.'s", by their own devices, would have accomplished a significant result.

They could go one relatively inexpensive step further if they captured their rooftop rainwater and used it for irrigation of lawn and landscape. If, by the year 2025 the distribution of housing is similar to today's, then we might anticipate a total of 600,000 new housing units. If these averaged 1,500 square feet each, then, in a 10-inch rainfall year we could capture around 17,000 acre-feet for outdoor irrigation from residential rooftops alone. Not a bad effort for the "A.T.'s" for probably a modest and highly cost-effective effort. Between these two activities our City's "A.T.'s" could make up nearly half of the additional water resources we will need to find even after we get all of our CAP (Central Arizona Project)expectation. *

The Texas Water Resources Institute newsletter for June 1980 contained an article which dealt with the re-use of water in a commercial setting:

"One of the best examples of residential water reuse is not in a home, but in a motel.
When planners for a new LaQuinta Motor Inn found what they considered the right location for an Inn in College Station, Texas, they were faced with a major problem. The city sewer line was not adequete to handle the volume of wastewater produced by the planned inn. Not only would the motel have wastewater from each of 114 bathrooms, but from all of the laundry operations each day as well.
The motel planners had two alternatives. They could select another location for their motel, or they could

* Kassander, Dr. A. Richard, "Residential Water Recycling and Runoff Uses," SAWARA **waterwords**, Vol. 2, No. 7, July 1983, pp. 2-3, Southern Arizona Water Resources Association, 465 St. Mary's Road, Suite 100, Tucson, Arizona 85705.

reduce the amount of wastewater which would enter the sewer.

LaQuinta management chose to build on the original site which faces the Texas A & M University campus. They promised the city of College Station, however, that wastewater volume would be less than half that which would normally flow from an inn of that size. The inn opened in January 1980 with a unique graywater treatment system which meets all city health and building codes. The system has indeed reduced water demand and wastewater volume by more than 50 percent.

All water from sinks and showers in the inn's 114 guest bathrooms is piped to four underground tanks. Each tank holds 10,000 gallons of the used water. The graywater is filtered and disinfected with chlorine, then piped to the laundry area where it is used to wash an average of 500 pounds of towels and sheets each day. From the laundry, the water goes back into the graywater storage tanks. There it is filtered, chlorinated, colored, and scented before being piped into each bathroom for toilet flushing. The colored and scented water is also used for watering landscaped areas around the motel." *

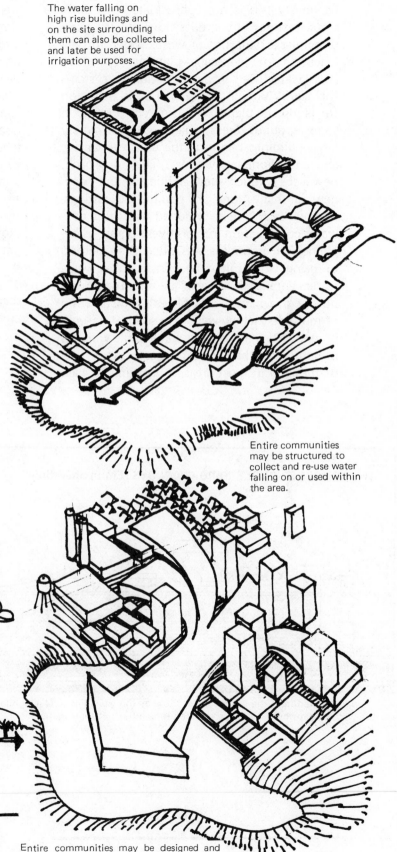

The water falling on high rise buildings and on the site surrounding them can also be collected and later be used for irrigation purposes.

Entire communities may be structured to collect and re-use water falling on or used within the area.

It may be possible to collect grey water and water falling on the site and to use that for later irrigation on the site itself.

* "Checking Into Reuse", **Texas Water Resources,** Texas Water Resources Research Institute, Texas A & M University, College Station, Texas 77843, Vol., 6, No. 5, June 1980, p. 2.

Entire communities may be designed and constructed to collect and re-use water falling on or used within the area.

Obviously this is not appropriate in all landscape settings but it does illustrate the basic principles of the use of waste water for the irrigation of landscape planting. In many areas water used in air conditioning systems for nearby buildings is later used in irrigation for landscape plants. This is maybe possible in some grounds areas which have extremely large buildings requiring the use of extensive air conditioning systems. This approach, however, is much more applicable and pertinent for institutional and commercial settings. As such it might be included as a part of a water conservation interpretive program as explained in grounds areas. One other method of using what might be construed as waste water entails the use of a self-jetting wellpoint equipment. This utilizes the installation of multiple shallow wells with self-jetting wellpoints to tap the ground water table which is presently less than 30 feet beneath the surface of the land in most areas. It is estimated each wellpoint would produce 10-50 gallons of water per minute. The concept of pulling large volumes of water from water tables is not new. New equipment, however, has been developed in recent years which makes this more economically feasible and energy efficient. The use of many shallow wells to produce water in the volumes required for irrigation is not as energy efficient compared to deep wells in that it takes less energy to lift a given amount of water 20 feet than it does to lift the same amount of water 300 feet. In this way water is used once again after it moves through the plant root zones in a particular grounds area. This may not be legal or allowable in all situations, but it is a means of re-using surface water once again for landscape purposes within a particular grounds area.

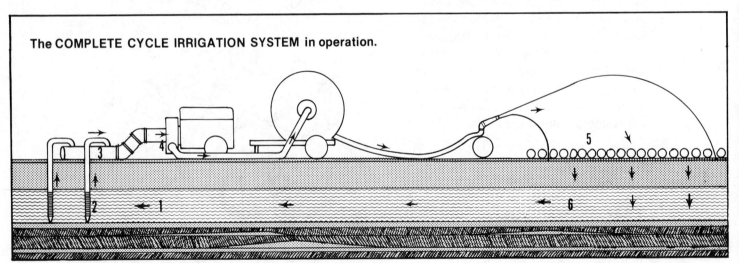

The COMPLETE CYCLE IRRIGATION SYSTEM in operation.

...water pulled from the ground water table by the wellpoint field is applied on the crops, in a short time, most of the water returns to the water table where it may be recycled time after time for irrigation.

*

*Complete Cycle Irrigation System, pamphlet, Complete Wellpoint Equipment, Port Orange, Florida 32019, p.2.

In a series of three articles on the characteristics and use of effluent water, **California Turfgrass Culture,** introduced the subject with a diagram which illustrated the process of water treatment prior to release for irrigation use.

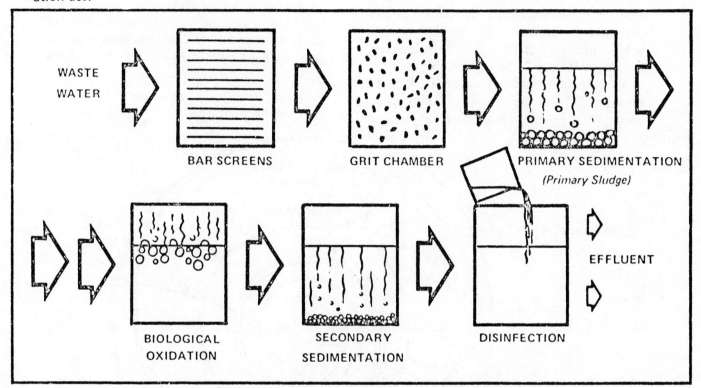

FLOW DIAGRAM OF PRIMARY AND SECONDARY SEWAGE TREATMENT *

The same source described the process in the following words:

"Sewage from most municipalities receives primary and secondary treatment before the waste water is discharged. Primary treatment consists of removal of large non-biodegradable material and grit by the bar screens and grit chambers after which most of the organic solids are removed in settling or sedimentation tanks. This would complete the process except for the chlorination to destroy microorganisms if primary treatment only were provided.

In secondary treatment, the primary effluent is further treated by aeration or biological exidation and

In secondary treatment, the primary effluent is further treated by aeration or biological oxidation and a second settling to remove additional solid materials before chlorination: the resulting effluent appears quite clear but still contains some organic material, various salts, nutrients, particulates and varying amounts of microorganisms.

Tertiary treatment, when provided, would remove most of these substances. Waste irrigation water if properly done provides the equivalent of tertiary treatment through the 'living filter' system."

* "A Three Article Series on the Characteristics and Use of Effluent Water", **California Turfgrass Culture,** Vol. 24, No. 4, Autumn 1974. p. 25.

It is obviously a play on words to indicate that an effective strategy for conserving water is to reuse water. All water is reused over and over again. As water is polluted or used it is purified and cleaned for reuse either through natural processes or by manipulated mechanical or chemical processes. The natural process takes a good deal of time and space, man-made purification takes less time but more money. The water used for landscape irrigation does not always need to be purified to the same degree as drinking water. The purification of used or polluted

of this may use water which is less expensive and more readily available than fully treated potable water, especially during water shortages or drought conditions.

Irrigating speeds up the application of water to the land. Water treatment speeds up the purification process and keeps the water out of the land and allows it to be used over and over again without ever entering the natural water cycle.

Purifying and recycling water for reuse relying on the natural water cycle takes time.

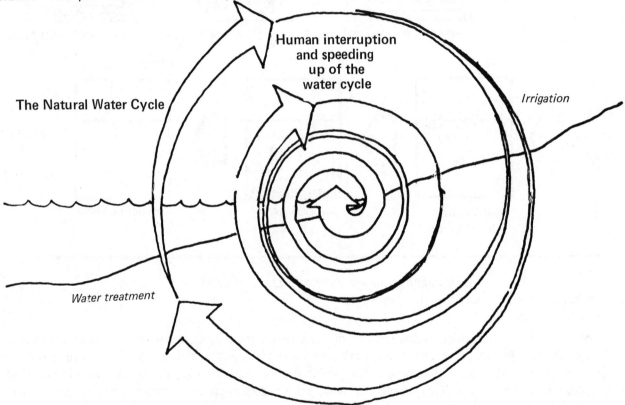

The Natural Water Cycle

Human interruption and speeding up of the water cycle

Irrigation

Water treatment

water is a multi-step process and some of the steps can be either skipped or replaced with natural purification actions when the partially treated water is used for landscape irrigation purposes. In these instances the application of the water to the landscape and the movement of the water through the soil may finish the purification process begun by man-made sewage treatment facilities. In these instances, the use of the water for landscape irrigation may be the final step in the purification process. All

This is why humans take matters into our own hands to speed things up by irrigating and mechanically and chemically purifying water. We irrigate because rainfall, which is a part of the water cycle, is not available when and where we want it and in the quantities we feel we need it. We build expensive purification plants because the natural cycle works too slowly or takes too much physical space to supply us with the water we need. We speed up the process and make it more compact.

Shallow pumping pulls water out of the ground and puts it right back where it is allowed. It is a technique to quickly reuse water and to short circuit the natural water cycle.

The depth of shallow pumping is relative and depends on the depth of available water and the legal restrictions on directly tapping ground water or aquifers.

Both shallow pumping and land treatment may be rigidly limited and controlled in certain area by health or water supply agencies.

Land treatment allows the water used for irrigation to enter the water cycle and be purified as it helps preserve vegetation. It is another means to short circuit the natural water cycle and to use water before it normally would be available.

Irrigation in agriculture quite often pumps water directly out of the aquifer and places it on the crops. This technique has not been used extensively in landscape settings except in some golf courses and parks in areas with high water tables.

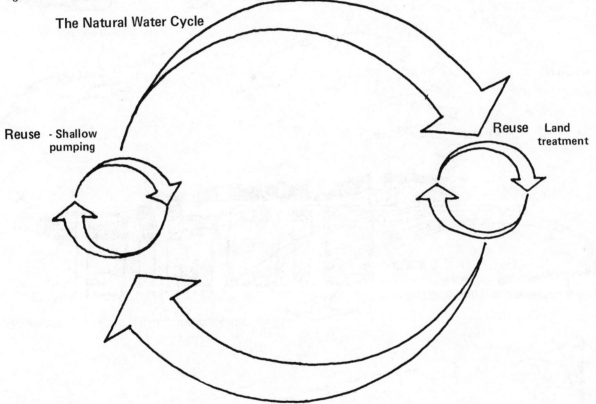

The Natural Water Cycle

Reuse - Shallow pumping

Reuse Land treatment

The reuse of water is actually using water for irrigation purposes before it goes all the way through the natural or man controlled water cycle.

Land application of partially treated sewage effluent provides aeration at the same time it provides a low level fertilizer to the plants and introduces the water back into the water cycle as the soil serves to purifiy the water in its move to the underground aquifer.

The prime purpose of land application of effluent water in the forest setting is to dispose of the sewage and reduce treatment costs while a secondary reason is to fertilize the forest trees.

The prime purpose of using partially treated effluent water on golf courses and in other recreation areas is to gain access to additional irrigation water at less cost while a secondary purpose is to use the recreational land as a water filter system.

Normally one of the final processes in water treatment is aeration or spraying partially treated water into the air to assist in the purification process.

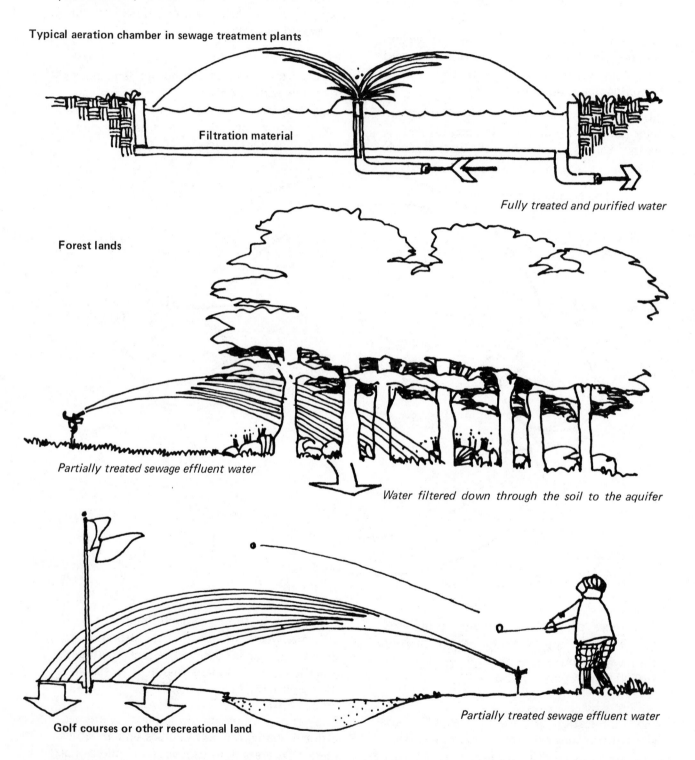

Typical aeration chamber in sewage treatment plants

Filtration material

Fully treated and purified water

Forest lands

Partially treated sewage effluent water

Water filtered down through the soil to the aquifer

Golf courses or other recreational land

Partially treated sewage effluent water

One other source of potential waste water which could be utilized for irrigation purposes in landscape areas has to do with the use of land disposal systems for sewage effluent and other waste waters. The U.S. Department of Agriculture, Forest Service, has worked extensively on examining the possibility of utilizing waste water in the irrigation of growing forest. Some of the information and data developed in the applications by the U.S. Department of Agriculture, Forest Service may be pertinent in the use of similar waste waters in the irrigation of some isolated grounds areas. As more refined waste water treatment is required the cost and energy requirements for performing this jump disproportionately. That is, a small gain in water quality represents a large increase in cost. Alternate solutions are being sought for waste water treatment and utilization. One of the most promising available alternatives is land based disposal systems incorporating the re-use and re-cycling of waste water. These land disposal systems offer several advantages. Among these are the abatement of pollution loads on surface water, the conservation and recycling of water and nutrients normally wasted and the utilization of nutrients in improved plant growth and site fertility as well as a very energy and cost efficient advanced water treatment. Normally all waste water treatment begins with conventional primary treatment consisting simply of separating water from settle sludge and flooding material. Such treatment removes approximately one-third of the biochemical oxygen demand (B.O.D.) and only a very small percentage of the nutrients so important in the accelerated eutrophication of surface water. Secondary treatment may follow a primary treatment and is a biological treatment system. After this secondary treatment in many instances the waste water may be discharged into nearby streams or waterbodies. This waste water is generally so high in nutrients that it causes lush aquatic plant growth or pollution of the water body into which it is discharged. In recent years a third or tertiary water treatment stage has been added to the secondary treatment process to remove some of the other troublesome nutrients. Because such tertiary waste water treatment programs are not always available, or even necessary in all park areas, it may be possible to use some of the secondarily treated waste water for irrigation in some specific park areas. The largest project of this type in the eastern part of the United States is at Pennsylvania University where crop and forest land is spray irrigated throughout the year. The project was started in response to problems associated with discharge effluent into local streams. The first problem dealt with the pollution of the famous trout stream by secondarily treated sewage and the second problem dealt with diminishing ground water supplies, the primary source of domestic water for the community. The irrigation of crops and forest land at Penn State resulted in successful pollution abatement, utilization of nutrients by vegetation and recharge of the ground water. Another type of land disposal system has been proposed as a result of research in Phoenix, Arizona, using infiltration basins. Treated sewage effluent is recharged to ground water and the dry salt river bed to be later withdrawn for irrigation purposes. A long term proposal visualizes the salt river flood plain developed into a green belt or golf courses, ball parks and trails maintained by irrigation or renovated sewage effluent withdrawn from the ground water. Infiltration basins are also well suited to waste water renovation and pollution abatement and coastal and glaciated regions where shallow ground water is prevalent. Basically there are two types of land disposal systems; one which includes higher plants as a part of the waste water renovation process and a second which does not include higher plants and depends entirely on physical, chemical and micro-biological renovation. Waste water applications to the vegetation soil complex is the same as intermittent application of small amounts of liquid fertilizer. Some nutrients are taken up by plant roots in essentially the same form as applied. Others are modified by micro-biological, chemical or physical processes, or are taken up by the plant or exchanged on the soil colloid, and still others are changed in form by the same processes and released as gas or reached soil horizon. The examples of the fertilizer content of municipal sewage effluent are illustrated in the following chart:

Fertilizer Constituent	Tucson, Arizona	State College, Pennsylvania
	Pounds per acre-foot	
Nitrogen	65	27
Phosphates (P_2O_5)	50	54
Potash (K_2O)	32	46

Therefore the two aspects may be identified in the use of this waste water as a potential source of irrigation water within a grounds area. The first of these would be the availability of water which, in this case, would include a low level of fertilizer solution. The second aspect would be the use of landscape area or the land for the renovation of the sewage effluent. Obviously great care must be taken not to utilize water of this type within grounds areas which might achieve heavy use. The following chart does show that this waste water was effective in stimulating the growth of Red Pine and mixed Oak with a wooded area:

Plot and Application	Year			
	1964	1965	1966	1967
	inches	inches	inches	inches
Red pine 1-inch	0.10	0.08	0.07	0.13
Red pine control	.10	.09	.12	.14
Red pine 2-inch	.07	.05	.07	.09
Red pine control	.13	.11	.12	.15
Mixed oak 1-inch	.16	.18	.16	.13
Mixed oak control	.15	.15	.16	.14
Mixed oak 2-inch		.21	.17	.22
Mixed oak control		.13	.12	.12
Mixed oak 4-inch		.22	.19	.23
Mixed oak control		.13	.15	.15 **

The following chart shows the relative effectiveness of the renovation of the waste water on a land application system:

Soil Depth (inches)	Nitrate		Phosphorous		Potassium	
	Conc.	Ren.	Conc.	Ren.	Conc.	Ren.
	(ppm)	(%)	(ppm)	(%)	(ppm)	(%)
6	10.3	24.3	0.11	98.5	11.2	28.7
24	8.6	36.8	0.57	92.7	8.7	44.6
48	7.6	44.1	0.02	99.7	7.5	52.2
72	10.1	25.7	0.03	99.6	7.7	51.0
Effluent Quality	13.6		7.84		15.7	***

* "Response of Vegetation to Wastewater Application", **Symposium on the Role of Trees in the South's Urban Environment,** University of Georgia Center for Continuing Education, Athens, Georgia, 1971, p. 23.

** Ibid. p. 25.

*** Ibid., p. 27.

The amount of land used for land disposal systems of waste water is relatively small. Drawing on the experience of Penn State, two inches of treated sewage could be applied per acre per week throughout the year and still maintain viable soil and biological systems. In their particular case at Penn State only 129 acres were needed to dispose of one million gallons per day. In this case it was the approximate output from a community of a population of 10,000. Odor at a land disposal site is not generally offensive, never approaching the septic smell of a polluted stream or the odor eminating from many of the lagoon storage plants. It is possible for irrigation to continue throughout the winter season if application rates are kept within the physical and chemical renovation capacities of the soil. Nutrients retained in the soil will be utilized by the plants during the next growing season. Ideally land disposal systems are best suited for small, rural or suburban complexes. Some cities are currently irrigating municipal golf courses and recreational areas with secondarily treated sewage. As cities expand each new sub-development in time to come will be required to set aside enough land for a small land disposal system. "Green belts" can be assured and maintained by use of this system while at the same time decentralizing the expensive collection and treatment of sewage.

Mr. A. C. Sarsfield, in an article in the November issue of *GROUNDS MAINTENANCE* Magazine, entitled, "Have You Considered Irrigating With Recycled Water?" makes the following point for institutional use of recycled water:

> Many people react negatively to the prospect of using effluent water for golf course irrigation because the word *effluent* carries the undesirable connotation of sewage. The terms *reclaimed* or *recycled water* connote patriotic conservation and environmental protection, more pleasant images. Water conservation is becoming more urgent, and recycling water is an obvious method to meet conservation needs.

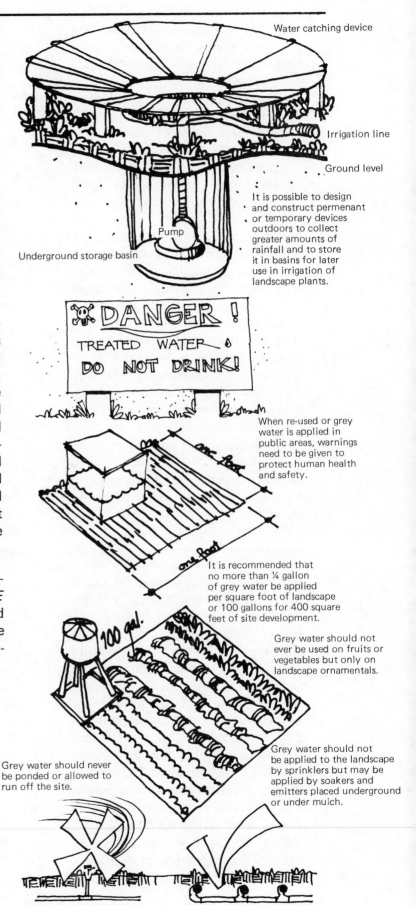

Water catching device

Irrigation line

Ground level

It is possible to design and construct permenant or temporary devices outdoors to collect greater amounts of rainfall and to store it in basins for later use in irrigation of landscape plants.

Pump

Underground storage basin

DANGER! TREATED WATER — DO NOT DRINK!

When re-used or grey water is applied in public areas, warnings need to be given to protect human health and safety.

It is recommended that no more than ¼ gallon of grey water be applied per square foot of landscape or 100 gallons for 400 square feet of site development.

Grey water should not ever be used on fruits or vegetables but only on landscape ornamentals.

100 gal.

Grey water should not be applied to the landscape by sprinklers but may be applied by soakers and emitters placed underground or under mulch.

Grey water should never be ponded or allowed to run off the site.

Helpful environmental controls may be incorporated into the automation. The following controls are among those offered:
- Moisture sensors to avoid over-watering.
- Rain switches to cut operation in the event of rainfall.
- Wind sensors that will stop operation when certain wind levels occur or directions change.

Virtually every effluent project requires its own special analysis. Although many potential problems exist, it is seldom that a major portion of them occurs on any one project. In most instances, the problems are little different from any other source. Success requires a re-evaluation of maintenance procedures, but many institutions have adapted and are achieving excellent results.*

Mr. A. C. Sarsfield, in his paper for the Northern California Turfgrass Council, entitled "How to Save Water Sensibly," makes reference to the use of recycled water in the following words:

The use of recycled water for irrigation of large public areas continues to be largely ignored, as it is for industrial processing use, with only a few notable exceptions, yet the impact on water conservation efforts could be vast. Wade L. Berry of the University of California at Los Angeles pointed out in a special report issued in 1976 that the Sanitation District of the City of Los Angeles is dumping close to 320 million gallons of wastewater into the ocean each day and the County Sanitation District about 360 million, making a total of nearly 700 million gallons per day, or over 2,000 acre feet of water lost from that basin each day. Only about 40 million gallons per day, or about 6% of that being dumped, is presently being renovated and reused. Statewide, about 8% of the total wastewater is being reused, most of it for irrigation. The cost of additional processing to achieve the necessary water quality has been a deterent in the past, but present requirements for increased treatment before wastewater can be disposed anywhere into the environment have made the additional costs for processing to irrigation quality relatively small. This present waste of a valuable and dwindling resource cannot be tolerated when looking to the long range future and the present drought situation should serve as an impetus to begin serious action. It must be realized that under the present situation virtually all water that goes down the drain is now lost, pumped to the treatment plant, then into the ocean. That water placed on the ground is used for plant growth, is evaporated into the atmosphere to create humidity and future rainfall, or finds its way downward to replenish our groundwater supplies.**

Professor Victor B. Youngner, in his article, "Using Effluent Water for Irrigation," makes the following points which seem to be applicable in other situations and circumstances:

The use of treated sewage effluent water for irrigation has been practiced for many years on a limited scale. Interest in this source of irrigation water is now on the increase and managers of many golf courses, parks and other facilities are considering its use. What are the reasons for this renewed interest? There are several answers depending upon one's point of view.

From the sanitary engineer's view it promises to be a safe method of waste disposal without polluting the environment. The conservationist and

---

* Sarsfield, A. C., "Have You Considered Irrigating with Recycled Water?, **Grounds Maintenance,** Vol. 14, No. 12, November 1979, p. 16.
** Sarsfield, A. C., "How to Save Water Sensibly", Northern California Turfgrass Council, p. 4.

hydrologist see it as a means of water conservation and recharging ground water reservoirs that have been seriously depleted. The user or potential user sees it as a new source of less expensive irrigation water.

Until recently little research has been devoted to use of sewage effluent for irrigation. People were entering into the practice with little knowledge of the numerous ramifications and potential hazards in its use. The user must fully understand these as he has the ultimate responsibility for the proper and safe management of the system. If something goes wrong the blame will be directed to him. He must work closely with State and County Health Departments and the State and Regional Water Quality Control Boards from the earliest planning stages. These agencies have established specific regulations on waste water disposal that are becoming more strict with time.

Waste-water recycling by sprinkler irrigation is feasible because the vegetation and soil act as a living filter system. As the polluted water moves through the soil, numerous constituents are removed or destroyed by the plant roots, soil microorganisms, and the soil itself. Thus, by the time the water reaches deep water-bearing strata where it might be removed for reuse, it is again of drinking-water quality.

However, successful recycling of waste-water requires that the user or potential user keep a number of considerations in mind. He must never forget the possible health hazards from biological and chemical constituents of the water. He must be certain that there is no runoff into surface waters and he must watch for possible plant toxicity. Above all, his irrigation system must be the best possible in design. Problems that may arise from faulty design when using high-quality water will be many times more serious when using waste-water.

Trouble-free waste-water irrigation is possible only if many factors are evaluated and considered during planning and construction. First, of course, is the quality of the waste-water. Sewage effluents are not the same but will vary greatly depending upon the source. Usually water derived primarily from domestic use will be satisfactory. However, if the source includes many industries the quality may be too poor because of toxic substances, especially heavy metals such as copper, zinc, cadmium and mercury. Other important water quality considerations are total dissolved solids which will indicate the salinity hazard; sodium absorption ratio (SAR) which, if it is high may indicate future soil structure and water infiltration problems; boron which is very toxic to many plants; and organic matter which can lead to plugging of sprinkler heads and valves.

If the area to be irrigated is open to the public, odor must be considered.

A thorough soil survey of the area to be used is highly recommended. A shallow soil over rock or hardpan may cause inadequately purified water to move horizontally into surface waters or through rock fissures into ground waters. Infiltration rates and hydraulic conductivity of the soil must be determined so that water application rates can be adjusted to avoid surface runoff or ponding.

Most sandy-loams are good as water will move into and through them at a sufficiently high rate while their exchange capacity and other characteristics will be such that good removal of dissolved and suspended constituents of the water will be accomplished. Sands and clays should be avoided if possible. Water will move too rapidly through sands and not rapidly enough through clays. If the water has a high SAR, clay soils may lose their structure in time and become very poor for plant growth or water purification.

Topography of the area must be such that there are no steep slopes which will lead to surface runoff. Nor should there be any depressions or pockets that will collect water on the surface. If there are ponds or streams in the area the sprinkler system must be designed so that absolutely no effluent water falls directly into them.

Depending upon the quality of the water, irrigation of all types of plants may not be equally desirable. In general, turfgrasses may be the best plants for this purpose. They take up large amounts of the nitrogen, phosphorous and potash found in the water. They will also accumulate large amounts of boron without showing toxicity symptoms. However, some turfgrasses are better than others. If salinity is expected to become a problem, salt tolerant grasses such as tall fescue, bermuda and St. Augustine grass should be selected.

Many ornamentals have a low tolerance to both salinity and boron. Selection of ornamentals, therefore, must be made with care. If plants of low tolerance must be used in some locations, a separate irrigation system using better water should be considered if at all possible.

If the "living filter" system is to work at its best on turfgrass, all clippings should be removed. If this is not done the substances taken up by the grass will be returned to the soil as clippings decompose and the necessary purification may not be accomplished.

Drift of irrigation water onto any crop in the area must be avoided. Health regulations relating to waste-water irrigation or contamination of crops are very specific and strict.

Finally, weather conditions must be considered. The direction and intensity of wind may determine the design of the irrigation system and the time of irrigation. Where projects are planned in areas of high rainfall, the user may be faced with the choice of irrigating during wet weather or storing the water in ponds for extended periods of time. Many contracts for waste-water require that the user accept a specified amount of water each day regardless of weather conditions. Temperature is another factor of importance. Will winter temperatures cause problems of frozen irrigation systems because the waste-water must be used each day? Will high summer temperatures produce high evaporation rates and an excessive accumulation of dissolved solids on plant and soil surfaces?*

Dr. Youngner goes on to conclude that article in the following words:

In summary, the potential user must thoroughly evaluate all aspects of waste-water irrigation in respect to his specific site and the quality of water available to him. The irrigation system must be designed and the site modified as dictated by such study. In some cases the study may indicate that irrigation with waste-water is not feasible or desirable at that location.

* Youngner, Victor B., "Using Effluent Water for Irrigation, **California Turfgrass Culture**, Vol. 24, No. 4, p. 27.

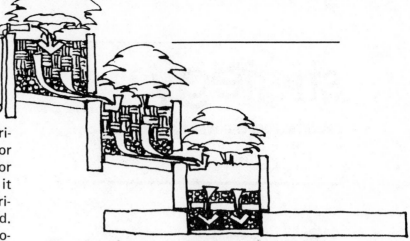

The "living filter" approach to waste-water disposal is not necessarily universal in its application.*

Much of the water traditionally used in irrigation has gone through tertiary treatment or has been fully purified and is acceptable for drinking water. In times of water shortage, it may be necessary to consider water for irrigation which has been less than fully treated. In this way valuable water is able to be provided to plants and the landscape is able to be used as a filter to help cleanse what would otherwise be regarded as "waste water" before it is returned to the water cycle as ground water.

One of the most obvious reuses of water is to allow unused water to flow down hill from one level to another in a series of planters or terraces. This has been extensively used in agriculture throughout history in all sections of the world, but needs to be anticipated in the original design in landscape projects. If water is applied at the highest elevation on a site and if the site is designed to encourage or guide the flow of water from level to level much of the same water can be used over and over on the same site. This can save water and curtail the need for additional water to be applied to the landscape plants.

In some cases, more elaborate planters or containers may be designed or developed which helps to guide or control the flow of water downward from plant to plant.

The reuse of water is essentially taking water out of the full cycle and using it for landscape irrigation at different times in the cycle. It is a relatively extreme strategy or a strategy used most often in extreme water shortages. The reuse of water is:

- short cycling the water cycle,

- using water before it is fully recycled, certain water can be used before its time,

- moving water from one use to another before it is fully recycled,

- using water a number of times before it is fully purified,

- using water for landscape irrigation after it has been used for other purposes and before it has been fully purified,

- using rather "dirty" water for irrigation rather than completely "clean" water.

The caveats which must be remembered in reusing water is that the water:

- be just clean enough,
- cause no damage to the environment,
- cause no danger to human health,
- cause no harm to the landscape,
- be only from certain sources or used for limited purposes previously.

* Ibid., p. 28.

strategy

"MAKING WATER WETTER"

 . . . additives may be used in water to make water either "wetter" or more effective in providing moisture to the plants. **99**

There are two types of additives which may be used in water to make water either wetter or more effective in providing moisture to the plants and landscape. The first of these is the wetting agent known as surfactants or adjuvants. These are wetting agents used to increase the capacity of water to penetrate stratified or hydrophobic soils. In an article in the January 1978 issue of *GROUNDS MAINTENANCE* Magazine, Dr. Ronald C. Smith states the following in regard to the use of these materials in improving the effectiveness or efficiency of water in penetrating and becoming available to help in the growth of landscape plant materials:

> In one case history, the manager of a grounds maintenance operation in Lakewood, Colorado, found places where his client's turf was browning out in irregular patches despite a properly functioning irrigation system. He increased the time on the automatic cyclers, but the turf area continued to turn completely brown.
>
> The adjuvant was applied via a pressurized sprayer, (about two quarts of

adjuvant in 600 gallons of water), and the irrigation cycles continued. Within two weeks the turf areas were returning to their normal green color.

The problem in this and similar locations was very poor soil mixing when the landscaping was originally installed. With total soil renovation unacceptable to clients, using adjuvants may overcome the shortcoming. When the soil mix has become partially stratified, it may be impervious to irrigation practices with plain water. With the adjuvant molecularly adhering to the soil particles, the soil overcomes its hydrophobic properties, allowing the water to more effectively wet all surfaces, especially in the capillary spaces where the water is needed for plant uptake by the root system.

In other landscape situations, the applications apparently made previously applied fertilizers available to plants. The manager reported "significant new growth" occurring on the plants shortly after the adjuvant was applied, with only the normal watering regime being followed.

The success stories with adjuvants do not stop here. They have long been used by maintenance supervisors to overcome poorly drained areas in the landscape, to make fertilizers, insecticides and fungicides more effective, and to make more water available to the plants with less of it being applied.

Water molecules have tremendous cohesive properties, clinging together in lakes, puddles and raindrops. This cohesiveness, or molecular bonding, is what makes it relatively difficult for water to move into hydrophobic surfaces or stratified layers near the turf surface. The water molecules stay together in relatively large droplets, allowing little surface coverage to take place, resulting in uneven wetting of the soil profile.

When automatic irrigation systems are functioning properly, we have a tendency to believe that water stress will not manifest itself, and that color and vigor of the plants will be normal. It is not until the plant material wilts or loses color that we question the wetting ability of the water as it has been applied. The right amount of the proper surfactant can cause water to lose some of its cohesive properties so it can enter rapidly into the soil profile and fill both the macro- and micropore spaces. This allows the water to more effectively wet all surfaces, especially in the capillary spaces where the water is needed for plant uptake by the root system.

As for the labor and related material savings, the application of fertilizer can be more effective when used with a surfactant—less fertilizer is needed for the desired effect. In addition, it has been observed that the use of a surfactant alone, in proper dilution, releases some locked up nutrients, resulting in increased plant growth and vigor. This could reduce the frequency of fertilizer application, saving money in both labor and materials. Control of snowmold or thatch buildup is facilitated with surfactant usage, as the chemicals used to control both are more effectively utilized in the turf eco-system.

However, not all adjuvants are equally effective, and some will cause plant toxicity under certain soil and weather conditions, if the concentrations are too high. Research has shown the non-ionic types to be the best under most conditions. It is suggested that the adjuvant be experimented with on a small scale before attempting wholesale use of it in your landscape situations. The right adjuvant should:
- Promote uniform root zone wetting.
- Overcome the effects of compacted soil.
- Eliminate localized drying and excessive wilting.
- Eliminate standing water.

Properly used, surfactants can be a boon from management, income producing, and cost reducing points of view. Surfactants will help get water into plant material to aid in its protection against winter desiccation. They help move water quickly through the soil profile to minimize disease proliferation, and to retain it over a longer period of time to minimize drought and heat stress.*

The beauty of this action is that the macropore spaces do not remain filled for long; the treated, non-cohesive water will respond quickly to the force of gravity, emptying these larger pores rapidly. While the water may lose some of its cohesive properties, it still retains its ability to adhere to soil surfaces with the right type and concentration of surfactant. The water adhering to these micropore spaces, known as capillary water, is what is available to plant root systems for growth.

The right surfactant for a particular use should:
- Be non-toxic to the plants in proper, effective concentrations.
- Be economical to use.
- Save labor.
- Save on material usage.
- Be available in both liquid and granular forms.

A small amount of surfactant added to the irrigation water in the Eastern or more humid regions of the country would allow for rapid penetration and utilization of water. In the desert regions of the West, granular applications would be more effective; subsequent irrigation or rainfall would wash the surfactant from the granular carrier into the soil profile.

Some grass species show heat and drought stress more easily than others, while some are disease-prone when the water stands on the surface for prolonged periods. Using the right surfactant will help move the water into the soil quickly and uniformly, resulting in more water being available to the turf with less being applied. Many golf course superintendents report 30-50% less water being used due to quicker penetration. *

One other additive which may be used in water to expand the capability of the water in providing moisture to the landscape plant is a super-absorbent material made by grafting man-made acrylic compounds to cereal grain starches and hydrolizing the combination. These materials were introduced as "super-slurpers" during the period from 1973-75. In an article by Kathy Copley, the editor of *GROUNDS MAINTENANCE* Magazine, in the September 1980 issue, entitled, "Super Absorbent Expands into Horticultural Uses," the following statements were made:

Absorbing 200 to 5,300 times their own weight of pure water in the laboratory, the gels established new standards of absorbency. According to its manufacturer, 1 pound of Terra-Sorb 200 will absorb 20 to 25 gallons of water, or about 50 times as much moisture as peat absorbs.

The absorbents maintain their water-holding ability for 6 months to a year or more. The material biodegrades in relation to the number of times it expands and contracts, absorbing and releasing moisture into the soil. The material expands to as much as 30 times its original size; the expansion may provide increased soil aeration. *

That article goes on to describe the following aspects of the use of this material as a soil additive:

Soil Additive

David Miller, USDA soils research leader at Prosser, Washington, has studied the effect of the absorbents on water retained by soils after irrigation. He says, "Although present costs of 'super slurper' may be prohibitive, except for specialized conditions . . . our data indicate that water retention of sandy soils can be greatly increased by treatment . . ." He added the absorbent at the rate of 0.5 percent by weight to the upper 60 centimeters (about 2 feet) of sand in laboratory soil columns. This treatment "increased the available water retained by the sand to nearly the same levels as that retained by a loam and a silt loam," he says. "This effect could also decrease wind erosion through maintaining a moist surface for a longer period after irrigation."

W. D. Shrader, agronomy professor at Iowa State University, says, "Sandy soil treated with 0.2 percent 'super slurper' by weight has about the same water-holding capacity as the best of the Corn Belt soils." Although complete modification of sandy soil would be prohibitively expensive, he says, "There are situations in which slight or localized increases in available soil water would be highly beneficial."

* Smith, Ronald C., "Making Water Wetter", **Grounds Maintenance,** January 1978, Vol. 13, No.1, p. 42.

** Copley, Kathy, "Super Absorbent Expands Into Horticultural Uses", **Grounds Maintenance,** September 1980, Vol. 15, No. 9, p.62.

He cites a field trial on a very sandy 30 percent slope on a dam construction site near Webster City, Iowa. The area was devoid of vegetation. Alta fescue was seeded in three sloping areas treated with 0.0, 0.1 or 0.2 percent of a super absorbent. After 3 months, fescue harvested from the 0.2 percent area weighed four times as much as that from the untreated area and twice as much as fescue harvested from the area that received 0.1 percent absorbent.*

The article concludes with the following statement concerning the implications of this material in grounds maintenance:

Implications
The majority of the research to date has been geared toward agricultural uses, but the knowledge gained is equally applicable to the grounds care industry. Growers can use the absorbents to grow better plants faster, possibly reducing the cost. Grounds managers can reduce the amount of water plants need and the frequency with which they need it, thus cutting the water and labor costs associated with irrigation. Sod growers and landscape contractors can increase the survival chances of sod. Revegetation specialists can increase seed germination and long-term survival rate on their projects. Interior planting experts can increase the time period between waterings, giving employees more time to spend on plant inspections and other maintenance.**

Obviously this sort of material has potential implications in use to reduce moisture requirements during extreme water shortages.

The surfactant helped to form a film around the soil particle which serves to hold the water in suspension for a longer period of time in the space between the soil particles.

Surfactants form a film around soil particles

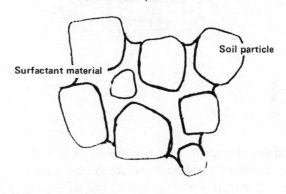

Helps to hold moisture in between soil particles

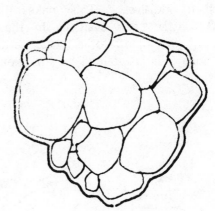

Water adhering to soil particles

Pushes small soil particles apart and allow water to flow and be held between them

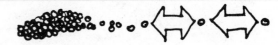

*Ibid., p.62.
**Ibid.,p.64.

Large soil particles (such as sand) allow water to percolate and evaporate too quickly

Small soil particles are too tightly packed and do not allow water to penetrate but force it to run off

As these materials are mixed with the soil they position themselves between soil particles. Then, as water is added, the adjuvant absorbs great amounts of water, expands pushing the soil particles apart and holds the water far longer than most soil types without such additives. This makes limited water "wetter" and available in the root zones of most plants for a longer period of time since it is is retained by the expanded adjuvant.

Surfactants coat soil particles and hold water close to each grain. This separates the particles and holds water in the spaces between.

Adjuvants respond to water by expanding and by holding great amounts of water for long periods of time.

Therefore the same materials can help either with soil that won't let water in or soil that won't hold it after it gets in. They do different things with different soils; they tighten some soils and they loosen other soils.

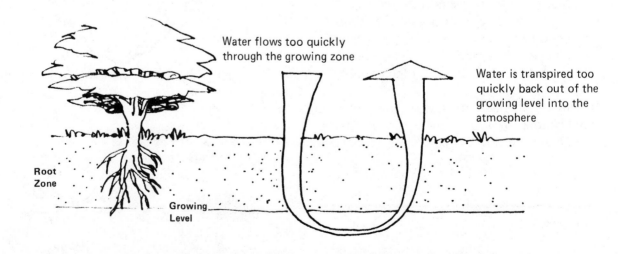

Water flows too quickly through the growing zone

Water is transpired too quickly back out of the growing level into the atmosphere

Root Zone

Growing Level

Small soil particles, tight bonding

Making water "wetter" is obviously not absolutely possible. Soil surfactants or adjuvants are a means to help the soil retain more of the available water and to loosen and lubricate soil to allow water to penetrate and be held in the spaces between soil particles. These materials absorb water and act as a water retaining gel when mixed with soil with either large or small particles. Water adheres to and is absorbed by these particles and is held in the spaces between soil particles when these materials are used. As soils are loosened and as moisture is held in the root zone, it is possible for roots to penetrate to a far greater extent to avail the plant of additional water in the soil.

Adjuvant particle added to tight soil expanding to loosen the tight soil

Surfactants and adjuvants are one other means to help existing water supplies to be used more effectively and efficiently during times of shortage. They can usually only be used in relatively small areas in planters or containers or around only the most indispensible plants in the landscape. In time, as the cost of these materials is brought down, the labor costs for periodically integrating them into the soil will be the only impediment to their widespread use. Hopefully, in time, improvements will be made in the length of time the materials are effective.

When water is added the adjuvant particle expands, opening up tight soil allowing water to be stored and to penetrate more effectively

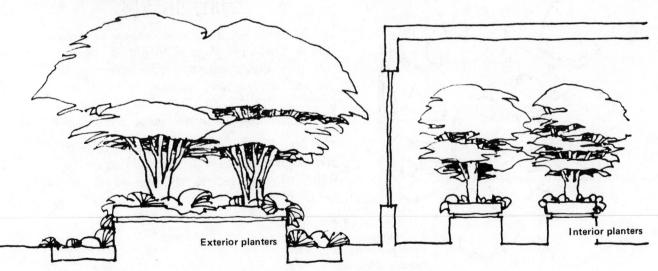

Exterior planters

Interior planters

Adjuvants are most useful and appropriate in small areas such as indoor or outdoor containers

Water applied
to adjuvant particle

Before water is applied

A soil which is too sandy will not hold water but will allow it to pass through the root zone where it is most usable to growing landscape plants. A soil which is too compacted will not allow the water to penetrate to the root level of the plants. Water which is applied to a heavily compacted soil may run off the soil surface and be wasted or lost as far as specific plants are concerned.

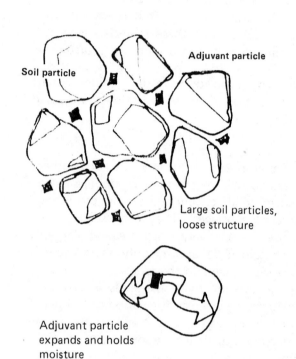

Adjuvant particle

Soil particle

Large soil particles, loose structure

Adjuvant particle expands and holds moisture

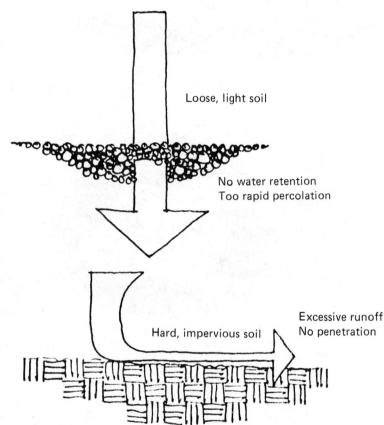

Loose, light soil

No water retention
Too rapid percolation

Hard, impervious soil

Excessive runoff
No penetration

After water is applied

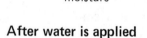

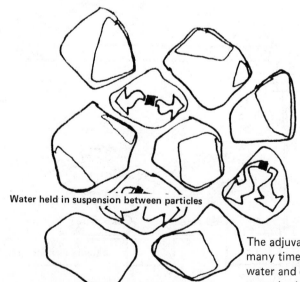

Water held in suspension between particles

The adjuvant particle holds many times its volume of water and expands to hold water in the spaces between soil particles

Soil additives are still rather expensive, they take a great deal of time to put in the soil and they don't last long once they are in the soil. They are, however, a valid consideration as an alternative or a strategy for conserving water in some situations.

The use of soil additives such as surfactants and adjuvants opens a new strategy as a result of new technology applied to an old problem.

strategy

ESTABLISHING WATER PRIORITIES

> 66
>
> . . .a series of priorities which determines what, when, how much, and how to irrigate plants with limited resources. 99

When there is plenty of water available, either through natural precipitation, or through readily available irrigation water, there is obviously little or no need to be concerned about what gets watered first or what gets watered last. However, if the water supplies, from whatever source, become more limited, it is possible and advisable to establish watering priorities. In case of a cutback, it is necessary to answer the questions of what gets neglected first and what gets neglected last; what gets watered first and what gets watered last, if you only have a limited amount of water to use to either enable plants to barely survive or to grow and flourish.

Many managers and homeowners establish a series of priorities which determine what, when, how much, and how in regard to irrigating plants with limited resources. A basic question which must be asked in establishing or re-establishing these water priorities for any landscape area has to do with what gets watered, where you place the limited water, when it gets watered, and how much water is used for each plant or each area.

The question of establishing watering priorities based on what can or should be watered will have to do with the individual needs of a specific plant or planting area, the amount of water available, and the relative importance of certain areas or plants. Turf obviously takes a certain amount of water. Different turf varieties take different amounts of water at different times during the growing season. Trees usually have much deeper root systems than do shrubs and ground covers, therefore, watering, to be of any help or use in saving large, mature trees, has to be very localized around the drip line of the trees and has to be done very deeply. Usually this is beyond the scope or capabilities of any irrigation or watering system. Large trees usually tap into the available ground water in a specific area. This is not the case, however, with relatively small trees or newly planted trees where traditional irrigation or watering practices are much more effective. This usually should be done through hand watering so that the amount of water placed around these small trees can be carefully monitored and controlled. Shrubs, on the other hand, range from very small, low-growing shrubs to very large tree-like shrubs. Usually, deep watering, especially early in the growing season, can have a decided impact on shrubs of all sizes. Therefore, watering priorities can be established specifically based on what to water or what needs extra water within the overall landscape. Watering priorities may also be established based on where the water specifically should be placed.

In periods of water shortage or drought, obviously water cannot be placed everywhere, and even if it could, it should not be placed uniformly throughout the entire landscape, as happens when natural precipitation in the form of rainfall occurs. Generally, in establishing water priorities, to conserve the maximum amount of water, the water should be used in the landscape areas which have the highest visibility, such as at the front entrance of a residence or in high use areas which need water to preserve the quality or the resilience of the plant material. This is especially true on athletic fields and the greens of golf courses. Locational priorities may also include watering specimen plants, or plants which are difficult or expensive to replace.

Some priorities may be established based on the concept of irrigation zones as often used in the southwestern United States. Various zones within the overall landscape would receive much more water and attention than would other specific zones. For instance, the interior garden courtyard of many homes in the American Southwest would contain many of the specimen or showy plants which require more water. The area outside this courtyard or around the edges of the house would be planted with drought resistant plants and would be on a lower priority or scale in the use of water to maintain these particular plantings.

Priorities for applying water in landscape settings may also be established specifically on *when* the water should be applied. The application of water to any plant or any area containing plants should be based on the growth cycle of each plant. Obviously this cycle is much different for different varieties. In some cases, especially in providing irrigation for large shrubs, or small trees, the water should be applied heavily in late winter or early spring. In ground cover or turf areas, since the root system is much shallower, the water should be applied in mid-summer when less natural precipitation occurs. In other plants, specifically flowering bulbs or in larger trees, water should be made available late in the autumn so that plants do not go into the winter in a dehydrated condition.

In periods of water shortage or drought, water should never be applied to plants on a regular predictable basis based on so much water applied each week or each month. It should vary from season to season depending upon the type of plant, the depth of its rooting system and its water requirements, the character, nature, and texture of the soil in which the plant is located, the amount of natural precipitation which has fallen or is available, the amount of available ground water which is available to the plants, and the temperature and humidity which pulls water through the plant and transpires it into the atmosphere.

Watering priorities should also be based on how much water specifically is needed. The decision may be made to apply less water to more plants so that everything in the landscape is maintained in a "near stress" condition or whether more water is used on fewer plants to save the most important, most expensive or the most difficult to replace plants and to let other plants survive if they can in the drought condition. Generally the priorities can be established by the grounds manager to provide for deep watering of plants less often because the root system in these plants is deeper or whether to provide shallow watering more often. This is especially the case in shallow rooting plants such as low shrubs, ground covers or turf areas. During periods of extreme drought or any type of water shortage it is advisable to learn to observe the plants daily to acertain signs of stress or of damage to the plants themselves. In this way, some sort of record may be made of what plants need how much water at certain times. Undoubtedly, in time to come, research will be undertaken in those areas faced with periodic droughts to provide the necessary information to assist in understanding the water needs of various types, varieties and sizes of plants. Until this is available for any given region it is wise to evaluate carefully the water needs of your own plants within your landscape area.

In establishing watering priorities it is also wise to consider how water is to be applied to plants and planting areas. Obviously there is a wide range of ways that the water can be applied. Some are inherently more efficient than others, however, in times of drought, it is wise to very carefully determine *how* best to apply just exactly the right amount of water to each plant or each planted area. This may require much more diversity in irrigation systems than would normally be the case if water were plentiful. The most water efficient and most appropriate system for application of water for the plant should be the only criteria in determining the means of applying water as a part of the overall establishment of priorities. Not the most energy efficient or even the most labor efficient method should be considered, but that which most efficiently uses the limited amount of available water should be the prime criteria. In some instances water applied by hand may be most carefully measured and evaluated as an individual plant is irrigated. Obviously this is costly and may use a great deal of energy to reach the site. However it does in some cases apply just exactly the right amount of water and no more to a specific plant. The use of sprinkler irrigation many times may be the most effective method of applying water. This is especially true if the sprinkler is installed carefully and is properly automated. The Northern California Turfgrass Council has prepared a brochure entitled, "How to Save Your Landscape and Save Water," and in that publication they cover some of the major points to observe in establishing water priorities in the use of sprinkler irrigation. The text of that publication is as follows:

Some General Observations:
Landscape professionals generally agree that in normal years most landscaping receives more water than is necessary. It should be kept in mind that through this emergency period, your goal should be to keep all planting in a near stress condition. That is, watered only enough to keep grasses and plant material alive. Professionals will in part accomplish this by a process called hardening off. In layman's terms this means to gradually extend the length of time between waterings. Over a period of months the plants have a tendency to require less water and become more drought resistant.

How to Sprinkle:
Automated irrigation systems offer the ultimate in both control of watering and water distribution. Because of coverage efficiency and the ability to precisely control operating time, volume can be accurately monitored. The typical automated irrigation system, properly installed and maintained, should offer a minimum of 40% saving in water over a manual system.

If a manual system is used, it should not be left unattended. While this type of system offers the same distribution of water advantages as its automated counterpart, lack of timing control requires close attention to prevent over-watering and unnecessary runoff. Most manual systems can be converted to automatic to maximize their efficiency.

If you do not have an irrigation system, use an oscillating (or wave type) sprinkler, or an impact drive revolving sprinkler for larger lawn areas. Watering by hand held hose is the most wasteful and inefficient method of irrigation and should be avoided if at all possible.

Drip or trickle irrigation, with its low precipitation rates, can be effective for some ornamental planting. Drip irrigation applies water through emitters strategically placed near the base of the plant. This tends to concentrate the water where it will do the most good, close to the root zone. Your landscape contractor or nurseryman can advise you as to the suitability of a drip system for your particular type of planting.

How Often and How Much to Water and When:
Obviously this depends on the type of plant material and the soil conditions involved. When your lawn turns a dull

gray green and loses its resiliency, it is approaching a water stressed condition and should be irrigated. Many shrubs will droop as they approach an absolute need for water. The objective of efficient irrigation is only to provide water to the soil surrounding the root area of the plant. To accomplish this, do not apply water more rapidly than the soil can absorb it. At the very first sign of saturation or runoff, turn off the irrigation system and allow the first watering to soak in for an hour or two before repeating the cycle.

As a general rule, shrubbery requires far less water than turf areas for stress maintenance. In most cases once a week should be sufficient, less often if plants are properly hardened off. Water only when stress signs appear.

All watering should be done at night or during early morning hours when wind and evaporation factors are at their lowest point. Do not water during the heat of the day.

How to Make Watering More Efficient:
• Thatch build-up in lawn areas should be removed as soon as possible. Thatch restricts penetration of water, air and nutrients.

• If soil is compacted, aeration (coring) is desirable to increase water penetration. Aerating should be done only during the spring months or after fall rains resume.

• Apply only balanced, low nitrogen content fertilizer. Use sparingly, if at all, during the summer months. This will promote slow growth.

• Mow grass higher and less often. Blue grasses and perennial ryegrass should be mowed at a 2 inch height. Don't let grass grow to more than twice the recommended mowing height.

• Eliminate weeds. They compete with grass and other plant material for water.

• Mulch beds to help retain moisture.

• Make sure that your sprinkler system is in good repair, that there are no leaks, and that heads are properly adjusted to eliminate any overspray on paved areas or buildings. Investigate the source of any unusual run-off, puddling or overly saturated areas.

• If you have an automated sprinkler system, make sure the controller is properly set to achieve minimum watering levels.

• If you are installing new landscaping, try to utilize plant materials that tend to be more drought tolerant. Your nurseryman or licensed landscape contractor can offer you assistance in selecting appropriate varieties.

• Remember that much of your indoor water can be recycled for use on exterior plant material to further extend water savings. Dish rinse water, a bucket with your morning shower, cleaning water with biodegradable soaps, and cooking water that would usually be thrown away are but a few sources of extra water that can be used for irrigation purposes.

How Much Water a Sprinkler Uses:
If you use a revolving sprinkler on a hose stand, most of them have a fractional number on the nozzle where the water comes out, usually stamped into the side. This tells you the nozzle size that determines the approximate amount of water discharged in gallons per minute as shown at the top of the next page.

Nozzle Size	Discharge in GPM	
	@50 psi	@ 100 psi
3/32	1.85	2.62
7/64	2.52	3.57
1/8	3.29	4.66
9/64	4.17	5.90
5/32	5.14	7.28
11/64	6.23	8.81
3/16	7.41	10.48
13/64	8.70	12.30
7/32	10.09	14.27
15/64	11.58	16.37
1/4	13.18	18.64

To find your total water use, multiply the approximate discharge rate figure for your sprinkler nozzle from the appropriate water pressure range column by the number of minutes of operation. For example, a sprinkler with a 5/32" nozzle operated for 15 minutes at about 50 pounds per square inch of water pressure will discharge about 77.1 gallons (5.14 gpm x 15 minutes). *

Dr. Ronald C. Smith in an article in the January 1980 issue of GROUNDS MAINTENANCE Magazine entitled, "Current Water-Use Research" points out that:

Conservatively, 40 to 50 percent of turf irrigation water is wasted—through runoff, excessive percolation from the root zone and evaporation caused by wind and high temperature. **

In any specific situation all of the alternatives for applying water or irrigating plants should be explored. Hand watering is labor intensive, but since someone is there it is possible to apply exactly the right amount of water and no more. Sprinkler irrigation can cover a much wider area of the landscape with very little labor involved. There is, however, a certain amount of waste in sprinkler irrigation.

It may be, however, water efficient in many landscape situations. Drip irrigation is increasingly being accepted to apply small amounts of water periodically directly around the root zone of individual plants. In some cases the most efficient method of applying water may be through the injection of water directly into the root zones. This is once again labor intensive, but does place water into an area in which there is little or no evapotranspiration back into the atmosphere. It is possible, however, that some of the water applied by this method may go down into the soil instead of staying in the immediate root zone. In other cases the use of soaker hoses may be the most appropriate means for applying water. In still other instances flooding an entire area may provide for uniform distribution of water to a limited depth around the roots of shallow rooting plants. The purpose of establishing any watering priorities is to provide just the right amount of water to the growing root zone around the base of each specific type of plant.

If water is short it is advisable to establish watering priorities in the use of that water to provide landscape irrigation. It is necessary in establishing those priorities to answer the questions, what, where, when, how much and and how to apply the limited amounts of water which are available.

The publication, SAVING WATER IN LANDSCAPE IRRIGATION, Leaflet # 2976, Division of Agricultural Sciences, University of California at Davis, suggests the establishment of water budget in a discussion of "If There Just Isn't Enough Water":

Even when there's no shortage of water, it's important not to irrigate too much. In a drought, however, you may not have enough water even to meet the normal needs of your plantings. In that case, here are some suggestions.

---

* **How to Save Your Landscape and Save Water,** Northern California Turfgrass Council, P.O. Box 268, Lafayette, California 94549.

** Smith, Ronald C., "Current Water Use Research", **Grounds Maintenance,** January 1980, Vol. 15, No. 1, p.- 42.

In the spring, make a "water budget" for the coming season. First, estimate the inches of water that will be available to your plants during the growing season by adding the amount already stored in the soil and the amount of irrigation water you expect to add. To estimate the amount of available moisture in the soil at the start of the growing season, determine the storage capacity of your soil reservoir. Then use the hand-feel test to estimate how full the reservoir is.

Second, determine the expected inches of ET loss during the growing season in your area. Then estimate your minimum requirement. Remember, the ET rates given are close to maximum. Many plants can get by with less. For shallow-rooted water-spenders you are determined to save, figure on replacing almost all of the potential ET loss. For deeper-rooted woody plants on deep soil, you should be able to get by on one-half ET, or even as little as one-fourth.

If the amount of expected available water is less than the minimum amount your plants will require, then you must decide how many square feet of landscape you will be able to irrigate during the coming season and how many square feet will have to go without water.

If necessary, make a priority list of which plants to save. Consider these points:

Most established drought tolerant plants on soil at least 4 feet deep should be able to survive in fairly good condition with no irrigation, if they start the growing season with a full soil reservoir. (Important note: for all trees and shrubs, fill up the soil reservoir at the start of the season, if possible—even if you have little water left for irrigation later on.)

Many other woody plants may need irrigation once or twice during the growing season. Fill up the soil reservoir early. Then divide the remainder of your available water into two equal amounts and apply them after the plants show symptoms of moisture stress. If you are extremely short of water, you may be able to irrigate only once.

During a drought, fertilize lightly if at all. Rapidly growing plants use more water.

Irrigate individual shrubs, trees or plant beds separately. In this way each one can be given the right amount of water. Even if your water supply is limited, don't try to spread it too thinly. When you do irrigate a plant, fill all or most of the soil reservoir.

Wait until symptoms of water stress develop before irrigating. By stressing each shrub, tree, or plant bed close to its limit, you can save as much water as possible while keeping the plants alive.

Check the soil moisture under non-irrigated trees and shrubs. Those that have not normally been irrigated or which you thought were benefiting from nearby irrigation actually may have been surviving primarily on winter rainfall. After an unusually dry winter or two, their soil moisture supply could be almost depleted. If it is, they may need special irrigation to survive.

Consider severe pruning, particularly of overgrown shrubs, hedges and vines that will grow back. This can both cut water use and revitalize the plants. Most shrubs will look better if the branches are thinned out or cut back to laterals rather than cut to stubs. This is particularly true of conifers, most of which do not sprout from old wood.

Severe pruning of trees to conserve water is more difficult, and should be attempted only in extreme drought conditions. To significantly reduce a tree's use of water, it must be cut back enough to markedly reduce its size. Otherwise, you merely expose previously shaded leaves to the sun and increase their rate of transpiration. Such severe pruning causes danger of sunburn or other injury.

It's easier to reduce water use of plants growing in containers. Just move them into a shaded area.

Remove some of the plants in crowded beds or low-priority plants that are growing close to others you want to save. This reduces competition for soil moisture. Turf may be the first to go but is easiest to re-establish later.

If no other water is available, it may be possible to irrigate outdoor plantings with household waste water—particularly rinse water. First, however, check with local health and building authorities. (Also see U.S. leaflet 2968, "Using Household Waste Water on Plants.")

Sprays to reduce transpiration (anti-transpirants) may increase the plant's chances of surviving critically dry periods. There are two types: reflecting materials, such as whitewash or white, water-based paint, that reflect sunlight and thereby reduce transpiration; and emulsions, of wax for instance, which plug many of the pores on the leaves. Reflecting materials are more effective when sprayed on the upper surfaces of the leaves; emulsions must be sprayed on the lower surface of each leaf where most, or all, of the pores are located. An anti-transpirant may reduce transpiration from a few days to several weeks, depending on the material, how well it is applied, environmental conditions, and the amount of new foliage produced by the plant after spraying.

A final step: You can start planning to replant part or all of your landscape with plants that require less water. But don't replant until more water is available. Even drought-tolerant plants require extra care and more frequent watering during the year or two required to get them established.*

It may be advisable each year for a grounds manager, especially in drought prone areas, to establish an overall water budget and to monitor carefully from year to year the amount of water which is used in a specific area. The individual home owner or grounds manager of necessity over the years will become extremely knowledgeable on rationing and prioritizing the use of limited amounts of water in landscape situations, especially in areas of perennial water shortages.

In times of water crisis, priorities may have to be developed as to where to water, what to water, how much to water, when to water and even whether to water.

Zones of use, importance and thus water levels may have to be established. The brochure "More Green Per Gallon" published by the City of Phoenix outlines the concept of priority zones or oases in the landscape.

" Many Phoenicians have already discovered one of the biggest benefits of arid landscaping: easy care. Saturday mornings are for tennis, not mowing. No hay fever. Lower water bills - and fewer dollars spent on fertilizer.

---

* **Saving Water in Landscape Irrigation**, Leaflet 2976, Division of Agricultural Sciences, University of California, Davis, California, April 1977, p. 3-6.

Actually, many arid landscapes do include some grass. They use a concept called "oases" or specimen lawns. Commonly this type of yard has a rockscape in the front and grass in part of the back yard. For most people, front yards are basically for decoration - the back yard is where they really live. Grass is grown only in those areas(usually next to the patio) where the yard is used for recreation.

Shrubs and trees that use more water are also placed near the house, with low-water demanding plants situated farther away. Incidentally, these landscape zones might just save you money for installing a watering system. The piping for sprinklers and bubblers can be concentrated near the house, leaving the more drought-resistant plants farther away to be watered by the summer monsoons and an occasional hose.

Many arid-country shrubs and trees grow quite large. Planting them near the house will offer welcome shade from the afternoon sun. With smaller shrubs, you may want to create groupings which will be easier to water.

Arid landscapes comprised of several green oases are naturals for bubblers or drip lines, two water-conserving systems that can be easily automated. Want green areas without mowing? Try courtyards, atriums and gardens. For this spot greenery, plant vines and ground covers(Lantana and verbena are used widely). An added touch is that many of these plants blossom with colorful flowers." *

A high priority plant on which to use water might be a prized specimen, a very large old plant which might be difficult, if not impossible to replace, a plant which might be difficult to grow or find again or a plant which is expensive to buy or replace. All of these might indicate a priority plant on which scarce water might be used.

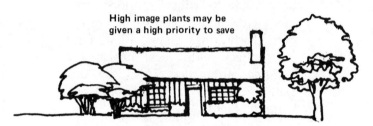

Specimen plants may be given a high priority in the use of scarce water supplies

In other cases, areas of high visibility may have the highest priority of water use in terms of shortage. These might be in the front of residences, around public buildings, in courtyards, on rooftops or at entrances to areas or complexes. If everything can't be saved or fully watered, maybe the high visibility areas are most important.

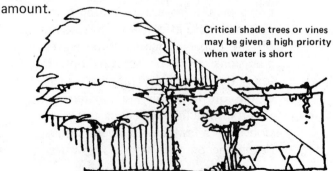

High image plants may be given a high priority to save

In order to preserve the environmental quality of an area, it may be important to make certain that major shade trees do not suffer during water shortages. Critically located areas of turf or vines growing on a trellis which would curtail dust or provide shade may need to be watered before other plants on a site or they may have to get all of the water if there is only a limited amount.

Critical shade trees or vines may be given a high priority when water is short

* **More Green Per Gallon,** Published by the City of Phoenix Public Information Office for the Water Conservation Office of the Water Conservation Office of the Water and Wastewater Department, September 1982, pp. 5-6.

It is possible to apply just a little water to a lot of plants or to apply considerable water to a few plants and neglect the rest.

How much?

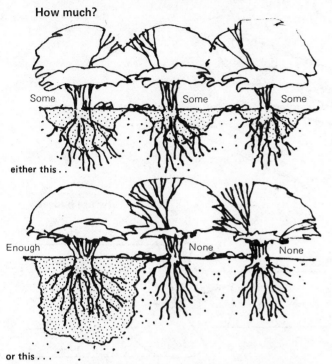

either this . .

or this . . .

In situations where water is very scarce, it may be possible to apply water at just the last minute to save a plant. If any vegetation goes too long without water it will die. As a plant begins to suffer there is a point at which water can be applied and the plant will be rejuvenated for a period of time before the process is repeated. When this happens, priorities need to be established as to which plants will be saved and at precisely what time the water will be applied. This can save water and even though it may not be good for the plant, it may keep it from dying.

ow much?

Watering less deeply and more often

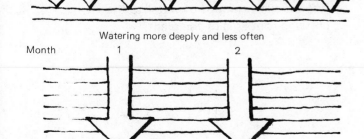

It is also possible to establish priorities by watering more often, using less each time or to water less often, using more each time. As matter of principle, it is better to water more deeply to encourage the roots to reach further down into the soil to bring up and use available moisture which may exist there. Shallow watering may encourage shallow rooting and thus make the plant unable to survive a drought because the roots cannot reach down to available water naturally occuring deeper down in the soil.

How often?

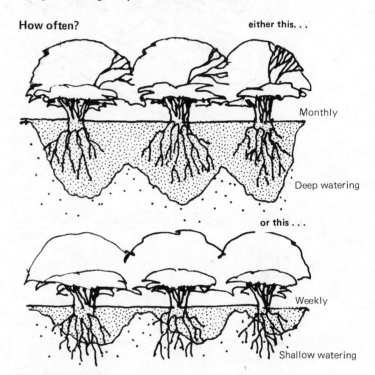

Water just at the last minute. . .

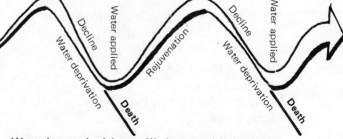

Watering priorities will be established during extreme water shortages whether they are done consciously or unconsciously. Care should be taken that these priorities be established carefully with a view to the long term interest of the most important areas of the landscape and the pleasure, comfort and safety of the users in years to come.

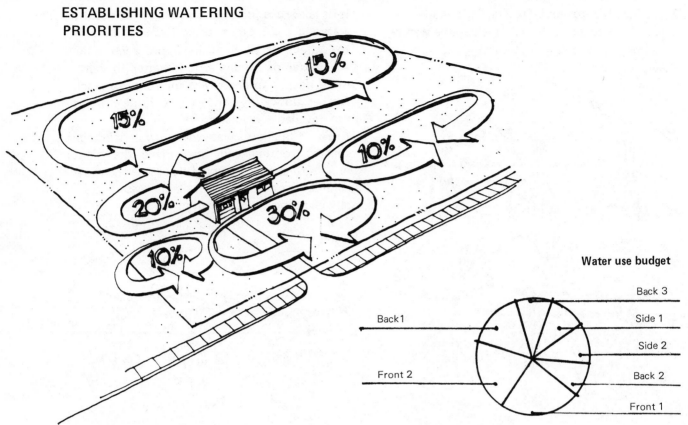

Water use budget

Back 1

Back 3

Side 1

Side 2

Front 2

Back 2

Front 1

What or Which Plants or Areas?
- turf
- trees
- shrubs
- ground covers
- newly planted vegetation
- established vegetation

Where if it Can't be Everywhere Uniformly?
- high visibility areas
- high use areas
- specimen plants
- difficult or expensive plants to replace
- zones of high or low watering

When?
- at the proper time in the growth cycle of each plant
- during seasons when there is generally little water
- safety net (at last possible minute) depends on the plant, the precipitation, the temperature, exposure and wind

How much?
- less on more plants—everything in a near stress condition
- more on fewer plants—save the most important, most expensive or most difficult to replace
- deep watering less often
- shallow watering more often

How?
- the most water efficient and most appropriate for the plants are the only criteria
- hand watering
- sprinkler irrigation
- drip irrigation
- injection
- soaker hose
- flooding
- just the right amount of water to the growing root area of the plant.

Water use allocation or priorities may have to be a part of a public education and awareness program. If people understand where water is being used or allocated, where it is not and why, they understand the seriousness of a water shortage and the possible methods of coping which can be applied in other situations or circumstances.

Water budgets for an area may be established for a week, a month, or a year either as a percentage of the total water available or as to the portions assigned to different parts of a site. This may have to be depicted graphically to communicate a concept or approach to staff or to users.

Watering Priorities - zones or areas

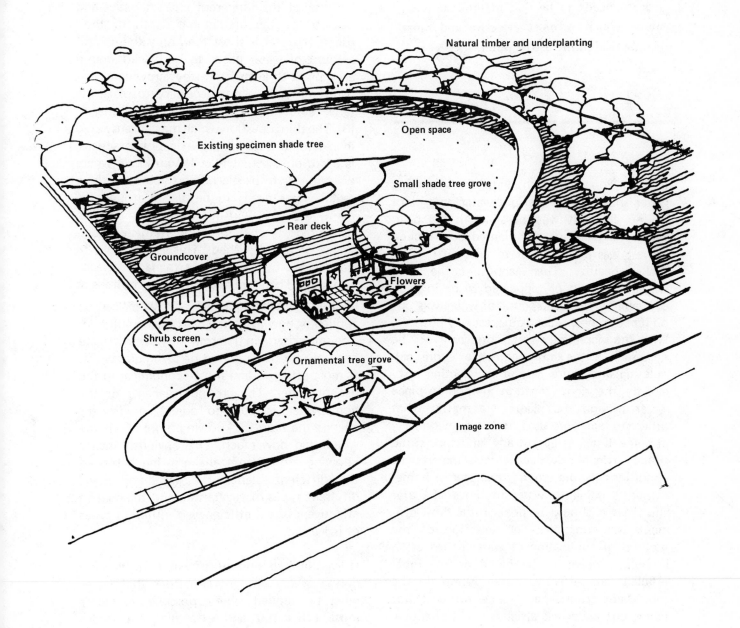

strategy

ALTER OR ADJUST IRRIGATION PRACTICES

The sole criteria in determining how to irrigate needs to be that method or technique which is most effective and most economical in the use of water.

It is no longer enough, with the increasing water shortages, to just put water on a plant in the cheapest way possible. In the past, when the plant or the planted area looked dry, it was possible just to water it until it looked healthy. Then each time the plant wilted, drooped or appeared to be in need of water, a certain amount of water was put on it in the cheapest and quickest way possible. With the increasing water shortages it will be necessary to be more objective, more calculating and more careful in selecting just exactly the right irrigation method to place water around the plants. No matter what other strategies are used, it may be necessary, at some time, in almost any landscape situation to irrigate or water plants during drought conditions. If the grounds manager or homeowner is going to water in times of water shortages it should be done in the most efficient way possible. The selection of the method of application of water or irrigation technique needs to be based on the most efficient and effective water use to do the job. Major criteria need to be, not cost, not labor, but water use efficiency and effectiveness. There are three basic questions which

need to be answered in ascertaining or determining the optimum irrigation practices. These are: (1) Where does water need to be placed? Some plants have roots so deep that irrigation does not quickly affect them. In other cases the roots are so shallow that water only need penetrate the soil to a limited depth. In any case, the water to be effective only needs to be placed around the roots of the specific plant. The next question that needs to be answered is; (2) How much water is needed? Different plants obviously have different water requirements. This is the case because of their inherent characteristics and because of the predictable depth of their roots. If water is short then only the correct amount of water needs to be placed around each plant to keep it healthy, growing or just barely alive. It is not necessary to place the same amount of water around all plants. (3) The third question which may be answered in regard to determining irrigation practices, is based on the first two. If you know where water needs to be placed and you know how much water needs to be placed around the plant, then the next question has to do with how precisely that irrigation is to be undertaken or accomplished. This is what has to be decided by the grounds manager in each situation. There are any number of options or methods or techniques of how water can be applied or how irrigation can be accomplished. The sole criteria in determining how to irrigate needs to be that method or technique which is most effective and most economical in the use of water. The grounds manager or the homeowner is able to adjust, modify or change the *how* by knowing more about the where and how much. This obviously means knowing more about the growing habits of the different plants, the water needs of different types of vegetation, and the relative effectiveness and efficiency of different types of irrigation.

If even limited amounts of water are available during severe drought situations that water must be applied, where possible, to plants most efficiently and effectively. In order to use this limited irrigation water most effectively, it may be necessary to alter significantly traditional irrigation practices. The concept behind this particular strategy is quite simple. Ideally, all plants used in a specific landscape should be able to exist on the amount of water which is naturally available to the plant material in that area. Realistically, however, some irrigation is essential, on some plants, at some time, in some situations, even in times of drought or water shortage. Everything cannot be the same as it had been in the past with plentiful or abundant water. Therefore, the irrigation practices used at other times need to be modified, changed, adjusted, adapted or made more efficient. This alteration may involve the method of application or water, the time of application of water or the amount of water which is applied to specific landscape plants. The essential aim of all irrigation practices, especially during times of extreme water emergency, is to apply just exactly as much water as is needed at exactly the right time so that there is no waste, no infiltration, and no direct evaporation or transpiration. Obviously it is not always possible to do that precisely and completely, therefore, the aim is to use any irrigation method which does as close to that as possible and to alter any previously used irrigation system so that it does do precisely that.

Irrigation needs and requirements will depend on the specific plants being used in a particular grounds area. Water is most effectively used at a time when the plant needs it and when it is applied in the most conserving manner exactly where the plant needs it. Irrigation water also needs to be applied at precisely the right time in the growth cycle of the plant and at a time when natural precipitation is not available. When more fertilizer is being used on any planting more water will be needed to help dissolve the fertilizer material and place it in suspension. Therefore, there is a connection between fertilizer use and water requirements. Different plants use moisture at different levels since their roots pull water from different soil horizons. In order to provide irrigation water to plants during dry periods most efficiently and

effectively, different watering programs should be established for trees, shrubs, ground cover and turf. Very large trees have roots which go deep into the soil. Generally if they have grown to any size at all they are able to survive in a geographic region with very little additional water even during the driest period. Smaller trees and shrubs with shallower roots are able to benefit from occasional deep watering during dry periods when no other water is available.

Different plant species have different water requirements. The original planting design should have been based on the natural ecological community and therefore the designer should have put in plants of similar water requirements near one another. Therefore, it should be possible within a grounds area to provide relatively uniform water quantities to the plants within one area of the landscape. The grounds manager also must ask the question in attempting to conserve energy and water, "What level of growth and development is needed or wanted in this specific plant?" Some plants and plantings, because of their extreme water needs, may have to be flooded and kept with a high level of water available to them, In still other instances the site manager may want specific planting areas to have lush and luxurious growth. In this case it will take a high amount of water which in some cases may be justified. If, on the other hand, the grounds manager wishes a specific plant or planting to have normal growth habits and patterns, the water applied to the plant should be very carefully controlled. In still other instances the plants, during extremely dry periods may be kept only in a state of very limited survival. One of the questions in regard to water usage and conservation that the grounds manager must also ask is, "How important is the area, or a particular plant?" In applying water to plants it is important to understand the plant's growth and dormancy cycle as well as the available moisture which the plant may receive through rainfall or snow melting.

The following is a diagram of the various water application decision options available to the homeowner or grounds manager.

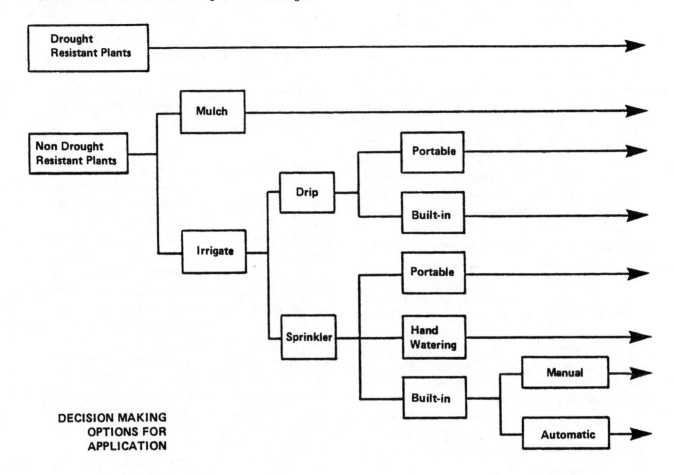

DECISION MAKING
OPTIONS FOR
APPLICATION

Obviously if you choose what will generally be drought resistant plants for use in a specific area there will be no further need for a consideration of irrigation. If the site manager selects non-drought resistant plants there are basically two options. The first of these is to provide adequate mulch over semi-drought resistant plants. This, once again, will call for no further action or activity in regard to irrigation by the grounds manager. If the decision is made to irrigate, the manager has two options.. The first of these is drip irrigation and the second is to select a form of sprinkler irrigation. If the grounds manager selects the drip irrigation option then there are several options. The first of these is portable drip irrigation and the second is a built-in system. If the landscape manager elects to use a form of sprinkler irrigation,

there are three options. The first of these is portable sprinklers, the second is handwatering and the third is a built-in sprinkler irrigation system. If the latter is chosen for use, there are two options once again for the manager. The first of these is manual irrigation and the second is automatic irrigation. In any of these built-in sprinkler irrigation system techniques there are certain limitations.

It takes a great deal of irrigation water applied to any site to equal the amount falling on a site in even a small and limited rain. The gallons per acre, the cubic feet per acre and the tons per acre of water falling on a site in rainfalls of different quantities are shown on the chart at the top of the next page. An equivalent amount of water would require a great deal of irrigation by any means.

Inches of Rainfall	Gallons per Acre	Cubic Feet per Acre	Tons per Acre
1	22,635	3,630	101.1
2	45,270	7,260	202.2
3	67,905	10,890	303.3
4	90,539	14,520	404.4
5	113,174	18,150	505.5
10	226,348	36,300	1,011.0

*

The following chart indicates water measurements and the volume of water delivered with different hose diameters and water pressure levels.

Water Pressure (Lbs.)	Hose Diameter						
	3/8"	13/32"	7/16"	1/2"	9/16"	3/4"	5/8"
30	2.6	3.2	3.8	5.3	7.2	9.3	14.5
40	3.5	4.2	5.0	7.0	9.4	12.2	19.0
50	4.3	5.2	6.3	8.8	11.8	15.3	24.0
60	5.2	6.2	7.5	10.5	14.1	18.3	28.5
70	6.0	7.3	8.7	12.2	16.2	21.0	32.7
80	6.8	8.3	9.9	13.9	18.5	24.0	37.3

Note: Table based on 50-foot hose length: For 25 feet multiply by 1.40; for 75 feet, by 0.80.   **

Because of these limitations it requires different amounts of time to put down one inch of water on 1,500 square feet of lawn or turf. The following chart shows the time required to put down 1" of water on 1,500 square feet of lawn for various hose diameters at 50 pounds per square inch of water pressure.

Hose I.D.	Gals. per min.	Time
7/16"	7.3	2 Hrs. 8 Min
1/2"	10.9	1 Hr. 26 Min.
5/8"	15.1	1 Hr. 2 Min.
3/4"	26.8	35 Min.

***

* Ibid., p. 116.

** Ibid., p. 121.

*** Ibid., p. 120.

In a draft of a publication (Miscellaneous Publication 39) developed by the Agricultural Extension Service of the University of Wyoming in Laramie, entitled "Watering of Lawns," the following table was given for the consumptive use of water for Kentucky Bluegrass:

| Period | Consumptive Use (inches) | |
	Laramie 7,200 ft altitude	Wheatland 4,700 ft altitude
April	2.37	2.79
May	3.53	4.74
June	5.58	6.06
July	5.74	7.16
August	5.15	5.02
September	3.21	3.12
October	1.67	2.64
TOTAL	27.25	31.53

*Consumptive use represents the sum of transpiration from the grass and evaporation from the soil. Any precipitation must be subtracted from the consumptive use to determine the amount of water to be applied by sprinkling.

This shows the increased water which is needed in lower altitudes and conversely the lesser amount of water that was needed for the same type of turf at a higher altitude. It also indicates the progressive need for water during the hot summer months.

At various seasons of the year and at various stages in the growing cycle of the plant irrigation needs and demands will depend, to a certain extent on the soil type and condition where the plant is growing. The soil composition will determine how much water it can hold and it will also determine how the water moves through the soil to be available to the plant. It is generally recommended that irrigation water not be applied to planting areas at a rate greater than one inch of water per hour. Separate valving should be provided for variations in demand such as in shady areas or in areas of full sun, areas of slope of over 6%, or in shrub, turf or flower bed areas. The following chart shows the water storage capacity of soils. This information was provided in a publication entitled "Saving Water in Landscape Irrigation," (Leaflet 2976), available from the Division of Agricultural Sciences at the University of California.

Water Storage Capacity of Soils. *

Soil texture	Inches of available water per foot of soil depth	Gallons per cubic foot of soil
Sand	1/2"–1"	1/3–2/3
Sandy loam	1"–1-1/2"	2/3–1
Clay loam	1-1/2"–2"	1–1-1/3
Clay	1-1/2"–2-1/2"	1–1-2/3

(An inch of water is the amount that would cover the surface 1 inch deep. 1-1/2 inches covering 1 square foot = 1 gallon.)

**

A diagram from the book ALL ABOUT FERTILIZERS, SOILS AND WATER, illustrates the growth cycle of various types of common turf grasses used throughout the United and Canada. Irrigation water must be applied when natural rainfall is not available, but to be effective it must be applied at precisely the correct time in the growth cycle of the plant. Turf needs more water during the prime growth period and as fertilizer is applied it may need even more water. The fertilizer granules need to be "watered in" and dissolved to reach the plant roots. Therefore there is a correlation between the need for food and water for plants at exactly the right time as the individual plant periodically grows and becomes dormant. Therefore not only the amount of water but also the timing of the application becomes a factor.

* Barnes, O'Neill, Borrelli, Pochop and Brosz, "Watering of Lawns", in **Water Requirements for Urban Lawns,** Wyoming Water Resources Research Institute, University of Wyoming, Laramie, Wyoming, Miscellaneous Publication 39, June 1977, p. III-88.

** **Saving Water in Landscape Irrigation,** published by the Division of Agricultural Sciences, University of California, April, 1977, Leaflet 2976, p. 7.

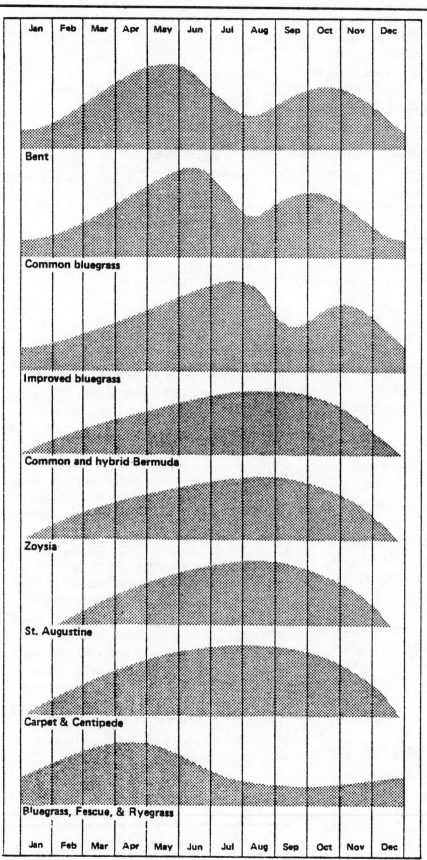

**GROWTH CYCLES
OF TYPICAL
LAWN GRASSES**

* **All About Fertilizers, Soils and Water,** Ortho Books,
Chevron Chemical Company, 575 Market St., San Francisco, California, 1979, p. 98.

There are numerous other charts that appear in other sources which would help the grounds manager in understanding more fully the rate of intake of water for various soils. The following chart is taken from the publication, *A GUIDE TO ESTIMATING LANDSCAPE COSTS.*

Soil Type	Clean Cultivation	Under Healthy Sod	Under Good Organic Mulch
Light (Coarse sandy loam)	0.8 In/Hr.	1.3 In/hr.	1.0 — 1.5 In/Hr.
Medium Light (Sandy loam)	0.5 In/Hr.	1.0 In/Hr.	0.8 — 1.3 In/Hr.
Medium Heavy (Silt loam)	0.3 In/Hr.	0.6 In/Hr.	0.4 — 1.0 In/Hr.
Heavy (Silt clay loam)	0.25 In/Hr.	0.5 In/Hr.	0.3 — 0.8 In/Hr *

A greatly simplified chart has been prepared by Mr. David Lofgren of the Institute for Maintenance Research in Salt Lake City, Utah. It outlines the maximum precipitation rates for various types of soil.

Light Soil—1" per hour or less
Medium Soil—1/2" per hour or less
Heavy Soil—1/3" per hour or less

One other aspect which must be taken into consideration in the application of water to plantings in grounds areas is the angle or degree of slope on which the planting is located. The steeper the slope the greater will be the runoff from the earth's surface, unless the water is applied more slowly. The following chart shows slope and its effect on water application or runoff. For instance, on a slope of 10-15% the water may have to be applied 20-45% more slowly to avoid runoff than would have to be done on a level site.

Grade of slope	Reduction of Infiltration
0% — 5%	0% — 10%
5% — 10%	10% — 20%
10% — 15%	20% — 45%
15% — 20%	45% — 60%
Over 20%	60% on Up

**

Great care should be taken as to the precise time of water usage in irrigation. This is not only seasonally, but also daily. Obviously irrigation is most important any time of the year when plant growth is underway and natural sources of water are not available. During the day the general recommendation for irrigation is either early morning or in the evening. This, of course, will depend on the type of irrigation technique or method utilized since the method of irrigation is correlated to the timing of the application. Any system which sprays water into the air should not be used either at mid-day or when it is extremely windy. During mid-day on a bright, sunny day with low humidity, much of the irrigation water sprayed into the air will evaporate and transpire into the atmosphere. By the same token, if spray irrigation techniques are used on an extremely windy day there is no guarantee that the spray pattern will be as originally intended. Much of the irrigation water will be deposited leeward of the spray head.

---

* **A Guide to Estimating Landscape Costs,** Van Nostrand-Reinhold Publishing Co., New York, p. 117.

** Ibid., p. 118.

In a pamphlet entitled "How to Save Your Landscape and Save Water," prepared by the Northern California Turf Grass Council, the following chart was presented to show how much water a sprinkler uses. The following chart was presented showing nozzle size, discharge at 50 pounds per square inch and gallons per minute at 100 pounds per square inch.

Nozzle Size	Discharge in GPM	
	@ 50 psi	@100 psi
3/32	1.85	2.62
7/64	2.52	3.57
1/8	3.29	4.66
9/64	4.17	5.90
5/32	5.14	7.28
11/64	6.23	8.81
3/16	7.41	10.48
13/64	8.70	12.30
7/32	10.09	14.27
15/64	11.58	16.37
1/4	13.18	18.64

*

The explanation given with that chart explained that to find total water use, it was necessary to multiply the approximate discharge rate figure for a sprinkler nozzle from the appropriate water pressure range column by the number of minutes of operation. For example, a sprinkler with a 5/32" nozzle, operated for 15 minutes at about 50 pounds per square inch of water pressure, will discharge about 77.1 gallons (5.1 gpm x 15 minutes).

The selection of appropriate irrigation techniques for a specific grounds area is the prime responsibility of the manager. Not in every area is irrigation possible or even necessary and not in all areas is some form of irrigation to be provided to certain plant materials.

However, faced with the need for some irrigation in some areas, the manager should be familiar with all of the options available and the relative merit of each. The previously

mentioned publication, *ALL ABOUT FERTILIZERS, SOILS AND WATER*, published by Ortho Books, mentioned the the need for care of applying water and suggested a number of different methods, some of which are applicable to park areas. This publication suggests:

- If you have shallow topsoil on top of hardpan, water lightly and frequently.
- Otherwise, water thoroughly and let the soil dry out somewhat before the next watering.
- Water early enough in the day that the leaves are dry by nighttime.
- In really hot and dry weather, don't be afraid to give the leaves of outdoor plants a cool shower.
- Don't use zeolite-softened water; do add gypsum to the soil if you want to use gray water.
- When irrigating clay or similar "tight" soils, apply water over short periods, separated by a soaking-in period at least twice the length of the application time—for example, 20 minutes on, 20 minutes off, 10 minutes on. For clay soils, use a sprinkler that emits water at as slow a rate as possible.
- Treat steep slopes as you would a clay soil, to minimize runoff.
- When irrigating sandy loams or other open soils, apply water in one continuous period.
- The best time to water is early morning when the sun and wind are both low.
- If you have the choice, water on the cooler days during the summer.
- Set sprinklers to avoid waste on sidewalks and driveways.
- Keep sprinkler heads clean to assure even distribution of water.

This publication goes on to list seven possible ways of applying water, which are:

Flooding—This technique is often used in areas with extreme summer heat and has only limited application in many areas.

* **How to Save Your Landscape and Save Water,** Northern California Turfgrass Council, P.O. Box 268, Lafayette, California 94549, p. 4.

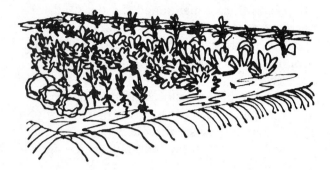

Underground Sprinkler Systems—This type of system is very convenient for large grounds areas with expanses of lawns. Good, even coverage is achieved with a minimum of guesswork. These can be installed on a timer for further convenience and regularity.

Soakers—A soaker hose can emit water slowly and economically. They do not disturb the soil structure and do not cause the crust formation common with overhead sprinklers.

Hose-end Sprinklers—Hose-end sprinklers are commonly used in residential projects and are sometimes used in certain critical areas within public landscapes. Because of their limited range, they are less convenient than a permanent sprinkler, but they are also much less expensive. Care should be taken in selecting the sprinkler best suited to the soil and the area to be watered in order to avoid wasting water.

Furrow Irrigation—Furrow irrigation is largely oriented toward agricultural production.

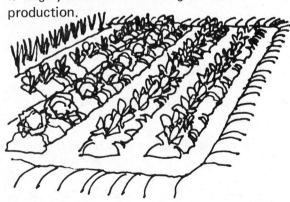

* Adapted from **All About Fertilizers, Soils and Water,** Ortho Books, San Francisco, California 94105, p. 80.

** Ibid., p. 80.

*** Ibid., p. 79.

**** Ibid., p. 80.

Porous Wall Systems—These porous wall systems help significantly to conserve water since they allow an osmosis-like, slow trickle along the entire length which provides a uniform flow for up to 400 feet.

Drip/Trickle Systems—These systems are becoming much more sophisticated in recent years and may provide a very innovative method or technique for the park manager to use in order to provide the maximum irrigation while still conserving a great deal of water and energy. *

---

* Ibid., p. 79.

** Ibid., p. 80.

Hand watering is very labor intensive. It also requires the use of energy to transport landscape maintenance staff to a site to water specific plants. There is, however, not much danger of overwatering plants with hand watering and there is extreme flexibility in placing the hose end in the exact location where water is desired. There is also relatively little permanent on-going expense to irrigate specific plants. It does require very tight management, coordination and a great deal of checking to determine precisely when plants need to be hand watered.

Portable sprinklers used in grounds areas require some labor and there is some overwatering. However, they do provide great flexibility while they do use a limited amount of energy for transportation of the staff and the equipment to a specific site.

Sprinkler irrigation systems require very little labor. They do allow for some overwatering and usually have relatively inflexible patterns. Sprinkler irrigations are quite often higher in cost. They are, however, excellent in areas for turf or ground cover irrigation.

In a study dealing with, "Measuring Lawn Water," the Wyoming Water Resources Research Institute explained the difficulty and the methods for measuring the amount of water required in lawn irrigation in the following way:

> "It is just about impossible to guess how much water is being applied to a lawn without some type of guidelines. In a study of lawn water application rates at the University of Wyoming, it was found that over 50% of the homeowners in a sample from Laramie and Wheatland overwatered their lawns. On the other hand, few homeowners underwatered. It was obvious that most homeowners did not realize how much excess water they are applying, whereas most will avoid underwatering by responding to visible water stress conditions. If an aesthetically pleasing lawn is to be maintained with a

minimum of water, the amount of water applied must be known.

There are several methods for determining the amount of water applied. These include (1) wetting the soil profile to a recommended depth, (2) using catch cans to calibrate the sprinklers, (3) metering the amount of water applied, (4) following average estimated application rates for specific sprinklers.

. . . The following table gives a general idea of the average application rates and size of wetted pattern for various sprinkler types without overlap. Note that application rates decrease as pattern sizes increase. *

Sprinkler Type	Pressure (lbs/sq-inch)		Avg. Application Rate (inches/hr)	Avg. Sprinkler Pattern Size	The Typical Application Rates For Various Types of Lawn Sprinklers*
Buried Head	Low	(10)	0.93	12 ft diameter	
	Medium	(20)	0.86	16 ft diameter	
	High	(30)	0.55	24 ft diameter	
Stationary	Low	(10)	1.81	12 ft diameter	
	Medium	(20)	1.01	16 ft diameter	
	High	(30)	0.82	25 ft diameter	
Impact	Low	(10)	0.50	20 ft diameter	
	Medium	(20)	0.26	25 ft diameter	
	High	(30)	0.22	40 ft diameter	
Rotating	Low	(10)	1.74	12 ft diameter	
	Medium	(20)	0.68	25 ft diameter	
	High	(30)	0.42	35 ft diameter	
Oscillating	Low	(10)	0.80	16 ft x 16 ft	
	Medium	(20)	0.35	30 ft x 30 ft	
	High	(30)	0.27	40 ft x 40 ft	
Traveling	Low	(10)	0.73	30 ft (width)	
	Medium	(20)	0.48	44 ft (width)	
	High	(30)	0.30	48 ft (width)	*

* Borrelli, John and Larry Pochop, "Measuring Lawn Water," in **Water Requirements for Urban Lawns** Wyoming Water Resources Research Institute, University of Wyoming, Laramie, Wyoming, p.-III-91.

In another article by the same authors dealing with,"Selection and Use of Lawn Sprinklers", other considerations and diagrams were presented in the following way:

One of the most likely causes of incorrect watering is the poor water distribution efficiency of the sprinklers used by most homeowners. Actually no sprinkler will distribute the water at equal depths over the entire wetted or sprinkler pattern. This unequal distribution will overirrigate in some areas and underirrigate in others. Most sprinklers do, however, give adequete distribution if overlapped and used properly. The trick is to select the best sprinkler for your situation and then use it correctly.

Each sprinkler will distribute the water in a different pattern. By pattern we mean not only the wetted area, but the relative depths of water within this wetted area. Shown . . . are the cross-sections of sprinkler patterns for the six most common types of sprinklers all operated at a medium pressure. Note that none of them have a very uniform depth of distribution. This points out the need to overlap sprinkler patterns.

*

* Borrelli, John and Larry O. Pochop, "Selection and Use of Lawn Sprinklers," in **Water Requirements in Urban Lawns,** Wyoming Water Resources Research Institute, University of Syoming, Laramie, Wyoming, p. III-93.

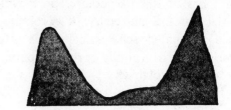

Buried Head

Impact

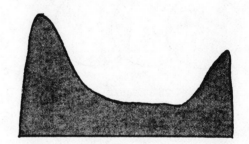

Oscillating

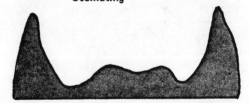

Rotating

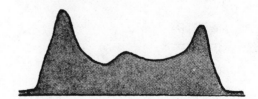

Traveling

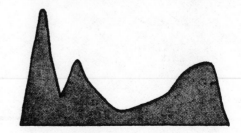

Stationary

The authors of this particular report, which took place at the University of Wyoming in Laramie, indicated schematically the effect of overlapping of various sprinkler patterns when seen in a plan view. This was shown in the following way:

In the draft publication entitled, "Watering of Lawns", from the University of Wyoming Agricultural Extension Service, the following statement was made in regard to water needs in that geographic area: **

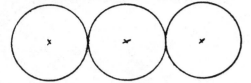

No Overlap

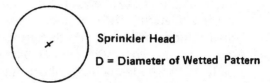

Sprinkler Head

D = Diameter of Wetted Pattern

Wetted Pattern

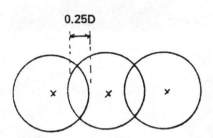

25% Overlap

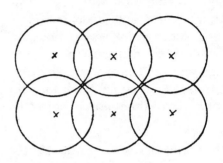

25% x 25% Overlap

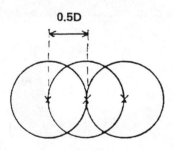

50% Overlap

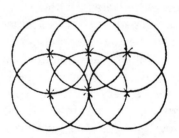

50% x 50% Overlap

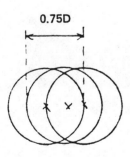

75% Overlap

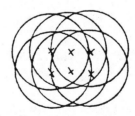

*

75% x 75% Overlap

** Barnes, John R., Patrick K. O'Neill, John Borrelli, Larry O. Pochop, Donald J. Brosz, **Watering of Lawns,** Agricultural Extension Service, University of Wyoming, Laramie, Miscellaneous Publication 39, June 1977, included in **Water Requirements for Urban Lawns,** Project Completion Report to Office of Water Research and Technology, U.S. Department of the Interior, Project B-035-WYO, Laramie, Wyoming, September 1979, p. III-87.

* Ibid., p. III-94.

A good way to minimize water application is to wait for water stress to appear in the lawn before irrigating. Some dry areas generally will appear between waterings due to spots with poor soil, poor distribution or water or other reasons. Water these small areas by hand with a drag hose to minimize water use. If larger areas than desired show signs of water deficiencies, decrease the time between major irrigations. However, be careful to avoid applying more than 1½ to 2 inches of water in any week.

To achieve a relatively uniform distribution of water, sprinkler patterns are overlapped so that more than one sprinkler set or sprinkler contributes water to an area. Hopefully the total application of water will be about the same in all areas. To measure the success of distributing water, a uniformity coefficient(UC) has been developed. A UC of 100 means a perfect water distribution has been achieved with all areas receiving the same depth of water. On the other hand, a UC of 70(the lowest recommended value) means at least 30% of the area will receive 120% or more of the average depth of water, and 30% of the area will receive 80% or less of the average depth of water. As an absolute minimum, no sprinkler should be operated so a UC of less than 60 is achieved.

Shown . . . are UC's for various sprinklers overlapped at various amounts. On comparing UC values for the three pressure levels, no sprinkler is acceptable according to the 70 minimum UC value until overlapped 75% in one direction or 25% x 25% in both directions. In general, the more the overlap of a sprinkler pattern, the higher the UC value. It should be noted that overlapped a sprinkler pattern in one direction only will not achieve a very high UC value.

Christiansen's Uniformity Coefficient (UC) for Lawn Sprinklers†

Sprinkler Type	Pressure (lbs/sq-inch)		Overlaps						
		0%	25%	50%	75%	25% x 25%	50% x 50%	75% x 75%
Buried Head	Low (10)	8*	18	38	54	29	66	86
	Medium (20)	30	38	54	75	45	69	93
	High (30)	27	44	50	68	56	71	95
Stationary	Low (10)	19	30	54	66	37	66	87
	Medium (20)	35	43	57	71	50	72	92
	High (30)	32	47	57	60	61	81	95
Impact	Low (10)	42	53	59	62	68	82	94
	Medium (20)	42	55	58	62	70	81	95
	High (30)	40	56	56	58	77	85	96
Rotating	Low (10)	10	17	37	55	22	53	79
	Medium (20)	26	31	50	64	35	63	85
	High (30)	40	51	57	70	57	67	89
Oscillating	Low (10)	33	33	49	53	38	56	79
	Medium (20)	43	38	51	61	45	63	86
	High (30)	49	48	61	68	49	70	91
Traveling	Low (10)	65**	57	67	90			
	Medium (20)	61	60	65	85			
	High (30)	61	66	68	86			

* A UC of 100 means a perfect distribution of water with respect to depth. The minimum acceptable UC for Sprinkler-systems is 70.

** A traveling sprinkler has an implied 100% overlap in one direction due to the forward movement of the sprinklers.

*

* Ibid., p. III-95.

Sprinkler Patterns*

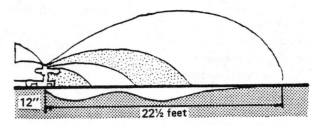

Pattern 1 is effective if you move sprinkler to overlap. Oscillating type and rotating "machine gun" type sprinklers make this pattern.

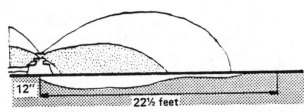

Pattern 2 has most water dropping on inside; you need successive overlaps. Whirling baffle type and fixed heads work this way.

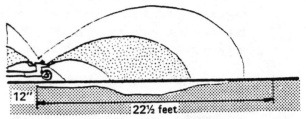

Pattern 3 is useful but erratic; most water falls 4 to 8 feet out. Plastic soakers, types with revolving arms, sieve types deliver water this way.

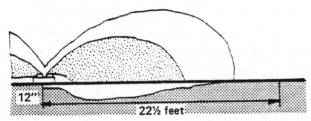

Pattern 4 cone spray soaks only a small area; for best results, turn water to half-pressure, move sprinkler often. One cone spray has two big holes like owl's eyes.

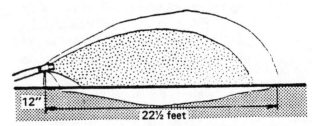

Pattern 5 fan spray throws most of water 7 to 14 feet from sprinkler. Nailhead spike type sprays water through slit in its head.

Root Depths of Seasonal Grasses

Cool-Season Grasses	Root Depth
Annual bluegrass	1 to 4 inches
Creeping bentgrass	4 to 18 inches
Colonial bentgrass	9 to 18 inches
Kentucky bluegrass	9 to 30 inches
Red fescue	9 to 30 inches
Tall fescue	18 to 48 inches

Warm-Season Grasses	Root Depth
St. Augustine	1½ to 6 feet
Zoysia	1½ to 6 feet
Bermuda	1½ to 8 feet

* Adapted from, **Basic Gardening Illustrated**, Lane Publishing Co., p. 19.

One of the more recently developed techniques for use in landscape irrigation is drip irrigation. Many professional grounds managers are very familiar with this technique since it is used to a great extent in agricultural and orchard irrigation. The concept behind drip irrigation is that small amounts of water are able to be applied through very small hoses in precise areas within a landscape area over an extended period of time. In this way the water is able to seep down into the soil to the root levels without causing excessive runoff. This requires, obviously, less water and at the same time also prevents drift or erosion. In an article in the June 1979 issue of GROUNDS MAINTENANCE Magazine, entitled, "Drip Irrigation in the Landscape . . . A Second Look," Mr. A.C. Sarsfield makes the following statement:

Drip irrigation is especially useful for highway plantings and median strips to prevent the wind drift of sprinkler irrigation from wetting the highway and passing vehicles. Using drip for public pedestrian areas in shopping malls or downtown mini-parks prevents wetting of people and sidewalks.

With areas containing more than one type of plant, drip irrigation becomes more complicated.

In landscaping various kinds, types and sizes of plant materials are often mixed. But different plants often require different amounts of water. Drip irrigation can be adapted to their requirements by using:

- Emitters that have different flow rates at the same operating pressure,
- Multiple emitters to apply more water to the root zones of the larger, thirstier plants,
- A combination of these alternatives.

Properly handled, the result on beds, ornamentals, and specimens can be excellent.

Conventional sprinkler irrigation is simply programmed to maintain a healthy soil moisture content throughout the irrigated area. When this is done, and the plant materials are reasonably compatible in their moisture requirements, each plant can draw the amount of moisture it needs from the total soil reservoir; the grounds manager does not have to be concerned about individual plant requirements. With drip, on the other hand, the primary means of saving water is through applying the required amount of water directly to the root zone of each plant, and only to that root zone. There is no overall soil moisture reservoir from which the plants can draw. Their only water source is their individual onion-shaped reservoir. Maintaining each reservoir at the proper level requires excellent planning by the grounds manager.

Much of this type of irrigation has been applied on the West Coast to ornamentals, especially during the severe drought and water-rationed years of 1976 and 1977. These specialized applications were very successful. Even with more plentiful water now available, systems are being installed combining sprinkler irrigation for lawn and turf areas with drip sections for ornamentals, trees, planter boxes and other specialized applications.

Since ornamentals are widely spaced, placing water only at the root zone can save significant amounts of water in extensive bed areas. Keeping most of the bed's surface dry constitutes an effective weed control measure. It also allows maintenance work to be scheduled when convenient, without regard to irrigation schedules. And the slow, deep and relatively uniform application of moisture directly to the root zone through a well-managed drip system usually results in superior growth and health of ornamentals.*

Drip irrigation systems provide water through at least four different systems off various laterals. These are:

Screw-in spray heads
Spaghetti tubes and nozzles
Drip emitters
Soaker/oozer

* Sarsfield, A.C., "Drip Irrigation in the Landscape . . .A Second Look," **Grounds Maintenance**, June 1979, Vol. 14 No. 6, pp. 18-20.

The following diagram shows the way in which drip irrigation is able to provide moisture in what has been called an onion-shaped form to the root zone of growing ornamental plants in park areas:

The Reed Technical Manual for Landscaping shows the following typical watering chart for drip irrigation systems:

Drip Irrigation

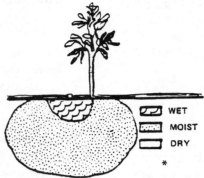

	WET
	MOIST
	DRY

*

The Reed Technical Manual for Landscaping shows the following typical watering chart for drip irrigation systems:

Typical Watering Chart for Drip Irrigation Systems

Type of Plant	No. of Emitters	Distance of Emitters from Plant or Tree	Emitter Location on Emitter Tubing	Total Watering Hours Per Week		
				Hot Weather	Warm Weather	Cool Weather
Ground Cover & Patio Plants	1	Within 1 Foot	For complete ground cover every 2 feet	12	6	3
Flower Beds & Vegetable Gardens	1 with Tee Cap and 2 feeder tubes distributing water to plants	Less than 36" when using feeder tubing	Between the two plants watered with feeder tubes	12	6	3
3' Shrubs	1	1 Foot	At Plant	12	6	3
10' Trees	4	1½ Feet	Equally spaced around tree	24	12	6
15' Trees	8	4 Feet	Equally spaced around tree	30	15	7
20' Trees and Larger	12+	5 Feet	Equally spaced around tree	36	18	9

This chart should be used as a guide for total weekly hours of watering. However, best results come from daily watering or watering every two days while not exceeding total hours per week indicated on watering chart.

The designer should take into account the water percolation and retention qualities of the soil which will affect the distance the emitter should be from the plant; the heavier the soil, the further away from the plant the emitter should be placed.   **

* **Drip Irrigation,** Leaflet, Division of Agricultural Sciences, University of California, Davis, California, 1979.p.4.

** **Drip Irrigation Technical Manual for Landscaping,** Reed Irrigation Systems, El Cajon, California, p.28.

The same publication illustrates the use of polyhose emitter ring around the base of the trees to provide on-going irrigation.

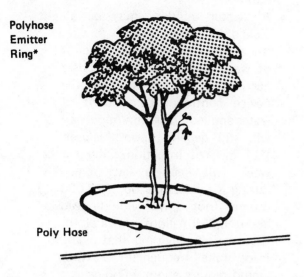

Polyhose Emitter Ring*

Poly Hose

That same publication shows the recommended emitter installation patterns as shown in plan view where the irrigation is provided by laterals off of the main water line and the use of double wrapped loops:

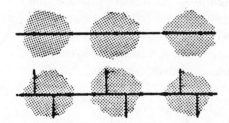

Recommended Reed emitter installation patterns
(As shown in top view illustrations)

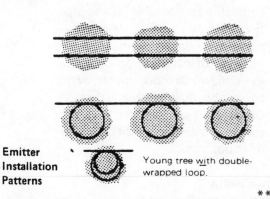

Emitter Installation Patterns

Young tree with double-wrapped loop.

**

* Ibid.,p.21.

** Ibid., p. 23.

There are many other methods of applying water to landscape vegetation that have different rates of efficiency, different levels of cost and require different amounts of labor. Injection of water directly into the root zone of plants is one of the most effective techniques but it is labor intensive and thus often costly.

It may be seen from the above that certain methods or techniques of applying water are more effective for certain types of vegetation under certain circumstances. Dr. Ronald C. Smith, in his article on "Current Water Use Research," states the following concerning the use of water and the waste of water utilizing various irrigation systems:

Continued growth and concentration of the population in cities and suburban areas make efficient water use increasingly important. Most Americans either overwater or underwater their landscape plantings.

A recent study, supported by the Texas Turf Irrigation Association, showed that an average of more than 700 gallons of water per day was used to maintain western landscape plantings. This figure compares with about 500 gallons of water for the same land area in the East.

In the areas studied, landscape irrigation represented from 26 to 80 percent of the total water consumed annually. At peak times, using this large amount of water for irrigation can create delivery and energy-consumption problems in a municipality. Thoughtful water use will reduce this load, reduce costs and minimize further government intervention.

Water Wasted in Turf Irrigation
The study supported findings of earlier reports that turf receives the most frequent irrigation of all landscape plants. Conservatively, 40 to 50 percent of turf irrigation water

is wasted—through runoff, excessive percolation from the root zone and evaporation caused by wind and high temperature.

Runoff, which results from applying too much water in too brief a time, can be corrected by watering for shorter periods or by using low-precipitation sprinkler heads. The city of Albuquerque, N.M., has a "fugitive water" law that imposes stiff fines on those persons who allow any water to run directly onto a non-plant area such as a street or sidewalk. This type of law may be adopted by other cities, especially in the Southwest.

Excessive percolation results from applying too much water over too long a period. This problem is generally limited to sandy or sandy-loam soils. Irrigation of these soils for 8 to 10 minutes saturates the root zones. To prevent drought stress, frequent irrigation would be necessary.

Evaporation results from ignoring wind patterns and velocities and attempting to irrigate during the higher daytime temperatures of midsummer. Early morning (4 to 6 a.m.) or early evening (5 to 7 p.m.) hours generally prove to be the best times for watering to minimize these effects.

Automated Monitoring of Irrigation Systems

The best way to accomplish efficient landscape irrigation is with some type of automatic monitoring system. Otherwise, plant material will be irrigated merely at the convenience of the operator, and either water will be wasted or underwatering will occur.

Systems may be automated in several ways:

- A battery-powered timer may be attached to the hose bibb to control irrigation frequency and duration.
- A "water minder" may be attached to the hose bibb to stop the water flow after the amount of water determined by the user has passed through. Although the device controls the *amount* of water applied, irrigation *frequency* will still depend upon the user. If 1 inch of irrigation water per week will keep a lawn green during a rainless period, a 10,000 square foot lawn would need about 6,250 gallons of water for that period. Dividing that figure into three frequencies a week would require about 2,085 gallons per setting for the inch equivalency.
- Fully automated, hydraulically or electrically actuated remote valves connected to a properly programmed controller provide the most accurate irrigation frequency and duration. Digital controllers allow the grounds manager to select certain stations for irrigation.

- Monitoring the soil's water content with rain gauges and tensiometers helps to avoid overwatering.
- Perhaps the greatest potential for controlling wasteful irrigation practices lies with "ET" (evapotranspiration) measurements. Knowing the rate of evaporation may help to determine how much water to apply during any irrigation. California agriculturists have successfully used ET readings to plan irrigation rates.

Native Plants

It appears that wherever native plant material is used in the landscape, less water is required. For example, buffalograss, crested wheatgrass and blue grama do quite well in most of the non-irrigated areas of the Southwest. Yet most residential and commercial properties prefer Bermudagrass or St. Augustine, which must be heavily irrigated to survive in this region. Landscape architects and horticulturists can save irrigation water by initially selecting drought-hardy native plant species.

The use of non-ionic adjuvants(surfacants) definitely helps in the efficient use of water. Where soils are tight or gradients are steep, the adjuvants are most effective. *

The grounds manager, in an area of extreme drought or water shortage, needs to carefully evaluate all of the possible methods of applying water and utilize that one of those which are most effective and efficient in applying the minimum amount of water to each of the landscape plants in the area. In a paper entitled, "How to Save Water Sensibly," and subtitled, "A Common Sense Approach to Water Conservation Programs for Urban Areas," which Mr. A. C. Sarsfield prepared for the Northern California Turfgrass Council, the following statement was made concerning consideration of irrigation programs:

Proposed severe irrigation bans seem somewhat surprising in view of the above, yet they have initially appeared in almost every original proposal for water rationing programs. Without consideration of the many factors involved, irrigation has been singled out for drastic cuts, probably because of its extreme visibility as opposed to less visible high waste users such as non-recycling car washes which are largely self-contained, and have also been initially labeled as a "non-essential use." This terminology has had detrimental effects, even though it has been changed in every case after the facts have been presented, and should certainly be avoided. Such as a classification is strictly a point of view of the person using it. If such terms need be used, perhaps "reasonable" and "unreasonable" use would be preferred. In the case of irrigation, reasonable use would be efficient application of sufficient water to keep plant materials alive in a stressed condition, while unreasonable use would be to over-apply water to a point of puddling or run-off or to waste water through system leaks or inefficiencies that can be reasonably corrected.

The hand held hose fallacy seems to be the first thought to surface in the initial panic situation of the realization of a drought emergency. It has been originally proposed in almost every such situation across the country. The theory seems to be that if a person must stand with a hose, he won't water as much because of the inconvenience. Experience has proven that the exact opposite is true. If plants start to wilt or die, the average householder will water more with a hose to keep them alive, will have no idea of the volume of water being applied, and will then waste water through inefficient application and overwatering of trouble spots.

Attempts to water with hoses were abandoned years ago by the landscape industry and professional grounds maintenance personnel as the most grossly inefficient method of applying water to landscaping, especially lawn and groundcover areas. It is because of this inefficiency that the hand held hose actually causes excessive water use. To understand, one must analyze the factors involved.

* Smith, Ronald C., "Current Water-Use Research," **Grounds Maintenance,** January 1980, Vol. 15, No. 1, pp. 42-43.

1. With no restrictive nozzle attached, a ¾" hose can easily discharge 10 to 12 gallons per minute or more depending on the pressure, the supply piping and the hose bibb. Smaller hoses may be slightly less.

2. When attempting to distribute this volume by hand direction of the hose, water is dispersed very unevenly, resulting in a mixture of over and under watered areas.

3. When dry areas show light or brown spots or plants start to wilt, more watering is done to revive them resulting in further over-watering of adjoining wet spots. This creates waste and encourages too frequent watering.

4. Water is applied faster than the soil can absorb it, leading to puddling and run-off.

5. In order to see, watering must be done during daytime hours when wind and evaporation losses are highest.

6. There is no control or monitoring over the length of watering time or the total volume of water used.

Irrigation systems have proven most efficient over years of use. Sprinkler irrigation efficiency has been documented many times in all areas of the country for all types of landscape application. More recently, drip irrigation has also proven extremely efficient for those relatively limited areas where it can be satisfactorily used. There are a number of factors that account for this.

1. Relating to the hose volume of 10 to 12 gallons per minute, this can be used to operate four or more properly spaced sprinklers that will distribute water uniformly over 1,200 square feet or more in the case of spray heads or 3,200 square feet or more in the case of rotary sprinklers.

2. The same volume of water will operate 600 to 720 emitters on a drip irrigation system of that type or over 1,400 feet of continuous drip irrigation tubing.

3. The volume used can be monitored accurately through sprinkler nozzling or fixed drip application rates and operating time.

4. These systems operate efficiently during night or early morning hours when wind and evaporation are at a minimum.

5. Distribution can be accurately and permanently controlled to avoid waste in gutters or on paving.

6. Automatic controls can provide exact minimum operating times and calendar programs for the application required.

7. The lower application rate plus the capability for accurately timed short repeat cycles during an application to allow the water to soak into the ground can virtually eliminate all run-off and puddling.

Documentation of Water Saving Through Automatic Irrigation

Since irrigation by hand held hose was abandoned years ago because of inefficiency, and accurate records of consumption and waste were virtually impossible to keep for that watering method due to the variabilities of the individuals hired for that purpose, no documentary records are available for direct comparison, to our knowledge. Mention is made of this because the point was researched at the request of some of those formulating early water rationing programs who originally proposed a hand held hose watering limitation.

The quick coupling system was the first step up from hand held hose watering. This consisted of underground supply piping which contained properly spaced special quick coupling valves permanently installed at ground level. Sprinklers of the proper size fitted with matching couplers were inserted manually into the valves for operation. Almost all of these systems have now been converted to automatically controlled permanent sprinkler irrigation systems for increased efficiency. Documentation of savings brought about by these conversions is the closest comparison available to hose watering. Scientific studies have proven that an average water savings of 66% was achieved through these conversions. Typical examples in California area:

> Cottonwood Country Club San Diego—Superintendent Bob Scribner, Documented water saving: 60%

> Los Angeles Country Club—Manager George Jacobs, Documented water saving: 67%

Even more dramatic water savings are those brought about by simply converting existing manually operated sprinkler systems to automatic operation. The primary reasons for these documented savings are basically those already listed for sprinkler system efficiency: night watering to eliminate evaporation loss; accuracy in automatic timing through elimination of the human factor; more uniform distribution because of less wind during night watering hours; and the capability to apply water in brief repeat cycles to allow soil penetration and avoid puddling and run-off.

Typical examples of water use comparisons between almost identical sprinkler irrigation systems controlled manually and automatically are these present from the records of the City of Pleasanton, California.

Total water used during 1976 for:
.Wayside Park, 7 ac.
(manual system)   2,184,160 Gal.
Heatherlock Park, 7.6 ac.
(automatic system)   1,344,904 Gal.

Direct gross savings
of water   839,256 Gal.

Additional water used by manual operation over automatic—62.4%
Corrected for additional .6 acres—76.3%

Total water used, last 8 months of 1976 for comparable strips of roadway landscaping:
Hopyard Road 2,000 lin. ft.
(manual system)   216,416 Gal.
Santa Rita Rd.,
2,500 lin. ft.
(automatic system)   179,500 Gal.

Direct gross savings
of water   36,916 Gal.

Additional water used by manual operation over automatic—44.7% (adjusted for additional 20% area)

To cite an example on a larger scale, Gene C. Reid, Director, Department of Parks and Recreation, City of Tucson, Arizona, maintained complete water use records on identical areas for operation before and after conversion from manual to automatic controls. Irrigated areas consist of:
- 58 parks covering 730 turf acres
- 13 miles of landscaped medians
- 22 miscellaneous landscaped areas

Updated automatic sprinkler systems consist of:
- 20,150 assorted sprinklers
- 142 automatic controllers
- 1,615 remote control valves
- 128.4 miles of control wire, and
- 36.5 miles of control tubing (hydraulic)

The water savings realized by converting manually operated sprinkler irrigation systems to automatic operation ranged from 38% to 43% on various individual areas for an average saving of 40.5% while still maintaining all landscaping at a high maintenance level.

All of the above are representative and fully documented examples. More can be provided if desired. Statistics such as these, repeated across the country are the most positive proof of the superior efficiency of automatic sprinkler systems and the folly of the hand held hose concept.

Drip irrigation for certain applications such as irrigation of ornamentals, supplemental deep watering for trees and large shrubs, many types of groundcover, and family vegetable gardens, has not been used extensively over a long period of time and much is still considered experimental. Because of this, there is no reliable documentation of savings through its use for these applications. Researchers and agricultural users who offer information on savings generally tend to place them in a range of from 25% to 50% less water, depending on the individual usage. These savings are achieved basically by placing the water only at the root zone of the plants rather than wetting the entire bed area as with sprinklers, thus the savings percentage is dependent to some degree upon the spacings of the plant material. In most cases, drip irrigation for the types of areas where they are suitable can be added to existing sprinkler systems to achieve additional savings or they may be installed independently.

One area of concern to most landscapers is the need for better information to the public regarding the danger of placing drip emitters next to the trunks of ornamentals and trees where the continuous moisture tends to create diseases such as root rot and crown rot. The public needs better information to properly use drip irrigation as a landscaping tool.

This documentation of savings through the efficiency of irrigation systems is not intended as a case in favor of requiring their use or for banning of of the hand held hose, or even the hose-end sprinkler which is somewhat more efficient in distribution if properly operated and monitored. It is intended as a case for allowing the continued use of existing sytems during the drought crisis as a means of saving landscaping through efficient distribution of the limited amount of water available, and to allow continued installation of such systems in the interest of increasing irrigation efficiency.*

This outlines considerations and selection of specific methods for use in irrigation programs. The TEXAS WATER RESOURCES NEWSLETTER, Vol. 6, No. 3, April 1980, contained an article entitled, "Breaking the Habit," which deals with ways to save water in lawn watering and covers the evaluation of some of the methods:

Does your lawn have a "drinking problem"? You may never be able to cure your lawn of its dependence on the water sprinkler, but you can certainly convince it to drink more moderately!

Chances are, you are giving your lawn at least 20 percent more water than it should have. This indulgence not only wastes water, but often damages the grass. Excess water robs plant roots of oxygen and also encourages plant diseases.

* Sarsfield, A.C., How to Save Water Sensibly, Northern California Turfgrass Council, P.O. Box 268, Lafayette, California 94549, pp. 4-6.

Limit Your Lawn

You probably don't realize how much excess water you are pouring on your lawn. You are much more likely to recognize when you are giving too little water than when you are encouraging immoderate drinking. As a matter of fact, a recent study found that more than half of all homeowners overwater their lawns while very few underwater.

An average of an inch and one-half of water applied once a week, according to the Texas Department of Water Resources, will keep most Texas grasses alive and happy. You will need to adjust this amount and time, however, for your lawn's soil structure, land slope, and condition as well as for the season of the year.

How do you know when your lawn has had enough? Water should penetrate the soil deeply enough to encourage firm and solid root growth. Ideally, you should water just enough to dampen the entire root system and water only when necessary.

Since it is almost impossible to guess how much water you are applying to a lawn, you should (1) test the depth of soil which is moistened, (2) use catch cans to measure depth of water applied, or (3) meter the amount of water applied.

To check how deeply the soil is moistened, push a large blunt screwdriver down until it meets resistance. Soil should be damp six to eight inches below the surface.

Place shallow cans or rain gauges to catch water at various distances from the sprinkler head so you can tell how many inches of water you have applied in a specific area. You must average the depth of water in the cans to determine the application over the entire area.

The most accurate method of determining the amount of water you are applying is to actually measure the water. In some cases you can read the city water meter at the edge of your property, but be careful not to use water for other purposes during the metering time. Meters that attach directly to the lawn hose can be purchased at a relatively low cost. Another way to measure water is to run a sprinkler into a container for one minute and then measure the amount.

You should determine the time it takes to apply the right amount of water. A simple wind-up kitchen timer or an alarm clock will help you to remember when to move the sprinklers. Better yet, invest in one of the timer-controlled sprinklers now on the market.

Bad Influences

One of the worst influences on your excessive-drinking lawn is an inefficient sprinkling system. No sprinkler will distribute the water at equal depths over the entire lawn area. This unequal application will overirrigate in some areas and underirrigate in others.

Each sprinkler distributes water in a different pattern. Pattern means not only surface areas covered by the sprinkler, but the relative depths of water within this area. The trick is to select the best sprinkler for your situation and then overlap applications for the most even distribution.

Homeowners generally water their lawns with one of five types of sprinklers: rotating, oscillating, stationary, impact, or traveling.

Rotating and oscillating sprinklers should be avoided because of their poor distribution characteristics. If used, they should be overlapped in both directions by 75 percent. A traveling sprinkler provides a relatively high uniform coverage without any overlap. Most traveling sprinklers, however, do not apply an adequate depth of water when crossing a lawn once. Traveling sprinklers, therefore, need to be run across the same area more than once.

Sprinklers that throw water high into the air cause poor distribution and excessive evaporation of the water. Large drops of water distributed in a low, flat pattern are more effective than a fine, high mist.

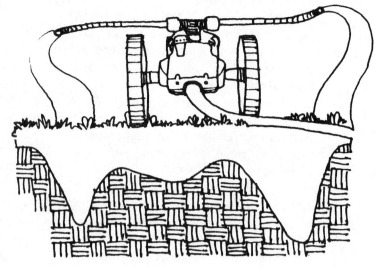

Cross Section of
Traveling Sprinkler Wetting Pattern

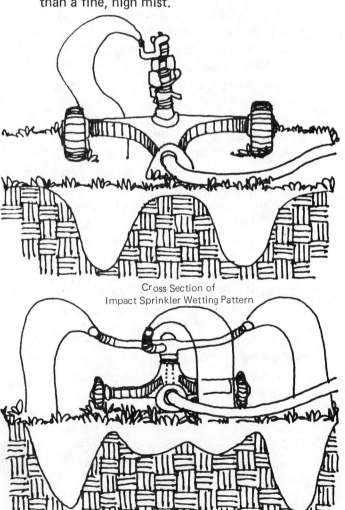

Cross Section of
Impact Sprinkler Wetting Pattern

Cross Section of
Rotating Sprinkler Wetting Pattern

Treatment For Problem Drinkers
Watering the entire lawn because of a few dry spots is wasteful and can be detrimental to the lawn in areas that tend to stay wet. Dry spots in the lawn may be caused by sandy or rocky areas or by heat reflected from buildings or concrete. Sunny or southern sides of buildings generally require more water than other parts of the yard. These areas should be watered with a soaker or an aerator attached to a garden hose rather than with a sprinkler. A good way to water grass near concrete is to push a root feeder into the soil 12 to 16 inches from the concrete. Force the water jets down to a depth of 4 to 6 inches. When the grass rises like a bubble, remove spike and repeat operation 12 to 16 inches further along the grass edge.

Trees and shrubs need to be watered to a depth of two to three feet. Use a root waterer or form basins around plants to hold water. After the second year, most plants should have established a root system to take care of their own water needs except during extended dry periods.

Happy Hours

You should give your lawn an especially good drink at the end of the growing season and again early in the spring. Lawns use a considerable amount of water during the winter in this southern climate. As a rule of thumb, during the growing season, you should water once a week for clay soils and twice a week for sandy soils.

Don't water just because it is a certain day of the week or because the neighbors are watering their lawns. If the grass has turned a dull gray-green, or if footprints remain visible as you walk across, then it is time to water.

Properly watered grass will develop a deep root system efficient in recovering soil moisture. Too frequent waterings can produce a lush grass with a shallow root system. Such grass may be especially vulnerable to drought damage and to certain diseases.

Water early in the day. Before 10:00 a.m. is best because rising heat later in the day tends to steal a lot of water by evaporation. There is another good thing about early morning watering: the grass leaves have a chance to dry off quickly. Water droplets left on leaves act like little magnifying glasses and can cause burn damage from hot sunlight.

Temperance Lessons

You can help your yard kick the habit of excessive drinking with a few of these water-saving tips:

• Add organic material (compost, peat moss, or ground bark) annually to improve sand or clay soil. A good loam soil—the combination of sand and clay—absorbs and retains water better than clay which takes in water too slowly or sand which losses water too quickly.

• Water slowly for better absorption.

• Aerate your lawn to help improve infiltration rate and prevent runoff from compacted areas.

• Raise the mower height one-half to one inch during the summer months. Taller grass encourages deeper root growth to take advantage of the soil moisture. Higher grass also provides more leaves to insulate the soil from heat and reduces evaporation.

• If you use a soaker hose, turn it so the holes are on the bottom to avoid evaporation.

• Fertilize your lawn at least twice a year to establish a grass with a water-efficient root system. During dry seasons, however, hold back on nitrogen fertilizers to keep plants from needing as much water.

• Control weeds. They are water gluttons.

• Don't water on windy days. And try not to water streets, walks, or driveways.

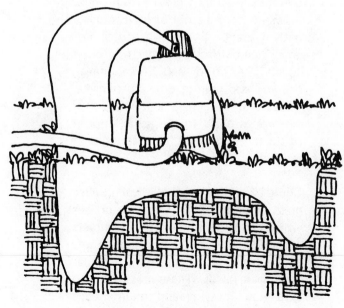

Cross Section of
Oscillating Sprinkler Wetting Pattern

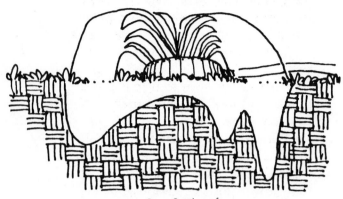

Cross Section of
Stationary Sprinkler Wetting Pattern

• Mulch shrubs and other plantings so the soils holds moisture longer. Mulching also controls weeds.

• Most importantly, learn what types of grass, shrubbery, and trees do best in your area and in your yard, and then plant accordingly. If you have a heavily shaded yard, for instance, no amount of water will make roses bloom!

On the Wagon

Put a part of your yard "on the wagon" by replacing thirsty grass with drought resistant ground cover or lower quality native grass. Good substitutes for grass include drought resistant ground covers, redwood bark, pea gravel, decomposed granite, or even concrete. Be careful though—a swimming pool evaporates close to the same amount of water consumed by the grass it replaces.

Could you live with a lower quality grass in your lawn? There are grasses which can survive most Texas summers without help, but they are not as soft or beautiful as grasses now popular for urban lawns. These grasses would save you mowing and maintenance time as well as water.

Trees and bushes native to your area would also save time and money. Once these plants are established, they would need little or no attention from you.

Total abstinence for your lawn is probably not your goal. You are willing to spend a reasonable amount of time, money, and water on plants and grass because they add beauty and value to your life and property. They also reduce energy needed to heat and cool your home.

You can, however, teach your lawn to drink more moderately by kicking some of your *own* overindulgent lawn watering habits.*

Leaflet No. 2976, "Saving Water in Landscape Irrigation," deals with the subject of how to irrigate without wasting water in the following words:

You can keep from wasting water in irrigating landscape plantings and reduce plant loss or damage in a time of water shortage. To do so you need the answers to three questions:

1. How much water do your plants use and, if necessary, how little can they get by on?
2. How can you give them as much water as they need without applying too much?
3. In a drought, what can you do to help them survive?

The answers to these questions depend on your location, climate, soil, and type of plant. This leaflet will help you find answers for your particular situation.

Soil Water Storage and Plant Waste Use.

To determine when to irrigate and how much water to apply, it helps

* "Breaking the Habit,", **Texas Water Resources,** Texas Water Resources Institute, Texas A. & M. University, College Station, Texas 77843, Vol. 6, No. 3, April 1980, pp. 1-4.

to know the water storage capacity of the soil where the plant roots are situated (the "soil reservoir") and the rate of water use by the plants.

The Soil Reservoir

Although the amount of organic matter makes some difference, the water storage capacity of a soil is determined mostly by soil texture— the size of the particles and their distribution.

Table 1 indicates the amounts of water that soils of various textures can store and make available to plants. Note that a fine-textured soil, such as clay, holds about twice as much water as a coarse, sandy soil.

TABLE 1:
WATER STORAGE CAPACITY OF SOILS

Soil texture	Inches of available water per foot of soil depth	Gallons per cubic foot of soil
Sand	1/2"—1"	1/3-2/3
Sandy loam	1"—1-1/2"	2/3—1
Clay loam	1-1/2"—2"	1—1-1/3
Clay	1-1/2"—2-1/2"	1—1-2/3

(An inch of water is the amount that would cover the surface 1 inch deep. 1-1/2 inches covering 1 square foot = 1 gallon.)

The storage capacity of your soil reservoir depends not only on the soil type but on the depth of soil that will be penetrated by plant roots during the growing season. When there is normal moisture in the soil, the top 3 or 4 feet can be considered the soil reservoir for most trees and shrubs. In dry periods, deep-rooted plants will draw water from farther down. Short-rooted plants, such as most grasses, have a more shallow soil reservoir.

One other factor may be important: The depth of the soil itself. If hardpan, bedrock or some other restricting layer is close to the surface, the soil reservoir will be limited accordingly. (Take care not to overirrigate shallow soils. They can easily become waterlogged.)

Water Use by Plants

Most irrigation water applied to plants goes out through the leaves as water vapor, while some evaporates from the soil. This is known as evapotranspiration—generally shortened to ET. The rate of ET is influenced by climate: sunlight, temperature, humidity, and wind. Because of differences in climate, ET rates are different in various locations and from season to season. It is important to have a rough idea of the amount of water used through ET by your landscape plantings. Otherwise you may put on too much or too little water to replace the loss.

Larger plants may use somewhat more water than grass, depending on their shape and exposure to the sun. Solid or almost solid plantings of shrubs or trees often use 10 percent or 20 percent more water than indicated in the table. A large solitary shrub or tree, because of its greater exposure to the sun and wind, may use two or three times as much water as a comparable area of turf. (Its larger root system compensates for the additional water use.)

You can use the ET rates to estimate the actual daily and seasonal amounts of soil moisture being used by your plants. However, one important point should be kept in mind: The ET rate is the *maximum* amount of water a plant will use if plenty of soil moisture is available. All plants can get by with less. Most woody plants can survive on half that much.

Water Spenders and Water Conservers

One other factor may make a difference in your particular irrigation requirement: Certain drought tolerant plants use significantly less water.

This is not true of all plants commonly considered drought tolerant. Some such plants, are "water spenders." They have extensive root systems and as long as some of their roots are in moist soil they can survive drought; but they still use relatively large amounts of water. Examples are eucalyptus and black walnut trees.

But other drought tolerant plants have naturally low rates of water use. Some of these ("drought evaders") become virtually dormant during dry periods. Examples are California buckeye and bermudagrass. Others ("water conservers") have ways of reducing water loss. Their leaves may be small, gray-colored, leathery, and arranged to reduce the amount of sunlight that strikes them or structured in other ways to save water. Many California native plants and plants from similar climates are of this type. Examples are ceanothus, manzanita, and olive.

Drought evaders and water conservers ordinarily use somewhat less water than other plants. In a drought, they can survive on far less.

How to Irrigate Without Wasting Water

Knowing the water storage capacity of your soil and the ET rate in your area, you can determine when to irrigate and how much water to apply.

When to Irrigate

One way to decide when to apply water is to observe the plants. This is particularly true in timing the first irrigation of the season, when you may not know how much moisture is in the soil reservoir or how fast it is being used. Symptoms of moisture stress vary with the kind of plant. Some are easy to spot and others are more difficult. Symptoms include wilting leaves; changes in appearance of the leaves (shiny leaves becoming dull, bright green leaves fading or turning gray-green); and heavy leaf fall and sometimes death of young leaves.

Another way to decide when to irrigate is to check the soil. The hand-feel test is quick and easy. Take a small sample of soil in your hand. Try to roll or squeeze it into a ball. If the soil will not mold into a ball, it is too dry to supply water to plants. If the soil will mold into a ball, rub it with your thumb. If the ball will not crumble, the soil is too wet.

If the soil can be molded into a ball that will crumble when rubbed, the moisture is probably about right. Sandy soils are an exception: They will crumble even when wet.

To get an idea of the moisture conditions throughout the rooting area, soil should be sampled in several locations and from several depths at each location—from six inches to three or four feet if possible. For the greater depths, you probably will need an auger or soil tube. If you use a shovel, be sure to fill up the hole and sample somewhere else the next time.

How Much Water to Apply?

Even if you have plenty of water, don't overirrigate. Too much water is not only wasteful, but it can be bad for plants. Develop a general idea of how much water the plants need by checking with the hand-feel test early in the season and, later on, estimating the rate of ET since the last irrigation and checking again with the hand-feel test.

Even if sufficient water will be available, your main goal is to use it efficiently by applying just enough water to fill up the soil reservoir, and waiting until the plants have used up at least half of the available soil moisture before adding more. If there's a water shortage, you may have to use less.

Do not irrigate frequently with small amounts of water. This wastes water through direct evaporation from the soil, and little will reach the deeper roots. Besides, too-frequent watering may encourage shallow rooting and may cause root rots and other diseases.

When you do irrigate, be sure to apply enough water—if you put on only part of the amount that the soil reservoir can hold, the upper soil will fill up to its water-holding capacity while the lower soil remains dry.

To put on the right amount of water, you need to know how fast it is being applied. This is fairly easy to determine if your water is metered. If it isn't, you can place 6 to 8 cans throughout a sprinkler pattern to measure the rate of application in inches per hour; or, run a hose into a garbage can or some other container to determine the gallons of water delivered per hour. (For example, a half-inch garden hose 50 feet long. with water pressure of 50 pounds, will deliver about 350 gallons per hour.) To convert gallons into inches of water: 1 gallon = 1½ inches of water covering 1 square foot.

How to Apply Water

Landscape plantings can be irrigated by running water into basins or furrows, or by use of sprinklers, soakers, or drip systems. Regardless of which method you use there are three basic rules:

Apply water uniformly. For example, be sure sprinklers distribute water evenly. If basins are used, be sure they are level. Avoid long furrows.

Eliminate or reduce runoff. Water that is applied by sprinkler faster than the soil can absorb it will run off and cause low areas to be over-watered and high or compacted areas to be under-watered. If you see runoff, get smaller nozzles; or stop irrigating and start again after an hour or two.

When irrigating individual plants, keep the water inside the dripline. A few of the roots may not be wetted, but less water will be wasted.

Properly designed and operated drip-irrigation systems apply water more efficiently than other systems because they allow a slower and more uniform application to a confined area. Drip systems are particularly efficient where plants are not close together.*

* **Saving Water in Landscape Irrigation,** Division of Agricultural Sciences, University of California, Davis, California, April 1977, Leaflet 2976, p. 7.

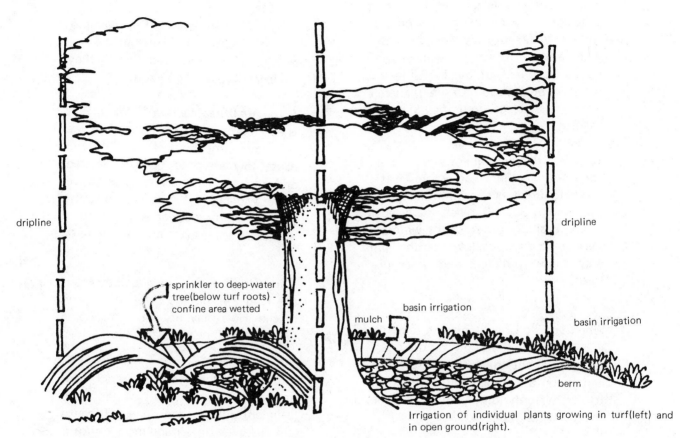

dripline

sprinkler to deep-water tree(below turf roots) - confine area wetted

basin irrigation

mulch

dripline

basin irrigation

berm

Irrigation of individual plants growing in turf(left) and in open ground(right).

There is no one method of irrigating landscape plants that is most effective and efficient under all circumstances at all times. The grounds manager or the home owner faced with a water crisis, and with a need to preserve landscape plants, should be aware of all of the possible methods of applying water and use only those in specific circumstances and situations which are most appropriate to save the maximum amount of water. A second factor which should be considered in altering irrigation practices is the timing of applying specific amounts of water. The time may be the time of day or the time of the year of growing season. Generally it is often recommended that sprinkling be done in the early morning hours. Some have suggested it be done as early as 4:00–6:00 a.m. In this way less water is lost to evapotranspiration into the atmosphere than would be the case if irrigation were done at midday. At the same time in most situations the wind speed is usually slowest during night or evening hours. Winds pick up during the day and thus cause a shift in sprinkler irrigation patterns. It is always advisable to avoid irrigation especially sprinkler irrigation of the landscape during midday. The reason for this is that a great amount of this water is wasted through evapotranspiration into the dry atmosphere. Therefore the water should be applied when there is no wind and when there is very limited sunlight. It should only be applied at levels at which it can be readily absorbed into the soil.

A third factor in altering irrigation practices has to do with the amount of water which is applied. The grounds manager or the homeowner should be very much aware of how much water an individual plant needs and when specifically the plant needs the water. In time to come, more information will be available concerning the water needs of the individual types of plants in specific geographical areas. In the interim, homeowners and grounds managers need to know the water needs of each of the plants or planted areas in a landscape area. This can be done through trial and error, it can be done through observation. One of the most common methods of measurement is the use of the tensiometer. Dr. Richard L. Duble in his article on "Sprinkler Irrigation Practices and Water Losses," has described the role and function of a tensiometer in the following words:

Moisture-indicating instruments called tensiometers may be used to measure the moisture status of the soil and indicate when irrigation is required. They consist of a porous cup, a vacuum gauge and a water-filled connecting tube between the cup and the gauge. When the cup is placed in the root zone of the soil, water is free to move through the porous wall and come to equilibrium with the soil water. As the soil dries, water moves from the cup and causes a vacuum to be indicated on the gauge; thus, the drier the soil, the higher the gauge reading. When irrigation water is applied or rainfall occurs, water returns through the porous cup and releases the vacuum, which lowers the gauge reading.

By placing the tensiometers at several depths and observing daily or weekly readings, it is possible to estimate how much irrigartion is needed and the depth to which water should penetrate to recharge the root zone.

Moisture readings with these instruments represent only a small area of soil that surrounds the cup; therefore, sufficient locations over the area should be established so that a representative measurement of soil moisture can be obtained.

Irrigation schedules based on tensiometer readings that indicate moisture stress are much more efficient in terms of water use than schedules established on a calendar basis.*

The publication, "Irrigating at Home . . . Do You Know When to Irrigate?", from the University of California, deals once again with tensiometers in the home landscape in the following words:

The wise use of water is important in California. Do you irrigate every day? In mixed plantings, frequent light irrigations may keep the lawn green but not provide enough water for shrub and tree roots. Frequent heavy irrigations generally waste water and fertility and cause root damage.

Do you irrigate every week or two? Infrequent heavy irrigations may be just what shrubs and trees need, but are not always compatible with good grass appearance.

"Periodic irrigation" in equal amounts at equal intervals is seldom correct. The best solution is a combination of several light irrigations for the turf with a less frequent heavier irrigation for deeper rooted plants, all properly timed.

Irrigating Your Lawn
Because lawn covers tend to be shallow rooted, they may need irrigating once or twice a week during the warm season—less often in cooler

* Duble, Richard L.,"Sprinkler Irrigation Practices and Water Losses," **Irrigation Journal,** March-April 1977, pp. 16-17.

weather. In no case is daily irrigation needed for established lawns. Daily watering may cause loss of nitrates and a yellowish-green appearance, invasion of weeds and diseases, soil compactibility, loss of deeper roots, and water waste.

On vigorous and well-fertilized lawns, irrigate at the first wilting symptoms (when the imprint of a footstep remains flattened for a few minutes).

If only parts of a lawn become dry, water distribution needs correction. Poorly performing or improperly spaced sprinkler heads, compacted soil, thatch accumulation, excessive application rates or steep slopes that produce runoff may cause such poor distribution.

The ideal time to irrigate is early morning. Evening irrigation in warm weather is not recommended because it encourages fungus diseases. Automatic systems can be set to start irrigating after midnight when the disease hazard is less, the turf is not in use, the water pressure is highest and most stable, and there usually is less wind.

When irrigating, operate the sprinklers for 30 to 60 minutes. If appreciable runoff starts in less than 30 minutes, modify the sprinkler system for lower application rate. Sprinkler heads are available for low application rates and good distribution. A temporary solution is to shut off the water when runoff starts, and complete the application later.

About 12 to 24 hours after irrigating, check the soil with a soil tube, auger, probe, or spade and note the depth of water penetration by change in color and feel of soil. If any soil in the root zone is dry, irrigate for a

longer period in future irrigations. If the soil seems quite wet, irrigate for a shorter time.

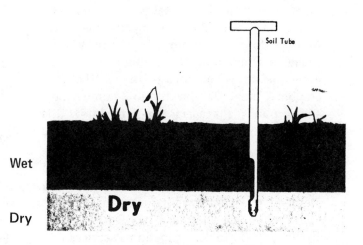

Irrigating Your Trees and Shrubs

Leaves of woody plants that are improperly irrigated become yellowish-green, stunted, curled, or brown-tipped and may fall prematurely. Since shrubs and trees do not show symptoms of water shortage until damage has been done, you will need to know the soil-water condition in the second and third feet of soil. A soil tube or probe can be used, but the best and easiest way to check this is with soil-water measuring instruments (tensiometers).

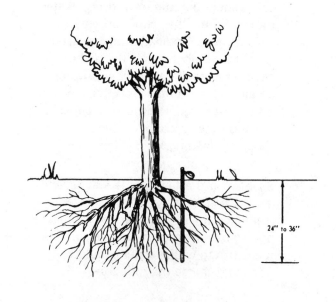

Install these at depths of 24 to 36 inches in the soil under trees or 12 to 24 inches under shrubs. When the instrument gauge shows a moderately dry reading (50 to 70), apply water for the length of time you think needed to rewet the soil. Check the gauge 12 to 24 hours after irrigating.

If the reading is 5 to 15, your irrigation was correct. If the reading is 0 to 5, use a shorter application next time. If the reading is more than 15, your next irrigation should be longer.

If tensiometers are not used, examine the soil weekly by inserting a soil tube or auger 2 or 3 feet into the soil. Irrigate when soil from the second or third foot crumbles instead of sticking together when you squeeze it in your hand. Several hours after irrigation, check again to determine soil wetness and depth of water penetration and decide if future irrigations should be longer or shorter or the same.

Use of Automatic Systems

Automatic irrigation systems, consisting of remote control valves operated by controllers, are common in professionally managed turf and landscaping. Similar systems are available for the home yard at modest cost. They deserve consideration because of the convenience, potential water saving, and better grounds appearance that can be obtained.

Controllers contain clocks and selector switches so that almost any desired irrigation schedule can be programmed. When your tests or gauge readings show that an irrigation is needed, set the controller to irrigate that night. Set the length of irrigation for each line to your best judgment. Check again after irrigation and reset the controller if necessary. Before you go away on vacation, you can program the controller to irrigate at definite intervals while you are gone. When you are at home you should adjust the intervals to reflect weather changes and your soil observations. It is possible to electrically connect tensiometers to the controller for completely automatic operation. Such operation applies water only when needed and eliminates the disadvantages of periodic irrigation.*

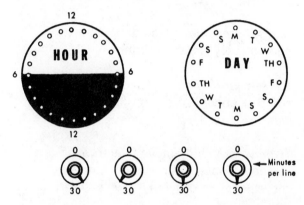

The publication, "Efficient Lawn Irrigation Can Help You Save Water," from the Division of Agricultural Sciences, University of California, Davis, indicates when turf needs watering in the following words:

> California has a Mediterranean climate characterized by long, hot, dry summers, and turfgrass must be watered to survive under these conditions. Because water is becoming scarce in California as demand continues to rise, we must learn how to use it efficiently and then put this knowledge into practice. This publication will broaden your understanding of turfgrass irrigation practices so that you can meet your lawn's moisture needs through more efficient use of water.

---

* **Irrigating at Home ... Do You Know When to Irrigate?**, Division of Agricultural Sciences, University of California, Davis, California, Leaflet 2745, September 1975, p. 2.

Check Your Lawn-Watering Efficiency

Time of day to irrigate. Irrigate early in the morning for healthy turf.

Amount to apply. Wet soil thoroughly to the depth of turfgrass roots.

Irrigation frequency. Irrigate when plants show stress. Frequency changes with season and weather. Avoid daily light irrigations.

Irrigation equipment. Your equipment should apply water uniformly.

Water runoff. Avoid loss due to run-off and poor distribution (on streets, sidewalks, etc.).

Remove thatch. Remove thatch which restricts water, air, and nutrient movement into your lawn's root zone.

Relieve soil compaction. Use a hand aerifier on compacted areas to assist water entry into soil.

Sun vs. shade. Water is used faster by plants in sunny locations than in shaded areas, so supplemental watering of sunny areas may be necessary.

Competition. Remember that tree and shrub roots in lawn areas compete with turfgrass roots for water.

Weeds. Remove weeds by hand or by use of an appropriate registered herbicide.

Low summer nitrogen fertility. Use fertilizer sparingly in summer.

General Concepts

California lawns include many grass species growing in a wide variety of soils, in many subclimates, and under different levels of maintenance. All of these factors influence lawn watering practices. Keep in mind: *the reason for irrigation is to maintain a supply of moisture in the soil for grass plants.* Ideally, maximum irrigation efficiency is achieved when the amount of water applied replaces water used by plants with no losses due to surface runoff and penetration below the roots.

When Turf Needs Watering

You can determine when your lawn needs watering by observing its appearance, and by examining its soil.

Look at your lawn. When a lawn changes color from bright green to dull gray-green, it needs water immediately. When stressed for water, your lawn will show footprints and will not "spring back" from normal foot traffic. If water is not applied at this time the gray-green hue will deteriorate to a tan color—and this indicates severe water stress and dead grass.

Examine the soil. Use a probe to check for soil moisture in your lawn's root zone. If soil feels moist or will form a ball when squeezed in your hand, its moisture level is adequate. This test can also be used to determine how often to irrigate.

Soil particle size (soil texture) influences water penetration and a soil's water-holding capacity. For example, sandy soils with large particles rapidly accept water but won't store large amounts of it. Match how often you water your lawn's soil type.

In summary, how often you should water your lawn depends on its appearance, or how moist its soil is, or both. Avoid daily, light irrigations.

How Long to Water

The goal of efficient irrigation is to wet the soil where grass roots are growing—no more and no less. Most turfgrass roots extend 4 to 6 inches into the soil but some penetrate to 12 inches or more. Generally, you should wet the top 6 inches of the soil thoroughly. Deeper root systems take in water from a greater soil volume, so lawns with deep roots can be watered less often than lawns with shallow root systems.

When watering to the depth of a root system, don't apply water more rapidly than the soil can absorb it. Avoid water runoff. To do so may require turning off sprinklers for 1 to 2 hours to let the water soak in before continuing irrigation. Repeat this cycle until the desired total amount of water is applied.

Factors impeding water penetration should be corrected. The two most common ones are thatch accumulation and soil compaction. Thatch is undecomposed organic matter that builds up between the leaf blades and the soil surface. Thatch restricts water, air, and nutrient movement into the root zone. A thick thatch layer should be removed in spring or fall by vertical mowing or by hand-raking. Heavy traffic on turfgrass compacts its soil surface. Compacted soil also restricts air, water, and nutrient entry and hinders root development. Compacted areas should be aerified (cored).

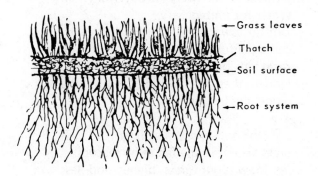

In summary, the length of time needed to water your lawn adequately is determined by the time it takes to thoroughly wet a lawn's soil to the depth of its root system. Grasses and soils differ, so irrigation schedules must be tailored to individual lawns. Remember, it is not uncommon to irrigate for ½ to 1 hour or longer at each watering to wet the soil adequately.

Sprinklers

Sprinklers should distribute water uniformly over the lawn. Check your sprinklers often and adjust or repair them as required. Hose end sprinkler devices with circular spray patterns tend to be less efficient than some other models because of runoff and waste. Plastic tubes that spray a light mist, and oscillating (or wave) sprinklers, apply water slowly and fit house-lot patterns better. On large lawns, part-circle impact-drive sprinklers can be effective.

Special Requirements

Landscape features influence irrigation practices. For example, turf on slopes in areas receiving reflected heat or much wind may require more irrigation than would turf not subject to these environmental factors. Check your lot for areas which may require special irrigation treatment. Some spots may require supplemental watering by hand.

Irrigation For Turfgrass Survival When Water is Limited

During low rainfall or drought years, some California areas may have limited, rationed, or restricted water supplies. Under these conditions, follow the guidelines below:

• Do not apply fertilizer to turfgrass except in the fall rainy season.

• Mow your grass higher and less often. Cool-season grasses (e.g. Kentucky bluegrass, perennial ryegrass) should be mowed at a 2-inch height, and warm-season grasses (e.g. bermudagrass, zoysiagrass) should be mowed at a ¾- to 1-inch height. Don't let your grass grow more than twice the recommended mowing height.

• Reduce weed competition. Drought stress encourages weediness in turf. Remove weeds by hand or use an appropriate registered herbicide to control broad-leaf weeds in turf, because weeds compete with the turfgrass for the limited amount of water available.

• Pay careful attention to water application. Follow the recommendations for efficient irrigation discussed above. Irrigate to root zone depth without runoff when your lawn shows a need for water.

What Will the Lawn Look Like Under Survival Management?

Under survival irrigation management, the lawn gradually will develop a spotty, thinned appearance. Some of the shallow-rooted plants will die first; the more stress-tolerant or deeper-rooted plants will remain green longest.

Management Alternatives

One management choice when water is limited or rationed is to *not irrigate* and let your lawn die, especially if there won't be sufficient water available to carry it through the period when irrigation is needed. In late fall or the following spring, when more water should be available, a new lawn could be planted to a more drought-tolerant turfgrass species.

Another management choice is to consider alternate landscaping which would include little or no turfgrass. Shrubs, groundcovers, mulches, and decorative rock could be used as replacements for turfgrass. This alternative is especially attractive in areas with yearly low rainfall or limited water availability.*

During times of water shortage it is essential that homeowners and grounds managers explore the possibility of altering their irrigation practices. They might do this through altering or evaluating all of the potential methods of applying water. They should also do this through evaluating the time of day and the time of the season in the year in which they apply this water. It is also necessary to understand fully the amount of water which is needed and which is supplied. This may be done through testing, record keeping or visual evaluation. Altering irrigation practices, in times of drought, is one other strategy which should be considered to use water efficiently in the landscape.

One other type of space age technology which may be applied to evaluating the need for irrigation of a specific landscape area is the use of infrared photography. Dr. Ricks Pluenneke in an article, "Using Infrared Photography to Illustrate Irrigation Problems," in the April 1981 issue of *GROUNDS MAINTENANCE* Magazine, explains how this might be done on a relatively large landscape area such as a golf course. He explains in that article how it is possible to take an infrared color photograph

---

* **Efficient Lawn Irrigation Can Help You Save Water,** Division of Agricultural Sciences, University of California, Davis, California, Turfgrass Management Series, Leaflet 2944, January 1977, pp. 1-3.

of a relatively large grounds area from an airplane and to see from that the areas which are under-irrigated or over-irrigated. He states that:

> In general, an infrared photograph will color healthy plants bright red to magenta and stressed ones pinkish to brownish. There is no magic in this approach; stressed plants (or areas) are simply more readily visible in a slide shot with infrared film than they would be with the naked eye.*

There is absolutely no way that within one short chapter in a book of this sort that it would be possible to suggest all of the ways in which water can be saved with altered or adjusted irrigation practices.

Those suggestions given in this chapter present only a very superficial overview and provide some of the many possible considerations in using irrigation in an increasingly water-short world. Basically a new view needs to be developed in reviewing how water is applied in times of water shortage. Cost of installation or amount of labor required may be less important than the water efficiency of a means of application.

A great deal of water can be saved in watching more carefully how it is applied and when it is applied. There are more options now than ever before and even more will be developed in time to save water and to use what water there is more carefully. Irrigation professionals should learn how to be more water efficient in application and should keep up with new technology. As they do this, these same professionals should be consulted and used in more situations but in new ways.

Water may be saved by spending money through consulting professionals and by using more sophisticated equipment. It may cost more in the short run to use less water, but in time it may mean the very survival of the softscape.

Altering irrigation practices and using irrigation water more efficiently are the ultimate strategies for water conservation in landscape design and management. After you have:

> Controlled water falling on the site,
> Selected drought resistent plants,
> Left plants in a stress condition,
> Erected wind barriers,
> Redesigned to use less water,
> Altered cultivation practices,
> Modified the soil,
> Expanded the use of mulch,
> Used anti-transpirants,
> Re-used water as much as possible,
> Made the water "wetter",

and studied every other means of conserving water and if you still need water; then, you need to:

> Establish watering priorities,
> Alter irrigation practices,
> Use irrigation water more efficiently.

If you need to water and if you have it, then apply it as carefully and efficiently as possible even if it takes longer and costs more.

---

*Pluenneke, Ricks, "Using Infrared Photography to Illustrate Irrigation Problems", April 1981, Vol. 16, No. 4, p. 34.

A Comparison of Irrigation Methods

This is a very perfunctory comparison of the effectiveness of different methods of applying water to landscape plants. Much more definitive research needs to be undertaken to carefully measure the water use, labor costs, time requirements and actual effectiveness of different equipment and techniques.

Application method	Water conservation advantages	Water conservation disadvantages	Comments
Hose			
By hand 	A rifle shot approach good control as to location and timing, good for newly planted trees and shrubs, low initial cost and investment,	Labor intensive, hand labor not good for turf or ground cover, unmeasured application can overwater, water can be wasted misapplied.	Takes some degrees of responsibility, judgement and attention, the most subjective as to where, how much and when, its effectiveness is totally dependent on the skill of the person applying the water.
Soaker hose 	Very little water is lost in evaporation, good for shallow watering, puts down a trench of water, good for hedges and shrub beds, can be used on windy days.	Labor intensive, has to be moved often, penetrates to different depths, non-uniform application, hose can be punctured to waste water.	Someone has to know when enough has been applied and to move the hose and place it correctly in another location, decisions are dependent on appearances, the amount of water is not apparant unless there is runoff, depth of penetration needs to be ascertained.
Perforated hose 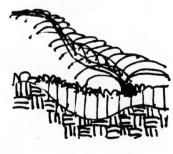	Good for shallow watering, inexpensive to buy or replace, easy to use for spot irrigation, linear in pattern, a long narrow spray for hedges and shrubs.	Some water is lost from evaporation, can't be used on windy days, non-uniform depth of application, has to be moved, put down each time and place to be used often, little or no control over where or how much water is applied, can cause runoff if used on slopes, hose can be punctured.	Takes knowledge to place it, to move it and to evaluate its effectiveness, very subjective and personal as to its placement and usage, can be effective if used by a knowledgable and sensitive person, but can be wasteful if used without care.

Application method	Water conservation advantages	Water conservation disadvantages	Comments
Sprinkler			
Hose end Rotating Machine gun Whirling baffle 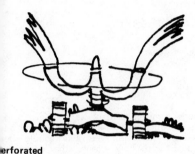	Very portable, inexpensive, light weight, comes in a variety of patterns and sizes, good for turf or ground cover, easily moved as needed to where it is needed, syringes foliage, the tops and filters down, one of the most commonly available devices.	Easily damaged, heavy evaporation, easily affected by wind, variable depth of penetration, generally circular pattern of coverage, full circle only, leaves some areas uncovered others undercovered, and some overwatered, wastes a good percentage of what it delivers, can malfunction since it is mechanical.	Depends to a great extent on who uses it, where it is used and how often it is used, all are judgement devices, used by amateurs generally who waste water because they do not know how, when or where to use them to be most effective for the landscape plants and to use the least water in the most effective way.
Perforated			
Fan spray Circular 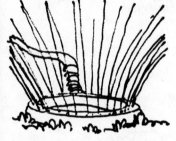	Inexpensive, portable, no moving parts to malfunction, syringes the plant surface and wets the soil surface, easily used by homeowners and amateurs, can be used on turf, ground cover, low shrubs and can be used under small trees, allows for great flexibility.	Either circular or fan pattern with little flexibility, tends to overwater or underwater, never allows water to penetrate fully to the root zone without long soaking of the foliage and losses in evaporation and runoff, shallow and limited throw or coverage, must be continually moved and can miss corners because of natural pattern of spray.	Depends totally on the knowledge, skill and judgement of the user, depends on where the unit is placed, how often it is moved and who makes a decision as to when it has applied enought water.
Oscillating			
	Usually provides a wide throw, covers a large area useful for trees, shrubs, turf or ground cover, can be used with larger hoses, allows for more penetration into the soil, gives a square or rectangular pattern, provides more even and uniform coverage of application.	Throws high in the air and wastes a great deal because of evaporation spray is carried by the wind, can break down or malfunction, can damage nearby plants, causes erosion if used on slopes.	The user needs to know when and where to use these units, especially as it relates to wind and slope, the unit has to be placed, moved and evaluated subjectively, the full sweep and pattern has to be understood, the settings on the sprinkler need to be adjusted to fit the situation, these devices are less subjective and are more able to be controlled than most other portable units.
Buried fixed head			
	Usually a part of an automated irrigation system so it is carefully monitored and controlled a variety of patterns are available, timers can regulate application time and rate, works well on turf, ground cover and shrubs.	May malfunction, needs to be a quality design and installation to be most effective, needs to be maintained, loses some water through evaporation into the air, high initial cost and upkeep, inflexible once installed doesn't work on large trees, may drift in the wind.	The most controlled method of application, can be timed, automated, attached to sensors and handled as objectively as any application method, the most careful and least subjective method, the variety of application devices allow it to be designed in great detail so that water is applied in exactly the right place, in the right amount and at the right time by knowledgeable professionals.

Application method	Water conservation advantages	Water conservation disadvantages	Comments
Drip 	Inexpensive, little waste, very water efficient, applies lesser amounts, can reach roots provides on-going water with little waste or evaporation, very flexible even after installation, has a wide variety of heads and application devices, has emitters, low volume sprinklers, mist sprayers, soaker tubes, can be measured, timed and controlled very accurately.	Can clog and malfunction easily, not well understood, a wide range of quality not always widely available, may apply water too shallow in the root zone, labor intensive to install, requires more maintenance, will not work well on turf, very limited for large trees.	Little human judgement is involved, especially if the unit is automated and connected to sensors, much more objective, measured, adjusted and modified than other water application methods, more of a professional device in most cases, can provide a very controlled and accurate application and is able to modified and altered.
Flooding 	Can be used in turf or shrub beds, can be used around large trees if a saucer holds the water, allows for minimum evaporation, generally allows for uniform depth of penetration, may be best used on ground cover or for small shrubs.	A very limited method, can encourage soil diseases, need to control the flow to where it is needed or wanted, requires monitoring and can cause erosion if used on slopes, the depths of penetration must be monitored.	Needs some judgement as to how high the damming device should be around an area, how often the area should be flooded and how deeply the water is penetrating. This is a human judgement call but in a much smaller area and under controlled circumstances, this technique needs to be set up by a knowledgeable person but can be administered by someone else with instructions as to how to administer it.
Furrow 	Can be used for some shrubs or flower beds, gets water to the roots, allows for soaking, very little evaporation, can best be used in very small areas of the landscape.	Not applicable for turf, ground cover or large trees, mainly an agricultural technique which can be used in vegetable gardens and in controlled areas, can waste water or cause erosion if the furrows are not maintained and controlled.	Trained judgement should be involved in locating and designing the furrows, and guidance should be given as to when to fill them and how often, this takes a great deal of time and labor to establish it for a very small area; once a design and a program is established, it can be administered easily with little waste of water.
Injection 	A laser-like accuracy of application, no waste, gets the water to the roots, can be done occasionally with certain vital plants, works best with large shrubs, small trees, equipment is relatively inexpensive, can also be used to apply liquid fertilizer at the same time as irrigation, no run-off or evaporation.	Can't work on turf or ground covers, very labor intensive for each injection, does not syringe or wet the leaves, equipment can break or clog, you never know when the plant has enough or when water is wasted.	Someone has to decide that water is needed around the roots of the plant, where exactly it should be applied, and when enough has been applied, the operator or user of injection devices requires unusual skills and sensitivity in timing and placement.

strategy

USE IRRIGATION WATER MORE EFFICIENTLY

Everyone, at all levels, in the green industry needs to understand all of the alternatives which are possible in using water more fully and more efficiently.

Mr. A. C. Sarsfield in his article, "Irrigation Devices for Water Conservation," in the May 1981 issue of *GROUNDS MAINTENANCE* Magazine, outlines a number of irrigation devices which can assist in improving irrigation or water efficiency. Mr. Sarsfield defines irrigation devices as follows:

> The term irrigation devices describes the many pieces of equipment that can be used in an irrigation system or can be added to it to perform functions that were not previously available or to improve control over the system and its water application.*

The first device that Mr. Sarsfield outlines is the computerized controller which can be added to an irrigation system.

> The recent explosion in electronic and computer technology has made everyone acutely aware of the use and advantages of automated irrigation systems.

* Sarsfield, A.C.,"Irrigation Devices for Water Conservation", **Grounds Maintenance,** May 1981, Vol.16, No.5, p. 14.

Assume that a system that distributes water at a rate of 0.6 inch per hour (0.01 inch per minute) must run through 3 cycles a week to provide a turf area with its minimum requirement of 1 inch of water. The system must operate 33 minutes per application to provide the correct amount of water. This exact scheduling can be accomplished with an electronic controller.

However, if this system used an electromechanical controller that operates only in increments of 10 minutes above the 30-minute setting, the system must operate 40 minutes per application, applying 1.2 inches a week, or 20 percent more than required. Even with a controller that will operate on 5-minute increments, three 35-minute applications will deliver 1.05 inches of water a week, or 5 percent more than required. These figures may have seemed inconsequential during the days of cheap, plentiful water, but soon this 20 percent waste will be thought intolerable, and even 5 percent unacceptable.

Precise timing, with the capability of programming repeat cycles in virtually any combination, is a great water saver during syringing and on slopes, newly seeded areas and tight soils where repeated short cycles can eliminate runoff.

The almost total flexibility in programming is also an advantage in tailoring irrigation to exact needs. Water need not be wasted on one area because it is tied to others by a rigid mechanical schedule.*

The next device outlined in that article is a soil moisture sensor or a tensiometer. This is described in the following way:

**Ibid., p.14-16.

More complete automation is achieved with the addition of monitoring devices to modify the time cycling, such as soil moisture sensors. The best known and most widely used sensor, especially in agricultural applications, is the tensiometer; gypsum blocks and other devices that measure soil moisture through electrical conductivity are also used.

The tensiometer measures soil moisture by recording the tension level within the soil. In its simplest form, it provides the irrigation manager with readings that can be used to adjust irrigation scheduling. It, and some other types, can also be incorporated into the controller or valve circuitry to prevent watering when there is sufficient moisture in the soil.*

Another device is the rain switch which is described in the following words:

Another water saver that also serves as a cutoff for the automatic irrigation cycle is the rain switch, which has a small cup or catchment, similar to a rain gauge, that fills with rain water. Most have an adjustment so that the amount or weight of water caught that will trip the system cutoff switch can be chosen and set. **

Another device mentioned in the article is the anemometer which is used to measure wind velocity and shuts off irrigation systems when winds are too high to irrigate effectively. Such a device will shut off or stop irrigation systems, thus eliminating uneven coverage, wasting of water. Such a device has safety implications when irrigation systems are established adjacent to highways, roadways or in median strips. By shutting off irrigation systems during excessively windy periods it eliminates a safety or traffic hazard of water blowing into or on automobiles.

Anemometers monitor wind velocity and eliminate irrigation cycles when winds are above preset levels. This eliminates water waste from wind drift, high evaporation and uneven coverage because of distortion in sprinkler patterns. ***

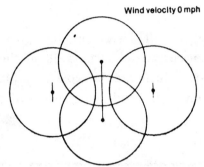

Wind velocity 0 mph

Spacing 65 percent of diameter

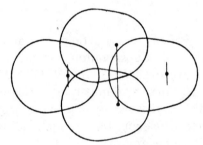

Wind velocity up to 5 mph

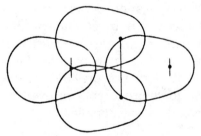

Wind velocity 5.1 to 10 mph

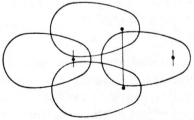

Wind velocity 10.1 to 15 mph

* Ibid., p 16.

**Ibid., p; 18.

***Ibid., pp. 18-22.

Flow monitors and pressure shutoffs may also be used to save water and to operate large irrigation systems more efficiently. Mr. Sarsfield also includes drip irrigation systems under devices, since they are not as widely used in landscape irrigation as they are in agricultural applications. In his article he has the following to say concerning the use of drip or trickle irrigation:

> Although drip irrigation has become big business and the equipment in use today can hardly be classified under the heading of special irrigation devices, most of its major advances have been in agricultural irrigation. Its use in landscaping has been rather limited, and in some areas of the country virtually nonexistent. Those who have not considered drip irrigation should take a closer look as the need to conserve water in the landscape grows.

> A drip system is not a cure-all for our irrigation problems. Golf course fairways will not be irrigated by drip systems in the near future, for example. On the other hand, there are many irrigation needs in landscaping that can be filled admirably with the proper drip equipment, and water can be conserved in the process.

> The primary areas in which the application of drip irrigation is rapidly growing are those in which the use of spray is objectionable. These include pedestrian malls, median strips and highway landscaping. The plantings are generally ornamentals and ground covers. The drip equipment is at ground level, perhaps with the supply tubing below ground, and is hidden by the plant material and bark or other decorative mulch.

> This same application can be carried into many landscape situations with good results. Its use in large bed areas with widely spaced ornamentals can save a considerable amount of water by limiting the wetted area to the root zone of each plant rather than saturating the entire bed. This also helps maintenance by reducing weed growth.

> The same basic application also does an excellent job of irrigating ground cover areas with little or no waste. Its very slow application at the plant root zone makes it an ideal way to irrigate steep slopes without water waste or erosion if the system is properly managed.*

Among the other devices mentioned in this particular article, were tree probes and the use of pipe or tile sleeves inserted vertically into the soil around the root zone of major trees. This article is concluded with the following statement concerning the relationship between water application and infiltration rates of various soils.

> To better appreciate the feasibility of this idea, some figures published recently by the University of California Cooperative Extension Service indicate that when comparing the infiltration rate of soils above pure sand, a sandy loam has the highest rate, 0.5 to 3 inches per hour; clay has the lowest rate, 0.01 to 0.4 inch per hour. To put this into perspective, it will take 20 to 120 hours to wet a clay-loam soil with an infiltration rate of 0.1 to 0.6 inch per hour to a depth of 1 foot, or 60 to 360 hours to wet it to a depth of 3 feet, where most tree roots are located. Water applied in excess of the infiltration rate will simply run off or pond. **

The type and amount of cultivation any planting receives will influence, to a certain extent, the amount of water required. The most heavily researched type of landscape

*Ibid., p. 18.

**Ibid., p. 22.

plant obviously is turf. In an article on "Water Use Rates and Turf Breeding Programs," by Dr. James Beard in the June 1981 issue of GROUNDS MAINTENANCE Magazine he spoke of cultural effects of water requirements in the following words:

Cultural effects.

The effects of specific cultural practices on the water use rate are not fully understood for each turfgrass species, but general guidelines can be presented.

Height of cut has a strong influence on water use; the rate doubles over the range of 0.25 to 1 to 5 inches in mowing height. This response is caused by the increased leaf area from which evapotranspiration occurs and a more extensive root system, which enhances the water absorption capability to support the higher evapotranspiration rate.

The water use rate is also significantly influenced by mowing frequency. As the mowing frequency of creeping bentgrass is increased from biweekly to weekly to 6 times per week, the water use rate increases 41 percent. This response is probably a result of the longer period during which the mower wounds are open, increasing the avenues through which evaporation occurs. Mowing with a dull, improperly adjusted mower increases the extent of wounding and would probably increase the water use rate. Actual experiments have not been conducted to confirm this effect.

Typically, turfs receiving no nitrogen fertilization will have a lower shoot density and a very low water use rate. As the nitrogen level is increased, the water use rate increases because of the increasing shoot density and associated leaf area. However, the rate can decline at excessive nitrogen nutritional levels, which have a minimal effect on shoot density but a significant effect in reducing the root depth and number.

A third cultural factor influencing the water use rate is the irrigation frequency. Turfs grown in soils that are irrigated to maintain a moist to wet condition will tend to have an increased water use rate. Studies have shown that turf irrigated three times per week requires 33 percent more water than does turf irrigated only when wilt is evident.

The specific amount of water conservation that can be achieved with any one of these cultural practices on a particular species cannot be stated because adequate data are not yet available. However, the relative responses reported should be comparable.*

An article entitled, "Improper Design is Largest Contributor to Water Waste," in the April 1981 issue of GROUNDS MAINTENANCE Magazine outlines the necessity for improved, careful and thoughtful design in the conservation of water in maintaining landscape vegetation during periods of drought. This article also outlines the various quantities of water which might conceivably be wasted under improper design guidelines.

The person or company that furnishes the irrigation design cannot be blamed for water wasted because of improper system design; the system design is based on the *client's budget*. Although the system may be adequate in coverage, the methods of applying that coverage may be very wasteful. The irrigation designer should discuss budget considerations versus water waste and equipment quality, two items that will suffer drastically if the budget is too low.

*Beard, James, "Water Use Rates and Turf Breeding Programs", **Grounds Maintenance,** June 1981, Vol. 16, No. 6, pp.14-16,82.

Fig. 1 shows a 10-ft.-wide, 88-ft.-long landscaped area that is watered with one row of full-circle spray heads down the center and part-circle heads on each end. The shaded area represents water that is wasted. Fig. 2 shows the same area watered with two rows of part-circle heads.

In both examples, pop-up spray heads with a 14-ft. diameter are used at a flow of 2 gpm on full-circle, 1 gpm on half-circle and 0.5 gpm on quarter-circle heads. Although the layout in Fig. 2 requires nine more heads than that of Fig. 1, the layout in Fig. 2 can be used in a number of ways to accomplish a very effective watering pattern.

Assume that the cost of the spray head is $5. The cost difference between the two layouts is $45, not including the cost of additional pipe and fittings.

Amount of Water Wasted

Assume that the precipitation rate of the spray heads is 1 inch per hour, a common rate among many manufacturers. In most areas of the country, the amount of precipitation required for good turf growth is 1.2 inches per week. The heads will need to operate 70 minutes per week to apply 1.2 inches of water. Based on watering 20 weeks a year, May through September, the amount of water wasted in a year by the layout in Fig. 1 is 4,958 gallons. The amount wasted in Fig. 2 is 248 gallons. The difference in water waste is 4,710 gallons.

Compare this landscaped area to the areas a municipality waters between traffic lanes. Using this design in Fig.1, a strip 1 mile long would waste 282,612 gallons per year; a strip 5 miles long would waste 1,413,060 gallons per year.

Assume that for budgetary reasons the system is installed with manual valves. Most soils absorb water at the rate of application illustrated for only about 20 minutes. Any water applied after 20 minutes will run off and can be considered wasted. If the system is unintentionally left on by the operator for 10 additional minutes, the amount of water wasted will be 180 gallons (18 gpm x 10 minutes).

If this is habitually done for an average of 10 additional minutes, the system will waste approximately 12,600 gallons of water per year. If a 1-mile-long landscaped area is watered this way by a manual system, approximately 756,000 gallons of water per year will be wasted. An automatic system is an important tool for water conservation.

Effect of Wind

Many of you will say, "Wind causes a lot of our waste and nothing can be done about that." However, you can use landscaping to reduce the effect and design the irrigation system to perform efficiently with existing wind conditions.

Notice the shaded areas in Fig. 3 and Fig. 4 that do not receive adequate coverage. However, in Fig. 5 *special arc* nozzles have been used to water the area. Dotted lines indicate the arc of coverage with no wind.

The prevailing wind will push the arc of coverage so the Fig. 5 layout is very effective.

Special *low angle* nozzles are another way to control the effect of wind, although in many instances these nozzles will provide only minimal effectiveness. A *combination* low angle/special arc would be ideal for use in controlling the adverse effects of wind.

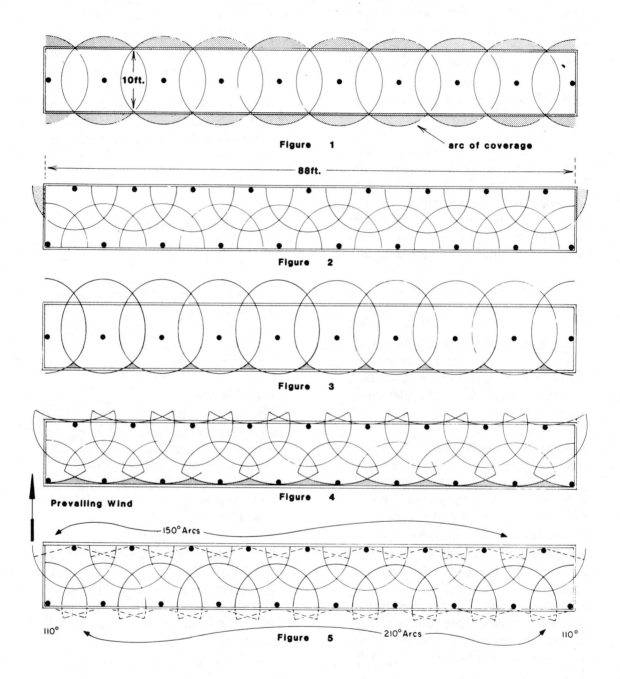

Figure 1

arc of coverage

88ft.

Figure 2

Figure 3

Prevailing Wind

Figure 4

150° Arcs

110°

Figure 5

210° Arcs

110°

Watering Corners

In Fig. 6 and Fig. 7 two methods of watering a corner are shown, but the layout in Fig. 7 is more desirable. If the locations of trees and other plantings prohibit the layout shown in Fig. 7, the layout of Fig. 6 could be used, although an alternative head location would move head *A* to location *B*. This would prevent damage to the head caused by vehicles making a right-hand turn into the drive from the street.

If head *A* is used in the location shown, the amount of money spent over the years in replacements, repairs or reinstallation could be very high. Also, if the head is broken off the piping, the amount of water wasted during 20 minutes of operation will be 140 gallons, a conservative figure based on ½-in. PVC at a water velocity of 6 feet per second.

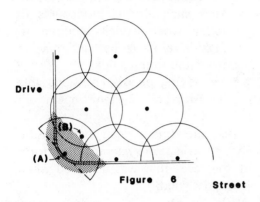

Figure 6

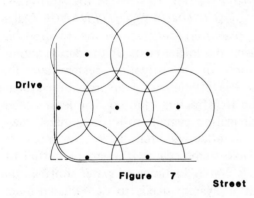

Figure 7

Choosing Equipment

The second most important item of concern is poor quality equipment, which continues to plague irrigation system installations throughout the country. It is caused by, but not limited to, lack of technical knowledge on the part of the irrigation designer, lack of concern by the client, local availability of products, improper irrigation specifications, lack of project supervision and inspection, and the ubiquitous but misleading phrase "or equivalent" writtten into specifications.

One of the most important aspects of a particular piece of equipment is the material used in its construction. Brass, bronze, rubber, plastics and stainless steel all have intended uses in the industry. Some may be more applicable than others in any particular situation or region.

The methods used to construct the equipment are also important. Many people expect more from a piece of equipment than it can actually deliver.

Wiper seals of poor quality material are undoubtedly subject to failure, in many instances within the first 5 years of use. A worn wiper seal can waste approximately 500 gallons of water per head per year. If the system has 100 heads, this represents a waste of 50,000 gallons of water per year. The additional cost involved with the purchase of good quality equipment actually saves money.

For example, assume that the spray heads in Fig. 2 cost $4 each and were of marginal quality. A top quality head could be purchased for $8. The difference in cost would be $76.

If the $4 heads were used and failed after 5 years of operation, the cost of replacing them then would be the current cost of the head plus labor, which would be much more than the extra $76 at the time of installation. The cost of using the inexpensive model would actually be more in the long run. This comparison can be adapted to all equipment, from pipe to controllers.

The best option an irrigation manager has is to examine the different equipment available and determine what is best in each given situation. The manager should keep in mind that the equipment he chooses is what he will have to use for quite some time.

A few items to consider when choosing equipment are:
- Type and quality of material,
- Ease of service,
- Parts availability and
- Quality of construction.

Maintenance

Maintenance is often assigned secondary importance once the irrigation system is installed. It should be of the utmost concern to anyone in charge of an existing system because even the best system available will need periodic maintenance. It would be advisable to check system operation at least once a week.

Grass should be kept trimmed around the spray heads to prevent deflection of the spray pattern. Special trimmers are available for this use. The cost of labor involved in trimming is much less than that of replacing turfgrass killed by lack of coverage. This trimming can be done during inspection of the system, further reducing labor costs.

Never use galvanized piping for connection to a brass or bronze valve or sprinkler head. The two metals will cause galvanic corrosion and must be separated by the use of dielectric unions. This is a major cause of valve and sprinkler head malfunctions.

Determining Precipitation Rates

To determine the approximate precipitation rate a section of sprinkler heads is applying, use the following formula:

$$\frac{gpm\ (one\ head) \times 96.25}{head\ spacing\ (ft.) \times row\ spacing\ (ft.)} = in./hr.$$

This will give an approximate rate so that timing and scheduling of irrigation can be more effective.

Some of the best investments an irrigation manager can make in maintaining an irrigation system are:
- Obtaining a plan of the system.
- Purchasing service manuals for the the equipment used in the system. Most manuals list procedures to follow when servicing equipment, include a parts list and have a troubleshooting guide.
- Employing people knowledgeable in irrigation system operation.

These investments can help ensure that an irrigation system will perform at the level that was intended when it was designed.*

An article by Mr. A. C. Sarsfield entitled, "Proper Irrigation Design" in the April 1981 issue of *GROUNDS MAINTENANCE* Magazine, places in perspective the relationship between the initial costs of the design and installation of an irrigation system and the water use efficiency of an irrigation system during its effective lifetime. The least expensive irrigation system to initially install may, over an effective lifetime, be the most expensive system because it wastes or inefficiently uses water. In times of water shortage the irrigation system needs to be designed much more carefully and more money may need to be spent on the initial design and installation to save water over the effective lifetime of the system. In this article Mr. Sarsfield outlines the necessity for efficiency and uniform coverage and the way in which a system may be designed to ultimately save a great deal of irrigation water.

Probably the greatest cause of waste is lack of uniform coverage. This is usually caused by stretching the sprinkler spacing pattern just a little to eliminate that extra row for the

* "Improper Design is the Largest Contributor to Waste Water", **Grounds Maintenance**, April 1981, Vol. 16, No. 4, pp. 26-28.

sake of cost, or failing to close the pattern to compensate for normally prevailing wind on the site. Sometimes it is just incorrect placement or failure to add sprinklers in those odd areas in which the standard pattern must be altered to fit. Whatever the reason, a lack of uniformity causes light spots in coverage that show up so glaringly in a turf installation.

These light spots usually receive some water, just not as much as the rest of the area. The solution? The easy way to compensate is to operate the system longer until the light spots get enough, but consider a hypothetical example in which 90 percent of the area has a relatively uniform distribution, but 10 percent consists of scattered weak spots. At this location, 1 inch of water a week is required to maintain the turf at the prescribed level. The weakest spots get only 3/4 inch; 90 percent received 1 inch. To get 1 inch of water on the weak spots, the system must be operated one-third longer. This means an application of 133 percent of the water actually needed to 90 percent of the area.

To put this waste into perspective, the unnecessary excess applied over a 16-week peak irrigation season alone would amount to 130,334 gallons per acre, or about 4.8 acre-inches. Projected over the 20-year life of the system, that totals more than 2.6 million gallons wasted per acre. Apply projected water rates to that, multiply by the number of acres under irrigation and decide whether additional capital investment to eliminate this situation might not be worthwhile.*

If water must be applied and if it is available to be applied, then, for irrigation water to be applied most efficiently it is vital to know *where* to water, *when* to water and *how much* to apply to each plant or area. As can be seen from the quotations above, the utilization of this strategy can save a great deal of water. There are a great many ways to know the answers to these questions. Among these are:

by observation - it is possible for the trained observer to see the signs of water stress, such as drooping leaves, falling leaves, the loss of turgidity, and the lack of new growth and vigor,

by testing - this is able to be done by checking the soil on top, in the root zone and in areas of the topsoil where plant roots seek water.

* Sarsfield, A.C., "Proper Irrigation Design: Getting the Decision-makers to do it Right the First Time," **Grounds Maintenance**, April 1981, Vol. 16, No. 4, pp. 16-18.

by using rain guages - to measure natural rainfall to compare this to local evapotranspiration.

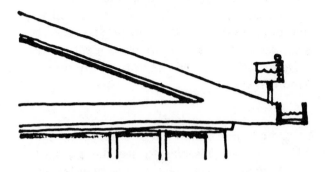

by using tensiometers - to measure moisture in the soil at different levels and at different times.

by using automatic timers - on irrigation systems, this must be used with some discretion since time is not the only consideration in determining the need for additional water.

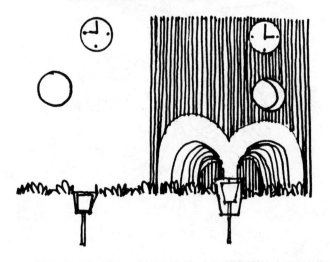

by using computer technology - which calculates the rainfall, evapotranspiration rate, the amount and timing of irrigation water applied and helps to guide decision making.

by using remote sensing - to be able to see dry areas in the overall landscape, which is best used on large scale areas.

Obviously a wide range of new technological innovations make it possible to use irrigation water more efficiently. However, homeowners and managers of small grounds areas need to use many of the traditional methods and older techniques of observation and testing because they may not have access to more sophisticated equipment. It is no less important at any scale to use all means available to make certain that whatever water *is* available will be used most efficiently *where* and *when* it is most needed.

Everyone, at all levels, in the green industry needs to understand all of the alternatives which are possible in using water more fully and more efficiently.

summary

This book is a beginning as a collection of state-of-the-art information. Hopefully it will be expanded, modified and updated in years to come to increase the basic knowledge which is currently available and which will become available as new research is undertaken.

This book is a sharing of information and experience. Newspapers, magazines, radio and television, all tell of water shortages, both current and impending. Water is scarce and it will become scarcer. More water is being used by fewer people for more purposes than at any time in history. Water is needed for many reasons including agriculture, industry, and urban and suburban areas. At the same time, however, there is a competition for available water resources. During times of water shortages there are restrictions and limitations on water use. One of the first areas affected by any water limitation is that which is used to enhance or preserve landscape development. In order to preserve the landscape development in extremely dry situations, locations or circumstances, it is necessary to explore a number of new strategies. Among those that were considered in this book were:

- Control water falling on the site to use it most effectively on the site,
- Select plants which require less water,
- Explore the possibility of soil modification,
- Expand the use of adjuvants and surfacants,
- Explore the use of anti-transpirants,
- Expand the use of mulch,
- Alter cultivation practices,
- Erect wind barriers,
- Establish watering priorities,
- Alter irrigation practices,
- Redesign or renovate areas to require less water.

Everyone in the landscape industry or involved in landscape operations, needs to be aware of the long and short term shortage of water. Everyone at all levels in the greens industry needs to understand all of the alternatives which are possible in using water more fully and more efficiently. This book is a beginning as a collection of state-of-the-art information. Hopefully it will be expanded, modified and updated in years to come to increase the basic knowledge which is currently available and which will become available as new research is undertaken.

The major purpose of this book has been to show that there are a large number of strategies which can be employed to conserve water and yet have the advantages provided by a significant landscape setting in any geographic or climatic region. To utilize as many of these strategies to use available water most efficiently is responsible landscape design and management of the environment.

No one way will save all of the necessary water. No one way is entirely appropriate for everyone in all situations. This is a shopping list and is a reminder of much that can be done. If one way doesn't save all that is possible, then other means need to be explored. All of the strategies need to be orchestrated and used when appropriate. There are other methods and techniques which have been or could be used not just to save water but also to use available water more responsibly and more carefully. This book is meant to focus attention on the problem and to show the state-of-the-art. The area of greatest potential is in the use of new technology in the irrigation industry and in the area of education of the public, of professionals, administrators, designers and managers. This book is meant to address that need for more information and educational materials.

bibliography

Addkinson, Roy with Douglas Sellick. **Running Dry: How to Conserve Water Indoors and Out.** Stein and Day Publishers, Scarborough House, Briarcliff Manor, New York, N.Y. 10510, n.d.

Adler, Jerry. "Are We Running Out of Water?" **Newsweek,** February 23, 2981, pp. 26-37.

Adler, Jerry. "Browning of America" **Newsweek,** Vol. 97, pp. 26-30, February 23, 1981.

Adler, Jerry. "Drought in the Northeast" **Newsweek,** Vol. 97, p. 20, January 5, 1981.

Albuquerque Areawide Wastewater Collection and Treatment Facilities Plan, (Draft E.I.S.) Lee Wilson and Associates, Santa Fe, N.M., February 1977.

Albuquerque/Bernalillo County Planning Department, Albuquerque/Bernalillo County Comprehensive Plan - Policies Plan, April 1975.

Albuquerque City Council Bill M-23. **Memorial Calling Upon the Mayor to Establish a "Conservation of Water Campaign in the City of Albuquerque".**

American Public Works Association, **Planning and Evaluating Water Conservation Measures,** Chicago, Ill. 1981.

Arizona Chapter, National Vegetation Committee, **Landscaping With Native Arizona Plants,** University of Arizona Press, Tucson, Arizona, 1973.

Arizona, State of. Cooperative Extension Service, College of Agriculture, The University of Arizona, Tucson, Arizona 85721. **Listing and Miscellaneous Information on Drought Resistant Plants.**

Baldwin, Richard "Conserving Water in the Landscape," **California Turfgrass Culture,** Vol. 27, No. 2, Spring 1977, pp. 2-3.

Barnes, John, et.al., "Optimum Lawn Watering Rates for Aesthetics and Conservation," **Journal AWWA,** Vol. 71, No. 4, April 1979.

Bandar, R.G., sup. ed. 1974. **Low Maintenance Gardening,** Sunset Books, Lane Publishing Co., Menlo Park, CA.

Bartel, Janice R., and Sage C. Belt, **A Guide to Botanical Resources in Southern California,** Museum Publications, Natural History Museum of Los Angeles County, 1972.

Baumgardt, John P. "Native Grasses for Low Maintenance" **Grounds Maintenance,** pp. 57, November 1978.

Beard, James "Water Use Rates and Turf Breeding Programs" **Grounds Maintenance,** June 1981, Vol. 16, No. 6, pp. 10-18, 82.

Beatty, Russell A. 'Browning of the Greensward" **Pacific Horticulture,** Fall 1977, pp. 5-7.

Beatty, Russell, **Drought Tolerant Plants,** class notes for L.A. 123, University of California, Berkeley, 1971.

Berry, Wade L., "The Use of Effluent Water in your Management Program," **California Turfgrass Culture,** Vol. 24, No. 4, Autumn 1974, pp. 26-27.

Beckett, Jackson, Raeder, Inc. **Michigan Soil Erosion and Sedimentation Control Guidebook,** prepared for the Michigan Department of Natural Resources, Bureau of Water Management, Lansing, MI, 1974.

Blane, Martha, "Drought Tolerant Plants", **Landscape West & Irrigation News, August 1982, pp. 12-15, 28.**

Bos, M.G. and J. Nugteren, "On Irrigation Efficiencies", Publication 19, International Institute for Land Reclamation and Improvement, Wegenngen, The Natherlands, 1974.

Breaking the Habit, Texas Water Resources, Vol. 6, No. 3, April 1980, College Station, TX.

Briggs, J., "There's No Synwater Industry to Bail Us Out" **Forbes,** Vol. 127, p. 154, March 16, 1981.

Bruvold, W. H., " Residential Water Conservation: Policy Lessons from the California Drought", Public Affairs Report, Bulletin of the Institute of Governmental Studies, University of California, Berkeley, Vol. 19, No. 6, December 1978.

Blane, Martha, "Drought Tolerant Plants", **Landscape West & Irrigation News,** August 1982, pp. 12-15, 28.

California Department of Water Resources, **A Pilot Water Conservation Program,** Bulletin No. 191, Sacramento, CA., May 1976.

California Department of Water Resources, **An Urban Water Conservation Conference Proceedings,** Los Angeles, CA., 1976.

California Department of Water Resources, **Calculating the Reduction in Urban Water Demand Due to Conservation,** Sacramento, CA., January 1982, (Draft Report).

California Department of Water Resources, Impact of Severe Drought in Marin County, California, **Bulletin 206, Sacramento, CA., 1979.**

California Department of Water Resources, **Water Conservation in California,** Bulletin No. 198, Sacramento, CA., May 1976.

California Department of Water Resources, **How to Save Water in the Landscape,** Sacramento, CA., 1974.

California Department of Water Resources, **Plants for California Landscapes: A Catalog of Drought-Tolerant Plants,** Bulletin 209, Sacramento, CA., September 1979.

California Department of Water Resources, **Vegetative Water Use in California,** Bulletin No. 113-3, Sacramento, CA., April 1975.

California Department of Water Resources, **Impact of Severe Drought in Marin County, California,** Bulletin 206, Sacramento, CA., 1979.

California Department of Water Resources, **The California Drought - 1977 Update,** Sacramento, CA., 1977.

California State Governor's Office of Emergency Services, **Community Water Management for the Drought and Beyond: A Handbook for Local Government,** Sacramento, CA., May 1977.

Canby, Thomas Y. "Our Most Precious Resource: Water." **National Geographic,** Vol. 158, No. 2, August 1980, pp. 144-179.

"Coast to Coast - Water Becomes a Big Worry", U.S. News and World Report, Vol. 81, p. 27, September 6, 1976.

Cotter, D.J. and F. Chavez, "Factors Affecting Water Application Rates on Urban Landscapes," **Journal of the American Society of Horticultural Science,** Mt. Vernon, VA., March 1979.

Cotter, D.J., and Don B. Croft, "Water Application Practices and Landscape Attributes Associated with Residential Water Consumption," New Mexico Water Resources Research Institute, **Technical Completion Report,** Project No. C-4060 NMEX, Las Cruces, N.M., November 1974.

Courtright, Gordon, **Trees and Shrubs for Western Gardens,** Timber Press, Box 92, Forest Grove, Oregon, 1979.

Cuneo, Katherine, **Water Conserving Gardening,** Marin Municipal Water District, 220 Nellen Ave., Corte Madera, CA. 94925, 1978.

Danielson, Robert E., Charles E. Feldhake and William E. Hart, "Urban Lawn Irrigation and Management Practices for Water Saving with Minimum Effect on Lawn Quality," (OWRT Project No. A-043-COLO) Colorado Water Resources Research Institute, Fort Collins, CO.(Completion Report 106), May 1981, 120 pp.

Drip Irrigation for the Home Garden and Landscape, Division of Agricultural Sciences, Leaflet 21205, University of California, Davis.

Drip Mist Watering Systems: Step by Step Planning and Installation Guide. flyer distributed by Care-Free Irrigation Supplies, Inc., P.O. Box 151, San Juan Capistrano, CA. 92693.

"Drought Resistant Plants". leaflet. Southern Arizona Water Resources Association, 465 St. Mary's Road, Suite 100, Tucson, AZ. 85705.

Drought Tips - How Much Irrigation Water Are You Applying? California Cooperative Extension Service, Davis, CA., n.d.

Duble, R.L., A.C. Novosad and W. E. Knoop, "Lawn Watering." **Fact Sheet L-1682,** Texas Agricultural Extension Service, The Texas A & M University System, College Station, Texas 77843.

Duble, Richard L. "Sprinkler Irrigation Practices and Water Losses," **Irrigation Journal,** March/April 1977, pp. 16,17,46.

Duffield and Jones, **Plants for Dry Climates,** HP Books, Tucson, Arizona, 1981.

Emory, Dara, **Native Plants for Southrn California Gardens,** Santa Barbara Botanic Garden Leaflet, Vol. 1, No. 12, 1969.

Eason, Henry, "The Approaching Water-Supply Crisis" **Nation's Business,** Vol. 71, No. 8, August 1983, p. 25.

Eason, Henry, "Making the Most of Less Water" **Nation's Business,** Vol. 71, No. 8, August 1983, p. 25.

Eason, Henry, "'The Approaching Water-Supply Crisis" **Nation's Business,** Vol. 71, No. 8, August 1983, pp. 22-24.

East Bay Municipal Utility District, **Water Conservation - Today and Tomorrow,** 1977, Oakland, California.

Editors of Sunset Books, **Basic Gardening Illustrated,** Lane Publishing Co., Menlo Park, CA., 1979.

"Fertilizer Injection Puts Water to Work." **Landscape and Irrigation,** Vol. 6, No. 6, April 1983, pp. 60-62, 87-92.

Flack, J.E., et. al., **Achieving Urban Water Conservation: A Handbook,** Colorado Water Resources Research Institute, Ft. Collins, CO., Report No. 80, September 1977.

Gibeault, Victor A., "Preparing Turf to Survive a Drought", **California Turfgrass Culture,** Vol. 27, No. 2, Spring 1977, pp. 9-11.

Gilbert, J.B. & Associates, **Water Conservation in Nevada,** Nevada Division of Water Planning, Carson City, NV., August 1979.

Gingrich, J. Clark, "GM Industry Report on Water", **Grounds Maintenance,** May 1977, Vol. 12, No. 5, pp. 19-25.

"Good Looking . . .Unthirsty," **Sunset Magazine,** October 1976, Lane Publishing Co., Menlo Park, CA.

Gulman, S.L. and H. A. Mooney. "Water Use by Plants" **Pacific Horticulture,** Fall 1977.

Haley, D.S.,Jr., **The Water Crisis,** Dutton, New York, 1966.

Harivandi, M. Ali., "Turfgrass Irrigation - More Knowledge Equals Less Water." **Landscape and Irrigation,** Vol. 6, No. 6, April 1983, pp. 80-85.

Hunt, Cynthia A. and Robert M. Garrels, **The Web of Life,** Norton, New York, 1972.

"Improper Design is the Largest Contributor to Water Waste," **Grounds Maintenance,** April 1981, Vol. 16, No. 4, pp. 26-28.

Irrigating at Home . . . Do You Know When to Irrigate? Leaflet 2745, Division of Agricultural Science, Davis, CA.

"Irrigation and Landscape Design Guidelines", unpublished material, Desert Water Agency, 1200 S. Bogie Rd., P.O. Drawer 1707, Palm Springs, CA 92263.

The Irrigation Association, **Sprinkler Irrigation, 4th Edition,** 13975 Connecticut Ave., Silver Spring, MD 20906, May 1982.

The Irrigation Association, "Wastewater Resource Manual," May 1982.

The Irrigation Association, **Sprinkler Irrigation Systems,** May 1982.

The Irrigation Association, **The ABC's of Lawn Sprinkler Systems,** May 1982.

The Irrigation Association, **Irrigation Technical Manual - Engineering Data,** May 1982.

The Irrigation Association, **Drip Irrigation: Principles, Design, and Agricultural Practices,** May 1982.

Israelson, O.W., and V.E. Hansen, **Irrigation Principles and Practices,** John Wiley & Sons, Inc., New York, 1962.

James, L. Douglas and Wade H. Andrews, **Water Conservation Information Dissemination During the 1977 Drought Emergency,** Utah Water Research Laboratory, College of Engineering, Utah State University, Logan, Utah 84322, June 1978, Water Resource Planning Series, Report P-78-002.

James, I.C., et.al. **How Much Water in a 12-ounce Can? A Perspective on Water-Use Information.** Pamphlet produced by the Geological Survey of the U.S. Department of the Interior, reprint from the U.S.G.S. Annual Report, Fiscal Year 1976, USGPO 1978-261-226/30, Washington, D.C. 1978.

Kittredge, Joseph, **Forest Influences,** The Effect of Woody Vegetation on Climate, Water, and Soil, with Applications to the Conservation of Water and the Control of Floods and Erosion, First Edition, 1948, McGraw-Hill Book Company, Inc., 394 pp.

Kramer, Jack, **Drip System Watering,** Norton, New York, 1980.

Krantz, B.A., **Soil and Water Management for Home Gardeners,** Agricultural Extension Service, University of California, Davis, CA., AXT-111 12 pp.

Lattie, James, "Public Education for Water Conservation," **Drought and Beyond, A Handbook for Local Government,** California Office of Emergency Services, Sacramento, CA., July 1977.

Linaweaver, F.B., Jr., et.al., **A Study of Residential Water Use,** Johns Hopkins University, prepared for FHA and HUD, Baltimore MD., February 1967.

Lupsha, Schlegel and Anerson, **Raindance Doesn't Work Here Anymore,** Division of Government Research, University of New Mexico, Albuquerque, NM, December 1975.

Marsh, A.W., **Questions and Answers about Tensiometers and Their Use.** Agricultural Extension Service, University of California, Davis, Davis, CA., Ext. 92, n.d.

Marsh, Albert W., Ralph A. Strohman, Stanley Spaulding, Victor Youngner and Victor Gibeault, "Turfgrass Irrigation Research at the University of California, Cooperative Extension Service Paper, University of California, Riverside, Riverside, CA., n.d.

Marsh, A.W., et.al., **Drip Irrigation,** Division of Agricultural Sciences, University of California leaflet 2740.

McNeil, Edward, "Irrigating at the Getty Museum", **Irrigation Journal,** January/February 1976.

Milne, Murray, **Residential Water Conservation,** California Water Resources Center, University of California, Davis, Report No. 35, Davis, CA., March 1976.

Model Ordinances, Department of Water Resources, Sacramento, CA., n.d.

Municipal Water District of Orange County, "Water Conservation Study," June 1982.

Nehrline and Nehrline, **Easy Gardening with Drought-Resistant Plants,** Dover Publications, Inc., New York, 1968.

Nehrling and Nehrling, **Easy Gardening with Drought-Resistant Plants,** Dover Publications, Inc., New York, 1968.

Nelson, John Olaf, **Water Conservation in New Residential Development,** proceedings of the Second Annual Conference of Watercare on Water Reclamation and Domestic Water Conservation, June 1975.

Nevada Division of Water Planning, "Water Conservation in Nevada," Information Series Water Planning Report 1, prepared by Brown and Caldwell, August 1979.

Northern California Turfgrass Council, **How to Save Water Sensibly,** (compiled by A.C. Sarsfield), Lafayette, CA., n.d.

Northern California Turfgrass Council, **How to Save Your Landscape and Save Water,** Lafayette, CA., 1978.

North Marin County Water District, **North Marin's Little Compendium of Water Saving Ideas,** Novata, CA., 1976.

North Marin County Water District, **Water Conservation in Novato,** Novato, CA, 1981.

Office of Appropriate Technology, **Guide to the Model Urban Water Conservation Garden,** Sacramento, CA., n.d.

Perry, Robert, **Trees and Shrubs for Dry California Landscapes,** California State Polytechnic University, Pomona, 1981.

"Planting Texas Style" **Texas Water Resources Newsletter,** Vol. 6, No. 4, May 1980.

Pluenneke, Ricks, "Using Infrared Photography to Illustrate Irrigation Problems," **Grounds Maintenance,** Vol. 16, No. 4, pp. 34-40.

Poge, William, "Tests Prove Tensiometers Conserve Water" reprint from **Landscape West & Irrigation News,** September 1982. Distributed by Irrometer Company, Inc., P.O. Box 2424, Riverside, California 95216.

Protect Your Investment . . . in a Landscape Irrigation System, Agricultural Extension Service Publication (ACT-313), University of California, Davis, California, 1971.

Reisner, M. "Are We Headed for Another Dust Bowl?" **Reader's Digest,** Vol. 118, p. 87-92, May 1981.

Residential Water Conservation: An Annotated Bibliography. EPA/HUD Office of Water Program Operations. (WH-595) FRD-16, Washington, D.C. 20460.

Robie, Ronald B., "California's Program for Dealing with Drought." **Journal AWWA,** Vol. 70, February 1978.

Robinette, Gary O., **Plants/People/ and Environmental Quality,** U.S. Department of the Interior, National Park Service, USGPO Stock No. 2405-0479, Washington, D.C. 1972.

Ronstadt, J. "Tucson's Nursery: Landscaping with Less Water and Low Costs" **Rural and Urban Roads,** pp. 27-28, February 1977.

San Diego Association of Governments, **Water Conservation Plan for the San Diego Region,** San Diego, CA., July 1981.

San Diego Home/Garden, **The Dry Garden,** San Diego County Water Authority, San Diego, CA., July 1981.

Sarsfield, A.C., "Irrigation Devices for Water Conservation" **Grounds Maintenance,** May 1981, Vol. 16, No. 5, pp. 14-22.

Sarsfield, A.C., "Proper Irrigation Design" **Grounds Maintenance,** April 1981, Vol.16, No. 4, pp. 14-24.

"Saving Water in Landscape Irrigation" Leaflet 2976, Division of Agricultural Sciences, University of California, Davis, CA.,

SAWARA waterwords, Newsletter, Southern Arizona Water Resources Association, 465 St. Mary's Road, Suite 100, Tucson, AZ. 85705.

"Self-guided, Low Water Use Plant Tour." U.S.D.A., Soil Conservation Service and Desert Water Agency, distributed by the Desert Water Agency, 1200 S. Bogie Road, P.O. Drawer 1707, Palm Springs, CA. 92263.

Smith, Ken L.,**40 Ways to Save Water in Your Yard and Garden,** Newbury Park, CA,1977.

Smith, Ronald C., "A Conservation Option . . .Drip Irrigation," **Grounds Maintenance,** January 1980, Vol. 15, No. 1.

Smith, Stephen. "Irrigation System Scheduling - Blueprint for Water Conservation," **Landscape and Irrigation,** Vol. 6, No. 6, April 1983, pp. 64, 65, 70-74.

Solomon, Ken and Malcom Kodoma, **Trickle Irrigation - Basic Questions and Answers from Rain Bird,** Rain Bird Sprinkler System Co, Glendora, CA. 1976.

Stroeh, J. Deitrich, "Public Response to Water Conservation," **Proceedings - 1978 Annual Conference of the American Water Works Association,** Atlantic City, N.J., June 25-30, 1978.

Sunset Magazine, "Frugality in Garden Water," Lane Publishing Co, Menlo Park, CA.1975.

Sunset Magazine, "For Summer-Dry California - Water Saving Planning Ideas," Lane Publishing Co., Menlo Park, CA. October 1975.

Sunset Magazine, "Drip . . . Its Time Has Come," Lane Publishing Co., Menlo Park, CA. May 1981.

Sunset Magazine, "Desert Gardening", Lane Publishing Co., Menlo Park, CA., June 1976.

Sunset Magazine, "Water Saving Planting Ideas" Lane Publishing Co., Menlo Park, Ca., Ocotober 1976.

Sunset Magazine Editors, **Western Garden Book,** Lane Publishing Co., Menlo Park, CA., 1979.

Texas Water Resources, Newsletter, Texas Water Resources Institute, Texas A & M University, College Station, Texas 77843.

University of California, Division of Agricultural Sciences, **Drip Irrigation for the Home Garden and Landscape,** University of California, Berkeley, 1976.

University of California, Division of Agricultural Sciences, **Efficient Lawn Irrigation Can Help You Save Water,** University of California, Berkeley, 1977.

University of California, Division of Agricultural Sciences, **Irrigating at Home . . .Do You Know When to Irrigate?,** University of California, Berkeley, 1977.

University of California, Division of Agricultural Sciences, **Saving Water in Landscape Irrigation,** Leaflet 2970, University of California, Berkeley, April 1977.

University of California, Division of Agricultural Sciences, **Soil and Water Management for Home Gardeners,** University of California, Berkeley, 1979.

University of California, Cooperative Extension Service, "Home Gardeners Get Drip Idea, Save Water," **News,** Riverside, CA., June 1976.

University of California, Cooperative Extension Service, **Saving Water in Landscape Irrigation,** Division of Agricultural Sciences, 1977.

United States Department of Agriculture, **Irrigation Water Requirements,** Technical Release No. 21, Soil Conservation Service, Engineering Division, April 1967, Revised September 1970.

U.S. Environmental Protection Agency, **Residential Water Conservation: An Annotated Bibliography,** Washington, D.C., 1972.

Van Dorn, A., "Water Conservation - A Worldwide Problem," **Intellectual,** Vol. 106, pp. 473-477, June 1978.

Wagner, K.K., "Water Crisis: It's Almost Here," **Forbes,** Vol. 124, pp. 56-63, August 20, 1979.

"Warning Water Shortages Ahead." **Time,** April 4, 1977.

Water Application Practices and Landscape Attributes Associated With Residential Water Consumption.,Wyoming

"Water Conservation and Operating Guidelines for Landscape Irrigation Systems" unpublished material. Desert Water Agency, 1200 S. Bogie Rd., P.O. Drawer 1707, Palm Springs, CA. 92263.

Water Conservation at Home, pamphlet, American Water Works Association, 6666 W. Quincy Ave., Denver, Co. 80235.

Water Conservation in California, Bulletin No. 198, Department of Water Resources, State of California, Sacramento, CA., May 1976.

"Water Conservation" (Information Bulletins) Department of Water Resources, State of California, Sacramento, CA.

Water Currents. Volume 1, Number 3, Fall 1982. Texas Water Resources Institute and the Texas Agricultural Experiment Station, College Station, Texas 77843.

Water Quality Affects Ornamental Plant Production, Division of Agricultural Sciences, University of California, Davis, CA., Leaflet 2995, 1979.

Water Research: A Sound Investment. Texas Water Resources Institute and the Texas Agricultural Experiment Station, College Station, Texas 77843, 1982.

Water. brochure. Southern Arizona Water Resources Association, 465 W. St. Mary's Rd., Suite 100, Tucson, AZ. 85705.

Water: Will We Have Enough to Go Around, U.S. News and World Report, 90:34-38, June 29, 1981.

Wheatley, Margaret Tipton, **Successful Gardening with Less Water,** Woodbridge Press Publishing Co., Santa Barbara, CA., 1978.

White, Anthony G. **Consumptive Water Use by Landscape Plants: A Brief Sourcelist for Landscape Architects,** Vance Bibliographies, (A-319), Monticello, Illinois, 1980.

Wiley, R.D. "Denver's Water Conservation Program" under "Management and Operations" **American Water Works Association Journal,** American Water Works Association, 6666 W. Quincy Ave., Denver, CO. 80235, July 1983, pp. 320-323.

Woffinden, A.J., "Advantages and Disadvantages of Using Effluent Water in Plant Management," **California Turfgrass Culture,** Vol. 24, No. 4, Autumn 1974, pp. 28-29.

Xeriscape 83. proceedings of conference, April 29, 1983, Anaheim Convention Center, Sponsored by the California Landscape Contractors (Long Beach/Orange County Chapter) and Municipal Water District of Orange County, P.O. Box 15229, Santa Ana, CA. 92705.

Xeriscape, brochure, Denver Water Department, Denver, CO., January 1982.

Youngner, Victor B., "Using Effluent Water for Irrigation," **California Turfgrass Culture,** Vol. 24, No. 4, Autumn 1974, pp. 27-28.

index